CONTENTS

Acknowledgments	vii
Introduction	ix
The Dallas Cowboys A–Z	3
America's Team Appendix	
The All-Time Dallas Cowboys Dream Team	246
A Cowboys Chronology—America's Team Year by Year	248
Ring of Honor: The Cowboy Hall of Fame	256
Cowboys Super Bowl Roundup	258
Cowboys Pro Bowl Honorees	263
Cowboys Season Records	266
The Eleven Best Books About the Cowboys	273
The Funniest Cowboys Quotes Ever	275
Bibliography	277

THE DALLAS COWBOYS ENCYCLOPEDIA

THE DALLAS COWBOYS ENCYCLOPEDIA

The Ultimate Guide to America's Team

Jim Donovan, Ken Sins, and Frank Coffey

A Citadel Press Book
Published by Carol Publishing Group

Copyright © 1996 Jim Donovan, Ken Sins, Frank Coffey
All rights reserved. No part of this book may be reproduced in any form, except by a newspaper or magazine reviewer who wishes to quote brief passages in connection with a review.

A Citadel Press Book
Published by Carol Publishing Group
Citadel Press is a registered trademark of Carol Communications, Inc.

Editorial, sales and distribution, rights and permissions inquiries should be addressed to Carol Publishing Group, 120 Enterprise Avenue, Secaucus, NJ 07094

In Canada: Canadian Manda Group, One Atlantic Avenue, Suite 105, Toronto, Ontario, M6K 3E7

Carol Publishing Group books may be purchased in bulk at special discounts for sales promotion, fund-raising, or educational purposes. Special editions can be created to specifications. For details, contact Special Sales Department, 120 Enterprise Avenue, Secaucus, N.J. 07094.

Manufactured in the United States of America
10 9 8 7 6 5 4 3 2 1

Library of Congress Cataloging-in-Publication Data
Donovan, Jim, 1954–
    The Dallas Cowboys encyclopedia / Jim Donovan, Ken Sins, and Frank Coffey.
        p.   c.m
    "A Citadel Press book."
    Includes bibliographical references (p.).
    ISBN 0-8065-1835-9 (pbk.)
    1. Dallas Cowboys (Football team)   2. Dallas Cowboys (football team)—History.   3. Dallas Cowboys (Football team)—Miscellanea.   I. Sins, Ken.   II. Coffey. Frank.   III. Title.
GV956.D3D66   1996
796.332'64'097642812—dc20   96-28736
                                                        CIP

ACKNOWLEDGMENTS

Thanks to Jeff Miller for his valuable contributions to the Jerry Jones-era players; Burk Murchison for his kind assistance in several areas, from his father to the Cowboys' 1960 opening day lineup; Gary Stratton for his knowledge and materials; Wayne "King of the Cards" Grove at First Base for the loan of his early years material; Jimm Foster at the Dallas Public Library for his photo knowledge and for "Willie, Lilly, George, and Jethro"; the tremendously helpful PR staff of the Dallas Cowboys; Joe Horrigan of the Pro Football Hall of Fame; agent Frank Weimann for putting it all together; editor Jim Ellison for a sure guiding hand; big, two-hearted Bob St. John for his generosity; and Carlton "Godfather" Stowers for everything. Thanks also to the many former Cowboys, especially Gary Wisener, who helped out. And (from Jim) to my wife, Judith, and Rachel, for putting up with it all. We couldn't have done it without you.

INTRODUCTION

The Dallas Cowboys Encyclopedia was designed to be the comprehensive guide to all things Cowboy. Every player ever activated by the Cowboys and on their All-Time Roster—even if for only a single game—is listed. That includes the 1987 replacement players, although their entries are, by necessity, brief.

Each player's main position is listed; in a few cases, where the player spent equal time or several years at different positions, more than one is listed. Besides players, there are entries of all sorts concerning America's Team, from The Catch to The Zero Club.

The authors have made every attempt to be comprehensive, but if you think we've left anything out that should be included, let us know. By the same token, we've made every attempt to verify the accuracy of the information in this book, but we would appreciate any errors brought to our attention so they can be corrected in the next edition.

Letters should be addressed to the authors, care of Carol Publishing Group, 120 Enterprise Avenue, Secaucus, NJ 07094.

We hope you enjoy reading *The Dallas Cowboys Encyclopedia* as much as we did writing it.

NOTE: the astute reader may notice that some entries for later, lesser Cowboys are longer than some for earlier, greater Cowboys. Several factors—heavier media attention, an increase in previously untracked statistics, etc.—have resulted in a wealth of material on the modern-day player. Rather than limit the information on a Cowboy by determining the length of his entry by the degree of his importance, we have elected to make the extra information available. This explains why, for instance, Kelvin Martin's entry is so much longer than Drew Pearson's. (Keep in mind also that as a rule offensive players, by the very nature of their statistic-heavy positions, will generate more information than defensive players.)

The Dallas Cowboys

ABRAMS, BOBBY
Linebacker, 6'3", 230 lbs., b. 4/12/67

After two years as a backup linebacker and on special teams with the New York Giants, Abrams was picked up on waivers by the Cowboys in September 1992 for the same purpose. The Michigan ex spent four weeks in Dallas, seeing action on special teams, and was released on October 6. He was picked up by Cleveland that year before returning to the Giants. He went into camp with the Cowboys in 1993 but was released early in the season; Miami picked him up for the rest of the year. He was signed by Minnesota in 1994.

ADAMS, DAVID
See Replacement Games

ADDERLEY, HERB
Cornerback, 6'1", 200 lbs., b. 6/8/39

Adderley, a first-round draft pick of the Green Bay Packers in 1961, came to the Cowboys in exchange for two players just two weeks before the 1970 season. The five-time All-Pro fit right into the Cowboy defensive scheme and provided Dallas with a solid corner for the next three years, two of which ended with Super Bowls. He led the Cowboys with six interceptions in 1971. The next year, his last, he was replaced during the season by Charlie Waters. He was amazingly quick—even Tom Landry couldn't get used to how far off his man he'd play—and he was a sure tackler. He also had two of the best hands in the league; if he went up for a ball, it was his. He rarely dropped one.

Herb Adderley zeroes in on a St. Louis receiver, 1970. *(From the collection of the Texas/Dallas History and Archive Division, Dallas Public Library)*

3

The man who Bart Starr called "the greatest cornerback to ever play the game" retired after the 1972 season with 48 career interceptions, and he was inducted into the Pro Football Hall of Fame in 1980.

ADKINS, MARGENE
Wide receiver, 5'10", 185 lbs., b. 4/30/47

After three All-Pro seasons with the Ottawa Rough Riders of the Canadian Football League, Adkins was signed by Dallas as a second-round pick in the 1970 draft. A great leaper with 4.4 speed in the 40-yard dash, he'd been a junior college All-American at Henderson City Junior College. He had a good preseason that year and the next, but he spent most of his Cowboy career returning kickoffs and punts. He had no receptions his first year, but in 1971 he had 4 for 53 yards. At the end of the year he was traded to New Orleans.

AGAJANIAN, BEN
Kicking coach

Agajanian was called "The Toeless Wonder," because of his right foot—he had lost the toes in an accident. A kicker with 13 different teams over 20 years, the New Mexico ex became the first kicking specialist when he played for the Philadelphia Eagles and Pittsburgh Steelers in 1945. He gained a reputation not only as a great kicker but also an excellent teacher. The Cowboys hired him in 1965 to work with their kickers, and he continued to do so through the Landry years. He was one of the leaders of the 1967 Kicking Karavan, which traveled to 28 cities looking for kickers.

AGEE, TOMMIE
Running back, 6'0", 235 lbs., b. 2/22/64

After spending his college career in the shadow of future first-round picks Bo Jackson and Brent Fullwood, Agee's five seasons as a Cowboy were spent primarily in the shadow of Emmitt Smith. A fifth-round

draft choice out of Auburn for Seattle in 1987, he came to the Cowboys as a free agent after three injury-riddled years with the Seahawks and the Chiefs. He started 11 games at fullback in 1990 and actually led the Cowboys in rushing with 59 yards in Smith's debut; he finished that season with what would be a career-best 213 yards. He led the running backs that year by averaging 4 yards per carry, and he gained 272 yards on 30 catches as a receiver out of the backfield. Once Smith asserted himself, Agee's role was greatly reduced; he never started another game. Most of his action on the playing field following the 1990 season was limited to special teams. In 1991 he had only 9 carries for 22 yards, and 7 receptions for 43 yards; the next year he had 16 rushes for 54 yards and only 3 receptions. His role outside of special teams dwindled even more after 1992, and after two more years with the Cowboys, he retired following the 1994 season.

Agee was recognized as a valuable force in the locker room throughout his Cowboy career. He was nicknamed "The Reverend" by his teammates for his positive influence at Valley Ranch. And even though he grew up in Alabama, he isn't related to the former major league outfielder of the same name who came from Mobile, AL.

AIKMAN, TROY
Quarterback, 6'4", 228 lbs., b. 11/21/66

Thanks to a late scoring drive by the Green Bay Packers against the Phoenix Cardinals in an otherwise meaningless game late in the 1988 season, the Cowboys "earned" the first pick in the 1989 NFL draft. That meant Dallas, and not Green Bay, could select the strong-armed quarterback from UCLA who had gained stardom after transferring out of the running wishbone offense of Barry Switzer's Oklahoma Sooners. Aikman teamed up with coaches Jimmy Johnson, whom Aikman had turned down

Troy Aikman

finished 11–5, beat Chicago in the playoffs and lost to Detroit, but it was evident bigger things were in store.

The Cowboys' 13–3 record the next season and wins over Philadelphia and San Francisco got them into the Super Bowl, where they destroyed the Buffalo Bills 52–17. Aikman was superb in all three games, especially the last; he was 22 of 30 for 273 yards with no interceptions and was voted the game's MVP.

The next year was more of the same. Aikman had one of the finest seasons ever by an NFL quarterback, hitting 69.1 percent of his passes while throwing only 6 interceptions. The Cowboys finished 12–4, and in the postseason Aikman completed 75.7 percent of his throws in wins against Green Bay, San Francisco, and Buffalo. In the 'Pokes' Super Bowl repeat win over Buffalo he was 19 of 27 for 207 yards with 1 interception.

Aikman's 1994 season was nearly as good, with a completion ratio of 64.5 percent. But this time the Cowboys couldn't get past the 'Niners in the NFC Championship Game. Three Dallas turnovers led to three San Francisco touchdowns in the first few minutes of play, and despite Aikman's heroics—30 of 53 for 380 yards—the final score was 38–28 'Niners.

The 1995 season saw Aikman guide the team to a 13–3 record with another superb year. He hit 64.8 percent of his passes with 16 touchdowns and only 7 interceptions, and in the playoffs he threw 4 TDs and just a single interception with a 66.3 percent passing. He capped the year with a 15 of 23 passing day on the way to a 27–17 Super Bowl win over the Pittsburgh Steelers in Tempe, AZ. Aikman called the third title his most satisfying because the team had to overcome great internal strife, including his own struggle to accept a Switzer coaching style that he considered too lax compared to the regimented Johnson.

Since 1991, Aikman and the Cowboys have been postseason fixtures, including the past four NFC Championship Games. Twice he broke team playoff records for passing

when recruited by him at Oklahoma State, and Switzer to win three Super Bowl titles in his first seven NFL seasons—a far cry from Aikman's early days in the NFL when critics were quick to question whether he could win the big one.

Aikman was thrown to the wolves in his rookie season, and he showed tremendous poise behind a porous front line. With a broken left index finger and a serious concussion, he made most All-Rookie teams despite losing every game he started. He followed his nightmarish 1–15 rookie season by leading the Cowboys to the brink of the playoffs in 1990, but he separated his right shoulder in week 15 against Philadelphia. The Cowboys lost that game and the finale at Atlanta to end the season. Aikman suffered 39 sacks that season and took another beating, but the offensive line was coming together. He hit 56.6 percent of his passes in leading the team to a 7–8 record as a starter.

The 1991 season was a sign of things to come. Aikman completed 65.3 percent of his passes to lead the NFC. The Cowboys accuracy, the first time while leading Dallas to the 1993 Super Bowl and the 52–17 rout of Buffalo at the Rose Bowl in Pasadena. Then again the following year, when the Cowboys rallied to beat the Bills, 30–13, in Atlanta, Aikman was 19 of 27 for 207 yards.

Aikman has become one of the most accurate passers in NFL history at 62.8 percent; only two San Francisco quarterbacks, Joe Montana and Steve Young, are ahead of him. Since the start of the 1991 season he has completed at least 60 percent of his passes in a remarkable 68 of his last 84 games. He ranks seventh on the all-time passing list with a career quarterback rating of 83.5, just behind Jim Kelly's 85.4. He holds over 30 Dallas passing records and should overtake Danny White's all-time completions mark of 1,761 in 1996, and a good year should vault him past White and Roger Staubach in career passing yards.

He is 10–1 in postseason play, where he shines; the bigger the game, the better he plays. He is the career record-holder for postseason completion percentage with 68.3 percent, and he has the second-highest quarterback rating in the postseason at 104.3, behind only Bart Starr's 104.8 mark. Although he has suffered several serious injuries, from a sprained medial collateral ligament to several concussions, no quarterback comes back quicker than Aikman. He's as tough as they come, and his five straight Pro Bowl selections (1991–95) indicates the respect of his peers. Troy Aikman is well on his way to securing a place in the Pro Football Hall of Fame as one of the greatest quarterbacks in NFL history. *Things Change,* a book he wrote for children about his life, was published in 1994 and became a bestseller.

ALBRITTON, VINCE
Strong safety/linebacker, 6′2″, 210 lbs., b. 7/23/62

Tom Landry had high hopes for Albritton when he made the team as a free agent

in 1984. Albritton's size and ability to deliver a rattle-the-fillings hit reminded the coaching staff of Ronnie Lott.

A University of Washington teammate of Cowboys reserve quarterback Steve Pelluer, Albritton had 42 total tackles in 1986 and 43 more in 1987. He also was the Cowboys special teams player of the year in 1987 and competed with Bill Bates for the starting strong safety job in the 1988 training camp.

His top season came as a member of the ill-fated 1–15 team of 1989 when he turned in 111 tackles, third on the team. But assorted leg injuries prevented him from living up to his promise, and Albritton's career ended in 1991. Albritton's greatest claim to fame may have been the fact that he graduated from McClymonds High School in Oakland, CA with rap star MC Hammer.

ALEXANDER, HUBBARD
Assistant coach

It appeared the 1995 title season would be Alexander's last as wide receivers coach with the Cowboys. But his rumored move to Nashville to become head coach of his alma mater, Tennessee State, turned out to be just that—a rumor. Alexander came to Valley Ranch as one of the University of Miami assistants who followed Jimmy Johnson before the 1989 season. During his ten years at UM, he developed such big-name receivers as Brian Blades, Brett Perriman, and a flashy guy named Michael Irvin.

ALEXANDER, RAY
Wide receiver, 6′4″, 193 lbs., b. 1/8/62

Alexander caught 88 passes for 1,590 yards in 1986. Unfortunately, those totals were amassed for the Calgary Stampeders of the Canadian Football League.

He was never able to approach those glittering numbers in the NFL, but the former college teammate of Nate Newton at Florida A&M was the Cowboys' best receiver in 1988, grabbing 54 passes for 788 yards and

6 touchdowns. Signed as a free agent amid some fanfare in 1987 due to his spectacular CFL stats, Alexander spent the entire season on injured reserve after breaking his wrist in training camp.

Injuries limited Alexander to one catch for 16 yards in 1989, his final year with Dallas.

ALLEN, ERMAL
Assistant coach

Allen, a former college quarterback at Kentucky, joined the Cowboys in 1962 as offensive backfield coach after 14 years as an assistant coach at his alma mater. In his first season, the Cowboys ranked second in the league in total offense, touchdowns, and points scored. He was made a special assistant in charge of research and development a few years later (primarily scouting other NFL teams and players) a post he kept until he retired in 1983.

ALLEN, GARY
Running back/wide receiver, 5'10", 183 lbs., b. 4/23/60

Acquired during the 1983 season after he was waived by the Houston Oilers in training camp, Allen served as a kick returner and backup running back. A sixth-round draft pick of the Oilers in 1982, Allen was switched to receiver in 1985, but the experiment failed. Allen made his biggest splash in 1984, when he became the second-leading punt returner in club history, behind Bob Hayes, with a 9.5-yard average in 54 attempts.

ALLEN, LARRY
Offensive guard, 6'3", 325 lbs., b. 11/27/71

Cowboy critics point to Larry Allen's sprained left ankle as one reason why Dallas couldn't beat San Francisco in the 1994 NFC Championship Game. The mere fact that Cowboy coaches preferred to have the injured rookie out on the field at right tackle in such a high-pressure situation, replacing the already-injured Erik Williams, is a testament to his ability. "I don't think anyone realizes the job Larry did for us," quarterback Troy Aikman said of Allen's 1994 effort.

Allen was drafted out of little Sonoma State in the second round in 1994. He began his rookie season quietly, seeing action as a third tight end in short-yardage situations the first three games, but when Mark Tuinei suffered back spasms the next game, Allen went in and acquitted himself well. He started the next game and played well, then went back to reserve duty. But when Erik Williams was injured in an auto accident on October 24 and was lost for the season, Allen moved into his spot at starting right tackle for good. The following year, he moved to guard upon Williams' return and made good on his considerable rookie promise, earning Pro Bowl and All-Pro honors in just his second year.

ALWORTH, LANCE
Wide receiver, 6'0", 182 lbs., b. 8/3/40

"Bambi" was already one of the pro game's all-time great receivers when the Cowboys obtained him in 1971 to take Lance Rentzel's place at wideout. He had been named to the AFL All-Pro team seven times in his career with the San Diego Chargers, topping 1,000 yards in receiving 6 times. But three injured ribs in a preseason game against Cleveland kept him out of the lineup for several games. When he returned halfway through the season, he was an effective and increasingly clutch receiver with 34 passes for 487 yards. In the Super Bowl against Miami, Alworth caught a seven-yard TD pass from Roger Staubach. The next year he saw less action, catching only 15 passes for 195 yards, but he had a touchdown in Dallas' come-from-behind victory over San Francisco in the playoffs. He retired after the season.

Lance Alworth

AMERICA'S TEAM

Bob Ryan, editor-in-chief of NFL Films, had just finished work on the 1978 Dallas Cowboys highlight film. He was finding it tough to come up with the right name. Pittsburgh had won the recent Super Bowl; how could he avoid a lame title for a second-place team, something like "Cowboys Never Give Up"? He remembered that everywhere he looked there was Cowboys paraphernalia; Dallas was on *Monday Night Football* most of the time and on a nationally televised Sunday game when they weren't. He realized there were Cowboys fans everywhere: they were a national team, like Notre Dame in college football, the New York Yankees in baseball, or the Boston Celtics in pro basketball. "The Dallas Cowboys—National Team" popped into his head; that wasn't exactly it...but "America's Team" had the right ring to it. The best-known highlight film in sports history was born.

The effect was overwhelmingly positive on the marketing side, but several players and coaches considered it a burden. Even Tom Landry said, "I think that title gave us a lot more trouble than it was worth." Some teams used the name as a motivational tool: the arch-rival Washington Redskins would watch the film the night before a Dallas game to work themselves into a frenzy. But the name, and the reasoning behind it, still seems right. Almost twenty years later, the Cowboys are just as popular as ever, with more fans nationwide than any other team.

ANDRIE, GEORGE
Defensive end, 6'6", 250 lbs., b. 4/20/40

A member of the original Doomsday Defense of the late sixties and early seventies, Andrie was a sixth-round draft choice in 1962 whose college, Marquette, didn't even have a football program his senior year (they had dropped the sport). "Bullwinkle," as he was branded by his teammates after his

George Andrie

favorite road-game TV viewing, played a strong defensive end position for the Cowboys for eleven years. He was a tough, smart pass rusher and a big-game player: in the Ice Bowl he picked up a fumble and ran it in for a TD, and he intercepted a swing pass and ran it to the one-yard line to set up a score against San Francisco in the 1970 conference playoff win that put Dallas in the Super Bowl. He retired after the 1972 season following a fine career that included five trips to the Pro Bowl and one All-Pro selection.

ANKROM, SCOTT
Safety/wide receiver, 6'1", 194 lbs., b. 1/4/66

The Cowboys liked Ankrom's potential when they drafted him in the twelfth round in 1989. Jimmy Johnson tried him first at wide receiver, then as a defensive back and a kick returner. Ankrom even filled in as a third quarterback after Troy Aikman was injured his rookie year. The former Texas Christian quarterback didn't turn many heads during his one-year stay with the Cowboys, for whom he played primarily as a safety. But Pete Koch certainly remembers him. Koch was playing defensive lineman for the Los Angeles Raiders during the 1989 preseason when Ankrom, at wide receiver, clobbered him with a bone-jarring block. Koch responded by attacking Ankrom. Two plays later, Ankrom's head was clear enough for him to catch a touchdown pass.

But Ankrom's main contribution was on coverage units, finishing third on the team in 1989 in special teams tackles. Arthroscopic surgery on his left knee forced him out of six games in 1989 and eventually ended his career. Ankrom was the first twelfth-round draft pick to make the opening-day roster since Norm Wells in 1980.

ARMSTRONG, JIMMY
See Replacement Games

ARMSTRONG, NEILL
Assistant coach

Armstrong had survived a tough four-year hitch as head coach of the Chicago Bears when he joined the Cowboys staff in 1982 to work with Ermal Allen in research and development. A native of Tishomingo, OK, Armstrong was 30–34 as the Chicago head coach and became the favorite whipping boy of Bears fans ("They Sent the Wrong Neil Armstrong to the Moon" read one sign at Soldier Field) before his firing following the 1981 season. That opened the job for former Cowboys assistant and ex–Bears tight end Mike Ditka.

Armstrong also was an assistant coach with the Minnesota Vikings, seven years as defensive coordinator, and he led the Edmonton Eskimos to the Canadian Football League playoffs three times during his six-year tenure in the Sixties.

Before retiring from the Cowboys in 1989, Armstrong helped prepare scouting reports on all players and teams in the league and contributed to the formulation of game plans after studying the tendencies of upcoming opponents.

ARNESON, BOB
Center/offensive guard, 6'3", 250 lbs., b. 1/7/51

A guard from Arizona, Arneson was the Cowboys' twelfth-round draft pick in 1973. He saw action over the next two years as a backup on the offensive line and on special teams. He spent one year with Washington and then retired from the NFL.

ASHER, BOB
Offensive tackle, 6'5", 250 lbs., b. 6/13/48

"Smasher" Asher, a highly touted second-round draft pick out of Vanderbilt, was acquired in a trade from Chicago for Craig Baynham and Phil Clark in 1970. He had good size and strength, and exceptional speed for a lineman, but playing behind Ralph Neely, Tony Liscio, John Niland, Rayfield Wright, and Blaine Nye left precious little time for a rookie. A knee injury kept him sidelined the next season, but he came back to play four years as a guard and tackle with the Chicago Bears before retiring.

AUGHTMAN, DOWE
Guard, 6'2", 260 lbs., b. 1/28/61

An eleventh-round draft pick in 1984, Aughtman joined the Cowboys as a long-shot defensive tackle from Auburn, but was switched to offensive guard, where the Cowboys thought he had a bright future. But the Alabama country boy who liked nothing better than chewing tobacco and cruising in his pickup truck never played again for the Cowboys after a shoulder injury short-circuited his career.

AVEZZANO, JOE
Assistant coach

How many NFL special teams coaches rate their own radio shows? Avezzano is part of *The Coach Joe Show* during the season. But it's obvious that Avezzano doesn't spend too much time worrying about his radio job. He was named the league's Special Teams Coach of the Year in 1991 and 1994. Before coming to Dallas in 1990, Avezzano coached offensive linemen for four seasons at Texas A&M; prior to that, he spent seventeen years at various colleges around the country. The New York native grew up in Miami and played high school football for fellow Cowboys assistant Joe Brodsky.

AWALT, ROB
Tight end, 6'5", 238 lbs., b. 4/9/64
The Cowboys thought they had acquired their new starting tight end from the Phoenix Cardinals when they traded for Awalt before the 1990 season. Well, they had... but it turned out to be Phoenix's Jay Novacek, who came to Dallas that same year via the NFL's old Plan B free-agency system.

Shoulder Pads and Aprons

Dallas Cowboys Who Opened Bars or Restaurants

- Dave Edwards—*The Handlebar*
- John Niland—*James Comedy*
- Craig Morton—*Wellington's, H.P. Cassidy's*
- Bob Lilly—*The Other Place*
- Rayfield Wright—*Balls*
- Lance Rentzel and Ralph Neely—*Pearl Street Warehouse*
- Dave Edwards and Mike Ditka—*The Sports Page*
- Harvey Martin—*Smokey John's, Recipe's, Lucifer's, Balls*
- Thomas Henderson and Ed Jones—*Playmaker's Plaza*
- Randy White—*Randy White's All-American Grill and Bar*
- Drew Pearson—*Drew Pearson's 88 Sports Cafe*
- Bill Bates—*Bill Bates' Cowboy Cafe*
- Deion Sanders—*Prime Time 21*
- Alfredo Roberts, Eugene Lockhart, Tony Dorsett, and Everson Walls—*The Cowboy Sports Cafe*

Awalt became Novacek's backup with the Cowboys. After averaging 38 catches in the three previous seasons with the Cardinals, Awalt only caught 18 passes in two seasons with the Cowboys, none for touchdowns.

When Awalt was a junior at San Diego State, he was stricken by Thoracic Outlet Obstruction Syndrome, the same neurovascular problem that troubled former major league star J.R. Richard. Awalt's situation was corrected by removing a rib and rerouting an artery and nerve. Awalt spent two years with the Buffalo Bills as a third-string backup before retiring from the NFL.

BABB, GENE
Fullback/linebacker, 6'3", 218 lbs.,
b. 12/27/34

The native Texan fullback from tiny Austin College in Sherman, TX was a 19th-round pick of the San Francisco 49ers in 1957. After two seasons there, he was released, and after a year as an assistant coach at Ranger Junior College in 1959, he signed with Dallas in 1960. He started at fullback for the Cowboys for much of the year, sharing the position with Walt Kowalczyk. In 1961 he moved to linebacker with the arrival of Don Perkins and Amos Marsh; he also saw some spot duty at fullback, though only as a blocker. He was traded to the Houston Oilers in 1962, playing there for two years before retiring.

BABINECZ, JOHN
Linebacker, 6'1", 225 lbs., b. 7/27/50

Babinecz was the Cowboys' second-round draft pick in 1972. He had played middle linebacker at Villanova, but during his two years in Dallas, he backed up the outside linebackers (infrequently) and played well on specialty teams. An injury sidelined him for the entire 1974 season, and he was traded to Chicago before the 1975 season. That year was his last in the NFL.

BAILEY, ROBERT
Cornerback, 5'7", 176 lbs., b. 9/3/68

Bailey played less than a year for the Cowboys, joining them in October 1995 after being released by Washington. He was drafted out of Miami by the Los Angeles Rams in 1991 and played there through 1994.

With the Cowboys he played primarily in their nickel defense and on special teams, and he had nine tackles and one pass deflection. He signed with Miami in 1996.

BAKER, JESSE
Defensive end, 6'5", 269 lbs., b. 7/10/57

A standout at Jacksonville State, Baker spent seven years with the Houston Oilers before signing with the Cowboys in 1986. He spent only part of the season as a backup defensive end before being released. He was picked up by his old team and spent his final two years with the Oilers before retiring after the 1987 season.

BAKER, JON
Kicker, 6'1", 170 lbs., b. 8/13/72

The Arizona State ex was drafted with a "big leg" reputation. Chris Boniol hadn't been getting the distance on his kickoffs that the coaches wanted, so Baker started the season as the kickoff specialist. But his kicking distance didn't measure up to his hype, and after three weeks, he was released and left the NFL.

BAKER, SAM
Punter/kicker, 6'2", 215 lbs., b. 11/12/30

One of the game's best kickers, Baker was known as a hellraiser off the field; he led every team he was with in fines. After five years with Washington and two with Cleveland, the former Oregon State running back (he also was a part-time runner in the pros, retiring with a 4.8-yard average) was traded to the Cowboys before the 1962 season. He had two strong years for Dallas, but he was

11

too wild even for Tom Landry; he was traded to Philadelphia before the 1964 season even though it left the Cowboys without an experienced kicker. He had averaged 45.1 yards punting (still a team record), never had a punt blocked, and hit 23 of 47 field goals. He had six strong years with Philadelphia and then retired. In fifteen years he kicked 179 field goals and 428 extra points.

BALDINGER, BRIAN
Offensive lineman, 6'4", 261 lbs., b. 1/7/59

Fun loving, hard working, and intelligent, "Baldy" was a backup at every position on the offensive line including tight end during his two stays with the Cowboys from 1982–84 and 1986–87. Baldinger graduated from Duke with a degree in psychology and could hold up his end of a conversation on subjects meatier than the execution of a trap block.

But the Cowboys gave up on Baldinger as injury-prone, and he moved on to have a productive career with the Indianapolis Colts and Philadelphia Eagles. Baldy's brothers, Gary and Rich, also played in the NFL.

BANKS, GORDON
Wide receiver, 5'10", 173 lbs., b. 3/12/58

Banks was a slightly built but smart player from Stanford who came to the Cowboys in 1986 after a productive career in the USFL. He had 187 receptions in 54 games for the Oakland Invaders but limited success in his 2 seasons (1986–87) with Dallas, catching 32 passes for 433 yards and 1 touchdown.

A stress fracture of his foot forced him to miss the final seven games of the 1987 season; Banks was out of football the following year. Active in the Fellowship of Christian Athletes, Banks remained associated with the team, conducting pregame religious services for the players.

BARKSDALE, ROD
Wide receiver, 6'1", 193 lbs., b. 9/8/62

Acquired in a trade with the Los Angeles Raiders in the summer of 1987 for cornerback Ron Fellows, the Cowboys felt Barksdale could provide a deep passing threat. Barksdale was from a long line of speedy Raiders receivers. He was a semifinalist in the 100-meter dash in the 1984 Olympic Trials and a three-time track All-American at the University of Arizona, but he never panned out in the NFL.

Barksdale started only one game for the Cowboys in 1987, caught 12 passes for 165 yards for a 7–8 team during the strike-shortened season, and was gone the following year.

BARNES, BENNY
Defensive back, 6'1", 185 lbs., b. 3/3/51

Signed as a free agent out of Stanford in 1972, Barnes was primarily a special-teams player and a good one (captain in 1974) until late in the 1974 season. He had just moved into the starting left cornerback position when he broke an ankle against Cleveland. The next year he was the busiest nonstarter on the squad playing on all specialty teams and serving as fifth defensive back in the rotation. In 1976 he took over at left cornerback when Mark Washington suffered two concussions early in the season; he won game balls for his play in wins over the Redskins and the Cardinals. Barnes was excellent on man-to-man coverage; in one game he limited Lynn Swann to 1 reception for 5 yards in 6 tries. He led the team in interceptions with 5 in 1978 and shared the team lead in interceptions and fumble recoveries in 1979. He was the starting left corner in Super Bowl XII (with one interception). In Super Bowl XIII he was the victim of a controversial interference call—Lynn Swann appeared to be running up *his* back—that moved Pittsburgh deep into Dallas territory in the fourth quarter and enabled them to score. Injuries were a problem throughout his career: he had foot surgery in 1974, 1977, and 1980, and an appendectomy the morning of the 1980 season opener that kept him out of five games. His last two years he played strong safety. Barnes retired before the 1982 season.

BARNES, GARY
Wide receiver, 6'4", 210 lbs., b. 9/13/39

Clemson ex Barnes had been a little-used offensive end on the 1962 NFL Champion Green Bay Packers. He was traded to the Cowboys after the season, and played one year in Dallas, catching 15 passes for 195 yards. In 1964 Barnes was dealt to Chicago for Maury Youmans, and he played there for a year before moving to Atlanta for two years.

BARNES, REGGIE
Linebacker, 6'1", 235 lbs., b. 9/23/69

A hometown high school hero from nearby Grand Prairie, Barnes was a standout at Oklahoma. After a year as a backup with Pittsburgh in 1993, he was out of football in 1994. But Barry Switzer gave him another chance with the Cowboys in 1995, and he made the team as a special teams player. He played through the first seven games and made four tackles before he was released on waivers October 19.

BARNES, RODRIGO
Linebacker, 6'1", 215 lbs., b. 2/10/50

The Cowboys' seventh-round 1973 draft choice, Barnes was a linebacker out of Rice who backed up Lee Roy Jordan at middle linebacker in 1973 and part of 1974. He was traded during his second year to New England and then to Miami in 1975. After a year with the Dolphins he was traded to Oakland, where he played one year (and saw some action in the Super Bowl) and then retired from the NFL.

BATEMAN, MARV
Punter, 6'4", 215 lbs., b. 4/5/50

Bateman was a third-round draft pick from Utah in the 1972 draft. His rookie year was disappointing as he averaged just 38.2 yards a punt, but a sprained ankle in the second game of the season bothered him. He improved in 1973, averaging 41.6 yards a punt, although he was still hampered by leg injuries. Early the next season he was traded to Buffalo, where he played four solid years and retired after the 1977 season.

BATES, BILL
Defensive back, 6'1", 210 lbs., b. 6/6/61

One of the most popular players in Cowboys history, Bates coupled marginal talent with extraordinary effort to forge a lengthy career. When he arrived as a long-shot free rookie agent from Tennessee in 1983, the Cowboys were still one of the NFL's power brokers. He was there when the franchise struck rock bottom in 1989 and remained a key contributor during their Super Bowl run of the 1990s. In the process, Bates transformed special-teams play into a legitimate role.

William Frederick Bates grew up a Cowboys fan in Knoxville, TN, and was living a dream when he was signed by Dallas to join a horde of free agents at the 1983 training camp. Bates wasn't fast by NFL standards, but he soon impressed Tom Landry and the coaching staff with his fanatical approach to hitting and special teams. Bates earned a roster spot for his kick coverage and abilities on the 4–0 pass defense.

As a rookie, Bates was named the league's Special Teams Player of the Year by the NFL Alumni Association. He led all nonstarters on the team with 84 tackles and also started two games at strong safety, one in the regular season and the other in the playoffs. Bates had arrived.

Bates picked up his production a notch

Bill Bates

in his second season. He again walked away with the award for the league's top special teams player, and his enthusiasm on kick coverage received so much attention that NFL executives created a spot on the two Pro Bowl units for a special-teams representative. Naturally, Bates was the first from the NFC. He also collected 5 sacks on blitzes, giving him 9 in two years.

In 1985, Bates again led the team's nonstarters in tackles, and he also added punt returns to his list of duties. The following year, he barged into the starting lineup at strong safety and remained there for three seasons, registering a career-high 124 total tackles in 1988.

Bates faced another stiff challenge in 1989 when Jimmy Johnson and a new coaching staff arrived at Valley Ranch. For Johnson, speed was the most important quality a football player could possess, and that was one area where Bates was lacking. It

seemed that if Bates wanted to prolong his career, he would have to do it somewhere else. But Bates' kamikaze attitude soon won Johnson over, and while Bates was no longer a starter, he was still a key member of the various passing-downs packages, while again leading the squad in special-teams tackles.

The Bates-Johnson relationship was cemented in 1990 when Johnson named Bates his special teams captain. The Cowboys were improving fast, and Bates would be a part of the rocket ride to greatness. Bates, playing the middle linebacker spot in the nickel defense, was second on the team with 7 passes defensed, made his 12th career interception and forced 2 fumbles.

Under the guidance of both assistant coach Joe Avezzano and Bates, the Cowboys developed one of the finest collections of special teams in the league. But Bates faced another career crisis in 1992, the Cowboys' first Super Bowl season under Johnson. Bates had a streak of 79 straight games snapped in the fifth week against Seattle when he suffered a torn anterior cruciate ligament in his left knee that required major surgery, the first serious injury of his colorful career. He continued to help coach the special teams, but he had to watch from the bench as the Cowboys captured Super Bowl XXVII.

Bates threw himself into his rehabilitation program with his typical vigor, and he picked up where he left off before he was hurt. He paced the 1993 team with 25 special-teams tackles for the regular season and contributed heavily to the nickel defense as the Cowboys rolled to victory in Super Bowl XXVIII.

Johnson's successor, Barry Switzer, did not have to be sold on Bates' value. Bates missed only one game in 1994, despite sustaining a fractured left wrist and broken thumb, then finished second on the 1995 team with 25 special-teams tackles, helping the Cowboys to their third Super Bowl title in four seasons.

At the age of 35, Bates is ancient according to the NFL's actuary tables. But he signed for the 1996 season and plans to keep playing as long as the Cowboys will have him.

A four-time winner of the Bob Lilly Award as the fans' most popular player, Bates and his wife, Denise, have five children, including triplets born in 1989. With an eye toward retirement as a player, Bates is a partner in a popular restaurant bearing his name and he operates a working ranch north of Dallas.

BATISTE, MICHAEL
Defensive tackle, 6'2", 305 lbs.,
b. 12/24/70

Batiste spent the 1994 training camp with the Cowboys as a free agent but was released before the final cut. He returned the following year and made a place for himself on the roster, seeing spot duty at defensive tackle, though he was active for only five games and no postseason play. A product of Beaumont (TX) Westbrook High School, Batiste played his college ball at Tulane University.

BAYNHAM, CRAIG
Running back, 6'1", 205 lbs., b. 7/24/44

While still a Georgia Tech junior, Baynham was taken in the 12th round of the 1966 draft. A year later, as a rookie with great speed, he played on specialty teams and split kickoff return duty with Walt Garrison, averaging a strong 28 yards on 12 returns. But in that year's conference playoff against Cleveland, he filled in for an injured Dan Reeves and scored three touchdowns in the 52–14 win. In 1968 he got a lot of work subbing for an injured Reeves, gaining 438 yards on 103 carries and grabbing 29 passes for 380 yards. He also was the frontline kick returner. But the next year was a disappointing one for him; behind a healthy Hill and Garrison, he had only three carries and no receptions. He was traded in 1970 to the Chicago Bears. After sitting out a year with an injury, he finished his career with one year at St. Louis. The man whose Dallas teammates nicknamed "John One Dozen"— because he would sign footballs "Craig Baynham—John 1:12"—became a pastor in later years.

BELDEN, BOB
Quarterback, 6'2", 210 lbs., b. 6/20/47

A twelfth-round draft pick out of Notre Dame in 1969, Belden was the number three quarterback behind Roger Staubach and Craig Morton in 1969 and 1970. He never saw any action and retired after his second year.

BENSON, DARREN
Defensive tackle, 6'7", 305 lbs., b. 8/25/74

A third-round pick in the 1995 supplemental draft, Benson played junior college ball at Trinity Valley Community College. The largest player on Dallas' 1995 defensive line, he was inactive the first eight games, but in the second half of the season he saw action in several games, including the playoff win over Philadelphia.

BERCICH, BOB
Defensive back, 6'0", 195 lbs., b. 11/9/36

Bercich was a Michigan State ex who came over from the New York Giants in 1960, the Cowboys' first season. He was a promising member of the Dallas secondary in 1960–61, but a concussion midway through his second year sidelined him for the season. He underwent a knee operation in August 1962 and couldn't come back; he was released just before the season and retired.

BERRY, RAYMOND
Assistant coach

A former Baltimore Colt, Berry was one of the all-time great receivers until he retired after the 1967 season. He hired on with the Cowboys for one year, 1968, to work with the receiving corps. He was head coach of the New England Patriots from 1984–89.

BETHEA, LARRY
Defensive lineman, 6'5", 254 lbs., b. 7/21/56

Nobody ever questioned Bethea's physical qualifications for NFL employment. Bethea was big, strong, and fast, the 28th overall selection in the 1978 draft. But Bethea was stuck behind All-Pro talents like Randy White and John Dutton for most of his career.

Bethea opened the 1979 training camp in a new position at left defensive end, as Cowboys defensive coordinator Ernie Stautner tried to plug the gap created by Ed Jones' decision to become a boxer and Jethro Pugh's retirement. But Bethea was found lacking and was back in a reserve role. "Nobody can tell me Bethea couldn't be as

good as anybody in the league," personnel director Gil Brandt said. "Sometimes it just takes longer for these big guys to develop." But Bethea never did.

He was involved in one of the key plays in franchise history, chasing San Francisco 49ers quarterback Joe Montana toward the sidelines late in the 1981 NFC championship game. Bethea was unable to track down Montana, who fired the infamous touchdown pass to Dwight Clark that gave the 49ers a 28–27 decision.

The Cowboys ran out of patience and Bethea played in the USFL from 1984–85 for the Michigan Panthers and Oakland Invaders before drifting out of football. He struggled with bouts of depression after football, and suffered financial setbacks that resulted in his being accused of stealing $64,000 from his mother. His life ended tragically when he committed suicide in 1987.

BEUERLEIN, STEVE
Quarterback, 6'2", 209 lbs., b. 3/7/65

The former Notre Dame star was content to come to Dallas before the 1991 season as an insurance policy for young Troy Aikman after starting for two seasons with the Los Angeles Raiders. The Cowboys cashed in when Aikman was lost five games from the end of the season; Beuerlein guided the team to victories the rest of the way and to the team's first playoff berth of the 1990s. He passed for 180 yards and a touchdown to lead Dallas to a 17–13 upset of the Bears in Chicago in the first round of the playoffs. But Aikman, who hadn't played since late November, was ready to play the following week at Detroit, a 38–6 Lions victory. The following year, Beuerlein threw only 18 passes and didn't even get in the 52–17 mugging of Buffalo in Super Bowl XXVII. So much for enjoying the caddy role; Beuerlein left for Arizona to become a starter. His odyssey has continued to Jacksonville and, for 1996, Carolina.

BIELSKI, DICK
Tight end, 6'1", 225 lbs., b. 9/7/32

This former Maryland grid star had been a steady receiver, occasional fullback, and spot kicker for five years with the Philadelphia Eagles. When he was left unprotected in the 1960 expansion draft, a desperate Dallas club picked him up. During his two years with the Cowboys, he started at tight end. He was a good blocker, and a clutch third-down receiver who often found a way to get open in the middle. In 1961 he had his most productive season ever: he had 26 catches for 377 yards and was named to the Pro Bowl. That year he was also the team's frontline field goal kicker, hitting 6 of 9 attempts. He was traded to the Baltimore Colts in 1962, and played there two years before retiring.

BISHOP, DON
Cornerback, 6'2", 205 lbs., b. 7/1/34

Bishop had played a year each for Pittsburgh and Chicago when the Cowboys claimed him on waivers before their inaugural season. The back out of City College of Los Angeles blossomed in Dallas. After a mediocre first year, he became a solid corner for the next five years. Bishop was voted to the Pro Bowl in 1962. He was fast, with good lateral movement; he led the Cowboys three straight years (1960–62) in interceptions, including eight in 1961, one less than the league leader. He underwent knee surgery before the 1964 season and split time as a starter that year with Warren Livingston at right corner; in 1965 he was primarily a backup. He retired after the 1965 season with a career 22 interceptions.

BJORNSON, ERIC
Tight end, 6'4", 230 lbs., b. 12/15/71

A former quarterback and wide receiver at the University of Washington, he turned heads at training camp in 1995 with

Don Bishop

his head and his heart. He saw special-teams work his rookie year, and in spot duty at tight end, Bjornson had 7 catches for 53 yards. Not anything to make Cowboy fans forget Jay Novacek just yet, but like Novacek, Bjornson is an accomplished kick holder.

BLACKWELL, ALOIS
Running back, 5'10", 195 lbs., b. 12/12/54

A backup running back out of the University of Houston from 1978–79, Blackwell, a fourth-round pick in 1978, was unable to overcome injuries during his brief career. He played in the NFC Championship Game and Super Bowl following the 1978 season.

BLACKWELL, KELLY
Tight end, 6'1", 255 lbs., b. 2/13/69

The former Texas Christian standout came to the Cowboys in August 1993 from the Chicago Bears in a five-player deal. He played in every game for the Bears in 1992, catching 5 balls. The intent was for Blackwell to succeed Alfredo Roberts as the primary backup tight end, behind Jay Novacek. Instead, Blackwell was released in early October with no receptions. That was his last year in the NFL.

BLAKE, JOHN
Assistant coach

The Cowboys' defensive line coach from 1993 through 1995, Blake resigned three weeks before Super Bowl XXX to become head coach at his alma mater, the University of Oklahoma, a position Blake called his "dream job." At 34, Blake became the youngest Division 1-A coach in the country and Oklahoma's first black head coach.

Blake's past includes connections with both Barry Switzer and Jimmy Johnson. A nose tackle for Switzer in his collegiate days (1980–83), Blake was an assistant at Tulsa and Oklahoma before Johnson hired him after the 1992 season. A popular, charismatic man, Blake believes in blending tenderness with toughness: "I think you need to show love to build self-esteem. That's how people get the best out of themselves."

Blake's departure came in the midst of prime college recruiting season. He was also involved in a controversy as he left the Cowboys. Late in the season, Blake told Switzer that quarterback Troy Aikman was singling out black teammates for public criticism during games. Aikman refuted the insinuation that he was a racist, and many teammates supported him, pointing out that the majority of Cowboys players were black.

BLAKE, RICKY
Running back, 6'2", 244 lbs., b. 7/15/67

He spent the 1991 season with the World League's San Antonio Riders, the Canadian Football League's Winnipeg Blue Bombers, and the Cowboys. Yet his nickname "Amtrak" referred to his bruising running style, not his mileage. He was in the process of rushing for 42 yards against Phoenix on November 3 when his season, and his NFL career, ended with a fracture of his right hip. His 80 rushing yards for the season, highlighted by a 30-yard touchdown run against Cincinnati in mid-October, were second on the team behind All-Pro Emmitt Smith. And no one can take away the fact that Blake was the first player to don the World League's memorable helmet cam.

BLOOPER BOWL

Dallas' first appearance in the Big Bowl, against the Baltimore Colts at the end of the 1970 season, was not a pretty sight. Between their ineffective offenses and hard-hitting defenses, both teams took turns giving the ball away. A succession of interceptions, fumbles, and fluke plays (all three working in Baltimore's favor, and two of them involving quite suspect calls by the officials) resulted in a 13–13 game, Baltimore ball deep in Cowboy territory, and time for one play. Rookie kicker Jim O'Brien kicked a 32-yard field goal as time ran out to win the game. The final tally: Baltimore—3 lost fumbles and 3 interceptions, Dallas—1 lost fumble and 3 interceptions.

BLOUNT, ALVIN
See Replacement Games

BOEKE, JIM
Offensive tackle, 6'5", 250 lbs., b. 11/11/38

Jim Boeke, out of Heidelberg, began his professional career the same year as the Cowboys, 1960. He spent four years with some ineffective Los Angeles Rams teams before he was traded to Dallas in 1964 for rookie fullback Les Josephson. An injury late that season gave him his chance, and he was a fine starter at left tackle for most of the next three years. A knee injury prior to the 1967 season slowed him down; that and the development of John Niland (Niland bumped Tony Liscio into Boeke's spot) made him the best reserve lineman in the NFL that year.

Boeke had excellent speed for a lineman, and he excelled at the open field cut block. But it was a play in the NFL Championship Game on New Year's Day, 1967, for which he is best remembered. With Dallas at the Packer one-yard line, on second down and trailing by a touchdown with less than two minutes, Boeke jumped offside. The pass to tight end Pettis Norman in the end zone was dropped, but the penalty moved Dallas back to the six. A dropped pass, then a short pass to Norman that was downed at the two, left Dallas with one more down. Meredith was hurried into a bad pass that was intercepted, and Green Bay ran out the clock to win 34–27. Boeke played one more year in Dallas, then finished his career with a final season at New Orleans in 1968.

BONIOL, CHRIS
Kicker, 5'11", 159 lbs., b. 12/9/71

The Louisiana Tech ex signed with the Cowboys as a free agent in April 1994 as the club collected candidates to succeed veteran Eddie Murray, who left for Philadelphia. Boniol won the job in training camp in Austin and went on to lead all NFL rookies that year in scoring and field goals with 22 of 29, and he didn't miss an extra point. His sophomore year he was even better: he missed only one of 28 field goal attempts during the 1995 season and helped the Cowboys build a 13–0 lead against the Steelers in the Super Bowl with field goals of 42 and 35 yards.

BORDEN, NATE
Defensive end, 6'1", 240 lbs., b. 9/22/32

After five years with Green Bay (the last four as the first-string defensive end) Borden was acquired in the 1960 expansion draft by the Cowboys. He was a starter at defensive end for much of that inaugural season; he also started in 1961 opposite Bob Lilly before Lilly moved to tackle. He played the next year for Buffalo, then retired.

BORRESON, RICH
See Replacement Games

BRAATZ, TOM
Linebacker, 6'1", 215 lbs., b. 5/12/33

Braatz was a Marquette product who had spent three years with the Redskins before Dallas picked him up in the 1960 expansion draft. He spent an uneventful year at right linebacker for the Cowboys that first year and then retired after a back injury before the 1961 season. He was player personnel director for the Atlanta Falcons for many years.

BRADFUTE, BYRON
Offensive tackle, 6'3", 245 lbs.

Not many of the pioneer members of the Dallas Cowboys' first year were rookies; the draft had already occurred when the Cowboys were officially made an NFL team. Bradfute, a Southern Mississippi gridder, was contacted in the spring of 1960 by Tex Schramm while he was still in college. After an invitation to training camp, he made the team and eventually earned a job as starting right tackle. An injury in training camp the next year sidelined him for most of that season, after which he called it quits.

BRADY, KERRY
See Replacement Games

BRANDT, GIL
Director of player personnel

Brandt was running a baby photography business in Milwaukee late in 1959 when Tex Schramm called to see if he was interested in doing some work for a new NFL franchise in Dallas. His pro football experience was limited to some part-time scouting he'd done for the Los Angeles Rams, which is how Schramm knew him. He didn't have much experience, but Schramm asked him if he might help sign some players. The request was complicated by the fact that, officially, there was no team yet (the NFL owners wouldn't meet until January 1960), so Schramm and Brandt made copies of the official NFL contract. Brandt used these counterfeit contracts to sign 28 players. When the mission was accomplished swiftly and smoothly, Schramm knew he had the right man for the job; he hired Brandt full-time to scout for talent.

And what a job he did. Brandt was largely responsible for the wealth of players the Cowboys found in places no other team looked. It was invention born of necessity in the early years: "When you don't have anything, you'll take whatever you can find," Brandt once said. And he found them everywhere—college basketball players and track stars, players from Europe, unknown free agents, low-round draft choices out of tiny colleges—and developed the Cowboy theory of drafting the best athlete available. He also established forty yards as the definitive distance by which to judge a football player's speed.

The 1975 draft, in which a Dirty Dozen rookies made the team, secured Brandt's reputation. But a few years later, after a decade and a half of success, he began to receive criticism for not coming up with enough superstars. Dallas' draft picks of the late '70s and '80s were, for the most part, miserable, marked by unproductive or injury-ridden choices. The Cowboys had set a high standard; the regularity with which they had developed All-Pros in the sixties and seventies was unbelievable. That, a long string of success-induced low draft choices, and the fact that the rest of the league had caught up to the Cowboys made Brandt's task tougher.

When Jerry Jones bought the team in 1989 and began cleaning house, the writing was on the wall. Brandt left the organization

he had served for thirty years soon after Tom Landry was fired.

BREUNIG, BOB
Linebacker, 6'2", 235 lbs., b. 7/4/53

Breunig was one of the Dirty Dozen 1975 draft picks who made the team as rookies. A third-rounder out of Arizona State, he became the special teams leader and a reserve linebacker his first year, although he missed four games with an injury. His second year, 1976, he started every game as the strongside linebacker, replacing long-time Cowboy Dave Edwards. He led the team with 3 fumble recoveries that year. In 1977 he was converted to middle linebacker after Lee Roy Jordan's retirement. He was a major factor in the Cowboys' trip to the Super Bowl that year, leading the team in tackles not only that year but five out of the next six. He was the perfect 'backer for Tom Landry's Flex defense—a savvy player and field leader, strong and fast, he was always where he was supposed to be and made few mistakes. In a game against Philadelphia he

Bob Breunig

had 18 tackles, 9 of them solo. He was named to three Pro Bowls (1979, 1980, 1982), and remained a starter until his last year, when a back injury sidelined him halfway through the season. He retired with 466 assisted tackles, second only to Lee Roy Jordan in Cowboys history.

BRICE, ALUNDIS
Cornerback, 5'10", 178 lbs., b. 5/1/70

The fourth-round pick out of the University of Mississippi in 1995, Brice finished the season as the backup at right corner behind the since-departed Larry Brown. Brice had an interception during his rookie season. As a senior at Ole Miss, he was chosen to wear the uniform number, 38, that belonged to Chuckie Mullins, the Rebel defensive player who was paralyzed while playing and later died.

BRIGGS, GREG
Safety, 6'3", 209 lbs., b. 9/19/68

Originally a fifth-round draft pick out of Texas Southern for the Cowboys in 1992, Briggs spent the '92 season on the physically unable to perform list with a hip injury. He went to camp with Cleveland the next two years but was cut before the season. As a member of the World League of American Football's Frankfurt Galaxy in the spring of 1995, he was second on the team with 48 tackles. He went to Cowboys training camp that summer but was released on final cuts; he signed with Dallas on September 20 after the team released kicker Jon Baker. He saw plenty of special teams action during the season.

BRIGHT, BUM
Owner

Texas A&M booster and oilman A.R. "Bum" Bright was the general partner of an eleven-man limited partnership that bought the Cowboys from Clint Murchison in 1984. The purchase price was $60 million, with

another $20 million for Texas Stadium. Bright changed little about the Cowboys, making Tex Schramm managing partner and building additional luxury boxes in the stadium. But as the Cowboys got worse in the late eighties, he became more vocal and public in his criticism of Tom Landry, even going so far as to ask Cowboys President Tex Schramm to fire Landry in 1988. Later that year, he decided to sell the team, and after sorting through dozens of serious offers, he accepted $150 million from a group fronted by Jerry Jones, a millionaire wildcatter from Arkansas.

BRINKLEY, LESTER
Defensive end, 6'6", 270 lbs., b. 6/13/65

Brinkley played for the Cowboys in 1990 after signing as a free agent, backing up Jim Jeffcoat and Tony Tolbert at defensive end. The product of Drew (TX) High School played his college ball at the University of Mississippi, finishing in 1988. He signed as a free agent with Pittsburgh in 1989 but was released before the season began.

BRINSON, LARRY
Running back, 6'0", 214 lbs., b. 6/6/54

Another of the Cowboys' free agent finds, Brinson was a reserve at fullback and running back from 1977–80. Injuries hampered his career when he missed almost all of the 1979 season with a dislocated shoulder, but Brinson also enjoyed a few moments of glory for the Cowboys.

Released at the end of training camp in 1978, Brinson returned to his alma mater, the University of Florida, as a graduate assistant coach. But when backup running back Doug Dennison went down with an injury in October, the Cowboys quickly called Brinson. He rushed for 96 yards and 2 touchdowns the rest of the way, with a 51-yard effort in the Thanksgiving Day rout of the Washington Redskins that included a 39-yard touchdown.

Brinson also played for the Seattle

Seahawks in 1981, when a knee injury halted his career.

BROCK, CLYDE
Offensive tackle/defensive end, 6'5", 265 lbs., b. 8/30/40

Brock was a free agent offensive lineman out of Utah State who played two years for the Cowboys (1962–63). He was a spot player on both offense and defense his first year; in 1963, when defensive end George Andrie went out for several weeks with a dislocated elbow, Brock took his place, with less than spectacular results. He was traded later in the year to San Francisco, and retired after the season.

BRODSKY, JOE
Assistant coach

A trademark of the Valley Ranch practice field since the arrival of the Jimmy Johnson coaching staff in 1989 is the straw hat that guards the smooth pate of running backs coach Joe Brodsky. He doesn't just coach backs, he prods them. Despite the fact that Emmitt Smith has been virtually unmatched in his production since coming into the NFL in 1990, Brodsky wasn't afraid to question Smith's work ethic a time or two. Brodsky was already on the University of Miami staff that Johnson inherited in 1984. He coached high school football in Miami for thirteen seasons before spending the next eleven with the Hurricanes.

BROOKS, KEVIN
Defensive tackle/end, 6'6", 273 lbs., b. 2/9/63

Brooks looked like a future star when the Cowboys drafted him out of Michigan in the first round in 1985. Personnel director Gil Brandt raved over Brooks' size, quickness, and agility. Other experts around the league weren't as sold on Brooks, however, pointing to a reputation as a college underachiever. As it turned out, the critics were on the mark.

Brooks finally won a starting job in 1987, replacing John Dutton, and he led all Cowboys defensive linemen with 67 tackles. Already unpopular with teammates, Brooks crossed the picket line during the 1987 players strike. He never was able to deliver on his potential, leaving the Cowboys following the 1988 season. Brooks played for his hometown Detroit Lions in 1989 after signing as a free agent, but he was out of football after two years there.

BROOKS, MICHAEL
Safety, 6'0", 195 lbs., b. 3/12/67

Brooks was a North Carolina State ex who played a year for San Diego before being picked up by Dallas in November 1990. He spent most of the year on the practice squad but was activated in December when injuries left the defensive secondary thin. He saw special teams action in the last three games of the season. A knee injury the next season, however, ended his NFL career.

BROTZKI, BOB
Offensive tackle, 6'5", 269 lbs., b. 12/25/62

A reserve lineman who played five games for the Cowboys in 1988, Brotzki also played two seasons for the Indianapolis Colts.

BROUGHTON, WILLIE
Defensive tackle, 6'5", 275 lbs., b. 9/9/64

Knee and neck injuries had apparently ended Willie Broughton's NFL career in 1988; he had played the 1985 and 1986 seasons with the Indianapolis Colts. But just as he was about to become a full-time salesman at Paul Harvey Ford in Indy, Broughton called his old coach from the University of Miami. The result was Broughton's recall to Dallas, where he contributed to Jimmy Johnson's first two rebuilding seasons. He started fourteen games in 1989 and played in the first four in 1990 before being shelved by a back injury. After a long layoff he played two years with the Raiders before retiring after the 1993 season.

BROWN, ERIC
Defensive back, 5'11", 175 lbs., b. 1/4/67

A free agent signed out of Savannah State in 1989, Brown saw limited backup duty in the secondary and on special teams. He was released after the season, his only one in the NFL.

BROWN, GUY
Linebacker, 6'4", 228 lbs., b. 6/1/55

Brown possessed the ideal size and speed for an outside linebacker, but injuries prevented him from reaching his potential. The Cowboys invested a fourth-round pick on the University of Houston prospect in 1977, and Brown spent most of his career as the backup for D.D. Lewis, Mike Hegman, and Anthony Dickerson before quitting in 1982 due to a neck injury. The deeply religious Brown was unable to translate his athletic skills into production on the field and this frustrated the defensive coaching staff during Brown's stay with the Cowboys.

BROWN, LARRY
Cornerback, 5'11", 186 lbs., b. 11/30/69

He arrived as an anonymous twelfth-round draft pick in 1991, familiar in the Metroplex only because he played in Fort Worth for Texas Christian. He left as a household name, the Most Valuable Player of Super Bowl XXX thanks to two second-half interceptions that sealed the Cowboys' third world championship of the nineties. The season wasn't all glamour and glory for Brown, though. In mid-November, his premature infant son died. "I considered taking time off, but the organization and the players supported me. That helped me get through all the hard times," said Brown.

Brown worked his way into the starting lineup in only his fourth NFL game, and he quickly became a standout at right corner. His best year was 1995, when he tied for the team lead with 6 interceptions, fourth in the NFC. He also became the only player in club history to return 2 interceptions for TDs in a single season.

The 2 Super Bowl pickoffs in one game tied a record, and the 77 total return yards set one. Not bad for a guy who was blamed for Jerry Rice's success in the previous year's NFC Championship Game. Shortly after the Super Bowl, Brown returned to his native California, signing as a free agent with the Oakland Raiders.

BROWN, OTTO
Cornerback, 6'1", 185 lbs., b. 1/10/47

Brown was a free agent rookie from Prairie View when he was asked to start the last few games of the 1969 season at cornerback. He performed adequately but was traded during the next preseason to the New York Giants, where he remained until retiring after the 1973 season. The arrival and immediate impact of both Cliff Harris and Charlie Waters made him expendable.

BROWNLOW, DARRICK
Linebacker, 5'10", 245 lbs., b. 12/28/68

Timing wasn't one of Darrick Brownlow's strong points. He played parts of the 1991 and 1994 seasons for the Cowboys (in between he played two years for Tampa Bay). Those were the last two seasons that Dallas hasn't won the Super Bowl. Called a human cork by his position coach at Illinois, Brownlow tried to emulate the style of a squatty linebacker who prepared for a tremendous pro career up the road from the Illinois campus—Mike Singletary of the Chicago Bears. Brownlow's main contribution to the 1994 effort was on special teams. He left Dallas for Washington, via free agency, in 1995.

BULLOCKS, AMOS
Running back, 6'1", 200 lbs., b. 2/7/39

Bullocks was a quick All-American halfback at Southern Illinois when he was signed by Dallas as a 20th-round draft choice in 1962. He backed up Amos Marsh and Don Perkins for three years (1962–64), finishing with a 5.9 rushing average his first year. On November 18 of that year he scored on a 73-yard TD run against the Chicago Bears, a club record until Tony Dorsett broke it in 1977. He saw less action the next year, and almost none in 1964; a bout of hepatitis sidelined him for most of the season. The Cowboys traded him to British Columbia in the CFL. After a season there he finished his NFL career with two years with the Pittsburgh Steelers. Then he went north again to play with Vancouver in the CFL.

BURBAGE, CORNELL
Wide receiver, 5'10", 189 lbs., b. 2/22/65

Signed as a free agent in the spring of 1987, Burbage had a few big moments with 7 receptions for 168 yards and 2 touchdowns. He was released in training camp in 1988, one of four times he was waived by the Cowboys, and was re-signed midway through the season. While he had little impact as a receiver, he developed into a threat as a return specialist, averaging 22.4 yards per kickoff return to finish second in the NFC. At the time, it was the highest finish ever by a Cowboys kickoff returner. Burbage also was a reserve receiver in 1989 and had 17 catches for 134 yards in that, his last season for Dallas.

BURKETT, JACKIE
Linebacker, 6'4", 230 lbs., b. 12/16/36

Burkett was a veteran linebacker who came to the Cowboys in 1968 after six years with the Colts and one year with New Orleans. An injury in 1968 sidelined him for most of the year, but the next year he backed up Chuck Howley, Lee Roy Jordan, and Dave Edwards before being traded back to New Orleans. He retired after a final year with the Saints.

BURNETT FIELD

The Cowboys' first practice field was Burnett Field, an old, abandoned baseball field on the Oak Cliff side of the Trinity River near the Houston Viaduct. Barnstorming major leaguers, including Ty Cobb in 1919, had played at the minor league facility, once called Steer Stadium. The playing field itself, just a long Meredith-to-Hayes throw from the levee, was fine, but the facilities were ramshackle. Hot water for showers was hard to come by, and rats chewed the tongues out of shoes and the padding from helmets; equipment had to be strung up on wires, high and away from the floor and walls. The training room was set up in what had been the ladies rest room, where the walls were painted pink. The dressing room was ridiculously small, and plenty of holes kept the building ice cold in winter. At least once the players set a large barrel of trash on fire to provide heat. But by the mid-sixties the Cowboys had moved their practice field to North Dallas, and Burnett was built over soon after.

BURNETTE, DAVE
See Replacement Games

BURTON, RON
Linebacker, 6'1", 245 lbs., b. 5/2/64

Burton was the surprise of the 1987 rookie class, a North Carolina free agent who placed himself in contention for a starting job the following year. Burton led the Cowboys in special-teams tackles as a rookie and started at middle linebacker in two of the final three games in his first NFL season. He made 17 tackles in the season finale against St. Louis.

In 1988 Burton moved to the outside, where he had 41 tackles over the final 8 games. But Jimmy Johnson's arrival as Cowboys coach in 1989 signaled Burton's departure. Johnson prized speedy linebackers and Burton was gone, first to Phoenix and then the Raiders.

BUTLER, BILLY
Safety, 5'10", 190 lbs., b. 7/10/37

Butler, a second-year man from Tennessee-Chattanooga, was an expansion-draft pick of the Cowboys from Green Bay in 1960. He started at safety that first year, his second in the NFL, and was Dallas' primary punt and kick returner. He was traded in 1961 and played a year at Pittsburgh and three with Minnesota (where he was also a halfback and returner) before retiring.

Singin' Stars

Dallas Cowboys Who Recorded Songs

- Don Meredith—*"Travelin' Man"*/ *"Them That Ain't Got It Can't Lose"*
- Buddy Dial—*"Hey Baby!"*, and an album of religious music
- Danny White—*I'm Just a Country Boy*, album
- Ed Jones—*"Funkin' on the Radio"*/ *"Doing the Dip"*
- Lance Rentzel—*"Looking Like Something She Ain't"*
- Troy Aikman—*"Oklahoma Nights"*
- Harvey Martin—*"No Safe Haven"*
- Walt Garrison, Randy White, and Jay Novacek—*Everybody Wants to Be a Cowboy*, album

CAFFEY, LEE ROY
Linebacker, 6'3", 250 lbs., b. 6/3/41

After a year with Philadelphia, seven years with Green Bay, and one with Chicago, Caffey was traded to Dallas just before the 1971 season to back up the linebacking corps. He had been an All-Pro with Green Bay, starting in two Super Bowls for them. Caffey provided experienced backup during the stretch run to the Super Bowl, and then he was traded to San Diego prior to the 1972 season. He retired after one year with the Chargers.

CALIFORNIA QUAKE

Butch Johnson developed this signature end zone dance in the late seventies. He scored a touchdown in a preseason game at Texas Stadium, looked up and saw a lady holding her hands straight up and shaking orgasmically. He did it back to her. Johnson's relatives in California saw it on a sportscast and told him that a reporter had said it looked like an earthquake. Johnson started calling it the California Quake. The response was hugely favorable; later, he began pulling out imaginary six-shooters and shooting them to add a Texas touch. He even worked with a ballet instructor to choreograph an entire routine. (Teammates thought this the height of irony, since Johnson was known as a bad dancer.) The dance did exactly what Johnson hoped it would—it got him a lot of publicity. David Letterman gave Johnson his Spike of the Year, and all the networks and major newspapers ran features on him.

One of the few who disliked the Quake was Tom Landry, who after the Cowboys'

third straight NFC Championship Game loss in 1982 announced there would be no more spiking—including dancing—on his team. That was the end of the California Quake.

CAMPO, DAVE
Assistant coach

One season as defensive coordinator, one Vince Lombardi Trophy. That alone should deem Campo's contribution in 1995 as a success. It was enough of a burden that previous defensive coordinators Dave Wannstedt and Butch Davis had parlayed their terms into high-profile head coaching jobs with the Chicago Bears and the University of Miami, respectively. But Campo's debut as a coordinator included the added challenge of working one Deion Sanders into the defensive mix when Sanders came to Dallas in part to spend time on offense. Because Campo had spent the previous four seasons as the team's secondary coach (he had previously spent two years at the University of Miami in the same capacity, and prior to that, sixteen years at ten other colleges), it was a challenge he was ready for—and one he met successfully. Under his direction, the Dallas secondary became one of the best units in the league.

CANNON, BILLY JR.
Linebacker, 6'4", 230 lbs., b. 10/8/61

Cannon was Dallas' first pick in 1984, and proved to be another one of Gil Brandt's draft-day gambles of the eighties that didn't pan out.

Cannon's pedigree was excellent. He was the son and namesake of the LSU

26

Heisman Trophy winner; at the time the Cannons were the third father-son combo to play in the NFL, joining Dub and Bert Jones and Ed and Brad Budde. Cannon was a superior athlete who had played four positions for the Texas A&M football team and was also a top major league outfield prospect who was drafted by the New York Yankees and Los Angeles Dodgers.

But Cannon also had a history of neck problems. There had been speculation that then-owner Bum Bright, a member of the Texas A&M board of regents, had pressured Brandt and Tom Landry into selecting Cannon. He played in only seven games before injuring his neck in his eighth game, forcing him to retire after one season.

CAPONE, WARREN
Linebacker, 6'1", 218 lbs., b. 8/14/51

Capone was with Birmingham in the World Football League when the 1975 season opened; when that league folded, Dallas signed him. The LSU ex joined the Cowboys before the tenth game and played on special teams the remainder of the season. He saw some action in the Super Bowl loss to Pittsburgh, then was picked up by the New Orleans Saints in 1976. He played a year there and retired after the season.

CARANO, GLENN
Quarterback, 6'3", 198 lbs., b. 11/18/55

Carano might have developed into an effective starting quarterback had he been just about anywhere but Dallas. Carano was stuck behind Roger Staubach and Danny White throughout his career in Dallas (1977–83) before moving on to sign with the Pittsburgh Maulers of the USFL for the 1984 season.

Carano was mostly confined to mop-up duty in the fourth quarter of blowout games, but when called upon in a pressure situation on Thanksgiving Day of the 1981 season, he delivered a victory. Danny White suffered a rib injury in the first half of the

game against the Chicago Bears, and the Cowboys trailed 9–3 when Carano took charge. Carano led the Cowboys on a fourth-quarter drive for the 10–9 victory, setting up the go-ahead touchdown with a 55-yard completion to Tony Hill. Carano started the following week in a 37–13 rout of the Baltimore Colts before White returned for the playoffs.

CARMICHAEL, HAROLD
Wide receiver, 6'7", 255 lbs., b. 9/22/49

One of the most intimidating receivers of his era, Carmichael was a Cowboys nemesis as a member of the Philadelphia Eagles from 1971–83. A four-time Pro Bowler for Philadelphia, Carmichael had been waived by the Eagles before signing with Dallas at midseason in 1983, his final NFL season, bailing them out of a shortage at wide receiver caused by injuries. Carmichael set the NFL record for most consecutive games with at least one reception (127) before the Cowboys halted the streak on December 21, 1980.

CARRELL, DUANE
Punter, 5'10", 185 lbs., b. 10/3/49

The Cowboys signed Carrell as a free agent in 1974, after the seventh game of the season. The Florida State ex had been with the Jacksonville Sharks of the World Football League until they folded. In his first game, against the St. Louis Cardinals the next week, he was named the game's MVP in a 17–14 victory. He finished the year with a respectable 39.8 average for 40 punts. He was traded to Los Angeles for a year, then to the Jets, and then to St. Louis before retiring after the 1977 season with a 38.9-yard average.

CARTER, JON
Defensive tackle, 6'4", 273 lbs., b. 3/12/65

The Cowboys' defensive line was a revolving door during the 1989 season, and one of the players who walked through was Carter, a fifth-round draft choice of the New York Giants in 1988.

Carter spent his rookie season on injured reserve, then was waived by the Giants in 1989. Carter signed with Dallas and played thirteen games for the Cowboys during the 1–15 fiasco of 1989, Carter's last season in the NFL.

CARVER, SHANTE
Defensive end, 6'5", 242 lbs., b. 2/12/71

After two seasons, the first-round pick out of Arizona State has become the poster boy for critics of the Switzer regime's draft system. Picked 23rd overall in the '94 draft, Carver struggled through his first two seasons as a Cowboy despite the fact that the team lost key defensive linemen such as Jim Jeffcoat and Jimmie Jones during that period. He saw some extensive playing time due to injuries to Charles Haley in 1995. He finished the season with only 2.5 sacks (a broken hand late in the season hampered him), but against Philadelphia in the playoffs he had a good game, and he had a career-high 5 tackles in the Super Bowl against Pittsburgh in a reserve role after Haley returned.

CASE, SCOTT
Safety, 6'1", 188 lbs., b. 5/17/62

An eleven-year NFL veteran, Case left Atlanta to sign with the Cowboys in 1995 to play for his old college coach at the University of Oklahoma, Barry Switzer. He finished the season as the backup to Darren Woodson at strong safety, while also playing in the nickel defense and seeing special-teams action. In a start against his old team he had 6 tackles, and in the Super Bowl against Pittsburgh he tied for third on the team with 7 tackles as well as forcing a fumble while seeing considerable action. His Super Bowl dream had become reality and was almost more than he could take in. "The grass was greener than I've ever seen it," he said. "And the ball was nice and brown. The lights were

brighter than I've ever seen. That's the Super Bowl; that's what it's all about."

CASILLAS, TONY
Defensive tackle, 6'3", 273 lbs., b. 10/26/63

There's something about trophies named for Vince Lombardi that agreed with Tony Casillas. As a defensive star at the University of Oklahoma, he won the Lombardi Trophy as college football's best defensive lineman in 1985. He joined the Cowboys in 1991, following five frustrating seasons with Atlanta, and he promptly helped Dallas win two Lombardi Trophies in the Super Bowls of 1993 and 1994. Casillas, who grew up in Tulsa, was the second player picked overall in the 1985 draft, behind Bo Jackson. In 1992, he was a key cog in a Cowboys defense that led the NFL in both overall defense and defense against the run. His first 2 years he led all defensive tackles in tackles, and in the 1992 post-season he led the team in sacks and tied for the team lead in tackles among defensive linemen with 12. Following the 1993 season, he left Dallas to sign with the New York Jets.

THE CATCH

The Cowboys were still considered the elite team of the NFC as the 1981 season got underway. Dallas had a galaxy of stars, all in their primes.

Tony Dorsett would go on to rush for a career-best 1,646 yards, running behind an offensive line anchored by Pro Bowlers Pat Donovan and Herb Scott. Danny White was coming into his own as a quarterback, and he had a fleet of inviting targets like Tony Hill, Drew Pearson, Ron Springs, Butch Johnson, Doug Cosbie, and Billy Joe DuPree. On defense the Cowboys boasted Charlie Waters, Harvey Martin, John Dutton, Randy White, Ed Jones, Bob Breunig, and a pair of excellent rookie defensive backs—league interception leader Everson Walls and Michael Downs.

If the Cowboys were the NFC's establishment, the San Francisco 49ers were outsiders, a young, emerging team that had finished 2–14 and 6–10 the previous 2 seasons. But the 49ers grabbed the Cowboys' attention in the regular season with a 45–14 rout of Dallas. Now the teams would meet for the NFC title on January 10, 1982, and the 49ers had won home field advantage.

The Cowboys seemed in command when they took a 27–21 fourth-quarter lead on Danny White's 21-yard touchdown pass to Cosbie and Rafael Septien's extra point. Five minutes remained, and young quarterback Joe Montana had to drive the length of the field.

Montana started from his 11-yard line. With the Cowboys opting for their 4–0 pass defense, he nickel and dimed his way down the field using 4 draw plays to Lenvil Elliott for 31 yards, a 14-yard reverse to receiver Freddie Solomon, and passes underneath deep coverage.

Twelve plays later, the 49ers had advanced to the Cowboys' six-yard line. On third down, Montana rolled out to the right, eluded the rush of Ed Jones and Larry Bethea, and as he was about to fall backwards out of bounds, launched a pass that some of the Cowboys who were on the field still swear Montana admitted he was throwing away, over the back of the end zone. But Montana's favorite target, Dwight Clark, had worked himself open behind Walls in the right corner of the end zone. Clark leaped as high as he could and pulled down the pass. Ray Wersching's extra point gave the 49ers a 28–27 lead with 51 seconds to play.

The Cowboys still had time for a miracle comeback. White threw a perfect pass to Pearson, but cornerback Eric Wright dived and barely grasped the back of Pearson's jersey and pulled him down at the 44. There was still time. But on the next play, White had the ball stripped by Lawrence Pillers while attempting to pass, and Jim Stuckey recovered. The 49ers ran out the clock and were headed for their first Super Bowl.

It was a devastating defeat and the beginning of a lengthy decline for the NFL's glamour franchise. That tailspin finally ended with a 1–15 disaster in 1989, Jimmy Johnson's first season as the Cowboys head coach.

CESARIO, SAL
See Replacement Games

CHANDLER, THORNTON
Tight end, 6'5", 245 lbs., b. 11/27/63

The sleeper of the Cowboys 1986 draft, the sixth-rounder from Alabama had his first two NFL receptions go for touchdowns. Chandler, Doug Cosbie's backup early in his four-year career, was primarily a blocker who split time with USFL retread Steve Folsom before he was swept out by Jimmy Johnson in 1989, his last year in the NFL.

CHEEK, LOUIS
Offensive lineman, 6'6", 295 lbs., b. 10/6/64

The Texas A&M ex spent one season on the Cowboys' roster, signing with Dallas through Plan B after playing for Miami in 1988 and 1989. He went on to play a year with Phoenix and a year with Green Bay before retiring from the NFL. He competed in rodeos into his sophomore year at Fairfield (TX) High School. A graduate in agricultural economics, he raises cattle on a 90-acre ranch.

CISOWSKI, STEVE
See Replacement Games

CLACK, DARRYL
Running back, 5'10", 218 lbs., b. 10/29/63

The Cowboys were looking for big things from Clack when they invested a second-round pick on the Arizona State ball carrier in the 1986 draft. But the San Antonio native was stuck behind Tony Dorsett and Herschel Walker, and his main contributions came as a kickoff return specialist. Like many of the Cowboys' high draft choices of the mid-eighties, Clack had the measurables—speed, size, strength—but injuries hampered his career, and he never panned out. After 4 uneventful years with the Cowboys (where his best year was 1988, when he had 11 carries for 54 yards and 17 catches for 126 yards), he was out of the NFL.

CLARK, MIKE
Kicker, 6'1", 205 lbs., b. 11/7/40

After five years as a steady kicker with Philadelphia and then Pittsburgh, Texas Aggie Clark was traded to the Cowboys for center Mike Connelly in 1968 following Danny Villanueva's retirement. He led the team in scoring each of his four years with the Cowboys. His first year he hit 17 of 28 attempts, then 20 of 36 in 1969. (That was the year he was nicknamed "Onside" by linebacker Dave Edwards for a botched onside kick in the mud against Cleveland in the playoffs.) He had a good year in 1970: 18 of 27 field goals, a clutch 26-yarder against Detroit in a 5–0 victory in the NFC playoffs, another against San Francisco, then 2 in the Super Bowl loss to Baltimore. But there were still concerns about his erratic kicking (he once completely missed the ball on a kickoff), and in 1971 he shared the kicking with newly acquired Toni Fritsch of Austria. Clark was moved to the taxi squad midway through the season after a loss to Chicago in which Clark missed 3 of 4 attempts, 2 inside the 30. But he was soon back, since Fritsch was injured much of the season; Clark finished 13 of 25, but he missed 3 attempts in the NFC Championship Game against San Francisco. He was injured in 1972, and sat out the year. The next year, his last, Fritsch became the frontliner and Clark his backup. He retired with a career field goal average of 57 percent.

CLARK, MONTE
Offensive tackle, 6'6", 260 lbs., b. 1/24/37

Clark, a standout player at USC, had played three years at defensive tackle for the San Francisco 49ers before the Cowboys traded for him early in the 1962 season. Landry immediately made him a starter on the offensive line for the remainder of the season. He was traded to Cleveland at the end of the year for Jim Ray Smith, and he played for the Browns until he retired after the 1969 season to join the coaching ranks. He later became head coach at San Francisco and then Detroit.

CLARK, PHIL
Defensive back, 6'2", 210 lbs., b. 4/28/45

The Cowboys' third-round draft pick in 1967 saw considerable action—primarily at safety—his rookie season due to Mel Renfro's injuries, and he recovered a fumble in the Ice Bowl against Green Bay. He had excellent speed, and he saw considerable action in the next two years. Assistant coach Gene Stallings was very high on him, and Clark was often stellar in practice drills, but it rarely translated into strong Sunday afternoons. A disappointing season in 1969, and an influx of defensive backs in 1970— the veteran Herb Adderley, and rookies Cliff Harris, Charlie Waters, and Mark Washington—made him expendable, and he was traded to the Chicago Bears. He played there a year and then retired after a year with the New England Patriots.

CLARKE, FRANK
Wide receiver/tight end, 6'0", 211 lbs., b. 2/7/34

Clarke was one of the rare exceptions among the 36 veterans the Cowboys picked from the 1960 expansion pool—he was a keeper. A wide receiver drafted in the third

Frank Clarke hauls one in against the Redskins, 1962. *(From the collection of the Texas/Dallas History and Archive Division, Dallas Public Library)*

round in 1957 out of Colorado, he had sat on the bench as part of a deep receiving corps at Cleveland, catching only 10 passes in 3 years. He had blazing speed, blocked well, and developed a habit of catching clutch third-down passes. After a sorting-out year in 1960, he led the league in average yards gained per reception in 1961 with 22.4, then beat that the next year with 1,043 yards on 47 receptions, and led the league with a 22.2-yard average and 14 touchdowns. He was also involved that year in one of the oddest plays in Cowboy—and pro football—history. Dallas was trailing Pittsburgh 21–14 in the third quarter when safety Jerry Norton intercepted Bobby Layne's pass on the 1-yard line. Eddie LeBaron dropped back into his end zone and hurled a bomb to a galloping Clarke at midfield. Clarke hauled it in and ran for an apparent 99-yard touchdown, what would have been the longest scoring pass in NFL history. But a penalty

flag had been thrown at the line of scrimmage; guard Andy Cvercko was called for holding defensive tackle Big Daddy Lipscomb—two yards deep in the end zone. The official awarded Pittsburgh 2 points for a safety. It was technically correct, but the rule would be erased from the books before the next season.

In 1963 Clarke finished with 43 catches, 833 yards, and a 19-yard average; in 1964, 973 yards on 65 catches and he was named an All-Pro. In his last few years he played primarily at tight end, and he never put up those kind of numbers again, although he remained a dependable clutch receiver through 1967. In the 1966 NFL Championship Game against Green Bay, he had 3 catches for 102 yards, and scored Dallas' last TD, a 68-yard pass from Meredith. When he retired after the '67 season, he had caught 281 passes for 5,214 yards and 50 touchdowns.

Dextor Clinkscale

CLINKSCALE, DEXTOR
Safety, 5'11", 195 lbs., b. 4/13/58

A member of the "Thurman's Thieves" secondary of the early to mid-eighties, Clinkscale earned the starting strong safety job in 1983, after two seasons as a nickel back and one on injured reserve. Another product of the Cowboys' extensive free agent network, the South Carolina State product was smart (Tom Landry called him "as smart as anyone we ever had") and instinctive, intercepting 9 passes for his career. He was traded after the '85 season to Indianapolis, where he spent one year before retiring.

COBB, GARRY
Linebacker, 6'2", 233 lbs., b. 3/16/57

As the Cowboys continued their downward spiral in the final years of the Tom Landry era, they were forced to turn to other teams' castoffs. This was the case with Cobb, a strong player for the Detroit Lions and Philadelphia Eagles for nine seasons

before he was released by the Eagles and signed by Dallas at the end of training camp in 1988.

By the third game of the '88 season, Cobb had moved up to the first unit at outside linebacker. In his first start against the New York Giants Cobb registered 10 tackles, and the following week against Atlanta he had 10 more, plus 2.5 sacks. Despite starting only 14 games, he tied for the team lead in sacks with 7.5, the most by a Cowboys linebacker since 1983, and he was third in tackles.

Cobb actually began his Cowboys career in 1979, when he was a ninth-round draft pick, but unable to make the talent-rich roster, he was released. The Lions picked him up, and he spent six seasons in Detroit before he was traded to Philadelphia for Wilbert Montgomery in 1985. Cobb's final season was in 1989 with Dallas.

COLE, LARRY
Defensive end, 6'4", 245 lbs., b. 11/15/46

Cole was an unheralded sixteenth-round draft pick out of Hawaii in 1968, but when Willie Townes went down almost halfway through the season with a thigh injury, Cole stepped in at right end and never came out. He was quick and a good pass rusher, and as steady as they come; he was also a man of quiet, self-deprecating wit, and one of the nihilistic Zero Club's charter members. When he retired after the 1980 season, he had played 13 years with the Cowboys and participated in 26 playoff games, a league record until broken by D.D. Lewis (27) the next year. Cole appeared in 5 Super Bowls, scored 4 touchdowns, and played every position on the defensive line.

He had a knack for coming up with a big play in a big game. His third-down tackle of Washington's John Riggins in the final game of the 1979 season gave the losing Cowboys one last shot at a victory; the resulting 35–34 win put them into the playoffs. His 4 career touchdowns were all against the Redskins. "Bubba" started at left

Larry Cole

end in both Super Bowl V and VI; in 1975 he moved to right tackle and started there in that year's Super Bowl. In his last five years he was an occasional starter and backup at bothend and tackle. He was the ultimate team player, although not much of a dresser; his teammates kidded him so much that he once showed up for a flight in new clothes with all the price tags still hanging out as a joke.

COLEMAN, ANTHONY
See Replacement Games

COLEMAN, LINCOLN
Running back, 6'1", 240 lbs., b. 8/12/69

Few people have the opportunity to play for two Dallas pro football teams in the same year. Lincoln Coleman did it in 1993, graduating from the Arena League's Dallas Texans to the Cowboys. He was placed on the active roster on November 17, just in time for the Thanksgiving Day game against Miami. In a game that will be remembered for Leon Lett's slide into infamy, Coleman replaced an injured Emmitt Smith and led the Cowboys in rushing with 57 yards. He finished the season with 34 rushes for 132 yards and 2 touchdowns. Back with the Cowboys in 1994, Coleman subbed for Smith against Washington and responded with 74 rushing yards. He was second on the team in rushing with 180 yards in 64 carries. He showed flashes of promise in his ability to run hard straight ahead, but weight problems contributed to his failure to fulfill that promise. The fairy tale for the product of Dallas' Bryan Adams High School and Baylor University ended in 1995 when the drafting of Sherwin Williams in the first round made Coleman expendable, and he was released before the season opener. He was signed by Atlanta but didn't make the cut.

COLEMAN, RALPH
Linebacker, 6'4", 215 lbs., b. 8/31/50

Drafted in the eighth round of the 1972 college draft, Coleman hung on for one year with Dallas before retiring after the 1972 season. That was his only year in the NFL.

COLLIER, REGGIE
Quarterback, 6'3", 207 lbs., b. 5/14/61

Collier wasn't the prototypical NFL quarterback, but his athletic ability intrigued the Cowboys. The Cowboys used a sixth-round draft pick on Collier in the 1983 draft, but Collier spent three seasons in the USFL. In 1985 Collier threw for 2,578 yards and rushed for 606 more for the Orlando Renegades. In 1986 Collier joined the Cowboys, who thought they'd signed a new-wave double-threat quarterback who would eventually replace Danny White.

But Collier didn't like to hang in the pocket and pick out receivers. He would scramble at the hint of a pass rush, running for 53 yards on 6 carries while completing 8 of 15 passes for 96 yards, 1 touchdown and 2 interceptions. Collier moved on to the Pittsburgh Steelers in 1987, his last year in the NFL.

COLVIN, JIM
Defensive tackle, 6'2", 250 lbs., b. 11/30/37

"Rocky" Colvin played four years with Baltimore, the last three as a regular, then was traded to the Cowboys before the 1964 season for tackle Guy Reese. He started every game of his three-year stay in Dallas and became an important part of a quickly improving defensive line. The Houston ex was an excellent pass rusher—quick, agile, and tough. He played most of 1965 with a badly injured knee and then a fractured elbow. After the 1966 season and the Ice Bowl loss to the Packers he was traded to the New York Giants, where he played one year on bad legs before retiring.

CONE, FRED
Kicker, 5'11", 195 lbs., b. 6/21/26

After seven years as the full-time kicker and backup running back for Green Bay Packer teams that never finished above .500, Cone retired to coach high school football. When he heard about the new NFL team in Dallas, he got the itch to play again. He contacted the Cowboys, who offered him a contract. That first Cowboy season, 1960, he made 6 of 13 field goals and 21 of 23 extra point attempts to lead the team with 39 points. After the season he retired once more to return to his alma mater, Clemson, where he worked with kickers for many years.

CONNELLY, MIKE
Offensive guard/center, 6'3", 235 lbs., b. 1/16/35

Connelly was cut by the Los Angeles Rams as a rookie out of Utah State in 1960 and was picked up by the Cowboys. He

Mike Connelly

became the regular center for the next four years, and his exceptional speed made him a standout on specialty teams. A former Marine, he worked hard to make the team; he was actually much lighter than listed, and would hide weights in his boxer shorts before weigh-in to give him an extra ten pounds. In 1965, after a preseason knee injury, he was a swing man at guard and center, sharing the snapping job with second-year man Dave Manders. The next year he saw even less action at center. When Manders went down with an injury in 1967, he was the full-time starter again and played well. He was traded in 1968 to the Pittsburgh Steelers for kicker Mike Clark; he played one year there and retired.

CONRAD, BOBBY JOE
Wide receiver, 6'2", 200 lbs., b. 11/7/35

Texas Aggie Conrad was the seventh all-time pass receiver in the NFL when he was acquired by the Cowboys in 1969, after eleven years with the Cardinals. He saw infrequent duty at wide receiver behind Bob Hayes, Lance Rentzel, and Dennis Homan and caught only 4 passes for 74 yards, then retired after the season.

COOPER, JIM
Offensive tackle, 6'5", 274 lbs., b. 9/28/55

The Cowboys have had their share of freak accidents, but none was as bizarre as Cooper's in 1984. Some teammates had gathered in a Dallas restaurant to watch a *Monday Night Football* game, and Cooper dislocated his ankle after slipping on a slick dance floor, forcing him out of the final nine games. "I've played football all my life, and I've never had an injury as serious as that one," Cooper said.

But Cooper, one of the most dependable linemen in Tom Landry's coaching tenure, bounced back to have one of his most solid seasons in 1985. A sixth-round pick out of Temple in 1977, Cooper was actually cut in training camp. But when Jim Eidson decided to undergo knee surgery, Cooper was invited back. He went on to play every position on the offensive line as a backup his first two years (his nickname was "Utility Man"). When Rayfield Wright developed leg problems in the 1979 preseason, Cooper became the starter. He played well, but when Wright returned with five games left Cooper was once more a backup. Wright retired after the season, and Cooper regained the job, winning a game ball from the coaches for his work in the playoffs against Atlanta. Consistent and competitive, Cooper remained a fixture at right tackle until midway through his last season in 1986.

COOPER, REGGIE
Linebacker, 6'2", 225 lbs., b. 7/11/68

Cooper was signed as a rookie free agent out of Nebraska before the 1991 season. He appeared briefly that season, his only NFL work, making 3 tackles on special teams. The Slidell (LA) resident was a first-team All-Big Eight Conference selection and second-team All-American as a strong safety with the Cornhuskers.

CORNISH, FRANK
Center, 6'4", 295 lbs., b. 9/24/67

Cornish's signing with the Cowboys in 1992 reunited him with quarterback Troy Aikman, whom he centered for at UCLA in 1987 and 1988. He was brought in to back up Mark Stepnoski at center and to provide depth at offensive guard. The move paid off with two starts in 1992 and three in 1993. He was drafted in the sixth round by San Diego in 1990 and started every game as a rookie at center. His father, also named Frank, played defensive tackle for Don Shula's first two Miami Dolphins teams in 1970 and 1971. Cornish went to the Minnesota Vikings after the '93 season then re-signed with the Cowboys late in the '94 campaign. He was released before the 1995 season.

CORNWELL, FRED
Tight end, 6'6", 233 lbs., b. 8/7/61

A better blocker than receiver, Cornwell started one game each in the 1984 and 1985 seasons. The Southern Cal product caught a total of 8 passes in his two-year career as the backup for Doug Cosbie.

COSBIE, DOUG
Tight end, 6'6", 238 lbs., b. 3/27/56

Until Jay Novacek's arrival as a Plan B find in 1990, Cosbie was the franchise's definition of a receiving tight end. "Cos" was the fourth tight end taken in the 1979 draft—behind Pro Football Hall of Famer Kellen Winslow, Dan Ross, and Ronnie Lee—and for his first three years he was the backup for an excellent tight end in his own right, Billy Joe DuPree.

The Santa Clara product took over the starting job from DuPree in 1982 and led all NFC tight ends that season with 30 receptions. His top season came in 1985 when he had 64 catches for 793 yards and 6 touchdowns. But his role in the offense plunged by

Doug Cosbie

more than 50 percent in 1986, mainly due to the arrival of Herschel Walker, who had to be used primarily as a pass receiver because Tony Dorsett was still the team's top running threat.

Cosbie surpassed DuPree's career tight end record for receptions in 1987 and has since been passed by Novacek. Described as "the consummate Cowboy" in a Dallas newspaper article, Cosbie was voted to three Pro Bowls and will be remembered as the best receiving tight end of the Tom Landry era. Injuries forced him to retire following the 1988 season. He was recently named head football coach and athletic director at Menlo College after several years as an assistant at Santa Clara, Stanford, and with the Sacramento Surge of the WFL.

COTTON BOWL

The Cotton Bowl was the home of the Dallas Cowboys for eleven years, until Texas Stadium opened six games into 1971. Built in 1930 and called Fair Park Stadium, it originally held only 46,200 spectators. But the stadium was gradually enlarged through the next two decades and renamed the Cotton Bowl in the forties. By 1960 it held 75,504; the cavernous arena on the State Fair of Texas fairgrounds seemed empty the first few years of the Cowboys' existence. College and high school football still received most of the ink and the attention in Dallas, and the pro games seemed anticlimactic after Friday evening and Saturday afternoon games. At one Cowboys game barely 8,000 spectators showed up. (Owner Clint Murchison liked to joke about the empty seats. When New York restaurateur Toots Shor sent him two box seats to the Cowboys-Giants game in New York, Murchison sent Shor 10,000 tickets—four full sections—to the Giants game in the Cotton Bowl.) The Cowboys shared the Cotton Bowl with their AFL rivals, Lamar Hunt's Dallas Texans, from 1960 through 1962, when the Texans moved to Kansas City and became the Chiefs. But it wasn't until the Cowboys began their winning-season streak in 1966 that they began to fill the stadium with consistently large crowds.

COURVILLE, VINCE
See Replacement Games

COW BELLES

Before the Dallas Cowboys Cheerleaders, there were the Cow Belles. The first cheerleaders for the team in the early sixties were teenagers—both male and female—from Dallas high schools. A woman named Dee Brock organized them, outfitted them in traditional cheerleader uniforms, and dubbed them "Belles" and "Beaux." They led classic cheers—"two bits, four

The Dallas Cow Belles and Beaux (1966)

bits" and all that—and received little attention as they exhorted Cotton Bowl crowds. They were displaced in the early seventies by the Dallas Cowboys Cheerleaders.

COWBOY JOE

The name given to the cowboy figure on the horse that was used on the Cowboys' promotional material in the early sixties. His last year with the Cowboys was 1963; he retired after the season.

CRAZY RAY

Former shoeshine boy Crazy Ray Jones began helping a friend sell pennants and later seat cushions for the Cowboys in the sixties when they were still in the Cotton Bowl. When he began entertaining fans by dressing in a Wild West cowboy outfit complete with chaps, hat, and six-guns, TV cameramen took notice of him. He was invited down onto the sidelines by the Cow-

boys in the mid-seventies to be their team mascot and cheerleader and has been a fixture ever since. Although he's not employed by the Cowboys, he's considered an honorary member. "He's as much a fixture at Texas Stadium as the star on our helmet," says Rich Dalrymple, the Cowboys' PR Director.

Jones had quadruple bypass surgery just before the 1995 season, the first time since the Cowboys' Cotton Bowl days that he wasn't on the sidelines for every home game. He did, however, recover in time for Super Bowl XXX, and he plans to continue leading cheers from the Texas Stadium for several years to come.

CROCKETT, WILLIS
Linebacker, 6'3", 220 lbs., b. 8/25/66

Out of Georgia Tech, Crockett was selected by the Cowboys in the fifth round of the 1989 draft, but spent the season on injured reserve with a knee injury suffered during training camp. He battled back to have a good preseason camp in 1990, but sprained an ankle and was released in early September. He was re-signed later that month and played in thirteen games that season, as a backup at middle linebacker and on special teams. He was released before the 1991 season, after his only season in the NFL.

CRONIN, GENE
Defensive end, 6'2", 230 lbs., b. 11/20/33

Cronin was a five-year veteran obtained by the Cowboys from the Detroit Lions in the 1960 expansion draft. A fine pass rusher, he played an injury-plagued year in Dallas and then was traded to the Washington Redskins before the next season. Cronin played two years there and retired, later becoming the director of player personnel for the Atlanta Falcons.

CVERCKO, ANDY
Offensive guard, 6'0", 240 lbs., b. 11/6/37

"Jiggs" Cvercko had been a rookie reserve lineman on Green Bay's championship team of 1960. He was traded to the Cowboys two weeks before the 1961 season opener and became a starter for much of the season. He played two years in Dallas, starting frequently, then spent 1963 with Cleveland and Washington before retiring.

DAHMS, TOM
Assistant coach

Dahms, a seven-year veteran of the NFL, was the defensive line coach with the Cowboys for their first season in 1960, and then also for two more. In 1962, his last with Dallas, he assisted Brad Ecklund and also was the Cowboys' chief scout.

DALLAS COWBOYS BLUEBOOK

The *Bluebook*, published each year from 1980 through 1989 by Dallas' Taylor Publishing, was basically a glitzed-up, hardback version of each year's *Cowboys Media Guide*, which were meant only for members of the media. Written by staffers of the *Dallas Cowboys Weekly*, the *Bluebook* evolved from a simple collection of records, statistics, and player bios its first year to full-scale articles, analyses, and interviews combined with full-color photographs in its later editions. It was discontinued after the 1989 season, not coincidentally the worst in Cowboys history.

DALLAS COWBOYS CHEERLEADERS

In the early sixties, a woman named Dee Brock was assigned to recruit and organize male and female cheerleaders for the Cowboys. She culled them from area high schools, outfitted them in traditional cheerleader costumes, and named them the Cow Belles and Beaux. They attracted little attention as they led traditional cheers—"two bits, four bits," etc.—from the Cotton Bowl sidelines. When the Cowboys moved into the ultramodern atmosphere of Texas Stadium in 1971, Tex Schramm decided that their image needed updating. He hired Paula Van Wagoner to design sexy new uniforms and local dance teacher Texie Waterman to conduct tryouts (grownups only this time, college girls or career women preferred) and to choreograph rock-n-roll dance routines. The new Dallas Cowboys Cheerleaders, in artfully revealing hot pants, halter tops, and go-go boots, owed more to the Rockettes and Vegas chorus lines than to megaphones and buck shoes, but they were a hit from their debut in 1972—helped tremendously by network TV cameramen focusing on the squad during timeouts. But it wasn't until January 1976 and Super Bowl X, when a Cheerleader winked at the millions watching around the world, that their popularity soared. There were two TV movies about them (the first—starring Jane Seymour—was for a while the highest-rated TV movie in history), several *Love Boat* appearances, a bestselling poster, and trading cards. Virtually every team in the NFL rushed to field copycat cheerleader groups; cheerleading would never again be the same.

For many years, until the Jerry Jones regime took over, Suzanne Mitchell, former secretary to Tex Schramm, directed the Cheerleaders' activities—often with an iron hand. She threatened, and often followed through with, legal action at the slightest hint of infringement on the Cheerleaders' trademark outfits and name, from the porno film *Debbie Does Dallas*, to the Texas Cowgirls (consisting of former Cheerleaders), and even a famous female impersonator who made a brief appearance in Texas Stadium. It is largely due to her efforts that the group's image has been maintained so well.

The Cheerleaders have made thousands of appearances for charity events, state

The Dallas Cowboys Cheerleaders

fairs, college halftime shows, telethons, and more than thirty USO tours. Though each Cheerleader receives only $15 a game, there's no lack of applicants; up to 2,000 young women try out each spring for the 36 spots on the squad. (They make decent money in personal appearance fees.) Today, while many of the copycat NFL cheerleader squads have disbanded, the Dallas Cowboys Cheerleaders dance on.

Steve Perkins as editor. The tabloid is published 32 times a year and provides action photos, game stories, interviews and profiles of players, inside information, and more. At its peak, in the early eighties, it had a circulation of over 100,000, a third of which were non-Texas subscribers. At a current circulation of 70,000, it remains the largest team publication in sports.

DALLAS COWBOYS WEEKLY

In the late sixties, there were two independent periodicals devoted to the Cowboys. The larger one was run by Bobby Collier and was entitled *The Cowboys Insider's Newsletter;* the other was associated with Bob Lilly (*Bob Lilly's Pro Report*) and was published by photographer Russ Russell. They joined forces in the early seventies, and soon reached a circulation of 35,000. The Cowboys bought the rights to the new publication in 1974 and installed Russell as publisher and veteran Cowboys beat writer

DALLAS RANGERS

The original name of the Dallas Cowboys football team was the Dallas Rangers. But owner Clint Murchison Jr. and general manager Tex Schramm found out that there was a Texas League minor league baseball team with the same name. Though there were rumors that the baseball club was going out of business, or moving out of the city, it didn't happen. So in May 1960, Schramm came up with the new name, and Murchison agreed to it. The Dallas Rangers became the Dallas Cowboys.

DALLAS TEXANS

The first team by this name was the last to drop out of the NFL. The Dallas Texans team of 1952 was actually the old New York Yanks franchise (formerly the Boston Yanks and the New York Bulldogs). After eight years of ineptitude, Yanks owner Ted Collins had sold his franchise to the NFL, who then awarded it to a syndicate of businessmen in Dallas. Although the city seemed like a good bet for a pro team—high school and college football were both tremendously popular—and the Texans had some good players (tackle Art Donovan, end Gino Marchetti, running backs Buddy Young and George Taliaferro), the team played dismal football in an empty Cotton Bowl. (Their biggest crowd at the 75,000-seat stadium was 17,000.) After their seventh loss without a win, the Dallas syndicate relinquished ownership to the NFL. The Texans became a permanent road team, operating out of temporary headquarters in Hershey, PA, but playing all of their games away. They won one game—a 27–23 victory over Chicago before 3,000 fans in Akron. The team folded after the season.

The Dallas Texans name was resurrected in 1960, when a new pro league called the AFL was formed by Texan Lamar Hunt. He planted his own team in Dallas. When Clint Murchison Jr. (a multimillionaire football fanatic who had considered buying the old Texans franchise himself) snagged an NFL franchise that same year, the two teams went head-to-head, not only in the same city but on the same playing field, sharing the Cotton Bowl. The Texans did not play well that first year, despite a record of 8–6, and both they and the Cowboys played before thin crowds. Before the 1961 season, the Texans challenged the Cowboys to a charity game, a publicity move that the NFL team ignored. That year the Texans struggled to a 6–8 record, but the next season they took the AFL title behind the coaching of Hank Stram, the passing of Len Dawson, and the running of Abner Haynes. But the team still lost money, playing before sparse crowds. If an AFL championship team couldn't make a profit in Dallas, it just wasn't going to happen. It was the final straw, and in May 1963, convinced that the Cowboys weren't going to leave, Hunt announced that the Texans would relocate to Kansas City, MO, and would change their name to the Chiefs. Dallas was now an NFL town.

DANIEL, TIM
Wide receiver, 5'11", 184 lbs., b. 9/14/69

Daniel was picked in the eleventh round of the 1992 draft out of Florida A&M but spent the entire season on the physically unable to perform list because of a right-hamstring injury he suffered during training camp. It was a similar story for 1993, when he made the 53-man roster but was deactivated every week when the team lowered to the NFL limit of 45 players. He was released after the season and was out of the NFL.

DANIELS, DICKIE
Safety, 5'9", 180 lbs., b. 10/19/44

Daniels was a free agent signed by the Cowboys out of Oregon's Pacific University in 1966. He was small but very fast, and he backed up safeties Mike Gaechter and Mel Renfro, and played well on kicking teams for three years. Then he was traded to the Chicago Bears in 1968. He played a season and a half there, then was traded to the Miami Dolphins where an injury kept him out of action, and he retired after the 1971 season.

DAVIS, BILLY
Wide receiver, 6'1", 199 lbs., b. 7/6/72

Davis played high school ball at El Paso's Irvin High School, then he went on to the University of Pittsburgh, where he climbed to third place in career receiving. Signed by the Cowboys as a rookie free agent in 1995 (the only rookie free agent to make the team that year), he was fifth on the team with 16 special teams tackles.

DAVIS, BUTCH
Assistant coach

Davis hooked up with Jimmy Johnson at Oklahoma State and rode the Johnson express through the national championship days at the University of Miami and the back-to-back Super Bowl wins with the Cowboys. He stayed on as defensive coordinator, a position he had gained in 1993, for Barry Switzer's first season in Dallas, then returned to Coral Gables to succeed Dennis Erickson as coach of the Hurricanes. An Oklahoma native, Davis earned a degree in anatomy and physiology while playing football at the University of Arkansas.

DAVIS, DONNIE
Wide receiver, 6'2", 235 lbs., b. 9/18/40

Davis was a sixth-round draft pick in 1962 out of Southern University. He caught 2 passes for 31 yards as a backup, then was released. Eight years later he played one more year in the NFL as a backup tight end with the Houston Oilers.

DAVIS, KYLE
Center, 6'3", 240 lbs., b. 10/1/52

One of the Dirty Dozen rookie draft picks to make the team in 1975, Davis was a third-round choice out of Oklahoma. He played on special teams and also saw some action snapping on punts, placements, and the shotgun. A knee injury in the preseason the following year kept him out of action in 1976. He was traded to San Francisco and played one year there in 1978 before retiring.

DAVIS, SONNY
Linebacker, 6'2", 220 lbs., b. 9/25/38

Davis was a fourth-round pick out of Baylor for the Cowboys in 1961; he was a converted wide receiver who spent the year

seeing limited action, backing up the linebacker corps. He retired after the season.

DEL RIO, JACK
Linebacker, 6'4", 240 lbs., b. 4/4/63

When Del Rio came to the Cowboys in 1990, Valley Ranch was practically his last-chance gas station. A four-year NFL veteran as a starter with both New Orleans and Kansas City, the USC product had been placed on waivers by the Chiefs. He regained a spark and was a valuable starter for the Cowboys for three seasons. That included sliding into the middle to replace Eugene Lockhart in 1991. He was the Cowboys' leading tackler that season and left afterward to join Minnesota as a free agent before reuniting with Jimmy Johnson in Miami in 1996. While at USC, he also was the number one catcher for a baseball team that featured future Oakland A's star Mark McGwire.

DENNISON, DOUG
Running back, 6'0", 210 lbs., b. 12/18/51

A free agent signed out of Kutztown State, where he was also a triple jumper and long jumper, Dennison specialized in doing what Emmitt Smith did twenty years later— getting into the end zone in short-yardage situations. He was a strong, explosive runner who earned a reputation as one of the best goal-line backs in Cowboys history. His first year with the Cowboys in 1974 he had only 16 carries, but 4 of those were for touchdowns. The next year he led the team in touchdowns with 7; he rushed 111 times for 383 yards. He had a 4-yard TD run in the Cowboys' playoff game against Minnesota, and saw some action in the Super Bowl loss. In 1976 he started at tailback for an injured Preston Pearson in 10 games and led the team in rushing (542 yards on 143 carries) and touchdowns (6). The arrival of Tony Dorsett in 1977 reduced his playing time; that year he had 60 yards on just 12 carries.

The next year was no different—75 yards on 14 carries—and he was traded to the Cleveland Browns in 1979. After a year there, one in the Canadian Football League, and two with the United States Football League, he retired after the 1984 season.

DEOSSIE, STEVE
Linebacker, 6'2", 250 lbs., b. 11/22/62

DeOssie made his mark with the Cowboys as a big hitter on special teams and short-yardage and goal-line situations, but the presence of middle linebacker Eugene Lockhart kept DeOssie from cracking the starting lineup. He chafed in the reduced role and was not content on special teams and as a situational player.

DeOssie's mouth got him in trouble with Jimmy Johnson's coaching staff soon after Johnson's arrival in 1989, and he was traded to the New York Giants. That proved to be a great break for the fun-loving, volatile DeOssie, and he went on to win a Super Bowl ring with the Giants following the 1990 season. DeOssie extended his career into the mid-nineties with the New England Patriots as a deep snapper, one of the more underrated skills in the NFL.

DETERS, HAROLD
Kicker, 6'0", 200 lbs., b. 1/16/44

Only one man recruited by the infamous Cowboy Kicking Karavan of 1967 actually played for Dallas—Harold Deters. He stayed on the taxi squad for most of the year, although he was activated for three games. He made 1 of 4 field goal attempts and was sent back down to the reserves. He was released just before the 1968 season, and retired.

DIAL, BUDDY
Wide receiver, 6'1", 190 lbs., b. 1/17/37

Dial was one of the league's star receivers at Pittsburgh for five years (his career average there was 26.8 yards per catch)

when he was traded to Dallas before the 1964 season. The former Rice All-American was happy to be back in Texas, and the Cowboys were glad to have him; he had burned them many times in the past, and the loss of Billy Howton left a big hole at flanker. But on the fourth day of camp, Dial tore a leg muscle and missed all but the last few games of the season. The next year he was healthy, but the injury changed his running style, and the usually surehanded flanker began to miss passes. He gained 283 yards that year, then 252 in 1966, his last. A back injury kept him out of the entire '67 season; he tried to make a comeback in training camp the next year, but it didn't work. He retired at the age of thirty, his final years with the Cowboys a huge disappointment to everyone. "It's something I've never gotten over," he said years later.

DICKERSON, ANTHONY
Linebacker, 6'2", 221 lbs., b. 6/9/57

Dickerson's football career appeared to be over in 1979. He left SMU following his junior year and signed with Calgary of the Canadian League, but the Stampeders released him after ten games in 1978.

He worked as a handyman at the Burbank Airport in California, then returned to his native area outside Houston and was taking business courses at the University of Houston when the Cowboys offered him a contract in 1980.

"Champ" Dickerson intercepted 2 passes in a game against San Francisco his rookie year and developed into a full-time starter by 1983, when he led the team in solo tackles, finished second in total tackles and quarterback sacks, and turned in a number of big plays. Dickerson was traded to the Buffalo Bills in 1985, his final NFL season.

DICKSON, PAUL
Offensive tackle, 6'5", 250 lbs., b. 2/26/37

Baylor ex Dickson had spent one year as a backup with Los Angeles before he was acquired by the Cowboys for their first year in 1960. "Suitcase" (he was nicknamed for his large hands) saw some action as a backup offensive tackle, then was traded to Minnesota in 1961. There he was converted to a defensive tackle; for the next ten years he backed up the front four of the Purple People Eaters. In 1971 he finished his career with a year in St. Louis.

DIEHL, JOHN
Defensive tackle, 6'7", 250 lbs., b. 1/27/36

The Virginia ex spent four years with Baltimore before he was traded to Dallas, just before the 1965 opener. He saw some backup action at tackle and then was traded to Oakland during the season; he played one year there and retired.

DIMANCHEFF, BABE
Assistant coach

Boris "Babe" Dimancheff played seven years in the NFL and coached for four before signing on with Tom Landry and the Cowboys in 1960, their first year. He coached the Dallas backfield for two years before moving on.

DIRTY DOZEN

The year 1975 was supposed to be a rebuilding year for the Cowboys. But eleven draft picks and one free agent helped Dallas to a 10–4 record and an appearance in Super Bowl X. In what is generally considered the best single-year draft in the history of the NFL, eleven of the Cowboys' eighteen draft choices (Randy White, Scott Laidlaw, Randy Hughes, Kyle Davis, Pat Donovan, Rolly Woolsey, Herb Scott, Bob Breunig, Burton Lawless, Mitch Hoopes, and Thomas Henderson) made the team, and several of them became Pro Bowlers and All-Pros in the ensuing years. Free agent Percy Howard didn't play much but did catch a touchdown pass in the Super Bowl. Mike Hegman, another 1975 draft pick, made the

team the next year and played twelve years for the Pokes. (Another free agent, quarterback Jim Zorn, was cut in favor of Clint Longley, despite having a fine training camp. He went on to become one of the best quarterbacks in the league with Seattle.)

DITKA, MIKE
Tight end/assistant coach, 6'3", 230 lbs., b. 10/18/39

The former All-American out of Pittsburgh had played six years for Chicago and two for Philadelphia before he was traded to the Cowboys in 1969 straight-up for a receiver named David McDaniels. With the Bears he had been Rookie of the Year (12 TDs, 56 catches for 1,076 yards) a five-time Pro Bowler, and four-time All-Pro, but injuries had caused his numbers to go down with the Eagles. Fiercely competitive, a great blocker, and a team leader, Ditka was a perfect fit for the team that couldn't win the big one. His numbers never approached those of his early years, but two seasons later

Mike Ditka

they won the Super Bowl against Miami, in no small part due to the extraordinary blocking of Ditka and Pettis Norman. The two tight ends alternated plays, much as they had all year, shuttling in plays to Roger Staubach. ("The Hammer"—nicknamed for his college basketball play—also scored the last Dallas touchdown, a seven-yard fourth-quarter pass.)

Ditka retired after the 1972 season to become a full-time assistant coach for the Cowboys, finishing his career with 427 catches for 5,913 yards and 43 touchdowns. In 1983 he was named the head coach of the Chicago Bears. He led them to a win in Super Bowl XX, then retired from coaching after the 1989 season.

DIXON, JAMES
Wide receiver/running back, 5'10", 184 lbs., b. 2/2/67

Dixon was a product of the University of Houston's zany Run-and-Shoot offense that produced some of the gaudiest stats in NCAA history. His three seasons as a Cowboy reflected the versatility of his UH football background. He was primarily a kick returner, but he also played wide receiver and running back. He came to the Cowboys in 1989, after being released during the preseason by Detroit. During the 1991 season, he even changed uniform numbers from number 86 to number 21 to play running back.

As a rookie in 1989, Dixon returned a kickoff 97 yards for a touchdown against Kansas City, marking the club's first kickoff return for a touchdown since 1985. He added a 90-yarder the following season against Green Bay. He had a good year in 1989 with 24 catches for 477 yards and a fine 19.9-yard average, tops on the team. He also was second in the NFC with a 25.1-yard average on 47 kick returns. In 1990 he worked as a backup running back, with 11 runs for 43 yards and only 2 catches for 26 yards. He was the team's leading kick returner again that

Act Naturally

Dallas Cowboys in the Movies

- Don Meredith—TV's *Banjo Hackett, "Crime Story,"* others
- John Niland, Craig Morton, D.D. Lewis—*Horror High*
- Jim Boeke—*North Dallas Forty, Heaven Can Wait*
- Ed "Too Tall" Jones—*Semi-Tough, Squeeze Play, The Double McGuffin*
- Drew Pearson, Jay Saldi, Ed Jones—*Squeeze Play*
- Duane Thomas—*The Dallas Cowboys Cheerleaders II*
- Thomas "Hollywood" Henderson—*Squeeze Play, Semi-Tough*
- Harvey Martin—*Mean Joe Green and the Pittsburgh Kid*

year. In 1991 he had no catches and no carries, but he returned 18 kicks for a 22.1-yard average. That was his last year in the NFL.

DOELLING, FRED
Safety, 5'10", 190 lbs.

Doelling, an unsigned free agent rookie out of Pennsylvania in 1960, started at safety for the Cowboys in their first season, his only year in the NFL.

DONALDSON, RAY
Center, 6'3", 300 lbs., b. 5/18/58

Donaldson, who spent thirteen seasons with Indianapolis and two with Seattle, was brought in to fill the void created when All-Pro Mark Stepnoski left for Houston. He hoped to make season number 16 a super season. And while it was, there was the crushing reality that a broken ankle suffered on Thanksgiving Day against Kansas City— in what at the time was considered a Super Bowl preview—kept him out of the big game itself. Despite his injury, he was voted to the Pro Bowl, the fifth time he received that honor.

DONLEY, DOUG
Wide receiver, 6'0", 178 lbs., b. 2/6/59

With Butch Johnson having been traded to Houston and Drew Pearson recovering from a car wreck that would end his career, Donley opened the 1984 season as the starter at wideout. Donley, the Cowboys' fastest receiver, had averaged 20.6 yards per catch in a reserve role in 1983.

Donley had 32 catches for 473 yards and 2 touchdowns in 1984, but recurring shoulder problems opened the door for Mike Renfro, acquired for Johnson, to emerge as the possession receiver complementing Tony Hill.

Known to his teammates as "White Lightning," Donley was too brittle to enjoy a sustained NFL career. After a brief fling with the Chicago Bears in 1986, Donley retired to a business career in Dallas.

DONOHUE, LEON
Offensive guard, 6'4", 245 lbs., b. 3/25/39

A San Jose State ex, Donohue was traded to Dallas from San Francisco in 1965 after three years there (the last two as a starter). He was a fine offensive guard despite several knee injuries. A tremendous pass blocker, he started for most of his three years in Dallas, including the two NFL Championship Games against Green Bay. Knee problems forced him to retire in 1968.

DONOVAN, PAT
Offensive tackle, 6'4", 250 lbs., b. 7/1/53

"Lurch" was one of the top tackles in the NFL in the late seventies and early

Pat Donovan

eighties, earning consecutive trips to the Pro Bowl from 1979–82.

One of the Dirty Dozen rookie draft picks who made the team in 1975, the Stanford ex was a defensive lineman in college. But the Cowboys converted him, as they had another Stanford defensive lineman, Blaine Nye, to the offensive line his first year. He subbed the next few years for both Ralph Neely and Rayfield Wright, and also played well on specialty teams. He was big, fast, strong, and intelligent. In 1977, he took over at right tackle when Wright went down with a knee injury. It was no coincidence that the Cowboys won the Super Bowl in Donovan's first season with the starting unit. The next year he moved to left tackle to fill the void created by the retirement of his mentor, Neely. A fractured wrist bothered him that year on pass blocking, but the next year he was voted to the Pro Bowl. That season marked the start of his four Pro Bowl appearances. Injuries in 1982 began to hamper him, and he retired after the 1983 season.

DOOMSDAY DEFENSE

The Doomsday Defense was a nickname bestowed on Dallas' defensive unit by *Dallas Morning News* sportswriter Gary Cartwright in 1970. It was the year of the Cowboys' first Super Bowl. Minnesota's Purple People Eaters led in most of the defensive categories, but Dallas dominated late, allowing only 15 points in the last 4 games of the season, and only 1 touchdown in the last 17 quarters of the year. The nickname quickly caught on, although despite the fame, only Chuck Howley was named to the All-Pro team that year. Actually, nine of the eleven starters—Larry Cole, George Andrie, Jethro Pugh, Bob Lilly, Dave Edwards, Lee Roy Jordan, Chuck Howley, Mel Renfro, and Cornell Green—had been playing together for several years. Only Green Bay veteran Herb Adderley and super rookie Charlie Waters were new to the unit. Much credit for the defense is due to its coordinator, Ernie Stautner, who began molding the unit upon his arrival in Dallas in 1966.

A few years later, after most of the original Doomsday squad had retired, Doomsday II was coined to describe the 1977 team that won the Super Bowl. They were first against the rush and yielded the lowest passing percentage in the NFC. That team was comprised of starters Randy White, Too Tall Jones, Harvey Martin, Bob Breunig, D.D. Lewis, Tom Henderson, Cliff Harris, Benny Barnes, Charlie Waters, Jethro Pugh, and Aaron Kyle. Doomsday Afternoon, a 1993 marketing ploy that included a poster, didn't catch on. Players featured on the poster were Leon Lett, Tony Tolbert, Robert Jones, Jim Jeffcoat, Tony Casillas, Russell Maryland, and Charles Haley.

DORAN, JIM
Wide receiver, 6'2", 210 lbs., b 8/11/27

In 1960, Doran was the first Dallas Cowboy to be named to the Pro Bowl. After nine years as first a dependable defensive end, then an offensive end on the great Bobby Layne-led championship Detroit Lions teams, Doran was the MVP of the 1952 NFL Championship Game. He was left unprotected in the 1960 expansion draft, and the Cowboys scooped him up. That first year with Dallas, he led the team with 31 catches and 554 yards. In the Cowboys' first game, against the Steelers in the Cotton Bowl, he had perhaps his best day as a pro, catching TD passes of 75 and 54 yards and finishing with 7 passes for 134 yards. (Dallas lost, 35–28.) He retired after the 1961 season with career totals of 212 catches, 3,667 yards, and a 17.3-yard average.

DORSETT, TONY
Running back, 5'11", 185 lbs., b. 4/7/54

Dorsett was the greatest runner in Cowboys history until the arrival of Emmitt Smith. During his eleven-year Dallas career, Dorsett rushed for 12,036 yards on 2,755 carries and scored 72 touchdowns. He added 3,432 receiving yards and still holds a share of an NFL record that can never be broken with a 99-yard touchdown run in 1983 against the Minnesota Vikings.

Known to friends and teammates as "The Hawk" or "T.D.," Dorsett arrived in Dallas as the 1976 Heisman Trophy winner, following a fabulous career at the University of Pittsburgh. He rushed for an NCAA record 6,082 yards and 58 touchdowns and led Pitt to the 1976 national championship with a 12–0 record. The flashy Dorsett broke or tied 14 NCAA records, was a four-time All-American and the first player in NCAA history with four 1,000-yard seasons and three 1,500-yard seasons.

Dallas was due to pick 24th in the first round of the 1977 draft, but the Cowboys pulled off a heist that would have made Willie Sutton proud, sending their first-round pick and three second-rounders to the Seattle Seahawks for the right to select Dorsett.

Coach Tom Landry brought the rookie along slowly, but by the middle of his first

Tony Dorsett

season, Dorsett had given the Cowboys' offense a crackle of excitement. With the breakaway threat of Dorsett providing balance, Dallas' passing game opened up with Roger Staubach throwing to Drew Pearson, Golden Richards, Billy Joe DuPree, Preston Pearson, and others.

The Cowboys swept to victories in the first eight games of 1977, won the last four to repeat as Eastern Division champs, and then marched through the playoffs. Dorsett rushed for 66 yards in a game dominated by the Dallas defense as the Cowboys crushed the Denver Broncos, 27–10, in Super Bowl XII in the Louisiana Superdome, the first Super Bowl played indoors. Dorsett's rookie-of-the-year numbers: 1,007 yards rushing, 273 more through the air, and a total of 13 touchdowns.

Dorsett could only get better, the experts insisted, and they were correct. He gained 1,325 yards rushing and 378 more in receptions, as the Cowboys won their last six games for another division crown and hit the playoffs on a roll. Dorsett and the Cowboys went on to face Dorsett's hometown team,

the Pittsburgh Steelers, in the Super Bowl. The Steelers had beaten the Cowboys three years earlier, 21–17, in Super Bowl X, and the teams were back at the Orange Bowl for another round. In one of the best Super Bowls ever, the Steelers prevailed, 35–31, despite 140 combined rushing and receiving yards from Dorsett.

Critics claimed Dorsett tended to run out of bounds rather than expose himself to big hits. Coach Tom Landry tried to limit Dorsett's carries, reasoning that a lighter workload would extend his career. Dorsett's defenders pointed out that his slender 185-pound frame wasn't built for constant pounding.

Few could argue with the results as Dorsett was voted to four Pro Bowls. His finest season came in 1981 when he amassed 1,646 yards, only 28 behind league leader George Rogers of New Orleans. Dorsett in 1981 established club records for yardage, carries (342), and 100-yard games (9). When Dorsett rushed for 100 or more yards, the Cowboys were 28–1.

But the Cowboys would not get to

another Super Bowl during Dorsett's career in Dallas. In 1986 Landry launched a grand experiment with the signing of USFL star Herschel Walker. Somehow, Landry had to devise a way to provide Walker and Dorsett with enough action to keep them both happy. Slowed by leg injuries, Dorsett gained only 748 yards in 1986 while Walker was rushing for 737 and scoring 14 touchdowns.

Dorsett and Walker posed together for the cover of the 1987 Cowboys media guide, but it was a pairing that was doomed to fail. Walker was used in various sets, and he was spectacular, rushing for 891 yards and catching passes for 715 more. Meanwhile, Dorsett brooded on the bench, gaining only 456 yards and scoring only 1 touchdown. Past his prime, Dorsett was traded to the Denver Broncos for a fifth-round draft pick in June 1988; he rushed for 703 yards in Denver after closing out a dazzling career in Dallas.

Dorsett was beset by tax problems and failed investments late in his career, but he recovered financially and remained a Dallas resident. Dorsett's son, Anthony, developed into a pro prospect as a defensive back for his dad's alma mater and was drafted by the Houston Oilers. Dorsett's autobiography, *Running Tough,* was published in 1988.

DOUGLAS, MERRILL
Running back, 6'0", 205 lbs., b. 3/15/36

Douglas was the second-line fullback for the Chicago Bears for three years. In 1961 the Cowboys picked up the Utah ex. As a backup, he had 5 carries for 24 yards. He played for Philadelphia in 1962 and then retired.

DOWDLE, MIKE
Linebacker/fullback, 6'3", 225 lbs., b. 12/6/37

The former fullback for Texas was drafted by San Francisco in 1960, then released after the final exhibition game. The Cowboys picked him up a few days before the regular season was to begin. He didn't play one down of offense that first year; the only action he saw was on special teams. Landry converted him to linebacker the next year, and he backed up Chuck Howley. He started several games, both for Howley and in the middle for Jerry Tubbs. When Lee Roy Jordan was drafted in 1962, Dowdle was expendable, and soon found himself traded to the 49ers. He was their starting middle linebacker until he retired after the 1966 season.

DOWNS, MICHAEL
Safety, 6'3", 212 lbs., b. 6/6/59

Downs joined Everson Walls as the two Cowboys free agent finds of 1981 training camp. Like Walls, Downs was a former Dallas-area high school star who started as a rookie. They combined to give the Cowboys one of the most solid secondaries of the eighties.

The soft-spoken Downs enjoyed his finest season in 1984, earning All-Pro and All-NFC honors. According to Tom Landry, "Everybody thought he should have gone to the Pro Bowl." Downs was Dallas' top interceptor with 7. He also had 3.5 quarterback sacks, knocked down 13 passes, forced 3 fumbles, recovering 2 of them. Against New Orleans, Downs had 9 tackles, intercepted 2 passes, knocked down a pass, recovered a fumble, and recovered a blocked punt as the Cowboys come back from a 27–6 fourth-quarter deficit to edge the Saints in overtime, 30–27.

Downs was a solid college player for Rice, but hampered by a pinched nerve as a senior, the scouts were scared away and he wasn't drafted. The Dallas South Oak Cliff High School product showed a playmaking flair from the start, however, and had 7 interceptions as a rookie—34 for his career. He also led the secondary in tackles for seven seasons from 1981–87, but struggled in 1988 and was released by the Cowboys in May 1989 after his last season in the NFL.

Cowboys Top Ten Rushing Days

237	Emmitt Smith	@ Philadelphia, October 31, 1993	(30 carries)
206	Tony Dorsett	vs. Philadelphia, December 4, 1977	(23 carries)
183	Tony Dorsett	@ NY Giants, November 9, 1980	(24 carries)
182	Emmitt Smith	@ Phoenix, September 22, 1991	(23 carries)
175	Tony Dorsett	@ Baltimore, December 6, 1981	(30 carries)
174	Emmitt Smith	@ Atlanta, December 21, 1992	(24 carries)
173	Herschel Walker	@ New England, November 15, 1987	(28 carries)
172	Emmitt Smith	vs. Philadelphia, December 6, 1993	(23 carries)
171	Emmitt Smith	@ Pittsburgh, September 4, 1994	(31 carries)
168	Emmitt Smith	@ NY Giants, January 4, 1994	(32 carries)

DUCKETT, KENNY
Wide receiver, 5'11", 183 lbs., b. 10/1/59

The Cowboys signed Duckett for the final three games of the 1985 season for special teams and wide receiver depth, though he didn't catch a pass. He also returned 9 kickoffs for 173 yards that year, his last in the NFL. He played for the New Orleans Saints from 1982–84.

DUGAN, FRED
Wide receiver, 6'3", 200 lbs., b. 3/2/35

Dugan spent two undistinguished years with San Francisco and then was picked up by Dallas in the 1960 expansion draft. He started for the Cowboys during the '60 season, catching 29 passes for 461 yards and 1 touchdown. The next year he was traded to the Washington Redskins, where he became Norm Snead's favorite receiver with 53 catches for 817 yards and 4 TDs in 1961. He played two more years there and then retired.

DULIBAN, CHRIS
See Replacement Games

DUNN, PERRY LEE
Running back, 6'1", 200 lbs., b 1/20/41

Dunn was a quarterback/defensive back out of Mississippi who was the Cowboys' fourth-round draft choice in 1964. Dallas converted him to fullback, and toward the end of the year, he became a starter after Don Perkins was injured, carrying 26 times for 103 yards and catching 2 passes for 30 yards. His second year he saw more action: 54 carries for 171 yards, and eight receptions. But the Cowboys drafted fullback Walt Garrison in the off-season, and Dunn went to Atlanta in the 1966 expansion draft. He played three seasons with the Falcons and one more with the Colts before retiring.

DUPRE, L. G.
Running back, 5'11", 190 lbs., b. 9/10/32

By the time he was selected by the Cowboys from the Colts in 1960, he was near the end of a short but fine career. (He had been instrumental in helping Baltimore win the overtime championship game against New York in 1958.) A celebrated Texas high school running back, he played his college

Cowboys Top Ten Passing Days

460	Don Meredith	@ San Francisco, November 10, 1963	(30 of 48)
406	Don Meredith	@ Washington, November 13, 1966	(21 of 29)
394	Don Meredith	@ Philadelphia, November 6, 1966	(14 of 24)
389	Gary Hogeboom	@ San Francisco, December 22, 1985	(28 of 49)
379	Troy Aikman	@ Phoenix, November 12, 1989	(21 of 40)
377	Danny White	vs. Tampa Bay, October 9, 1983	(29 of 44)
362	Danny White	vs. Atlanta, October 27, 1985	(27 of 47)
359	Danny White	@ Washington, December 13, 1987	(27 of 49)
358	Don Meredith	vs. NY Giants, September 18, 1966	(14 of 24)
354	Danny White	vs. Miami, October 25, 1981	(22 of 32)

ball at Baylor, where legendary announcer Kern Tips gave him his nickname, "Long Gone." In the Cowboys' winless first season, he played a major role in their one tie, against New York; he scored three TDs. He also led the team in rushing (with a meager 362 yards), but the next year saw the arrival of Don Perkins and Amos Marsh in the backfield, and Dupre retired after 1961 to work for GE in contract sales.

DuPree, Billy Joe
Tight end, 6'4", 225 lbs., b. 3/7/50

A key member of the Cowboys' Super Bowl teams of the mid- to late-seventies, DuPree was the ideal tight end for the Cowboys system under Tom Landry. "BJ" was big enough to block outside linebackers and defensive ends during his era when all players were smaller, yet he was mobile enough to serve as a legitimate pass-catching threat. Toward the end of his career, he split time with Doug Cosbie, giving the Cowboys one of the most feared tight end duos in the league. DuPree had 92 consecutive starts before Cosbie won the starting job in 1982.

DuPree was the Cowboys' first-round draft pick in 1973. He became a starter in his

Billy Joe DuPree

rookie year and led the team in receiving yardage with 392 on 29 catches. He lost the starter's job to Jean Fugett in 1975 after a series of injuries hampered him, but he regained it the next year when Fugett signed with Washington. He had 42 receptions for

680 yards that year; in 1977 he had 4 catches for 66 yards in Super Bowl XII. He led the team in 1978 with 9 touchdowns on 34 catches, and he had a TD in the Super Bowl loss to Pittsburgh. DuPree was extremely durable; he played in every game of his eleven-year career, and he started every game from 1976 through 1981, after which Doug Cosbie won the starting job. He was fast (Landry liked to run him on an end-around), and he blocked well. He was voted to the Pro Bowl three years (1976–78) and retired after the 1983 season. DuPree entered the construction business after retirement, and has also worked for the City of Dallas.

DUTTON, JOHN
Defensive tackle, 6'7", 268 lbs., b. 2/6/51

After six seasons as an All-Pro defensive end for the Baltimore Colts, Dutton was acquired by Dallas in a major trade in 1979 and developed into a fine left tackle.

The Cowboys had to fill a void at end after Ed Jones took a hiatus to become a heavyweight boxer and Jethro Pugh retired. Dutton had refused to report to the Colts in a contract dispute with skinflint owner "Tiger Bob" Irsay, and the Cowboys sent Baltimore first- and second-round draft picks for Dutton on October 9, 1979, twenty minutes before the trading deadline. Dutton played through frequent injuries during his first season with the Cowboys.

When Jones abandoned his boxing career prior to the 1980 season, Cowboys defensive coordinator Ernie Stautner shifted Dutton to left tackle, where he split time with Larry Cole. Cole retired following the 1980 season, and Dutton took control of the position in 1981.

Dutton's absence due to a badly bruised left thigh in the 1981 NFC title game

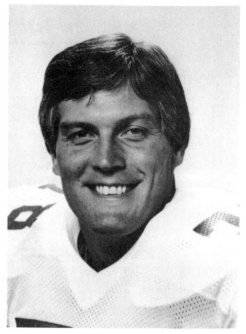

John Dutton

against the San Francisco 49ers was a major blow to the Cowboys' defense. Many have said that if Dutton had been on the field, the Cowboys would have done a better job controlling Joe Montana and the 49ers offense in that pivotal game. San Francisco's 28–27 victory on Dwight Clark's miraculous fourth-quarter catch has been singled out by many NFL historians as the beginning of the Cowboys' fall from grace in the eighties.

Dutton's best season came before he joined the Cowboys, when he led the Colts with an astounding 17 sacks in 1975. Slowed by an accumulation of injuries, Dutton's final season came in 1987.

DWYER, MIKE
See Replacement Games

EASMON, RICKY
Defensive back, 5'10", 160 lbs., b. 7/3/63

The University of Florida product was a reserve defender for the Cowboys in 1985. He also played for the Tampa Bay Buccaneers in 1985 and 1986.

EAST, RON
Defensive tackle, 6'4", 245 lbs., b. 8/26/43

East was a free agent from Montana State, signed by the Cowboys in 1967. He spent four years ably subbing for tackles Jethro Pugh and Bob Lilly, then was traded to San Diego. He played there regularly for three years, then tried the WFL for a year, and finished his career with a year in Cleveland.

ECKLUND, BRAD
Assistant coach

Ecklund, a former All-Pro center in the NFL, was the Cowboys' offensive line coach in their first two years (1960–61) and then coached the defensive line for two years. He left the Cowboys after the 1963 season.

EDDY, JIM
Assistant coach

Eddy joined the Cowboys' staff as linebackers coach in 1993 after becoming the fall guy for the biggest collapse in NFL playoff history: He was the defensive coordinator of the Houston Oilers team that watched a 31–3 halftime lead against the Buffalo Bills in the playoffs turn into an incredible 34–31 defeat. Lost in the emotion of the move was that Eddy was part of three playoff teams in his three seasons in Houston. Eddy was seriously considered for the Cowboys' defensive coordinator position, a job that went to Dave Campo following Butch Davis's departure for Miami in 1995. A popular figure among his NFL peers, Eddy cut his pro coaching teeth in Canada. His career included head coaching stops with Saskatchewan and Montreal.

EDWARDS, DAVE
Linebacker, 6'2", 225 lbs., b. 12/14/39

Signed as a free agent offensive end out of Auburn in 1962, Edwards played thirteen years for the Cowboys and was a

Dave Edwards

53

fixture of the Doomsday Defense of the early seventies. After a year on the taxi squad as an offensive lineman, he saw considerable action in 1963 after injuries to the linebacker corps. He started off and on in 1964, but by 1965 he was a starter. He made himself into an outstanding outside linebacker in the next few years.

He wasn't exceptionally fast, but he had great strength; opponents found it extremely difficult to run against him, and he made few mistakes. As a strongside linebacker, it was his job to control the line of scrimmage, especially against the sweep. But no matter what tight end or pulling guard they sent against him, he'd keep them inside with his immensely strong hands. Chuck Howley and Lee Roy Jordan got all the ink, and the Pro Bowl and All-Pro selections, but his teammates and opponents knew how good he was. One of his finest moments was against Cleveland in the penultimate game of 1970. A doubtful starter due to injuries, Edwards intercepted two passes in the mud to lead the Cowboys to a 6–2 victory that catapulted them into the playoffs. He was the unsung hero of the Doomsday Defense.

EDWARDS, DIXON
Linebacker, 6'1", 225 lbs., b. 3/25/68

Drafted in the second round out of Michigan State in 1991, Edwards spent five seasons with the Cowboys, leaving following the Super Bowl XXX triumph to sign with Minnesota for a hefty pay raise. He was a dependable, durable player, missing only a few starts during his last three years with Dallas—and those were the result of a different pass coverage scheme.

After spending his first two years as a reserve linebacker and special teams standout, Edwards moved into the starting lineup when Vinson Smith was traded in training camp 1993. He soon established himself as Dallas' starting strongside linebacker. He combined excellent speed for pass coverage with solid strength to play the run. In 1994 Dixon was third on the team with 104 tackles. After recording 6 tackles against

Green Bay in the 1994 Divisional Playoff Game, he dislocated his right shoulder in the NFC Championship Game at San Francisco and later underwent off-season surgery. The following year, his last with Dallas, he was back in action and again was third on the team, this time with 109 tackles, and he was tops among linebackers in the playoffs with 16 tackles.

EDWARDS, KELVIN
Wide receiver, 6'2", 204 lbs., b. 7/19/64

Signed as a free agent after starting his career in New Orleans in 1986, Edwards was a promising player for Dallas from 1987–88. Edwards starred for the Cowboys replacement team during the strike of 1987, catching 14 passes for 272 yards and 3 touchdowns and adding a 62-yard touchdown off a reverse during the three games during the strike.

A few weeks after the regulars returned, Edwards was back in the starting lineup, where he remained for the rest of the '87 season. The Cowboys were looking for Edwards to cement his roster spot in 1988; he seemed on his way to a big season, catching 5 passes for 93 yards in the first three quarters of the '88 opener. But after suffering a season-ending knee injury in the fourth quarter of the game, Edwards never fully recovered and never caught another pass in the NFL.

EIDSON, JIM
Offensive guard, 6'4", 260 lbs., b. 5/10/54

A second-round draft pick in 1976, Eidson saw little action in his only year in Dallas, although he occasionally was a deep snapper on punts and placements. An injury kept him sidelined all of 1977; he retired after the season.

ELAM, ONZY
Linebacker, 6'2", 225 lbs., b. 12/1/64

After two years with the New York Jets, the Tennessee State product was picked up on waivers by the Cowboys. He was on hand as a backup linebacker and special teamster for Dallas' nightmare 1989 campaign. He was released after the season and was out of the NFL.

ELLIOTT, LIN
Kicker, 6'0", 182 lbs., b. 11/11/68

The Texas Tech ex was the regular kicker for the Cowboys' 1992 title team before being replaced by veteran Eddie Murray after two games of the 1993 campaign. The Cowboys, playing without holdout Emmitt Smith for the first two games in 1993, lost to Washington and Buffalo. In the 13–10 loss to the Bills, Elliott missed from 49 and 30 yards and was gone. His presence in a Cowboy uniform in 1992 was unlikely—trying to win the job in training camp, he missed the first three preseason games because of a groin pull. He won the job by hitting 3 of 4 field goal attempts in the last two preseason games. Elliott finished the season third in NFC scoring, tops among rookies, despite struggling through the first half of the year. He went on to play for Atlanta and then Kansas City.

ERKENBECK, JIM
Assistant coach

Erkenbeck was a tough-talking, chain-smoking former Marine who seemed drafted out of central casting to play the role of the typical offensive line coach. The San Diego native could be brutally honest, but he could also praise lavishly when situations warranted.

The Cowboys hired Erkenbeck in 1987 as the successor to long-time assistant head coach and line coach Jim Myers, and Erkenbeck was on Tom Landry's staff for two years before Jimmy Johnson's arrival in 1989.

Erkenbeck had coached all over the football map. He started as a high school head coach in his hometown, moved on to an assistant's job at his alma mater, San Diego State, then was an assistant in the Canadian Football League and the USFL. Erkenbeck got his first NFL job in 1985 as line coach for the New Orleans Saints. After the Cowboys, he was on the Kansas City Chiefs' staff from 1989–91.

EVERETT, THOMAS
Safety, 5'9", 183 lbs., b. 11/21/64

The acquisition of Everett, a holdout at Pittsburgh, before the 1992 season was an example of how Jimmy Johnson slowly added talent to his roster to produce back-to-back Super Bowl champs. Everett had played college ball at Baylor and five years as a starter for the Steelers. He was traded to the Cowboys on September 20, and by mid-season was a force at strong safety; he was voted to the Pro Bowl that year. After two seasons, Everett signed with Tampa Bay. One of ten children, Everett's family was from Daingerfield, TX. He won the first Jim Thorpe Trophy as the nation's best college defensive back in 1986 at Baylor.

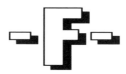

FALLS, MIKE
Offensive guard, 6'1", 240 lbs., b 3/3/34

Falls, out of Minnesota, began his professional career with Toronto in the Canadian Football League in 1956. After two years in the military, he played a year in New York. He was traded to the Packers, who cut him, then was picked up by Dallas the week before their 1960 opener; by midseason he had won the starting right guard position. The next year, Falls was a backup, and knee problems ended his career in 1962. He joined the clergy and became an Episcopal chaplain.

FELLOWS, RON
Cornerback, 6'0", 180 lbs., b. 11/7/58

Fellows was a solid, if unspectacular, corner for the Cowboys from 1981–86 before his trade to the Los Angeles Raiders in 1987, where he ended his career the following season.

Fellows won the starting right corner job after Dennis Thurman was moved to safety in 1984. A college receiver at Missouri, Fellows was shifted to the secondary after he was drafted in the seventh round in 1981. He served as a nickel defensive back his first three seasons and was considered one of the league's best situational defenders during that span. His best season was in 1983, when he was the team's number-one kickoff return man and also had five interceptions for 139 yards.

FIELDINGS, ANTHONY
Linebacker, 6'1", 237 lbs., b. 7/9/71

Fieldings originally signed in 1993 with the Bills out of Morningside College in Iowa.

He was released at the end of training camp. The same scenario happened the following season. He played during the spring of 1995 with the World League of American Football's Rhein Fire, where he was the team's MVP. He signed with the Cowboys in July as a free agent, and made the team in training camp. Fieldings played on special teams and nickel defense situations the first four games, then was released on waivers after the fifth game of the season.

FISHBACK, JOE
Safety, 6'0", 212 lbs., b. 11/29/67

Fishback established himself as something of a special-teams legend during his two seasons with Dallas. He played three seasons on special teams with the New York Giants (who signed him in 1990 as a free agent out of Carson-Newman), the New York Jets, and the Atlanta Falcons before arriving in Dallas in October 1993. In his first game, he recorded two special-teams tackles against San Francisco. Later that year, he missed five games due to arthroscopic surgery, although he came back to play well. He finished with 29 regular-season tackles on special teams in his two years. He was released after the 1994 season and retired.

FISHER, RAY
Defensive tackle, 6'3", 230 lbs., b. 2/12/34

Fisher was an Eastern Illinois product who was picked up from Pittsburgh in the 1960 expansion draft. He was injured before the season started, sat out the year, and then retired.

FITZGERALD, JOHN
Center, 6'5", 260 lbs., b. 4/16/48

The Cowboys' fourth-round pick in 1970, Fitzgerald played ten solid years for Dallas. He had been a defensive tackle at Boston College, and he had bounced around the offensive line his rookie year, which he spent on the taxi squad. He saw more and more action the next few years; in 1973, his size and speed (4.0 in the 40-yard dash) helped make him starting center, following the retirement of Dave Manders. For years, he was the only center to snap the ball in the spread formation. "Fitz" wasn't the world's greatest athlete, but the big Irishman had an All-Pro sense of humor and an upbeat view of life. He was president of the Cowboys' Iro-American Club, calling his fellow offensive linemen "Four Irishmen and a Scott"—sons of Erin Pat Donovan, Tom Rafferty, Jim Cooper, and Fitzgerald, along with African-American guard Herb Scott.

Fitzgerald started in three Super Bowls. His athletic skills may have been limited, but his leadership, attitude, and

John Fitzgerald

desire made up for any shortcomings. "He tries so hard all the time," line coach Jim Myers said. "He may be the toughest we've got." Fitzgerald also took pride in his snapping skills in the shotgun formation. "It has shed a little light on me," he said. "When people talk about how different guys have sixty percent completion averages, they don't realize mine is ninety-nine, and that's with a couple of drops."

Fitzgerald anchored the offensive line until 1980, although several injuries (knee and elbow surgery, back spasms, foot trouble) made him consider retirement more than once. When the foot trouble sidelined him midway through the 1980 season, Robert Shaw took over the job. Fitz planned on one more year, but a preseason thigh injury, and then another knee injury in 1981, moved him to the injured reserve list the entire season. He retired after that season with more games logged at center than any other player in Dallas history. A native of Southbridge, MA, Fitzgerald remained in Dallas working as an insurance executive.

FLAHERTY, HARRY
See Replacement Games

FLEMING, CORY
Wide receiver, 6'1", 216 lbs., b. 3/19/71

The Cowboys had hoped Fleming might help fill the 1995 void created by Alvin Harper's defection to Tampa Bay. Not quite. Though he had a good preseason, during the regular season he caught more flak from fans than passes (6 of the latter for 83 yards). That season was a success, however, compared to his time with San Francisco. He was chosen by the 49ers in the third round of the 1994 draft, but was released without ever signing a contract or even reporting to training camp. What a surprise, considering Fleming was such a standout at the University of Tennessee, where he broke Harper's school record for career touchdown catches. Fleming signed as a free agent with Dallas in 1994, but was activated for only five games and had no receptions. He was released after the 1995 season.

THE FLEX

The Flex defense was Tom Landry's variation on his own 4–3 defense that he had designed (around Hall of Fame middle linebacker Sam Huff) as an assistant coach with the New York Giants in the fifties. The 4–3 had proved amazingly successful, helping win championships in 1956 and 1958 for the Giants, and it later became standard equipment for every NFL team. But by the time he got to Dallas, Landry saw the need to refine the basic 4–3, to make it effective against all offenses, including the multiple formations that had risen to solve it. "Lombardi wrote *Run to Daylight*," said Landry, "and we wanted to take away the daylight."

He developed a defense that, for all its vaunted complexity, was fiendishly simple at its core. (Landry claimed it was based on engineering principles.) The problem with it—and the reason so many players found it difficult to master—was that it violated the basic instinct of a player. Instead of moving immediately toward the ball, each player first secured his assigned area, his "gap," in a coordinated response to the action of the offense. Only then could he move toward the ball; freewheeling, follow-your-instincts play was not permitted. In effect, the Flex stifled a player's natural impulse to pursue and insisted that he wait for the ball to come to him. (Only the middle linebacker had more than one gap to control.)

The Flex required a discipline that often took years to learn. Until then, players acted on faith. Some never could muster that faith, that discipline, and they never mastered the Flex. "It took a lot of character to play the Flex," said Landry.

With the Cowboys, Landry began installing the Flex from the start. Many of the older castoffs from other teams refused to learn this new system; old dogs, it seems,

couldn't learn new tricks. Most of them moved on in a year or two, through their own wishes or through Landry's. It took several years before those early Dallas defenses were nearly as good as the offenses. (In their second year of existence, the Cowboys were already second in the league in offense.)

But by 1965 it was starting to work. Dallas was getting the best—and some of the quickest and brightest—players around, thanks to personnel director Gil Brandt, and they were finally beginning to believe in the Flex. After the two Championship Game losses to the Packers, the Flex was achieving a mythic reputation for its "intricacy" and "complexity." When put into effect by players such as Bob Lilly, Jethro Pugh, Lee Roy Jordan, and Chuck Howley, the scheme looked positively frightening. With athletes like Jordan and then Breunig running the Flex, and leading a cast of like characters, it was unbeatable through the seventies. And it was so daunting to other teams that only San Francisco (whose coach, Dick Nolan, had been a defensive coach under Landry) dared to attempt it in the early seventies.

But smart teams gradually learned to beat the Flex—first Pittsburgh, then Oakland, and then other teams figured out how to do it. There were other reasons for Dallas' decline in the eighties—bad draft picks, aging greats, etc.—but Landry's refusal to modify or scrap the Flex was a factor. The Flex met its demise in 1989 with the arrival of owner Jerry Jones and coach Jimmy Johnson, who put it out of its misery. It now exists only as a legend parents tell children of on cold winter nights—and cool Sunday afternoons.

FLOWERS, RICHMOND
Safety, 6'1", 180 lbs., b. 6/13/47

Flowers was an All-American wide receiver and a world-class hurdler at Tennessee, but the Cowboys made him a second-round draft pick in 1969 with defense in mind. They converted him to a defensive back, and during the 1970 season he shared starting honors with rookies Charlie Waters and Cliff Harris. He also served on specialty teams, leading the Cowboys in kickoff returns in 1969. But he saw little action the following year, and early in the 1971 season, he was traded to the New York Giants, where he started at strong safety through 1973. He finished his career with two years in the WFL.

FOLKINS, LEE
Tight end, 6'5", 220 lbs., b. 7/4/39

Folkins was a rookie end out of Washington on Vince Lombardi's first championship team in Green Bay, in 1961. The next year, "Snake" was traded to the Cowboys for a future draft choice (he had incurred Lombardi's wrath by accidentally knocking out an official in a preseason game). He quickly won the starting tight end job and had a good year receiving—39 catches for 536 yards and 6 touchdowns. The next year was almost as good (31 catches for 407 yards), but his numbers fell drastically in 1964 (only five for 41 yards). He played mostly on specialty teams, and was also pressed into service as a punter the final two games of the season. He was traded just before the 1965 season to the Pittsburgh Steelers. He had an unimpressive year there and retired after the season.

FOLSOM, STEVE
Tight end, 6'5", 240 lbs., b. 3/21/58

The well-traveled Folsom played for the Cowboys from 1987–89. With Doug Cosbie injured for most of the 1988 season, Folsom helped fill the void.

Although he was used primarily as the second tight end on running downs, Folsom also caught 9 passes for 84 yards in 1988. Folsom was Dallas' top receiving tight end for the 1–15 team in 1989, finishing second on the team with 28 catches for 265 yards and 2 touchdowns, while starting all 16 games.

Following brief stints with the Philadelphia Eagles in 1981 and the New York Giants in 1982, Folsom played three seasons for the USFL's glamour team, the Philadelphia-Baltimore Stars.

FORD, BERNARD
Wide receiver, 5'9", 168 lbs., b. 2/27/66

A free agent signed out of Central Florida in 1989, Ford played one season for the Cowboys, catching 7 passes for 78 yards and 1 touchdown. He caught on with the Houston Oilers for one season in 1990 and then retired from the NFL.

FORD, ROBERT
Assistant coach

Ford, who has been on the Cowboys' coaching staff since 1991, can relax in the knowledge that his name will never be erased from the NCAA record book... as long as a football field remains 100 yards long. As a wide receiver at the University of Houston, Ford caught 2 touchdown passes for 99 yards. Coaching stops for the native of Belton, TX, have included the USFL's Houston Gamblers (one year), Texas Tech, and Texas A&M. With the Cowboys, Ford has coached tight ends.

FOWLER, TODD
Fullback/tight end, 6'3", 226 lbs., b. 6/9/62

A native of Van, TX, fifty miles east of Dallas, Fowler—nicknamed "Country"—was a second-team all-state tight end at Van High School, where he was coached by his father, Mal, who played fullback for TCU in the early fifties.

Fowler came to the Cowboys in 1985 with impressive credentials from the USFL. He rushed for 1,003 yards and had 301 yards in passes for the Houston Gamblers in 1984. Dallas tapped him in the first round of the supplemental draft of USFL players in 1984, but he never lived up to his promise during his Cowboys career from 1985–88, contributing mostly on special teams.

Fowler moved in at fullback for the injured Timmy Newsome in the final half of the 1988 season, finishing with more catches (10) and receiving yards (64) than in his three previous seasons combined for the Cowboys. A knee injury forced Fowler's retirement.

FRANCIS, RON
Cornerback, 5'9", 201 lbs., b. 4/7/64

Francis' injury-plagued Cowboys career lasted from 1987–90. A second-round pick, Francis began his career in 1987 as the first rookie defensive back to start for the Cowboys since 1981, but the following year, he suffered a dislocated shoulder in the Blue-White training camp scrimmage and was sidelined for two months.

Francis opened the 1989 training camp battling his former Baylor roommate and teammate, Robert Williams, to regain his starting right cornerback spot. Francis, Williams, and another teammate, Broderick Sargent, played in the same offensive backfield at Baylor before Francis was moved to defense.

When Williams went down with a knee injury early in the 1989 season, Francis was back with the starters and responded in that first game against the Giants with his fourth career interception. He finished the 1989 season as the team leader in deflected passes with 10. He played the next year but saw little action, and was traded to the Patriots before the 1991 season. He failed to make the team and retired from the NFL.

Francis's brother, James, was an All-American linebacker at Baylor and the first-round draft choice of the Cincinnati Bengals in 1990.

FRANCKHAUSER, TOM
Defensive back, 6'1", 195 lbs., b. 5/26/37

The very first Dallas Cowboy to touch a football in a regular-season game was this former wide receiver out of Purdue. After a year with the Los Angeles Rams, he was selected by the Cowboys in the 1960 expansion draft. He received the opening kickoff from the Pittsburgh Steelers in Dallas' first game. In that long season he returned 26 kickoffs (a league high) for 526 yards (a 20.2–yard average). An excellent tackler, he was a starter at cornerback for most of his two years with Dallas (1960–61), except for a few months of National Guard duty in 1961. He then was traded to another expansion team, Minnesota. He played there 3 years before retiring and returning to Dallas, after the 1964 season.

FRANK, BILL
Offensive tackle, 6'5", 255 lbs., b. 4/13/38

Frank, a free agent out of Colorado, played three years with Vancouver in the Canadian Football League. He was signed by the Cowboys the week of the ninth game of the 1964 season, saw little action, and was released after the season.

FRANKLIN, BOBBY
Assistant coach

Franklin spent seven years as a defensive back with the Cleveland Browns before retiring after the 1966 season. After a year as an assistant at Georgia Tech, he coached the Dallas secondary from 1968–72.

FREDERICK, ANDY
Offensive tackle, 6'6", 255 lbs., b. 7/25/54

A reserve lineman from 1977–81, Frederick was a fifth-round pick from New Mexico in the 1977 draft who spent his career stuck as a backup behind Ralph Neely, Rayfield Wright, Pat Donovan, and Jim Cooper. Another Cowboy who made the switch from a college defensive lineman, he stepped in as a starter during injury emergencies in 1978 and 1980. In the days before megabuck contracts, Frederick spent one off-season as a self-employed house painter.

He spent five years after the Cowboys with Cleveland and Chicago, before a foot injury ended his career.

FRITSCH, TONI
Kicker, 5'7", 185 lbs., b. 7/10/45

In 1970, when Tex Schramm noticed that four of the top six field-goal records belonged to soccer-style kickers, a light bulb appeared over his head. Those four weren't even first-division pros in that sport. What if a really good soccer player tried kicking field goals—how good might he be? He proceeded to spend more than $30,000 scouting Europe, and sending himself, Gil Brandt, and coaches Tom Landry and Ermal Allen to view the results. They brought three kickers back to Dallas. The only one that stayed had been a right winger on Austria's national team; they signed him on the day he hit 29 of 30 field goals at 40 yards.

His first year, 1971, Fritsch was on the taxi squad, but halfway into the season, Landry, unhappy with his erratic veteran

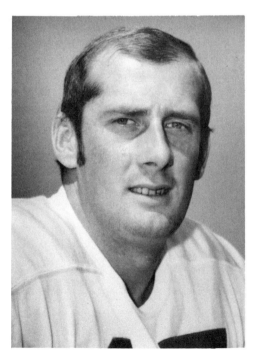

Toni Fritsch

kicker, Mike Clark, switched kickers, activating Fritsch and waiving Clark onto the taxi squad. Fritsch looked good hitting 5 of 8 attempts, including 3 of 4 and the game-winner in a pivotal game against St. Louis, but he pulled a hamstring muscle in practice after the next game and Clark took over for the rest of the year. But the next year, Clark was injured, and Fritsch hit 21 of 36 attempts and led the league in extra points (36/36). Clark was back the next year, but only as Fritsch's backup. Fritsch again led the league in extra points (43/43) and hit on 18 of 28 field goal attempts. A knee injury kept him sidelined all of 1974, allowing Efren Herrera a chance to show his excellent form. The next year saw Herrera sit out the year with an injury; Fritsch had a good but not great year, missing 2 extra points and hitting 22 of 35 field goal attempts. He was traded in 1976 to San Diego after missing only 1 three-point try in the playoffs. He was an active kicker through 1985 with Houston, New Orleans, and the USFL, and retired with a 68 percent average.

FROST, KEN
Defensive tackle, 6'4", 250 lbs., b. 11/17/38

Frost was a free agent out of Tennessee (he had flunked out) and was signed by the Cowboys in 1961. A big, strong tackle, he played regularly two years with Dallas and then retired after the 1962 season.

FRY, BOB
Offensive tackle, 6'4", 240 lbs., b. 11/11/30

A third-round draft choice out of Kentucky for the Rams in 1953, Fry played five full seasons as a starter for Los Angeles (and spent two in the military) before he was picked by Dallas in the 1960 expansion draft. Fry was known as a master of the hidden hold. He was the Cowboys' starting left tackle for five seasons, and retired just as the offensive line was beginning to earn respect around the league. Since then he has held coaching spots with Atlanta, Pittsburgh, and the Jets.

FUGETT, JEAN
Tight end, 6'3", 220 lbs., b. 12/16/51

Fugett was only twenty when he reported to the Cowboys' summer training camp. A thirteenth-round draft choice out of Amherst in the 1972 draft, he ended up alternating with veteran Mike Ditka as one of Dallas' two regular tight ends and saw action on the specialty teams. He had good speed for a tight end, and there was some talk about making him a wide receiver. He caught 7 passes for 94 yards that year. The next year, a big first-rounder named Billy Joe DuPree stepped into a starter's role in his rookie season; Fugett backed him up and had a healthy 168 yards on 9 catches for a 19-yard net average, tops on the team. His numbers dropped in 1974—4 receptions for 60 yards—but in 1975, he took over the starting job when DuPree suffered several injuries that limited his playing time. Fugett caught a career-high 38 passes for 488 yards that year, his final one in a Dallas uniform, and he started in the Super Bowl. (He had 1 catch for 9 yards.) He was signed by the Washington Redskins the next season and spent four years with them before retiring; he led the club in receptions and yards in 1977.

GAECHTER, MIKE
Defensive back, 6'0", 190 lbs., b. 1/9/40

Gaechter was a wiry 9.4 sprinter in the 100-yard dash from the University of Oregon when Gil Brandt signed him as a free agent in 1962. (He and Mel Renfro had teamed on the 440-yard relay team to set a 40.6 NCAA record.) In the next few years, he earned a reputation as a hard-hitting strong safety; his rookie year he had a 100-yard interception return for a TD against Philadelphia.

He won a cornerback job from Warren Livingston, four games into his rookie season, and finished the year with 5 interceptions. He also returned the occasional punt and kickoff, something he would do over the next few years. But several games into 1963 he went to safety, where he'd stay until he retired. That season saw him set the Cowboys' single-game record with 121 interception yards against Washington. A broken elbow sidelined him four games into 1964, and when he came back, he was primarily a backup. But he won back his starting job at safety the next year. Gaechter was complex, smart, and unpredictable; when he ruptured his Achilles tendon in the meaningless Playoff Bowl at the end of the 1969 season, ending his career, he filed a lawsuit against the Cowboys and their team doctor. He finished his career with 21 interceptions.

Mike Gaechter (27) deflects a 1967 pass. Flanking him are Mel Renfro (20) and Cornell Green (34). *(From the collection of the Texas/Dallas History and Archive Division, Dallas Public Library)*

GAINER, DERRICK
Running back, 5'11", 240 lbs., b. 8/15/66

Gainer spent two seasons in Dallas as a special-teams player and running back. He began with Cleveland in 1990, and also played with the Los Angeles Raiders in 1992 before signing with the Cowboys the following September. His 1992 totals with Dallas consisted of 2 special-teams tackles. In 1993, his last year as a Cowboy, he rushed 9 times for 29 yards, and had six catches for 37 yards in an unsuccessful attempt to become Emmitt Smith's primary backup. He was traded to the Raiders after the season, but he didn't make the team and retired from the NFL.

GALBRAITH, SCOTT
Tight end, 6'2", 255 lbs., b. 1/7/67

With hobbies like being a deputy probation officer in the Los Angeles Police Department, it's obvious Galbraith is a tough guy. For the 1993–94 seasons in Dallas, his hobbies included being the Cowboys' second tight end in the short-yardage offense. Signed in November 1993 after injuries to Alfredo Roberts and Jim Price, he quickly established himself as a key blocker in the Dallas running game and distinguished himself on special teams. He had played three seasons with Cleveland, including thirteen starts for the Browns in 1991. He got a measure of revenge against Cleveland when he caught a one-yard touchdown pass (his only reception of the season) against the Browns in 1993. His role was the same in 1994; he had 4 catches for 31 yards behind Novacek. With the arrival of rookie tight ends Kendall Watkins and Eric Bjornson, he was gone. He was signed by the Redskins in 1995 as a backup tight end.

GANT, KENNETH
Safety, 5'11", 189 lbs., b. 4/18/67

Where else but Dallas could a special-teams player out of tiny Albany (GA) State become a national phenomenon, all because of a silly stance on kickoffs? That's what happened with Gant, whose Shark Dance became a staple of national telecasts. Gant was a ninth-round draft pick in 1990, and he made an instant impression on special teams. He led the special teams with 25 tackles in 1991 and played cornerback in some of the Cowboys' multiple defensive back alignments. He was moved to safety for 1992 and responded with several big plays. He tied for the team lead in interceptions (3) and forced fumbles (3). A shoulder separation during the 1994 preseason slowed him, although he excelled in the season opener. He reinjured the shoulder several games later and then underwent arthroscopic surgery for a sprained right knee, all of which kept him out of action until the season finale. He forced a fumble on a Green Bay kickoff return during the playoffs, which Joe Fishback recovered to set up a Jay Novacek touchdown catch. For the record, Gant did do more than play on special teams and dance. He provided some depth in the secondary, especially in the expanded nickel package. Gant left Dallas in 1995 to play for Tampa Bay in a similar capacity.

GARRETT, JASON
Quarterback, 6'2", 195 lbs., b. 3/28/66

Some might think a Princeton grad (signed as a free agent in 1993 after stints with San Antonio of the the World League and the Ottawa Roughriders of the Canadian Football League) would be smart enough not to waste his time as the Cowboys' third-string quarterback. Cowboys fans didn't consider it a waste on Thanksgiving Day 1994, when Garrett stepped in for the injured Troy Aikman and Rodney Peete. All Garrett did was establish a team record by scoring 36 second-half points in a 42–31 victory over the Packers. Garrett also started a game in 1993, a 20–15 victory over Phoenix, after beating out Hugh Millen for the backup spot behind Aikman. In 1995, he was 4 of 5 for 1 touchdown in the fourth quarter in a loss to

San Francisco, after Aikman and Wade Wilson left with injuries.

GARRISON, WALT
Running back, 6'0", 210 lbs., b. 7/23/44

"Puddin," as his teammates called him, was a cowboy long before Dallas drafted him out of Oklahoma State, in the fifth round of the 1966 draft. He was active on the rodeo circuit so when the Cowboys offered him a Pontiac Grand Prix as part of his bonus, he said he'd rather have a two-horse trailer and a new Stetson. He inherited the fullback job when Don Perkins retired after the 1968 season, and he gave the Cowboys rock-solid play there through 1974. Speedy he wasn't, but he was one of the toughest ever to wear the Cowboy stars. In the 1970 Championship Game against San Francisco, he left the game early on with a cracked ankle, but soon returned to gain 71 yards on 17 carries, and he caught the winning touchdown. The next year, he gained 74 yards on 14 carries in Super Bowl V against Miami. He was a strong receiver out of the backfield, and led Dallas with 40 receptions in 1971. It was his first love, rodeo, that ended his football career when he tore up a leg bulldogging a steer in Montana. He retired after the 1974 season with a 4.3-yard average and 3,886 yards in nine years.

GAY, EVERETT
Wide receiver, 6'2", 209 lbs., b. 10/23/64

The University of Texas product was the surprise of 1988 training camp before injuring his knee on July 21. Gay regained his health and caught his first pass against the New Orleans Saints in October, and then was the team coleader with 5 catches the following week against the Chicago Bears. Later in the season, against the Cleveland Browns, Gay averaged 20.7 yards on 3 catches.

Tall and fast, the fifth-round pick in

Walt Garrison hammers out four more yards against the Rams, 1970. (*From the collection of the Texas/Dallas History and Archive Division, Dallas Public Library*)

1987 had little exposure to a pro-style passing offense at Texas and spent his rookie season in 1987 on injured reserve, learning the Cowboys' system. Gay was traded to Tampa Bay in 1989, where he finished his pro career after one year.

GENT, PETE
Wide receiver, 6'4", 208 lbs., b. 8/23/42

Gent was a good basketball player for Michigan State, and he turned down an offer from the NBA Baltimore Bullets when the Cowboys signed him as a free agent. He played five years for the Cowboys from 1964 through 1968. He saw little action his first year, but in 1965 he caught 16 passes for 233 yards. His best year was 1966, when he split time with Buddy Dial, then replaced him, as starting flanker; he had 27 catches for 474 yards and 1 touchdown. On October 30, 1966, against the Pittsburgh Steelers, he scored on an 84-yard reception from Don Meredith. The next year he backed up Lance Rentzel and Bob Hayes at flanker and split end, and in 1968, after surgery for a broken ankle and a wrecked knee, he worked at tight end in passing situations. Though he wasn't particularly fast, he had great hands, and he was a good blocker, but a bad knee prevented him from seeing much action his last couple of years. He was traded to the Giants after the 1968 season, but New York put him on waivers, and he retired. He worked for a while for a Dallas ad agency as an account executive, then for a printing firm. In 1973 his novel _North Dallas Forty_ was published; it was clearly based on his Cowboy experiences. The book became a bestseller and later a fine movie. Gent moved to Wimberley, TX, and wrote four more sports novels, none coming close to his first in impact or sales. In 1996 he published _The Last Magic Summer: A Season with My Son_, a memoir about coaching his son's Connie Mack baseball team.

GESEK, JOHN
Offensive guard, 6'5", 282 lbs., b. 2/18/63

Gesek was acquired by the Cowboys in September 1990 from the Los Angeles Raiders for a fifth-round draft pick. He went on to become a solid addition to Dallas' offensive line, starting at right guard for most of his four years as a Cowboy and playing a key role in Emmitt Smith's league-leading rushing numbers in 1991, 1992, and 1993. He was signed by the Washington Redskins in 1994.

GIBBS, SONNY
Quarterback, 6'7", 225 lbs., b. 10/25/39

The tall TCU star with a rocket for an arm was the biggest disappointment of the young Dallas scouting system. In 1962, when he was a junior, the Cowboys made him their first selection, a future pick. A year later, he signed with Dallas. But he showed little aptitude for signal-calling in the NFL, and he never played in a regular-season game. He played the next year in Detroit, where he threw 3 passes for 1 completion and one interception, then retired.

GILLMAN, SID
Assistant coach

The former longtime San Diego Chargers coach was hired in 1972 by Tom Landry as a special assistant to Ermal Allen in the scouting and research department. He left after one season to become the head coach of the Houston Oilers for two years.

GOGAN, KEVIN
Offensive lineman, 6'7", 306 lbs., b. 11/2/64

Gogan was a goofy, gregarious character, popular with teammates, who was predicted to have a short career. But when the

1987 eighth-round pick from the University of Washington inherited the starting right tackle job after Phil Pozderac decided to retire following the '87 players strike, Gogan grabbed the job and held it for virtually all of the rest of that year and the next two seasons. Gogan impressed in his starting debut, making a strong showing against Philadelphia Eagles All-Pro defensive end Reggie White.

In 1991, the Cowboys saw a hole at left guard, and the versatile Gogan was plugged into that gap. Gogan performed well there for a unit that paved the way for Emmitt Smith to lead the league in rushing with 1,563 yards, and that same unit also provided the kind of pass protection that enabled Michael Irvin to pace the league in receiving yardage with 1,523. Dallas' offensive line was one of the team's most dramatically improved positional groups, permitting 2 sacks or less in 11 of 16 games, and 1 sack or less in 8 games.

When Nate Newton was shifted from right tackle to left guard, making room for sensational young tackle Erik Williams, Gogan became the line's number one backup in 1992, starting only one game as the Cowboys marched to the Super Bowl title. Gogan was back in the starting lineup at right guard in 1993, and his excellent play helped the Cowboys to a second straight Super Bowl championship.

Gogan was an accomplished athlete despite his massive size. He was among the team's best racquetball players and, in high school, was a standout catcher and first baseman.

When Gogan received a generous free agent offer from the Los Angeles Raiders during the spring of 1994, the Cowboys' salary cap problems made it difficult for them to counter with a competitive bid. Gogan's departure represented the loss of one of the team's most accomplished locker room comics and a close friend of quarterback Troy Aikman.

GONZAGA, JOHN
Defensive end, 6'3", 250 lbs., b. 3/6/33

Gonzaga had been an offensive lineman for five years with San Francisco, until he was selected by the Cowboys in the 1960 expansion draft. Landry converted him to defense, and he started and saw plenty of action that first Cowboy season. He was traded in 1961 to Detroit, where he played five years, then finished out his career with a season in Denver. He was one of the few noncollege players to make it in pro football.

GONZALEZ, LEON
Wide receiver, 5'10", 162 lbs., b. 9/21/63

An eighth-round pick from Bethune-Cookman in 1985, "Speedy" Gonzalez turned in an impressive performance in his rookie training camp to earn a roster spot. Sure-handed, Gonzalez played in a pro-style offense in college and caught five passes for 93 yards in the 1985 preseason. He spent the 1985 regular season as a punt returner and backup to starting wide receiver Mike Renfro, but bad feet that eventually required surgery ended his first season in December. Gonzalez caught 3 passes for 28 yards for the Cowboys, and after Dallas waived him, he played for the Atlanta Falcons in 1987, ending his NFL career there.

GOWDY, CORNELL
Defensive back, 6'0", 192 lbs., b. 10/2/63

Gowdy was a free agent pickup who played in the nickel defense in 1986. He moved on to the Pittsburgh Steelers, the team that signed and released him as a 1985 rookie. Gowdy played for Pittsburgh in 1987–88 and then retired.

GRANGER, CHARLIE
Offensive tackle, 6'2", 240 lbs.

Granger was a free agent signed by the Cowboys out of Southern University in 1961.

He was traded during the year to the St. Louis Cardinals, and retired after the season.

GRANGER, NORM
Fullback, 5'9", 220 lbs., b. 9/14/61

Granger was a burly Robert Newhouse-type fullback who made the team in 1984, as a fifth-round rookie from Iowa. He played in fifteen games as a rookie, mostly on special teams, and backed up starter Timmy Newsome. Granger sat out 1985 and 1986 with various injuries, then joined the Atlanta Falcons in 1987, his last year in the NFL.

GREEN, ALEX
See Replacement Games

GREEN, ALLEN
Punter/kicker, 6'2", 215 lbs., b. 2/15/38

Green had been a center and linebacker at Ole Miss who had only begun kicking midway through his senior season. He was drafted by the Giants, then traded to Washington; Dallas acquired him in 1961 for his kicking abilities. Green's 30-yard field goal with seconds remaining in the season opener against Pittsburgh gave the Cowboys their first-ever regular season win. But it was to be his first and last hurrah; he made only 5 of 15 field goals that season and had a 36.7-yard punt average. He was traded back to the Packers, and then cut, his career finished.

GREEN, CORNELL
Cornerback/safety, 6'4", 211 lbs., b. 2/10/40

The man who made All-Pro four times and went to five Pro Bowls never played a down in college. He was an All-American basketball player at Utah State before he suited up for the Cowboys in 1962. (He put his hip pads on backwards the first time he wore equipment.) But "Boards," as his teammates called him—the joke was that he had

Cornell Green recovers a fumble against the Redskins, 1972. *(From the collection of the Texas/Dallas History and Archive Division, Dallas Public Library)*

such bad hands for a basketball player—quickly established himself as the best cornerback in the NFL in the late sixties. He took over the left corner spot late in his first season and kept it for eight years. When Mike Gaechter tore his Achilles tendon and retired from football in 1970, Green moved to strong safety and earned a fifth trip to the Pro Bowl. He retired in 1975 after 13 years and 34 interceptions, and still holds the Cowboy record for interception yards in a season with 211.

GREGG, FORREST
Offensive tackle, 6'4", 250 lbs.,
b. 10/18/33

Vince Lombardi called him "the finest player I ever coached." In fourteen years with the Green Bay Packers, the SMU ex was an eight-time All-Pro, a seven-time Pro Bowler, and an integral member of two Super Bowl winners. He had retired and was working in Dallas when Landry persuaded him to give it one last go. So he finished his career with one year (1971) as a backup in Dallas, where he picked up another Super Bowl ring. He entered the coaching ranks and, over the next several years, became head coach at Cleveland, Cincinnati, and Green Bay.

GREGORY, BILL
Defensive tackle, 6'5", 240 lbs., b. 2/14/49

Gregory was a rookie in 1971, a third-round draft pick out of Wisconsin, when he was asked to fill in for Jethro Pugh (appendicitis) in a pivotal late-season game against Los Angeles. He was in on 9 tackles, more

than any other defensive lineman. He went on to play seven years in Dallas as an able backup on the defensive line, most of the time behind Pugh and Bob Lilly, and then Larry Cole at defensive tackle. He was traded in 1978 to Seattle, where he played three years before retiring.

GREGORY, GLYNN
Wide receiver/defensive back, 6'2",
200 lbs., b. 7/6/39

Gregory was a Texas high school football legend and an All-American at SMU when he was picked by the Cowboys in the ninth round of the 1961 draft. He started several games in his career in the defensive secondary, but worked primarily as a backup; he also filled in occasionally at wide receiver. He spent time on the 1963 taxi squad and then retired at the end of the season.

GROTTKAU, BOB
Offensive guard, 6'4", 230 lbs., 3/22/37

After two years with Detroit, this Oregon ex was traded to the Cowboys a few weeks before the 1961 season opener. He backed up the offensive line that year and then retired.

GUY, BUZZ
Offensive guard, 6'3", 250 lbs., b. 3/20/36

Melwood "Buzz" Guy had spent two years as a backup with the New York Giants when he was acquired by the Cowboys in the 1960 expansion draft. He started a few games during the 1960 season, then was released.

HACKETT, PAUL
Assistant coach

Tom Landry had always served as his own offensive coordinator, but in 1986 he finally admitted the job had become too time-consuming to handle alone. Hackett brought a major reputation as a budding genius after three years under Bill Walsh as quarterbacks/receivers coach for the San Francisco 49ers.

Hackett was a college quarterback in the sixties at Cal-Davis, coached at his alma mater, then moved on to the University of California, which featured a wide-open offense. He also was an assistant at Southern Cal, then spent two years as quarterback coach of the Cleveland Browns before joining the 49ers.

Hackett's tenure as offensive coordinator under Landry was a muddled one; he and Landry didn't see eye to eye, and in his last year in Dallas, Landry was calling most of the plays. Hackett was swept out with the 1989 hiring of Jimmy Johnson and a new staff. He moved on to the University of Pittsburgh as quarterbacks coach, then spent three seasons as the Panthers' head coach. Hackett joined the Kansas City Chiefs as offensive coordinator in 1993.

HAGEN, HALVOR
Offensive guard, 6'5", 255 lbs., b. 2/4/47

Hagen was a third-round draft choice out of Weber State in 1969. He spent his rookie season at defensive end, seeing little action except for specialty teams. The next year he saw some work at offensive guard and center, then was traded before the 1971 season to New England. He spent two years there and three in Buffalo before retiring.

HAIL MARY

In 1974 the Cowboys had finished 8–6, failing to make the playoffs for the first time since 1966. The next season was to be a year of rebuilding; gone before the season opener were Cornell Green, Bob Lilly, Bob Hayes, John Niland, Walt Garrison, Calvin Hill, Pat Toomay, and Efren Herrera. After a 2–4 preseason with a squad that would keep thirteen rookies, the demise seemed even more evident. Opponents chuckled when Landry dusted off the old spread, or shotgun, formation, but it became astonishingly effective. The thirteen rookies and a nine-year veteran discarded by the Pittsburgh Steelers, Preston Pearson, quickly melded into a winning ballclub. The team finished with a 10–4 record and met the heavily favored Minnesota in the divisional playoffs.

It was a bitterly cold day in Minneapolis, December 28, 1975. With less than two minutes left in a punt-filled defensive struggle, the Cowboys were trailing 14–10. They had the ball on their own 9-yard line when they began driving. Staubach threw 5 passes in the drive—all 5 to Drew Pearson, including a clutch 22-yarder on fourth down to stay alive. On that one, Pearson stutter-stepped out of bounds at the fifty with 24 seconds left.

Staubach lined up in the shotgun formation. Pearson lined up wide to the right. When the ball was snapped Pearson took off toward the cornerback, Nate Wright. He faked to the inside, then raced for the sideline. Staubach hurled a long, high pass. Wright was running alongside Pearson as the slightly underthrown ball came down toward them. There was contact, and then Wright was on the ground. The ball came down at the five-yard line in Pearson's hands; he

Charles Haley

juggled it and then trapped it between his right elbow and hip as he stepped backward into the end zone. When the referee signalled a touchdown, Pearson turned and tossed the ball into the stands. Said Staubach later, "I never had a more eerie sensation on a football field than during the aftermath of our touchdown. The crowd was so shocked there wasn't a sound from the stands. It was as though all of a sudden we were playing in an empty stadium. The silence, as they say, was deafening." Later in the locker room he called it a Hail Mary pass—thrown up as a prayer—and the name stuck.

HALEY, CHARLES
Defensive end, 6'5", 255 lbs., b. 1/6/64

The Cowboys' triumph in Super Bowl XXX in Arizona gave Haley the distinction of collecting five Super Bowl rings, three with the Cowboys and two with San Francisco. His mere presence on the field at the

Super Bowl was shocking considering he had 1) retired in the off-season after Dallas' 30–20 loss in the previous season's NFC Championship Game, and 2) all but retired late in the 1995 season, after yet another back injury appeared to end his season. But it's tough to go by what Haley says, which isn't much during the season, when his rule is to talk to reporters only when he has to on game day. He underwent back surgery in early December and was back with the Cowboys for the postseason. Even a subpar Haley was the team's most talented pass rusher; he is perhaps the NFL's fiercest pass rusher, his style an unstoppable mix of speed, quickness, strength, and technique. He capped the year in typical Haley fashion, by saying the Cowboys' defensive coaches didn't do a good job during the season. Unlike the 49ers, the Cowboys have taken a hear-no-evil approach with Haley. That's one reason why there are three Lombardi Trophies, vintage 1990s, at Valley Ranch.

Haley's presence on the team made an

immediate impact beginning with his training camp acquisition from the 'Niners in 1992. He helped make the Cowboys' defense the best in the NFL, and the pass defense move up to fifth from twenty-third. He climaxed the year with an excellent Super Bowl showing against Buffalo. The following season, he played with constant lower back pain, but in the big games, he came through with big plays. He missed five games due to the injury. After offseason back surgery, he enjoyed his best season as a Cowboy. He led the team with 12.5 sacks and forced more fumbles than any other defender. He missed the last three games of the 1995 season due to more back surgery, but still registered 10.5 sacks late in the year. In the Super Bowl he was superb, with 5 tackles, 1 sack, and 3 quarterback pressures. He was selected to his second consecutive Pro Bowl (fifth overall).

HALL, CHRIS
Safety, 6'2", 184 lbs., b. 4/25/70

The Cowboys went seeking a defensive back to make big plays when they selected Hall out of East Carolina in the ninth round of the 1992 draft. He didn't last through training camp in Austin before being released, but he returned to the Cowboys as a free agent in April 1993 and played with the team for one season, his only one in the NFL.

HALL OF FAME

Seven members of the Pro Football Hall of Fame have been elected based on their accomplishments with the Cowboys.

Bob Lilly was the first in 1980, followed by Roger Staubach in 1985, and Tom Landry in 1990. Tex Schramm was inducted in 1991, Tony Dorsett and Randy White in 1994, and Mel Renfro in 1996.

HAMEL, DEAN
Defensive tackle, 6'3", 276 lbs., b. 7/7/61

Relations between the Redskins and the Cowboys having been rocky since the early seventies, it was surprising that the rivals were willing to commit to the 1989 trade that sent the "Tasmanian Devil" from D.C. to Dallas for a fifth-round draft pick in 1990. Hamel was a part-time starter for the 'Skins the previous four seasons, and stepped in as a starter for the Cowboys, despite joining the team only three days before the final preseason game. He dropped from ninth on the team in tackles during the 1–15 campaign of 1989 to 17th in 1990, when the Cowboys chased a playoff berth and finished 7–9. He was out of the NFL after the season.

HANNAH, SHANE
Offensive guard, 6'5", 345 lbs., b. 10/21/71

A second-round pick in the draft, Hannah was moved over to guard by the Cowboys upon his arrival in camp in 1995, after playing left tackle for Michigan State University. He suffered a torn lateral meniscus and strained ALL in a preseason game against Buffalo, underwent arthroscopic surgery a week later, and was on the injured reserve list during the entire season. For his size, Hannah possesses unusually quick hands for pass blocking. As a junior at Michigan State, he was given the Gerald R. Ford "Up Front Award" that goes to the top offensive lineman.

HANSEN, WAYNE
Linebacker, 6'2", 230 lbs., b. 10/6/28

Hansen played a variety of positions—linebacker, offensive and defensive tackle, guard, and center—from 1950 through 1958 with the Chicago Bears, after a college career at Texas Western. He retired for a year, then was persuaded by the Cowboys to come back for one more year in 1960. He saw a fair amount of action after linebacker Jack Patera was injured four games into the season, then retired in 1961.

HARDY, DARRYL
Linebacker, 6'2", 230 lbs., b. 11/22/68

Originally a tenth-round draft pick of the Atlanta Falcons in 1992, Hardy went to training camp with Dallas in 1994, but was released before the season. He was claimed off waivers from Arizona in October 1995 and saw action on special teams in mid-season. His finest moment was a Christmas night victory over, ironically, the Cardinals, for which he received a game ball for his special-teams work.

HARPER, ALVIN
Wide receiver, 6'3", 208 lbs., b. 7/6/67

Four years in the shadow of Michael Irvin was more than the University of Tennessee star could bear, so following the Cowboys' loss to San Francisco in the NFC Championship Game of January 1995, Harper bailed out on the pursuit of another Super Bowl ring to sign as a free agent with Tampa Bay. His reward was a fat contract and plenty of free time the following January. Not that the Cowboys told him to get lost. His numbers continued to improve during his stay at Valley Ranch as he developed into Dallas' "home-run" receiver.

Dallas' second pick in the 1991 draft, Harper had 20 catches for 326 yards and a 16.3-yard average his rookie year. He caught more than 30 balls each of his final three seasons in Dallas with yardage totals of 562, 777, and 821, and he led the NFC with a 21.6-yard average in 1993. He was even better in 1994, with an amazing 24.9-yard average. In the playoffs, he was phenomenal: 88 yards in his first postseason game, in 1991; 3 catches for 117 yards against San Francisco, one a tremendous leaping catch for a 38-yard gain, and a later catch for 70 yards, both of which set up Dallas touchdowns; a 45-yard TD pass in Super Bowl XXVII; a game-breaking 42-yard pass in the 1993 NFC Championship Game victory over San Francisco, and 3 catches for 75 yards in Super Bowl XXVIII; and 2 grabs for 108 yards against Green Bay in the 1994 playoffs. But in the 1994 NFC Championship Game loss to the 49ers, he was effectively defended by Deion Sanders, acquired before the season especially for that purpose;

Harper had only 1 reception for 14 yards in his final game as a Cowboy.

HARPER, DAVE
Linebacker, 6'1", 220 lbs., b. 5/5/66

Harper played college ball for Humboldt State, an NCAA Division II school located about 275 miles north of San Francisco. He was the first Humboldt player to perform in the annual East-West Shrine Game. His college career also included stops at Weber State and the College of the Redwoods. Harper saw special teams action in 1990 with the Cowboys and then retired from the NFL.

HARRIS, CLIFF
Safety, 6'0", 190 lbs., b. 11/12/48

Harris was another of the Cowboys' scouting system's gems—an unknown out of tiny Ouachita Baptist College in Arkadelphia, AR, he was signed as a free agent in 1970. He battled draft pick Charlie Waters for the starting nod at free safety that year, won the job, and looked good until a military obligation limited his playing time the second half of the season; Waters then took his place and was spectacular.

But the next year, Harris won the job back. He also led the Cowboys in kickoff and punt returns, averaging 28 yards on 29 kickoff returns, fourth in the NFL. He led the team in returns again in 1972, but then turned most of those duties over to other Cowboys. "Captain Crash" was known as one of the hardest hitters in the league: said Tom Landry, "He only knows how to play at one speed, and that's full speed." His first trip to the Pro Bowl was in 1974, and he made the trip every year until he retired after the '79 season, a total of six appearances. Harris was also voted All-Pro four times, from 1975 through 1978. He and good friend Charlie Waters gave the Cowboys the best safety tandem in the NFL from 1976 until Waters suffered a serious preseason injury in 1979. Harris was in his share of big plays in

Cliff Harris

the playoffs, too: he intercepted a pass in the 1971 playoff win against Minnesota, and he had another in the win over San Francisco in the NFC Championship Game. In 1975 he intercepted a pass in that year's NFC Championship Game victory at Los Angeles, and in 1978 he again snared one against the Rams. His final playoff interception was the next year, in a 27–24 first-round loss to Philadelphia. He retired—prematurely, most observers felt—after the 1979 season at the age of 31.

HARRIS, DURIEL
Wide receiver, 6'0", 188 lbs., b. 11/27/54

The Cowboys were looking for an offensive spark for the 1984 stretch drive when they picked up Harris on waivers from the Cleveland Browns, in mid-November. He had been an outstanding player for the Miami Dolphins from 1976–83, eventually becoming the second-leading receiver in club history, with 266 receptions for 4,510 yards and 18 touchdowns.

But Harris, who grew up in Port Arthur, TX, as a neighbor of future NFL great Joe Washington, was at the end of the line by the time he joined the Cowboys. Harris caught only 1 pass for 9 yards for the Cowboys, and then retired after the season.

HARRIS, JIMMY
Defensive back, 6'1", 180 lbs., b. 11/12/34

Harris, a less than spectacular player out of Oklahoma, was the subject of a celebrated court battle between the 1960 Cowboys and their crosstown rivals, the AFL Dallas Texans. After retiring from the Rams with a couple of years in the NFL, he signed with the Texans. But the Rams contended that they had traded his rights to the Cowboys, and that this nullified any other contract. Though he stayed with the Texans, legal actions prevented him from playing a complete year. When the court found for the Cowboys in the summer of 1961, Harris played a year for Dallas and then retired.

HARRIS, ROD
Wide receiver, 5'10", 183 lbs., b. 11/14/66

The signing of Harris as a free agent in 1990 was a homecoming for the former star from Carter High School in Dallas. He was a three-year starter at Texas A&M, was drafted by Houston in 1989 and released, and was picked up by New Orleans for a year before hooking up with the Cowboys. His year with Dallas was highlighted by punt returns; he handled 12 for 63 yards, and he had 2 kick returns for 44 yards. He was traded to Philadelphia during the year, played through 1991, when he led the team in punt and kick returns, and then was released and out of the NFL.

HAYES, BOB
Wide receiver, 5'11", 187 lbs., b. 10/20/42

Olympic gold medal sprinter Hayes was known as the world's fastest human when he was drafted by the Cowboys in 1964 out of Florida A&M. He also held several records, including the world's record of 9.1 seconds in the 100-yard dash. His first year, he caught 46 passes for 1,003 yards and 12 touchdowns and redefined the phrase "deep threat"; when he learned how to catch a football in the next few years, he became *really* dangerous.

Throughout the sixties, Bob Hayes defined the phrase "big-play receiver" for the Cowboys. "Speed-O," as he was nicknamed by teammates both for his singular trait and an early sixties song, had moves as well as speed; he became a tremendously exciting and elusive punt returner, and led the league in 1968 with a 20.8-yard average, the highest since 1952 and still a Cowboys record. He holds the Cowboys record of yards for receptions in a single game with 246. And he was so fast, he changed the face of defensive coverage: no one man could keep up with

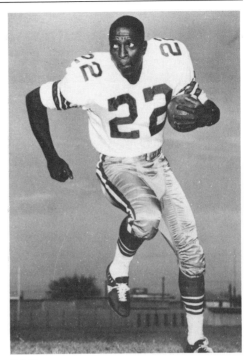
Bob Hayes

him, so the zone defense was invented to contain Bob Hayes. Toward the end of his career, defensive secondaries also began using tactics such as bump-and-run coverage that further reduced Bullet Bob's advantage in man-to-man foot races. Hayes was a lackadaisical blocker, and soon even his decoy value was weakened; his last few years were undistinguished. In 1974 he lost his starting job to Golden Richards, and was traded the next year to San Francisco. He played part of the season and had 6 catches for 119 yards, then was placed on waivers and not claimed. He retired with 7,414 yards and 71 TDs. The loss of the spotlight was tough on Hayes, who had grown up in a Jacksonville slum area called Hell's Hole, and in 1977, after returning to Dallas, he was found guilty of drug dealing (Hayes claims it was a racially motivated frameup) and spent almost ten months in the state prison. His conviction for cocaine trafficking was later overturned.

Cowboys Top Ten Receiving Days

246	Bob Hayes	@ Washington, November 13, 1966	(9 catches)
241	Frank Clarke	vs. Washington, September 16, 1962	(10 catches)
223	Lance Rentzel	vs. Washington, November 19, 1967	(13 catches)
213	Tony Hill	vs. Philadelphia, November 12, 1979	(7 catches)
210	Michael Irvin	vs. Phoenix, September 20, 1992	(8 catches)
203	James Dixon	@ Phoenix, November 12, 1989	(6 catches)
203	Kevin Williams	vs. Kansas City, November 23, 1995	(9 catches)
195	Bob Hayes	vs. NY Giants, September 18, 1966	(6 catches)
190	Frank Clarke	@ San Francisco, November 10, 1963	(8 catches)
188	Drew Pearson	@ Detroit, October 6, 1975	(6 catches)

HAYES, WENDELL
Running back, 6'0", 205 lbs., b. 8/5/41

Hayes was a free agent out of Humboldt State signed by the Cowboys in the summer of 1963. He showed promise in camp, but a thigh operation sidelined him for all but the last two games of the season. He returned 2 kickoffs for 48 yards in the season finale against the Cardinals, then was traded before the 1964 season to Denver. He sat out a year with another injury, then saw plenty of action in the next couple of years as their starting halfback. In 1968 he went to Kansas City, where he was a busy backup until he retired after the 1974 season.

HAYNES, TOMMY
See Replacement Games

HAYS, HAROLD
Linebacker, 6'2", 230 lbs., b. 8/24/39

Hays was a Dallas future pick in the fourteenth round of the 1962 college draft. When he finished his eligibility at Southern Mississippi and signed with the Cowboys a year later, he saw considerable action his first year filling in for an injured Lee Roy Jordan until he was injured himself in the twelfth game. He was a good reserve linebacker the next three years, filling in for starters like Jordan, Howley, Tubbs, and Edwards; then, in 1966, Tom Landry made him the first captain of the specialty teams in the club's history. In 1967, he was the only backup linebacker, and he had three interceptions. He was traded to San Francisco in 1968, after D.D. Lewis was signed, and spent two years there before retiring.

HEALY, DON
Defensive tackle, 6'3", 265 lbs., b. 8/28/36

An offensive guard chosen by the Cowboys from the Chicago Bears in the expansion draft of 1960, Healy was converted to a defensive lineman and stayed around for two years. He played one year for the AFL Buffalo Bills, then retired after the 1962 season.

HEGAMIN, GEORGE
Offensive tackle, 6'7", 355 lbs., b. 2/14/73

Drafted out of North Carolina State in the third round in 1994, Hegamin came to the Cowboys with the reputation of a dominating blocker. It was something the Dallas brass were still waiting to witness after two seasons. He played in only two games as a rookie and wasn't much of a contributor during the 1995 season; the only action he saw was during the final drive against Philadelphia on January 7. The departure of Ron Stone and the retirement of Derek Kennard would seem to give Hegamin a tremendous opportunity to move up on the Cowboys' offensive board in 1996.

HEGMAN, MIKE
Linebacker, 6'1", 228 lbs., b. 1/17/53

Hegman was an effective but unspectacular outside linebacker for the Cowboys for thirteen seasons. He was a member of the Dirty Dozen draft class of 1975, but he didn't make the team that year as a seventh-round draft pick. The next year he did.

A college teammate of Ed "Too Tall" Jones at Tennessee State, Hegman participated in 18 playoff games, helped win 6 NFC

Mike Hegman

East titles, and appeared in 2 Super Bowls. He became a full-time starter with four games left in the 1979 season when Tom Landry released Thomas "Hollywood" Henderson, and he stayed there until a broken leg late in the 1987 season forced him to miss the last few games of the year. He was a steady player who made few mistakes; toward the end of his career he was replaced on obvious passing situations, but he was tough against the rush.

Hegman's top season was in 1985, when he registered 79 tackles and 5.5 sacks. He turned in a career-high 85 tackles in 1980, his first full season as a starter, and, in 1986, he led all Cowboy linebackers in passes defensed with 6 even though he was replaced on passing downs.

The biggest play of his career may have come in Super Bowl XIII, when he stripped the ball from Pittsburgh Steelers quarterback Terry Bradshaw and raced 37 yards for a second-quarter touchdown.

Injuries prevented a more glittering career. A dislocated elbow during the 1980 playoff opener knocked him out of the rest of postseason play, and in 1981, he broke a bone in his right forearm, missing five games. His most serious ailment was a broken leg in a game against Washington in December 1987; it ended his season and career.

HEINRICH, DON
Quarterback, 6'0", 182 lbs., b. 9/9/31

Heinrich was obtained in the 1960 expansion draft from New York, where he had backed up Charlie Conerley for six years. He never saw much playing time save for a single year. The 1956 championship Giants had a unique quirk: third-year QB Heinrich would start each game, then the veteran Conerley would trot in after a quarter and play the rest of the way. "The theory behind it," Tom Landry said later, "was you'd have Heinrich come in and probe the defense, see what they were doing, and you could discuss it with Conerly during the first quarter on the sidelines." Said teammate Kyle Rote, "Heinrich wasn't the greatest passer in the game, but he had a great football mind, a real instinct for the game."

But despite 1956, Heinrich had never had much of a chance to prove himself as an on-the-field leader, and he hoped to find that opportunity in Dallas. It never happened. Just before training camp, Eddie LeBaron was signed, and Heinrich spent the season splitting backup duties with rookie Don Meredith, whom he worked with constantly. Though he set an NCAA pass completion percentage record at the University of Washington, his lifetime NFL average was 40 percent, and he didn't even reach that in Dallas. He retired after that first season to return to the Giants as a coach, and a year later, he was one of several backups to Cotton Davidson on a horrible 1–13 Oakland Raiders team. In his final year, he completed only 10 of 29 passes. He later published an annual predraft football magazine entitled *Don Heinrich's Scout Report*.

HELLESTRAE, DALE
Center/offensive guard, 6'5", 286 lbs., b. 7/11/62

The owner of a business administration degree from Southern Methodist University, Hellestrae parlayed his special role as an extremely reliable long snapper into a high-profile position. After all, how many NFL long snappers do restaurant commercials and have radio shows? Not bad for a career backup who was drafted in the fourth round by Buffalo in 1985, went to the Los Angeles Raiders in 1989, and came to the Cowboys in 1990 for a fourth-round pick in 1991. But Hellestrae has a job as deep snapper as long as he wants it; in 378 regular-season snaps with the Cowboys, he has never had a punt blocked or a snap fumbled. He grew up near Phoenix and operates a Cookie Bouquet franchise there.

HENDERSON, THOMAS "HOLLYWOOD"
Linebacker, 6'2", 221 lbs., b. 3/3/53

Arguably the most controversial, frustrating, misunderstood, and reviled Cowboys player of all time. A gifted athlete and flamboyant personality, Henderson had a nose for the ball, a nose for publicity, and a nose for drugs.

A first-team Little All-American at tiny Langston (OK) University as a defensive end, Henderson was the Cowboys' number-one pick in the 1975 draft, the 18th player taken overall. Henderson was a little-known prospect, but the Cowboys again had done their homework.

Henderson was a rookie reserve outside linebacker and a ferocious special teams player when the Cowboys lost Super Bowl X. By 1976, his second season, Henderson was a starter and a star. In 1977, he helped the Cowboys win Super Bowl XII over Denver.

Super Bowl XIII matched the Cowboys with the mighty Pittsburgh Steelers. During the week of pregame hype, Henderson made national headlines when he questioned Steelers quarterback Terry Bradshaw's intelligence, saying, "Bradshaw couldn't spell cat if you spotted him *c* and *t*." Bradshaw had the last laugh, however; after the 35–31 Steelers victory, the MVP quarterback said, "Ask Henderson if I was dumb today."

During the game, Henderson would later admit, he snorted cocaine on the sidelines, and played brilliantly anyway. One season later, Henderson had drunk and snorted his way out of Dallas, alienating coach Tom Landry and his teammates with declining performance, poor work habits, and an attitude that produced dissension.

Henderson drifted from San Francisco to Houston to Miami, and by 1981, at the age of 28, injured and addicted, his football career was over. Still, Henderson hadn't hit bottom. In 1984, after a cocaine party with two underage girls, Henderson was sentenced to jail for having sex with a minor.

It was in jail that Henderson began rebuilding his life, joining Alcoholics Anonymous and remarrying. After twenty-seven months in prison, he was released and subsequently wrote a candid, cautionary autobiography, *Out of Control: Confessions of an NFL Casualty,* written with Peter Knobler, which appeared in 1987.

No longer "Hollywood," Henderson has been sober for more than ten years. He lives in his hometown of Austin with his wife, Diane, and is an alcohol and drug abuse counselor and motivational speaker.

HENDRICKSON, STEVE
Linebacker, 6'0", 250 lbs., b. 8/30/66

In the not-so-memorable season of 1989, Henrickson contributed one of the plays that helped make the year so forgettable for Cowboy fans. In an October game against Kansas City, a personal-foul call against Hendrickson for hitting an opponent while he was already out of bounds wiped out an 89-yard punt return for a touchdown by Derrick Shepard. But give Hendrickson credit for not letting his one dismal season with the Cowboys get him down. He went on to become a special-teams star with San Diego for several years.

HENDRIX, MANNY
Defensive back, 5'10", 181 lbs., b. 10/20/64

Another athlete converted to football by the Cowboys after playing another sport in college, Hendrix was a solid basketball player at Utah, finishing his career as the Utes' eighth-leading scorer of all-time.

Mindful that about two decades earlier they had converted former Utah State basketball player Cornell Green into an All-Pro defensive back, the Cowboys brought Hendrix to 1986 camp as a raw free agent. Hendrix played football as well as basketball and starred in track as a Phoenix high school athlete, but it took some time to adjust to the pro game. He was released before the

start of the 1986 season, but was signed again following the third game.

Hendrix got his first NFL start in the final game of the 1987 season against St. Louis, leading the team with 11 tackles and knocking down a pass to earn a coaches' game ball.

Hendrix had his most productive season in 1990, starting eleven games, including the final ten, for a pass defense that led the NFC and ended the season with streaks of not allowing an opposing passer to throw for 300 or more yards. But Jimmy Johnson continued to upgrade his pass defense, and Hendrix's career ended following the 1991 season, after which he moved on to college athletics administration.

HENDRIX, TIM
See Replacement Games

HENNINGS, CHAD
Defensive tackle, 6'6", 288 lbs., b. 10/20/65

Good things came to those who wait. The Cowboys learned that during the sixties when they waited for a Navy quarterback named Roger Staubach to complete his military obligation. A similar scenario played itself out in 1988 with the team's eleventh-round selection of Hennings out of the Air Force Academy. That selection didn't come to fruition until 1992, when Hennings had fulfilled his four-year Air Force commitment (he flew an A-10 Warthog and escorted the planes that dropped supplies in northern Iraq and southern Turkey, during the Gulf War). Hennings slowly moved into the rotation of defensive linemen; in 1994 he got plenty of playing time and recorded 7.5 sacks, second on the team. He had several starts late in the 1995 season and made 56 tackles, more than his previous three years combined, and recorded 5.5 sacks. The Iowa native grew up on a 900-acre farm and underwent pilot training in Wichita Falls, TX, about 100 miles northwest of Dallas.

HERCHMAN, BILL
Defensive tackle, 6'2", 245 lbs., b. 3/10/33

A Texas native and a former Texas Tech grid star, Herchman had played for the San Francisco 49ers for four years. He was traded to the Cowboys before 1960, their first season, and became their starting defensive right tackle for the next two years. He was traded to the Houston Oilers and played there one year before retiring after the 1962 season.

HERRERA, EFREN
Kicker, 5'9", 190 lbs., b. 7/30/51

At UCLA Herrera led the nation's kickers in scoring in 1973. He was drafted in the seventh round by Detroit and cut by them and several other teams before signing with the Cowboys as a free-agent, three games into 1974. After the new pickup, Mac Percival, proved dreadful as injured Toni Fritsch's replacement, Herrera responded with a steady performance the rest of the season. He didn't miss a single extra point and hit 8 of 13 field goals, several of them providing the difference in Dallas wins. The 5'9" Herrera even made some jarring tackles on kickoffs. He hurt a knee in the following preseason; the surgery kept him out for the year. Toni Fritsch had a good year in his stead, but during the 1976 preseason a healthy Herrera made him expendable, and Fritsch was dealt to San Diego.

Herrera responded with an incredible year: no missed extra points, and 18 of 23 field goal attempts (with no misses inside the 30-yard line) to tie for the league lead with a 78 percent average. In the playoff loss to Los Angeles, he booted a 44-yarder on his only attempt. He missed two extra points in 1977, but hit 18 of 29 three-point attempts to lead the league with a 62 percent average, good enough to make the Pro Bowl and the All-Pro team. In the playoffs, he went wild, hitting on all 4 of his attempts, but he only hit 2 of 5 in the Super Bowl win over Denver. That was his last year in Dallas; a contract

couldn't be agreed upon in 1978, and he was shipped to the Seattle Seahawks. He had several excellent years there and one with Buffalo before retiring after a year in the USFL.

HERVEY, EDWARD
Wide receiver, 6'3", 179 lbs., b. 5/4/73

Hervey began his college career as a quarterback at Pasadena City College, later becoming a receiver at the University of Southern California. He was picked by the Cowboys in the fifth round of the 1995 draft. He has an intense work ethic honed by growing up in Watts and Compton, CA. Fans in Dallas got a sneak preview of his skills when he had 3 catches for 99 yards in USC's rout of Texas Tech in the 1995 Mobil Cotton Bowl Classic. He led the Cowboys in the preseason with eight receptions but was inactive every game of the regular season.

HICKEY, RED
Assistant coach

An NFL player, assistant coach, and head coach since 1941, Howard "Red" Hickey joined Tom Landry's staff in 1964 as the offensive end coach. He left after the 1965 season.

HIGGS, MARK
Running back, 5'7", 188 lbs., b. 4/11/66

Undersized but athletic, Higgs was an eighth-round pick from Kentucky whose vertical leap was measured at 43 inches prior to 1988 training camp. Higgs brought a reputation as a tough inside runner and blocker, but he played sparingly on special teams in five games as a rookie.

Higgs was signed by the Philadelphia Eagles in 1989 as an unprotected rookie and showed he could play in the league, picking up 184 yards on 49 carries. But when the Miami Dolphins signed him as a free agent in 1990, his career took a definite upswing. In 1991 he turned in one of the best performances by a running back in Dolphins history, gaining 905 yards on 231 carries. He led the team in rushing the next two years and was traded to Arizona in 1994.

HIGHSMITH, ALONZO
Running back, 6'1", 237 lbs., b. 2/28/65

Many of Jimmy Johnson's former players at the University of Miami thrived under him at Valley Ranch. That wasn't the case with Highsmith, who appeared headed for stardom when Houston made him the third player picked overall in the 1987 draft. He rushed for about 1,000 yards for the Oilers; the problem was those yards were compiled over three years, not one. Highsmith was traded to the Cowboys in September 1990, coming off knee surgery. His Cowboys contributions were minimal: 19 carries for 48 yards in 1990. Early in the 1991 season, he was traded to Tampa Bay, where he was a replacement back for two seasons. He was released after the 1992 season and out of the NFL.

HILL, BILL
See Replacement Games

HILL, CALVIN
Running back, 6'3", 230 lbs., b. 1/2/47

When Dallas made a halfback from Yale their first choice in the 1969 draft, it startled the country. It was actually another triumph for the Dallas computerized scouting system. Hill was a great athlete—he held school records in the long jump and the triple jump—and an extremely intelligent player who thrived in Landry's complex offensive system. In training camp, he was first tried at tight end, then linebacker, but settled in at running back after Dan Reeves was injured. He went on to win Rookie of the Year honors after rushing 204 times for 942 yards and a 4.6-yard average. (He also completed all 3 of his passing attempts, 2 of them for touchdowns.) Only a jammed big

Calvin Hill

toe from November on kept him from rushing for 1,000 yards. Over the next five years he would lead the Cowboys in rushing three times (1972–73–74) and in receiving twice (1972–73), and make four Pro Bowl teams and two All-Pro squads. Injuries moved him in and out of the lineup over the next two years, but in 1972 he gained 1,036 yards on the ground and caught 43 passes; against San Francisco in the conference playoff, he gained 125 yards on 18 carries. The next year he had 1,142 yards and 32 catches, and rushed for 97 yards in the conference playoff against Los Angeles, but he was injured for the subsequent loss against Minnesota. His final season with the Cowboys, 1974, he had 844 yards but only 12 receptions. He finished his six-year Dallas career with 5,009 yards on 1,166 carries, an average of 4.3 yards per carry. In 1975 he jumped to Hawaii in the

WFL, then played a backup role for the Redskins for two years, and the Browns for four, until his retirement after the 1981 season.

HILL, ROD
Cornerback, 6'0", 193 lbs., b. 3/14/59

The Cowboys have a reputation for finding talent in the most unusual locations, and they pulled off the surprise of the 1982 draft when they used the 26th pick of the first round to select little-known speedster Rod Hill from Kentucky State.

Cowboys personnel director Gil Brandt felt he'd pulled off the heist of the draft, but the joke was on Brandt. Hill's work habits were suspect and his cocky attitude soured teammates. Hill once proclaimed that he was a fanatic on college basketball. Grumped veteran teammate Dennis Thurman, "I wish you were a fanatic on learning to play cornerback in the NFL." Hill also liked to play Pac-Man and do Richard Pryor impressions.

But he contributed little on the field as a rookie except for an 89-yard kickoff return to set up a critical field goal in a 37-26 playoff victory over Detroit, tying for the second-longest kickoff return in postseason history. Hill negated that kickoff return in the NFC title game, however, when his fumbled punt deep in Dallas territory was recovered by Washington on the Cowboys' 11-yard line. The recovery led to a John Riggins touchdown and a 14-3 Redskins lead at halftime.

In 1983, Hill averaged 7.7 yards per punt return and 18.7 yards per kickoff return, but he couldn't win a starting job. Hill was given an opportunity to win it at right cornerback with Thurman's move to safety in 1984 training camp, but he was again a flop, and the exasperated Cowboys traded him to the Buffalo Bills. Hill drifted on to the Detroit Lions and Los Angeles Raiders before moving on to the Canadian Football League, where he played for several years.

HILL, TONY
Wide receiver, 6'2", 202 lbs., b. 6/23/56

Hill was among the elite receivers in the NFL in the late seventies and early eighties, teaming with Drew Pearson and Butch Johnson to give the Cowboys one of the league's top receiving trios. Hill had almost identical seasons in 1979 and 1980, catching 60 balls each year for over 1,000 yards.

Hill broke all of former San Francisco 49ers All-Pro Gene Washington's records at Stanford, catching 140 passes for 2,225 yards and 18 touchdowns during his four-year college career. Hill was not that highly regarded by pro scouts, however, and the Cowboys were able to get him in the third round of the 1977 draft that also gave the Cowboys Tony Dorsett in the first round. The Cowboys got the third-round pick that they used for Hill from the Philadelphia Eagles in a trade for former All-Pro guard John Niland.

The son of a Bay Area mailman,

Tony Hill

"Thrill" Hill became a starter in 1978, catching 46 passes for 823 yards and 6 touchdowns. In 1979, Hill's impact was fully felt as he became Roger Staubach's deep target, earning his second straight Pro Bowl berth. He turned a quick screen pass into a 22-yard touchdown with two minutes left to beat the Chicago Bears in September, and he grabbed an eight-yard touchdown with 39 seconds to play on December 16 to wrap up a dramatic comeback victory over the Washington Redskins, clinching the NFC East title for Dallas.

His heroics continued in 1980 when his 28-yard scoring catch with 45 seconds remaining lifted the Cowboys over the St. Louis Cardinals in a game in November.

In the 1983 regular-season opener against the hated Redskins, Hill was at it again, catching Danny White touchdown passes of 75 and 51 yards to spark the Cowboys comeback from a 23–3 halftime deficit to a 31-30 victory. Hill also set a Cowboys playoff record with 9 receptions against the Los Angeles Rams in a 1983 defeat in the wild card game.

Injuries—and a weight problem in his later years—prevented Hill from putting up even more impressive numbers. Despite missing five games due to injury in 1984, he caught 58 passes, 2 short of his career high, and he led the team in receiving yards for the seventh straight season with 864. Projected over a sixteen-game schedule, Hill would have caught 84 passes for over 1,200 yards. In 1983 he missed four games due to an injured foot, limiting his totals to 49 catches for 801 yards. In 1984 Hill hurt his shoulder in the season opener and was out for the next five games.

When he was healthy, Hill was a game-breaker, standing second on the Cowboys' all-time list for receiving yards (7,988) and third in catches (479); he caught passes in 72 straight games and finished his career in 1986 with 26 100-yard games—although some pointed out his reluctance to run pass patterns over the middle.

"Tony's our big-play guy," coach Tom Landry said in 1985. "He has that ability to make the key play. He threatens the defense because he has the excellent burst of speed to get under a ball that's deep. He's a very explosive player, the type that can turn a short play into a deep play in a hurry."

After retirement, Hill continued to make Dallas his home, working as a broadcaster, businessman, and high school football coach.

HILL, TONY
Defensive end, 6'6", 250 lbs., b. 10/23/68

Hill's arrival in Dallas was a capsule of the Jimmy Johnson era of draft trading. Hill, who played at Tennessee-Chattanooga, was selected with a pick that Johnson got from Detroit, in a trade for a pick obtained from Washington. You couldn't blame the Cowboys for having big plans for Hill after he capped his rookie season with a couple of solid 1991 playoff performances against Chicago and Detroit. But the balance of his Dallas career was consumed by injuries. He played little in 1992, dogged much of the season by a hamstring pull. He never truly got back into peak condition. The Cowboys were forced to part company before the 1993 season, with an injury settlement. He never played in the NFL again.

HODSON, TOMMY
Quarterback, 6'3", 195 lbs., b. 1/28/67

If a Cowboy fan blinked, he probably missed Hodson's stint with the Cowboys during the 1994 season. In mid-November, the Cowboys sought an emergency number-three quarterback, behind Jason Garrett and Rodney Peete, while Troy Aikman was unavailable because of injury. Dallas actually wanted to sign longtime backup Mike Pagel, but he couldn't pass the team's physical. Enter Hodson, who played four seasons with New England. Hodson was signed, wasn't needed the following weekend, and was promptly released the following weekend, because of a fluke situation that resulted in Hodson's salary putting the team over the NFL salary cap. He was signed by the Saints in April 1995 as a backup.

HOFFMAN, STEVE
Assistant coach

Hoffman has been the Cowboys' assistant coach for kickers/quality control since leaving the University of Miami with the Jimmy Johnson group in 1989. That means he coordinates computer scouting of opponents, and he provides internal analysis of the Cowboys' own tendencies and productivity. He was also an offensive coordinator for two seasons in Italy. Hoffman has acquired a reputation for developing unknowns into effective kickers from his work with free agent rookie kickers Chris Boniol, Lin Elliott, Ken Willis, and punter John Jett.

HOGEBOOM, GARY
Quarterback, 6'4", 207 lbs., b. 8/21/58

In Dutch, Hogeboom means tall tree. In Dallas, it was a name synonymous with tall expectations in the eighties.

Drafted in the fifth round in 1980 as a lightly regarded prospect from Central Michigan, Hogeboom inherited the roster spot created by Roger Staubach's retirement. His early contributions reminded nobody of Staubach, as Hogeboom attempted only 8 passes in mop-up situations in his first three seasons.

But fans, media, and even some teammates were disenchanted with Staubach's successor, Danny White, and Hogeboom developed almost a cult following that eventually exploded into the franchise's latest quarterback controversy. He looked the part: strong-armed, tall, able to read defenses, and mobile enough to avoid a pass rush.

Hogeboom's performance in the NFC Championship Game on January 23, 1983 against Washington fanned the flames. With 19 seconds left in the first half, Hogeboom

Gary Hogeboom

took over for White, who had been flattened by Redskins defensive end Dexter Manley and left groggy with a concussion. Hogeboom converted his first 6 third-down situations and finished with 14 completions in 29 attempts for 162 yards and 2 touchdowns, getting the Cowboys as close as 14–10 on a TD strike to Drew Pearson. But he also threw 2 interceptions, and the Cowboys fell to the Redskins, 31–17.

Hogeboom made no secret of his desire to supplant White, but he remained the backup in 1983. When the White-led offense fizzled in a 24–17 loss to the Los Angeles Rams in the wild card game, the public clamor for Hogeboom gained steam during the off-season. The Boomer Bandwagon was bolstered by a very unscientific newspaper poll that contended overwhelming player support for Hogeboom over White, the quarterback for three straight losing efforts in NFC Championship Games and a wild card knockout in 1983.

Coach Tom Landry had been a staunch White supporter, but in 1984 he bowed to public pressure and installed Hogeboom as the starter. The Cowboys opened with victories in four of their first five games behind Hogeboom. But the off-season retirement of Drew Pearson, Harvey Martin, Pat Donovan, Billy Joe DuPree, and Robert Newhouse had created a severe talent drain, and a series of injuries crippled the offensive line.

Landry turned the offense back to White by mid-season, but it didn't really matter who was quarterbacking the Cowboys. They were in a serious decline, dropping 4 of their next 7 games, including a humiliating 14–3 upset to the hapless Buffalo Bills. White held off Hogeboom's challenge in 1985, and the Cowboys dealt the disgruntled backup to the Indianapolis Colts in 1986.

Hogeboom played for the Colts from 1986–88; he experienced a series of injuries and mixed success. He moved on to the Phoenix Cardinals in 1989, then spent a year with Washington before retiring.

HOLLOWAY, JOHNNY
Cornerback, 5'11", 182 lbs., b. 11/8/63

Holloway impressed coach Tom Landry as a rookie in 1986, after making the transition from college wide receiver to pro defensive back. The Kansas product and Houston native had an interception, 15 tackles, and 4 passes defensed with the nickel defense in 1986, his only season in the NFL.

HOLMES, CLAYTON
Cornerback, 5'10", 181 lbs., b. 8/23/69

The Cowboys' third-round pick from Carson-Newman in 1992, Holmes played fifteen games as a rookie in 1992 as a reserve defensive back and kick returner with 3 returns for 70 yards. He also was second on the team with 15 special teams tackles. He spent the following year on injured reserve after tearing ligaments in his right knee in a preseason game. After a complete rehabilitation, he saw some action at both corner spots and on special teams; he returned 5

punts for 55 yards and 4 kickoffs for 89 yards. In 1995, following Kevin Smith's Achilles tendon injury in the first week of September, he moved into the starting lineup at left corner. He returned to a reserve role in late October with the arrival of Deion Sanders. He also had several punt and kick returns subbing for the injured Kevin Williams, including a 46-yard kick return against Green Bay. He finished the year with 34 tackles. Holmes was released shortly after Super Bowl XXX, having missed much of the 1995 title season after being suspended by the NFL for violating the league's drug policy.

HOLT, ISSIAC
Cornerback, 6'2", 201 lbs., b. 10/4/62

Holt, who played five years for Minnesota, was one of the best products of the mammoth October 1989 trade that sent Herschel Walker to the Vikings. He moved in as a starter the following season despite having suffered a dislocated left shoulder late the previous year, and he led Dallas in interceptions in 1991 with 4. Holt was a hard hitter who made some big plays; he ran two of his interceptions as a Cowboy back for touchdowns, and he had several blocked punts, one for a safety. He had two as a backup in 1992, and saw action in the Super Bowl against Buffalo. The highlight of his pro career came in 1986, when he grabbed eight interceptions for the Vikings. He retired after the 1992 season.

HOMAN, DENNIS
Wide receiver, 6'1", 180 lbs., b. 1/9/46

Homan played on three straight bowl teams for Alabama before his selection as the Cowboys' first draft pick in 1968. But he was playing behind two exceptional receivers: Bob Hayes and Lance Rentzel. His first year he caught only 4 passes for an impressive 22-yard average. Early in his sophomore season, he averaged 20 yards on 12 catches filling in for an injured Bob

Hayes. He had only 7 catches for 105 yards his final year in Dallas; he saw some action in the Super Bowl loss to Baltimore, but didn't catch a pass. He was traded to Kansas City in 1971 and spent two years there as a backup before retiring.

HOOPES, MITCH
Punter, 6'1", 210 lbs., b. 7/8/53

Hoopes was the Cowboys' eighth-round draft pick in 1975 and one of the Dirty Dozen rookies to make the team that year. He stepped in as a starter and performed adequately, averaging 39.4 yards on 68 punts. (He also had an unplanned run on fourth and 13 for a first down in the season opener against Los Angeles.) But the Arizona ex was expendable the next year with the signing of quarterback/punter Danny White, and was traded to San Diego before the season. He punted for Houston, Detroit, Philadelphia, and in the USFL before retiring after the 1983 season.

HORTON, RAY
Safety, 5'11", 190 lbs., b. 4/12/60

Jimmy Johnson had high praise for Horton, a Plan B pickup from Cincinnati (where he spent six years) in 1989, when he said Horton "has more savvy than any player on this team." As a starter at free safety for most of his Dallas career, he was the quarterback of the defense, and he helped put together one of the best pass defenses statistically in the NFL. In 1990 Dallas led the NFC in pass defense, and despite a season hampered by illness and injury (a left knee sprain in late September slowed him throughout the year), Horton was a big reason for that ranking. "When you're injured, I think you play a little smarter," Horton said. He was a mainstay in the Cowboys' secondary for four seasons, totaling 5 interceptions, and retired after the 1992 championship season.

HOUCK, HUDSON
Assistant coach

The first battle between the 1996 Cowboys regime and new Miami Dolphins coach Jimmy Johnson was fought in the months following Super Bowl XXX—over Houck, and the Cowboys won. Houck was hired in 1993 by Johnson to coach the Dallas offensive line. Three years later, Johnson tried to bring Houck to Miami, but Cowboys owner Jerry Jones managed to keep Houck on the Valley Ranch staff. Houck's stint with Dallas included the selection of a team-high three offensive linemen to the 1995 Pro Bowl: Nate Newton, Mark Stepnoski, and Mark Tuinei. In his three years Houck has molded the Cowboys' offensive line into one of the strongest in team history. Prior to his Dallas move, he coached dominant offensive lines at Seattle and the Los Angeles Rams, and before that, spent several years at the University of Southern California, his alma mater.

HOUSER, JOHN
Offensive guard/center, 6'3", 240 lbs., b. 6/21/35

Howser, out of Redlands University, had played three years with the Los Angeles Rams before he was claimed on waivers by the Cowboys for their debut season. He started at center, then in 1961 played mostly at guard. The next year, he suffered a knee injury in an exhibition game. After sitting out the season, and after a second knee injury, he was signed by the St. Louis Cardinals, where he played one year before retiring.

HOUSTON, BILL
Wide receiver, 6'3", 210 lbs., b. 8/22/51

Houston was an unknown free agent out of Jackson State signed by the Cowboys in 1974. He saw limited duty save for special-teams work, catching 6 passes for 72 yards. That was his only year in the NFL.

HOWARD, CARL
Cornerback, 6'2", 188 lbs., b. 9/20/61

A free agent find in 1984, Howard gave the Cowboys improved special teams work as a rookie, earning game balls for kick coverage in wins over Green Bay and Indianapolis. He also got playing time as the third cornerback in nickel situations in his only season for the Cowboys.

HOWARD, DAVID
Linebacker, 6'2", 230 lbs., b. 12/8/61

Howard played two seasons for the Cowboys after being acquired in the October 1989 Herschel Walker transaction. He shared the strongside linebacker spot with Jack Del Rio for the balance of the 1989 season and all of the following season. In 1991 he was acquired by the New England Patriots; he played two years there before retiring from the NFL. The Long Beach State product got his pro start with the USFL's Los Angeles Express.

HOWARD, PERCY
Wide receiver, 6'4", 210 lbs., b. 1/21/52

Howard had been a fine rebounding and scoring forward on the Austin Peay basketball team. The Cowboy computer picked him as one of those fine athletes—like Cornell Green and Pete Gent—who might make the transition to football successfully. He made the team in 1975 as a free agent (he and eleven rookie draft picks were the Dirty Dozen), and caught nary a pass during the season, although he did run back two kickoffs and saw action on the kicking teams. But late in the fourth quarter of Super Bowl X against Pittsburgh, he went in for the injured Golden Richards. He raced past defender Mel Blount to snag a Staubach pass for a 34-yard touchdown. It was the only

time he touched the ball all day. In next year's preseason he was having a good game against Denver when he injured a knee on a reverse. It took three operations before the knee was fixed, and by then his football career was over.

HOWARD, RON
Tight end, 6'4", 225 lbs., b. 3/3/51

Howard was a free agent basketball player with no football experience when the Cowboys signed him in 1974. He became a fierce hitter on the special teams that year and the next, but playing behind Billy Joe DuPree and Jean Fugett didn't leave much of an opportunity for action. He didn't catch a pass in either year (although he was in for a few plays in Super Bowl X), and the next year, he went to Seattle in the expansion draft. He had an excellent year there in 1976 (second on the team in receptions) and for two more solid seasons. He played the 1979 season as a little-used backup in Buffalo, then retired.

HOWLEY, CHUCK
Linebacker, 6'3", 230 lbs., b. 6/28/36

"Hogmeat," as his teammates called him, came to the Cowboys in 1962 after a two-year stint with the Chicago Bears from 1958–59. He'd been the Bears' number-one draft pick in 1957 after his senior year at West Virginia. In his rookie season, he cracked the starting lineup at linebacker, but a knee injury and subsequent surgery four games into 1959 sidelined him for the rest of the year. A year later at training camp the state of his health was still unclear. The Cowboys, desperate for talent, and willing to gamble on a player with his ability, gave the Bears two future draft choices for him.

Howley soon established himself as one of the best outside linebackers in the game. He made six Pro Bowl teams, and he was one of the pillars of the Doomsday Defense of the late sixties and early seven-

Chuck Howley returns an interception. *(From the collection of the Texas/Dallas History and Archive Division, Dallas Public Library)*

ties. The young man from Wheeling, WV was extremely quick (at West Virginia he had lettered in five sports—football, diving, track as a sprinter, gymnastics, and wrestling), and he was an intuitive gambler who reacted to a play instantly. There were few better open-field tacklers in the NFL. In 1966 he had the longest fumble return in Cowboy history, a 97-yarder for a TD against the Chicago Bears. He was a big-play athlete who saved his best for the big games; he is still the only player from the losing team to be named the Super Bowl Most Valuable Player—in a 16–13 loss to Baltimore in 1971, in which he intercepted 2 passes and recovered a fumble. His play in the next year's Super Bowl was almost as good, as Dallas demolished Miami 24-3. It was also the site of his greatest embarrassment: he intercepted a Bob Griese pass early in the fourth quarter at midfield and ran back what looked like a sure TD. But he slipped and fell at the nine-yard line with no Dolphin near him.

Howley retired after the 1973 season to run his successful uniform-rental and dry cleaning business. He was named to the Ring of Honor in 1977.

HOWTON, BILLY
Wide receiver, 6'2", 190 lbs., b. 7/3/30

After seven fine years at Green Bay and a disappointing one with Cleveland, two-time All-Pro Howton was the second-leading receiver all-time, behind Don Hutson, when he was signed by the Cowboys in 1960. The former Rice All-American became a steady recipient of Eddie LeBaron and Don Meredith passes those early years; his specialty was the down-and-out, and he was a smart runner with the ball. His teammates called the skinny redhead "the Fox." He caught 56 passes for 785 yards in 1961, then 49 for 706 the next. His last year, 1963, he gained 514 yards on 33 passes. He retired after 12 years with 503 catches for 8,459 yards and a 16.8 average.

HOYEM, LYNN
Center, 6'4", 225 lbs., b. 6/27/39

Hoyem was drafted out of Long Beach State by the Cowboys as a future in the nineteenth round in 1961. A year later, after he had finished his college eligibility, he signed with the Cowboys and played the next two years primarily on specialty teams. He was traded to Philadelphia in 1964, and spent four years there before retiring after the 1967 season.

HUGHES, ED
Assistant coach

Tom Landry had coached Hughes from 1956 through 1958, when Hughes played cornerback for the Giants. In the interim Hughes had coached for the Dallas Texans, Denver, Washington, and San Francisco before assuming head coach duties at Houston in 1971. He was an assistant with St. Louis in 1972, and he coached the Dallas offensive backfield through the 1976 season.

HUGHES, RANDY
Safety, 6'4", 210 lbs., b. 4/3/53

All-American Hughes was a fourth-round draft pick out of Oklahoma for the Cowboys in the great 1975 draft. He quickly became a reliable backup to starting safeties Cliff Harris and Charlie Waters. In Super Bowl XII, he picked off a pass and recovered two fumbles in the first half of the Cowboys' victory over Denver. When Waters sat out 1979 with an injury, Hughes performed ably; he was fourth on the team in tackles and made two of the season's most important defensive plays—a 68-yard interception return against Cincinnati that set up an important score, and a 23-yard interception against Philadelphia that set up another. In 1980, with Harris retired, Hughes planned on making the free safety job his own. But a series of shoulder separations kept him out much of the season; he returned for the last five games, but dislocated the shoulder again in the first playoff game, and had surgery the next day. When he dislocated it yet again in the 1981 preseason, he knew it was time to call it quits.

HUMPHREY, BUDDY
Quarterback, 6'2", 200 lbs., b. 9/29/35

Humphrey, who led the nation in passing at Baylor his senior year, was a second-round draft choice of the Rams in 1959. After two and a half years of inaction, he was traded to the Cowboys late in 1961, as a backup to LeBaron and Meredith. That year he threw two passes and completed one. He was traded before the 1962 season to the Cardinals, to back up Charley Johnson.

HUNT, JOHN
Guard/tackle, 6'4", 256 lbs., b. 11/6/62

Hunt made the roster as a reserve as a ninth-round rookie in 1984. Hunt spent seven of the first twelve weeks of the season on injured reserve and did not see action in the other five games, but when a rash of injuries struck down the players ahead of him on the depth chart, Hunt was pressed into service. He replaced injured starters Kurt Petersen and Howard Richards late in the season, but the former Florida star was out of the NFL by the 1985 season.

HUNTER, MONTY
Safety, 6'0", 201 lbs., b. 1/21/59

Monty "Big Game" Hunter was selected in the fourth round of the 1982 draft out of tiny Salem College in West Virginia, another in a series of small college gambles the Cowboys favored in the eighties. Hunter brought a reputation as a big hitter, but contributed primarily on special teams in his lone season with the Cowboys. He later was signed by the St. Louis Cardinals and Washington Redskins.

HURD, JEFF
Linebacker, 6'2", 245 lbs., b. 5/25/64

The Kansas State ex signed with Dallas as a free agent in 1987. He was released before the first preseason game, resigned for the replacement team, released again, then signed again late in the season and saw special teams action, recording four tackles. A serious knee injury kept him sidelined over the next two years, and he retired after the 1989 season.

HURT, ERIC
Cornerback, 5'11", 171 lbs., b. 5/11/57

A reserve defensive back out of San Jose State who made the roster as a free agent rookie in 1980, Hurt was with the Cowboys for one season, playing in the nickel defense and returning 4 kickoffs for an 18-yard average in an injury-plagued year. It was his only season in the NFL.

HUSMANN, ED
Defensive tackle, 6'0", 235 lbs., b. 8/6/31

Husmann, out of Clemson, spent five years with the St. Louis Cardinals, then was signed by Dallas in the expansion draft of 1960. He started the first game, and he also filled in on the defensive line that year. The next year he was signed by Houston and spent five years there before retiring.

HUTCHERSON, KEN
Linebacker, 6'0", 220 lbs., b. 7/14/52

Hutcherson, out of Livingston State, was the Cowboys' fourth-round draft choice in 1974. He played exclusively on special teams that year, and was picked up by the San Diego Chargers in 1975. But a leg injury sidelined him that year; it was his last in the NFL.

HUTHER, BRUCE
Linebacker, 6'1", 230 lbs., b. 7/23/54

A free agent gem from New Hampshire, a school not known for its football, in 1977, Huther developed into a solid backup and savage hitter who was chosen the team's special teams player of the year in 1978 and 1979.

Huther was among the strongest Cowboys, able to bench press more than 400 pounds. He turned in one of the biggest plays of his career in Super Bowl XII, recovering a fumbled punt in the victory over the Denver Broncos. After a year with Cleveland and one with Chicago, Huther came back from injuries to play for Dallas again in 1983, then went to the USFL one year before retiring.

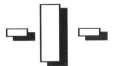

ICE BOWL

On the last day of 1967, a capacity crowd of 50,861 diehard Packer backers braved Lambeau Field's 13-below-zero weather (it would reach minus 20, the coldest December 31 in Green Bay history) to see their veteran Packers take on the upstart Dallas Cowboys in the NFL Championship Game. The Packers had barely beaten the same team in the same game the year before, 34–27, and it was a rematch everyone looked forward to.

The frozen field and a 15-mph wind made play almost impossible—and es-pecially hard on the Cowboys, whose offense relied on speed and deception, factors negated by the elements. (It was so cold that the college marching band that was to perform at halftime fled before the opening kickoff.) The Packers took an early 14–0 lead, but the Dallas defense, which had 8 sacks to Green Bay's 1, took matters into its own hands. Willie Townes hit Bart Starr on a pass attempt, and George Andrie grabbed the ball and ran it 7 yards into the end zone. A fumbled Green Bay punt led to a field goal that cut the margin to 14–10 at halftime.

Dallas went ahead in the fourth period

Green Bay quarterback Bart Starr (15) has just dived through for the game-winning touchdown in the Ice Bowl. Chuck Mercein (30) helps him up as Jerry Kramer (64) disentangles himself. Jethro Pugh kneels behind Kramer. *(From the collection of the Texas/Dallas History and Archive Division, Dallas Public Library)*

91

Cowboys Top Ten Runs From Scrimmage

99	Tony Dorsett	@ Minnesota, January 3, 1983 (TD)
84	Tony Dorsett	vs. Philadelphia, December 4, 1977 (TD)
84	Herschel Walker	vs. Philadelphia, December 14, 1986 (TD)
77	Tony Dorsett	@ St. Louis, October 9, 1977 (TD)
77	Tony Dorsett	@ Washington, September 5, 1983
75	Tony Dorsett	@ New England, September 21, 1981 (TD)
75	Emmitt Smith	vs. Washington, September 9, 1991 (TD)
73	Amos Bullocks	vs. Chicago, November 18, 1962 (TD)
71	Amos Marsh	vs. NY Giants, October 15, 1961
70	Amos Marsh	@ Washington, November 4, 1962

on a surprise 50-yard option pass from half-back Dan Reeves to Lance Rentzel. In the next ten minutes, both teams wasted long drives. When the Packers got the ball back with 4:50 left, they hadn't scored a point for almost 38 minutes; the Dallas defense had not allowed them more than 14 yards on any of their 10 possessions. After the Packers ran back a Dallas punt 9 yards to their own 32, Starr started pushing them downfield. Nine well-mixed plays later, they had moved to the Dallas 1. First down, less than a minute left. Two Donny Anderson runs failed, each followed by a Starr time-out. With no time-outs left, and 16 seconds on the clock, the Packers spurned a tying field goal and tried one last running play. Starr took the snap and slipped into the end zone behind guard Jerry Kramer's block of Jethro Pugh for the winning touchdown. In the thirteen seconds remaining Meredith could only throw two long futile bombs. As time ran out, thousands of fans rushed onto the field to rip down the goalposts. The Cowboys trudged into the locker room, where Andrie, Pugh, and Mel Renfro were treated for frostbite. Said owner Clint Murchison when he stopped by to offer his condolences, "The day wouldn't have been too cold if we had won."

Three points about this, one of pro football's most famous plays : 1) Pugh had a great game against Kramer, with several pressures and sacks; 2) Kramer was probably offsides (he as much as admitted it in his bestselling *Instant Replay*: "I came off the ball as fast as I ever have in my life. I came off the ball as fast as anyone could. In fact, I wouldn't swear that I didn't beat the center's snap by a fraction of a second. I wouldn't swear that I wasn't actually offside on the play"); and 3) center Ken Bowman's block on Pugh was probably more important than Kramer's.

IRVIN, MICHAEL
Wide receiver, 6'2", 205 lbs., b. 3/5/66

After eight seasons, Irvin had rewritten the Cowboys record book in most receiving categories. Flamboyant on and off the field, Irvin also had his share of legal scrapes, including an indictment for cocaine possession in the winter of 1996.

Nobody could question Irvin's character on a football field, however. He is among the most feared receivers in the game, a physical receiver who loves to mix it up. "Playmaker," his vanity license plates read. And so he is.

Michael Irvin

In his first eight years in the NFL, Irvin left Drew Pearson, Tony Hill, Bob Hayes, and his other Cowboy predecessors in the dust. He was the franchise's all-time king of receptions (527), receiving yards (8,538), consecutive games with at least one catch (81), and most games with 100 or more yards (36). In 1995 he established single-season marks for catches (111), yardage (1,603), and 100-yard games (11).

Dallas' first-round pick in 1988, the University of Miami star debuted with a flourish as the first rookie to start at wide receiver for the Cowboys since Bob Hayes in 1965. He caught a touchdown pass in his first game, finished the season with a per-catch average of 20.4 yards, tops in the NFC, and contributed 32 catches for 654 yards and 5 touchdowns.

Irvin was on pace to collect almost 70 catches and over 1,000 yards in 1989 when he went down with a season-ending knee injury. The rehabilitation period would extend into the 1990 season, raising doubts about whether he would ever reach his potential.

But Irvin is a determined man, the product of an impoverished childhood in a family of seventeen brothers and sisters. Those who hesitated at the dinner table went hungry, and that's Irvin's philosophy on the field. Irvin was back by the fifth game of the 1990 season and returned to the starting lineup by mid-November. His 20 catches for 413 yards and 5 touchdowns were a prelude to a monster 1991 season.

Irvin established himself as one of the elite receivers by grabbing 93 passes for 1,523 yards and 8 touchdowns. The consensus All-Pro finished with the sixth-highest yardage total and eighth-best for receptions in league history, also establishing team marks. Irvin further demonstrated his ability to step up in the big games with 9 receptions for 167 yards in two playoff contests.

The Cowboys in 1992 would take the next step in their development and Irvin was among the leaders of the parade, finishing second in the league in yardage (1,396), seventh in receptions (78), and pacing the NFL with a per-catch average of 17.9 yards. Irvin also had someone else to attract the attention of opposing safeties in the person of speedy first-round pick Alvin Harper. Irvin capped off his season with 6 catches in each of the three playoff games, including 114 yards and a pair of first-half touchdown grabs as the Cowboys rolled past the Buffalo Bills in Super Bowl XXVII.

There was more of the same for Irvin in 1993, resulting in another Super Bowl triumph over the Bills. Irvin was second in the league in yardage (1,330), third in catches (88), and had five 100-yard games. He was voted to his third straight Pro Bowl berth, then caught 16 passes for 215 yards in the playoffs as the Cowboys collected their second straight Lombardi Trophy.

Dallas missed its third straight Super Bowl in 1994, but nobody was pointing an accusing finger at Irvin. He caught 79 balls for 1,241, scored 6 touchdowns, and returned to the Pro Bowl. In the 38–28 defeat to San

Francisco in the NFC Championship Game, Irvin distinguished himself with 12 receptions for 192 yards and 2 touchdowns.

The Cowboys barged back into the Super Bowl following the 1995 season, beating the Pittsburgh Steelers, and Irvin again made his presence felt in the big game with 76 yards on 5 catches, all for first downs. That allowed him to surpass Pearson's club record of 67 post-season receptions. During the regular season, he caught 111 passes (fifth in the league) for 1,603 yards (fourth in the NFL) and 10 touchdowns.

Throw in a fifth consecutive Pro Bowl berth, most ever by a Cowboys receiver, and it's difficult to argue with those who insist he's the greatest pass-catcher in the franchise's history. If he can keep his off-the-field problems from interfering with his football career, he has some spectacular years still to come.

IRVING

The Dallas Cowboys moved to the city of Irving in 1971, a suburb on the western edge of Dallas, upon completion of Texas Stadium—so technically speaking, they are the Irving Cowboys. That name was never seriously considered, however.

ISBELL, JOE BOB
Offensive guard, 6'1", 240 lbs., b. 7/7/40

The Houston standout free agent played four years in Dallas (1962–65) and was one of Landry's first messenger guards, shuttling in plays from the sidelines when he wasn't injured. After sitting out much of the 1965 season, he went on to play for Cleveland, Houston, and finally Cincinnati before he retired.

JACKSON, TIM
Safety, 5'11", 192 lbs., b. 12/7/65

Jackson was a ninth-round pick by the Cowboys out of Nebraska in the 1989 draft. He saw some action on special teams and was released after the season, his only one in the NFL. Jackson, whose nickname was "Action," had been a star at Dallas' Skyline High School.

JACKSON, WILLIE
Wide receiver, 6'1", 205 lbs., b. 8/16/71

A second-generation wideout from the University of Florida (his three seasons as a starter for the Gators allowed him to finish second in career receiving yardage and catches at the school), Jackson appeared to have a bright future with the Cowboys when he finished third in preseason catches in 1994 and made the opening day roster. But he was deactivated for every game, and then left unprotected in the 1995 expansion draft. The Jacksonville Jaguars plucked him in the eleventh round.

JAX, GARTH
Linebacker, 6'2", 222 lbs., b. 9/16/63

An eleventh-round pick in 1986, following an injury-riddled career at Florida State, Jax was released on the final cut of his rookie training camp, but one week later the Cowboys re-signed him when Mike Renfro was placed on injured reserve. Jax was a special teams performer and backup right linebacker as a rookie, but a broken hand limited his 1987 season to three games.

Traded by the Cowboys to Phoenix in 1989, Jax forged a lengthy career with the Cardinals into the mid-1990s.

JEFFCOAT, JIM
Defensive end, 6'5", 280 lbs., b. 4/1/61

Durable and consistent, Jeffcoat's twelve seasons with the Cowboys spanned the end of the Tom Landry era, Jimmy Johnson's short but spectacular run of two Super Bowl titles, and Barry Switzer's first season as Dallas' head coach.

James Wilson Jeffcoat arrived with considerable promise in 1983 as a first-round pick out of Arizona State, a New Jersey native who grew up a New York Giants fan. (The Cowboys passed up Dan Marino to take Jeffcoat.) Jeffcoat wasn't the most impressive of athletes, but he quickly impressed the coaching staff with his work ethic. He also found two imposing ends ahead of him his rookie season: Pro Bowlers Harvey Martin and Ed "Too Tall" Jones.

But Martin's star was fading, and Jeffcoat took over in 1984 as the starting right end. He finished the season with 11.5 sacks, second on the team to Randy White, and recovered a key fumble in the end zone against New Orleans that tied the game at 27-all with less than three minutes to play. The Cowboys had rallied from a 27–6 deficit at the start of the fourth quarter, and won in overtime, 30–27.

Jeffcoat continued to shine in 1985, learning to be more aggressive by watching films of former Cowboys defensive linemen Bob Lilly and George Andrie. Long hours of study after practice paid off when Jeffcoat finished with 12 sacks, second to Jones, and keyed two of Dallas' most important wins. In a November victory over Washington, he sacked Redskins quarterback Joe Theismann a club-record 5 times and led the team with 11 solo tackles. Against the Giants in mid-December, he intercepted a tipped Phil

95

Jim Jeffcoat pressures 49ers quarterback
Steve Young.

Simms pass and rumbled 65 yards for a touchdown as the Cowboys wrapped up another NFC East title.

In 1986 Jeffcoat paced the Cowboys in sacks with a career-best 14, and in 1987 he again proved to be a nemesis against his once-favorite team, returning another tipped Simms pass 26 yards for a touchdown to help beat the Giants.

Jeffcoat had a knack for the big play, huffing and puffing 77 yards with a fumble recovery for his fourth career touchdown in a 1989 game against the Redskins. After being on the receiving end of two batted passes for TDs, Jeffcoat returned the favor in 1991 when he tipped a pass that was caught and returned by linebacker Dixon Edwards 36 yards for a touchdown against the Cincinnati Bengals.

Johnson was stockpiling talent along the defensive line, and in 1992 Jeffcoat was shifted to a reserve role, behind fellow New

Jersey transplant Tony Tolbert, as a pass-rushing specialist. Jeffcoat wasn't happy about his removal as a starter, but he thrived in his new job, recording a club-leading 10.5 sacks in 1992 en route to his first Super Bowl ring and the Cowboys' first world championship since the 1977 season. Jeffcoat was named to *Pro Football Weekly's* all-backup squad at defensive end, and he also filled in at tackle for the first time since 1986.

Jeffcoat remained a productive player in 1993, and at the end of the season he topped all active Cowboys with 669 career tackles and 86.5 sacks. He was back in the starting lineup in November of 1993, moving in for the injured Charles Haley, then returned again back with the starters in consecutive games in December, as Haley's back continued to ache.

In the regular-season finale against the Giants, Jeffcoat proved he could still contribute, leading the defensive line with 7 tackles, 2 sacks, a forced fumble, and 3 quarterback pressures to clinch another NFC East title. Jeffcoat had at least half a sack in all three playoff games following the 1993 season, teaming with Haley on a critical third-down sack of Buffalo Bills quarterback Jim Kelly early in the third quarter of Super Bowl XXVIII.

Jeffcoat added 8 more sacks in 1994 and 1 more in the playoffs, but free agency and the salary cap conspired to lower the Cowboys' deep talent pool. There wasn't much money left to pay a tenured reserve like Jeffcoat, and he accepted a lucrative contract offer in 1995 from the Bills.

JENNINGS, KEITH
Tight end, 6'4", 251 lbs., b. 5/19/66

Jimmy Johnson didn't strike gold every time as a master talent evaluator. When Jennings was picked in the fifth round of the 1989 draft from Clemson, Johnson boasted that Jennings "really looks like the complete tight end we're looking for." But Jennings lasted only one season, and the Cowboys added veteran tight ends Jay Novacek and Rob Awalt from Phoenix the following season. Jennings went on to play several years as a backup tight end for the Chicago Bears.

JENSEN, JIM
Running back, 6'4", 225 lbs., b. 11/28/53

Jensen was the Cowboys' second-round pick in the 1976 draft. He had been a premier running back at Iowa State, and had also earned track letters as a hurdler and shot-putter. But Dallas was deep in running backs, and he spent the year on specialty teams. He was paired with Butch Johnson as a deep back on kickoff returns, running back 13 for 313 yards. He was traded to Denver a week before the following season's opener. Jensen played four productive years there (missing 1978 with a bad knee), then spent two years as a backup with Green Bay before retiring after the 1982 season.

JETT, JOHN
Punter, 6'0", 184 lbs., b. 10/11/68

Punters are often judged on what they don't do, rather than what they do. In the case of Jett, who joined the Cowboys as a free agent in 1993 and displaced eight-year veteran Mike Saxon, he hasn't put Dallas in difficult situations with blocked punts or shanks. He led the NFL in percentage of punts downed inside the 20-yard line in each of his first two seasons, and was eighth in his third. Each season, his yardage average has hovered around the 41-yard mark—41.8, 41.9, and 40.9. In 1995 he tied for second in the NFL in fewest number of punts returned at 22.

JOHNSON, BUTCH
Wide receiver, 6'1", 192 lbs., b. 5/28/54

One of the more outspoken and outrageous personalities in Cowboys history, Michael McColly "Butch" Johnson chafed in his role as a backup behind two of the greatest receivers in Cowboys history, Drew Pearson and Tony Hill. Johnson was never able to supplant Pearson, Hill, or Golden Richards during his Cowboys career from 1976–83, but he still made his share of memorable plays as a part-time receiver. He choreographed one of the most famous touchdown dances ever in the NFL: the gyrating California Quake.

Johnson was a tough competitor who prided himself on making clutch receptions. None was bigger than his diving 45-yarder for a touchdown in the third quarter of Super Bowl XII, putting the Cowboys ahead of the Denver Broncos, 20-3. Johnson scored another Super Bowl TD the following year against the Pittsburgh Steelers, a four-yard grab from Roger Staubach late in the game that pulled the Cowboys to within 35–31, the final victory margin.

A third-round draft pick from Cal-Riverside in 1976, Johnson tasted limited action with the offense his first four seasons.

Butch Johnson

His primary early contributions came on special teams. As a rookie, he returned 45 punts for a 10.9-yard average and 28 kickoffs for a 24.8-yard average, both career highs, and his 9 punt returns in a game against Buffalo tied an NFL record. He caught only 5 passes playing behind Pearson and Richards.

In 1977, Johnson alternated with Richards as play messenger, but he finished with only 12 catches for 135 yards. The next year, a second-year player named Tony Hill started opposite Pearson; Johnson contributed only 12 catches for 155 yards in 1978, then an injury forced him to miss the first five games of 1979. Nevertheless, Johnson contributed to two victories in the 1979 season: a diving 19-yard third-down catch to spark a fourth-quarter rally over the New York Giants, and a 17-yard grab in the fourth quarter for the winning touchdown in a playoff-clinching victory over the Philadelphia Eagles. He finished the year with 6 catches for 105 yards.

But Johnson wanted more involvement with the offense. That's where the real money was. Coach Tom Landry increased Johnson's role in 1980, and Johnson responded with 19 receptions for 263 yards and 4 touchdowns. He caught a 35-yard touchdown pass that sent the Cowboys ahead, 27–13, late in the third quarter of an NFC wild card playoff victory over the Los Angeles Rams.

When Hill was injured in 1981, Johnson had his longest stint with the first unit, starting the first six games. He took advantage with 25 catches, 552 yards, and 5 touchdowns, tying with tight end Doug Cosbie for the club lead. "Butch makes the tough plays in tough situations," quarterback Danny White said, acknowledging Johnson's ability to catch passes across the middle, unlike Hill. All 5 touchdowns contributed significantly to Dallas victories, and Johnson's one-handed 20-yard reception set up the Cowboys' first touchdown in the NFC title game against the San Francisco 49ers, a game the Cowboys would eventually lose. In 1982 he had 12 grabs for 269 yards, with games of 76 and 73 yards in the playoffs.

In 1983 Johnson established career highs with 41 receptions and 561 yards, but his outspoken ways and flamboyant on-field personality finally wore thin with Landry. Johnson was traded to the Houston Oilers in 1984 for possession receiver Mike Renfro. Johnson was dumped by the Oilers after three weeks of training camp, however, then signed with the Denver Broncos, for whom he finished his career in 1984–85. He had a good year in 1984, but halfway through the next season, he was replaced as the starting wide receiver by a fast rookie out of Arizona, Vance Johnson. He retired after the season.

Toward the end of his stay with the Cowboys, Johnson was asked if he was happy being a well-regarded backup on one of the elite teams in pro football. "Happy? Happy isn't in my vocabulary," replied Johnson, who nevertheless possessed a quick wit and fun-loving personality.

JOHNSON, JIMMY
Head coach

Jimmy Johnson talked the talk and walked the walk.

His first Cowboys team in 1989 went 1–15. No Cowboys team had ever lost that many games, and there were cries for his head—and that of new owner Jerry Jones. But just three years later, the 'Pokes steamrollered the Buffalo Bills to win their first Super Bowl in fifteen years. That kind of success is a hallmark of Johnson football teams.

James William Johnson, a native Texan, grew up on the Gulf Coast in Port Arthur, where he earned all-state honors as a two-way lineman in high school. At Arkansas he became All-Southwest Conference, and helped lead the Razorbacks to the 1964 national championship. His roommate was a scrappy over-achiever named Jerry Jones.

Johnson earned a degree in psychology in 1967. He was already a two-year coaching veteran: at Louisiana Tech in 1965, then Picayune (MS) High School the following year. After a year at Wichita State, two years at Iowa State, three years at Oklahoma, four years at Arkansas, and two years at Pittsburgh (all assistant coach positions), he was hired to rebuild the losing program at Oklahoma State in 1979. He brought the school plenty of national attention and two bowl invitations as he compiled a 29–25 record over 5 seasons. Johnson was named Big Eight Coach of the Year following his first season, and it clearly wasn't long before a major program came calling.

The school was Miami, and Johnson was ready. His first year, the Hurricanes only went 8–5, but over the next four seasons they chalked up a 44–4 mark, two Orange Bowl wins, a national championship in 1987, and two second-place finishes in 1986 and 1988. They won 36 straight regular-season games from 1985–88, the fifth-longest streak in NCAA history.

Jimmy Johnson

So when old teammate and soon-to-be-owner of the Dallas Cowboys, Jerry Jones came calling, Johnson was ready for the next step. He and Jones roared into town in February 1989 like a tornado. Johnson had a vision in his head of what he wanted his team to be and went about it in typical Johnson fashion—damn the reactions, full speed ahead. He cleaned out the deadwood from the Cowboys team in short fashion, and started to look at anyone and everyone. It soon was obvious that Johnson had an uncanny eye for talent. He and Jones made an outrageous forty-five trades in his first four years, many of them Plan B free agents, and thirty-two of the fifty-four college players they drafted earned a roster spot on the team. All six of Dallas' first-round draft choices between 1989 and 1992 went on to be Super Bowl starters, and the 1991 draft is one of the greatest in Cowboys history.

But that came later. That first year was a nightmare. Not since the Cowboys' first year in 1960, when another first-year coach,

Tom Landry, was attempting to put together a team that matched the one in his head, did Texas Stadium see as many one-year (or one-game) wonders. Johnson ran them in and ran them out; if they couldn't play, they didn't stay. He stripped the roster to the bare bones, cutting legendary veterans and promising newcomers alike. The results on the scoreboard weren't pretty—the 1–15 finish had the entire town screaming, especially since these were the two guys that fired local legend Tom Landry—but in this case looks were deceptive. Johnson had traded the most valuable Cowboy, super running back Herschel Walker, to Minnesota for a pile of draft choices and players in what would be called the greatest trade in NFL history. Number-one draft choice Troy Aikman showed promise and signs of leadership, and Michael Irvin looked like a budding superstar until he went out with a knee injury.

Things got better quickly. The following year the Cowboys had a shot at a .500 season and even the playoffs, until the last week of the season. A Troy Aikman shoulder separation in the previous game sidelined him for the finale against Atlanta, and replacement Babe Laufenberg couldn't get it done against a strong Atlanta rush. But the turnaround season earned Johnson NFC Coach of the Year honors, and by the end of the year, rookie Emmitt Smith was running like a Hall of Famer. The key, however, was a no-name defense that was first in the NFC against the pass and fourth overall.

The two years of wheeling and dealing paid off in 1991. For the first time since 1985, the 11–5 Cowboys made the playoffs, and advanced to the second round, where they were soundly trounced by a motivated Detroit squad. But the offense, led by the Aikman-Irvin-Smith axis, was explosive: Smith and Irvin led the league in yardage, and Aikman was the hottest signal-caller in the NFL until he went down with a sprained knee with a month to go.

The following year everything clicked. The Big Three all had strong years, supplemented by the best pass-catching tight end

in the NFL—Jay Novacek—and an ice-breaker offensive line. Nearly twenty players rotated into a defense that gave up the fewest rushing yards in the league, and posted one of the lowest pass-completion percentages—and didn't send one player to the Pro Bowl. The youngest team in the NFL roared to a 13–3 record, then blitzed Philadelphia and favored San Francisco on the way to Super Bowl XXVII. The 52-17 pasting of the Bills presaged a team of destiny.

Not only did the Cowboys have the best and the deepest talent in the league but smart negotiating by Jones avoided salary cap problems. Dallas entered the 1993 season virtually undamaged by free agency. For the first time in years, a Cowboys team was favored to win it all—and they did, in much the same fashion and with most of the same faces. A 12–4 finish and the NFC East crown—won in a thrilling overtime victory in the season finale over the Giants—got them a first-round buy in the playoffs. Wins over Green Bay and San Francisco catapulted the Cowboys into a rematch with Buffalo in the Super Bowl. The script was different but the denouement was the same—another Dallas triumph, this time by a 30–13 score.

Johnson, throughout the team's ascendance, had developed into a master motivator. The psych major possessed an uncanny ability to prepare his team mentally, for the gimmes as well as the death matches. A few days before the second NFC Championship Game, against the 49ers, he called into a sports talk show from a car phone and pulled a Joe Namath: "We will win the ball game," he said over the air, "and we're going to beat their rear ends." *The Dallas Morning News* bannered it the next day. Said a bemused George Seifert, the 'Niners' head coach, "The man's got balls." Coaches just didn't issue bulletin-board material to help stir the other team to a fever pitch. But the bottom-line, no-excuses mentality it thrust onto the Cowboys worked. Final score: Dallas 38, San Francisco 21.

But the biggest surprise was still to

Cowboys All-Time Rushing Leaders

	Att.	Yards	Avg.	Long	TDs
1. Tony Dorsett (1977–87)	2755	12,036	4.4	99t	72
2. Emmitt Smith (1990–)	2007	8956	4.5	75t	96
3. Don Perkins (1961–68)	1500	6217	4.2	59	42
4. Calvin Hill (1969–74)	1166	5009	4.3	55	39
5. Robert Newhouse (1973–83)	1160	4784	4.1	54	31
6. Walt Garrison (1966–74)	899	3886	4.3	41	30
7. Herschel Walker (1986–89)	802	3388	4.2	84t	26
8. Roger Staubach (1969–79)	410	2264	5.5	33	20
9. Ron Springs (1979–84)	604	2180	3.6	46	28
10. Amos Marsh (1961–64)	427	2065	4.8	71	14

come. Insiders knew that the Jones-Johnson friendship had been a strained one for several years; they increasingly disagreed on many aspects of running the team, chiefly the degree of Jones's participation. But the announcement on March 29 that Johnson was leaving the Cowboys—eight days after an alcohol-assisted confrontation at the NFL owners' meeting in Orlando—created nearly as much of a stir as Landry's firing five years before.

Johnson was immediately offered the head coach position in many NFL cities, but there were only a few NFL situations that excited him. He took a TV job as a color commentator; by his second year he was receiving good reviews and settling into a relatively cushy job. But the one team he coveted, the Miami Dolphins, had a disastrous year in 1995, and when owner Wayne Huizenga came a-courting in the spring of 1996, Johnson couldn't resist. Another NFL coaching legend—Don Shula—was eased out to make room for Johnson. This forced "retirement," however, was handled a bit more smoothly. No one doubted that somehow, some way, Jimmy Johnson would turn the thing around.

JOHNSON, MIKE
Cornerback, 5'11", 185 lbs., b. 10/7/43

Free agent Johnson played in the same backfield with Gale Sayers at Kansas, but he was converted to a defensive back after only one Cowboy summer camp practice in 1966. He was a punishing tackler, and in his second year he became a starter; after settling in, he finished strong with 5 interceptions. The next year, 1968, a shakeup in the secondary midway through the season left him on the bench. He lost his self-confidence on the field during the course of 1969, and was traded to Chicago and later released on waivers before the 1970 season.

JOHNSON, MITCH
Guard, 6'4", 245 lbs., b. 3/1/42

Johnson was a 17th-round draft pick out of UCLA in the 1965 draft. He played one year for Dallas as a backup on the offensive line, and then was traded to Washington, where he played two years, and then went to Los Angeles for two final years.

Cowboys All-Time Receiving Leaders

	No.	Yards	Avg.	Long	TDs
1. Michael Irvin (1988–)	527	8538	16.2	87t	50
2. Drew Pearson (1973–83)	489	7822	16.0	67	48
3. Tony Hill (1977–86)	479	7988	16.7	75t	51
4. Tony Dorsett (1977–87)	382	3432	9.0	91	13
5. Bob Hayes (1965–74)	365	7295	20.0	95	71
6. Jay Novacek (1990–)	339	3576	11.0	49	22
7. Emmitt Smith (1990–)	301	1951	6.5	86	4
8. Doug Cosbie (1979–88)	300	3728	12.4	61t	30
9. Frank Clarke (1960–67)	281	5214	18.6	80	50
10. Billy Joe DuPree (1973–83)	267	3565	13.4	42	41

JOHNSON, UNDRA
Running back, 5'9", 199 lbs., b. 1/8/66

Johnson had been selected by the Atlanta Falcons in the seventh round of the 1989 draft, but was waived and signed with the New Orleans Saints in mid-October. The West Virginia product was on the move again in late November when he was released by the Saints and signed by the Cowboys. He played one game for Dallas in his only NFL season.

JOHNSON, WALTER
See Replacement Games

JOHNSTON, DARYL
Fullback, 6'2", 242 lbs., b. 2/10/66

He has rushed for only 685 yards in seven years, yet has become something of a cult figure throughout the NFL. For that, credit former Cowboys quarterback and current radio color man Babe Lautenberg who nicknamed the personable Syracuse University grad "Moose." It's no coincidence that Johnston has been the lead blocker for Em-

mitt Smith's assault on the NFL rushing record book. And don't assume that someone called Moose has the IQ of a wooly mammoth. He graduated first in his high

Daryl Johnston

school class of 290 in Youngstown, NY, with a grade point average of 4.0. Since the Pro Bowl began selecting fullbacks, Johnston grabbed the first two NFC selections. When he rushed for 111 yards in 1995, that gave him back-to-back 100-yard seasons for the first time. (Maybe he gets his toughness from his sister, JoAnn, who played goalkeeper for the University of Rochester's two-time national championship soccer team.) Though he's known primarily for his devastating blocking, Johnston has been successful 19 of 23 times he's run on third or fourth down for a first down during his career. He's also a valuable receiver out of the backfield, averaging 31 catches a season from 1991–95. The second-round 1989 draft pick is also extremely durable; he's never missed a regular-season or playoff game in his career.

JONES, DALE
See Replacement Games

JONES, E. J.
See Replacement Games

JONES, ED
Defensive end, 6'9", 275 lbs., b. 2/23/51

"Too Tall" Jones was one of the premier defensive ends in the NFL for more than a decade. The Tennessee State ex was the Cowboys' first-round draft pick in 1974. He learned his trade, his first year, from vets Larry Cole and Pat Toomay, then moved into a starter's job the next year. He remained a starter through 1989, his last year—not counting 1979, when he took the year off to try his luck at professional boxing. Jones did win all his fights, but six less-than-impressive victories over second-rate club fighters didn't impress anyone, and Jones returned to the Cowboys the next year. The training he had undergone for boxing made him an even better football player. He was voted to three straight Pro Bowls (1981–82–83) and two All-Pro teams (1981–82). He was one of the most feared pass rushers of all time, and his imposing height made many a quarterback alter many a pass. No one was more dependable, and he remained amazingly agile and fast deep into his career; he led the team in

Ed Jones rushes Cleveland Browns quarterback Gary Danielson.

Cowboys All-Time Passing Leaders
(Minimum 1500 Attempts)

	Att.	Comp.	Pct.	Yards	TDs	Int.	Rating
1. Roger Staubach (1969–79)	2958	1685	57.0	22,700	153	109	83.5
2. Troy Aikman (1989–)	2713	1704	62.8	19,607	98	85	83.5
3. Danny White (1976–88)	2950	1761	59.7	21,959	155	132	81.7
4. Don Meredith (1960–68)	2308	1170	50.7	17,199	135	111	74.7

sacks several of his last seasons. As good as he was during the regular season, he was even better in the playoffs. Jones retired with 105 sacks, 1,032 combined tackles, and 693 solo tackles, all good for third place in Dallas record books, and he is the only Cowboy to play fifteen years (and 224 games) in Dallas.

JONES, JAMES
Running back, 5'10", 203 lbs., b. 12/6/58

Jones was the most heartwarming story of the 1984 season, coming back from a serious knee injury that sidelined him for two and a half years. Jones was activated for the eighth game of the 1984 season and finished with 7 rushes for 13 yards and 7 catches for 57 yards, including an 8-yard touchdown grab against St. Louis, the only touchdown of his career.

A third-round pick from Mississippi in 1980, Jones averaged a team-leading 5.3 yards per carry in 1981, as Tony Dorsett's backup. His 59-yard touchdown run against the Baltimore Colts in December was the second-longest run from scrimmage of the 1981 season. In the playoffs following the 1981 season, Jones was Dallas' second-leading pass receiver with 5 receptions for 32 yards.

As a rookie in 1980, Jones sparkled in his debut with 45 yards in 10 carries while filling in for Dorsett (slowed by leg cramps) in the opener at Washington. But Jones

made his biggest rookie contributions on special teams, setting a club record for punt returns (54) and punt return yardage (548), breaking Butch Johnson's previous marks. Against the Los Angeles Rams in the NFC wild card game, Jones had 153 yards in kick returns, including a 43-yard punt return in the first quarter.

The knee injury Jones suffered in the 1982 preseason sidelined him until 1984, his last in the NFL, when he had only 8 carries and 7 receptions.

JONES, JERRY
Owner

Millionaire wildcatter Jerral Wayne Jones was deep sea fishing in September 1988, in Cabo San Lucas, when he read in a day-old San Diego newspaper that Dallas Cowboys owner H.R. "Bum" Bright was looking for a buyer for the team he'd bought in 1984. Within minutes, the former Arkansas Razorback defensive lineman (co-captain of the 1964 national championship team) was making a long distance phone call to Dallas. By spring 1989 he had bought the team, beating out dozens of other bidders that included Los Angeles Lakers owner Jerry Buss, a Japanese group, and a group fronted by Roger Staubach.

On Saturday morning, February 25, 1989, a deal was made—for about $150 million and the stipulation that Jones was

Jerry Jones

bringing in his old college roommate Jimmy Johnson, head coach at Miami, to replace Tom Landry. Jones and Tex Schramm helicoptered down to an Austin golf course to tell Landry that he was no longer the coach of the Dallas Cowboys. In an awkward scene, Jones did the dirty work, even though the job, by all rights, was Bright's—or Schramm's—to do. But Jones was castigated as The Man Who Fired Tom Landry. A badly orchestrated press conference that evening made things worse. Several years, three Super Bowls, and one head coach later, Jones is the toast of the town, and the most powerful owner in the NFL.

JONES, JIMMIE
Defensive lineman, 6'4", 276 lbs., b. 1/9/66

Despite popular opinion, Leon Lett's goal-line fumble, courtesy of Buffalo's Don Beebe, wasn't the most newsworthy event involving a Cowboys defensive lineman dur-

ing Super Bowl XXVII at the Rose Bowl. Jones tied a Super Bowl record when he recovered a pair of offensive fumbles, one of which he returned two yards for a touchdown. The Cowboys' third-round draft pick in 1990 out of the University of Miami had size, speed, and quickness, and he was a major factor in the Cowboys' defensive-line rotation for four seasons, before leaving via free agency in 1994 to play for the Los Angeles Rams. Not bad for someone who didn't play football as a high school senior in Okeechobee, FL, because family obligations forced him to hold down a full-time job. Miami coach Jimmy Johnson had film on Jones' performance as a junior, and offered him a scholarship based on that.

JONES, ROBERT
Linebacker, 6'2", 237 lbs., b. 9/27/69

It would be difficult to find a recent Cowboy career as jumbled as Jones' stay at Valley Ranch. He was a first-round draft pick out of East Carolina in 1992, and became the first Dallas rookie to start at linebacker since Lee Roy Jordan in 1963. He finished second on the team in tackles and earned NFC Defensive Rookie of the Year honors. But in his second season, Jones was benched, and the critics howled that the Cowboys had wasted the draft pick. Then Ken Norton left the team for San Francisco via free agency before the 1994 season, and Jones responded by returning to the first team. That year, the defense led the league in fewest yards per game, and Jones had a team-high 162 tackles, an effort that earned him All-Pro honors. He started throughout the 1995 Super season, recording 100 tackles despite missing four games and most of another with a strained abdominal muscle. He played almost exclusively against the run, rarely in passing situations, and he had a career-high 6 tackles for losses in 1995. Jones was second on the team with 8 tackles in Super Bowl XXX. In the offseason, he signed a five-year, $10 million contract with St. Louis.

JORDAN, LEE ROY
Linebacker, 6'2", 215 lbs., b. 4/27/41

Lee Roy Jordan, according to Bear Bryant "the finest athlete I ever coached," was the inspirational leader of the first Cowboy championship teams. He was Dallas' first-round draft choice in 1963 after an All-American career at Alabama. Though he was small for a middle linebacker, he was unbelievably tough. His hands were massive, and he gained a reputation for ripping ball carriers apart; it wasn't long before he earned the nickname "Killer." Assistant Coach Ernie Stautner said, "If Jordan weighed as much as Dick Butkus, they'd have to outlaw him from football."

He played at outside linebacker his first year; a kidney injury sidelined him the last six games. The next year he moved to the middle, his natural position, and never left. Few defensive players ever marshalled the intensity Jordan did on big downs; he was the vocal leader on the field, exhorting his teammates individually, and demanding they step up to big-play level. He was never satisfied with anything less than the best, and he transmitted that kind of fire to his teammates the way few leaders in any sport ever have. And he worked harder than anyone else, watching endless film and studying assignments, tendencies, keys of both the opponents and his fellow Cowboys. (The last five years of his career, he de-

Lee Roy Jordan *(From the collection of the Texas/Dallas History and Archive Division, Dallas Public Library)*

manded that his contract include a projector for his home.) He had 32 interceptions over the years, an impressive number for a linebacker. He was a five-time Pro Bowler and two-time All-Pro, and he was finally inducted into the Ring of Honor in 1989 (bitter contract disputes with Tex Schramm had kept him out previously) after a superb 14-year career at middle linebacker.

KELLER, MIKE
Linebacker, 6'3", 220 lbs., b. 12/13/49

The Cowboys' third-round draft pick out of Michigan in 1972 saw mostly specialty teams action in his first year with Dallas. He missed the entire '73 season after undergoing shoulder surgery, and retired before the '74 season started.

KENNARD, DEREK
Offensive guard, 6'3", 320 lbs., b. 9/9/62

One practice beneath the scorching Austin sun during the summer of 1995 was enough to convince Kennard that there was no way his chronic hip problem would allow him to play another year in the NFL. But the Cowboys convinced him to return a month later. And when starting center Ray Donaldson was lost for the balance of the season with a fractured right ankle on Thanksgiving Day, Kennard emerged as Dallas' new center, starting all the way to the Super Bowl.

Kennard came to the Cowboys in 1994 following eight seasons with the St. Louis-Phoenix-Arizona Cardinals and New Orleans. He started all sixteen games that year at right guard. After Super Bowl XXX, he was released by the Cowboys in February 1996.

KER, CRAWFORD
Offensive guard, 6'3", 285 lbs., b. 5/5/62

The Cowboys had high expectations for "Big Daddy" Ker when, in the 1985 draft, they invested a third-round pick on the University of Florida lineman. Ker missed eleven games as a rookie due to a back injury, but in 1986, he won a job with the first unit at right guard, and he stayed with the starting unit for the next five years.

Ker was durable, starting forty-two straight games during one stretch. But in 1989 new coach Jimmy Johnson soon became disenchanted with Ker, who received unconditional free agency in February 1991 and then signed with the Denver Broncos. He played there a year and then retired.

Ker's first appearance with the starting unit came in the 1986 preseason opener in London, where his parents (natives of Scotland) once lived, and where his father served as a royal guard at Buckingham Palace before emigrating to the United States.

KICKING KARAVAN

In early 1967, Cowboy Personnel Director Gil Brandt launched a coast-to-coast search for kickers—in other words, someone to replace the less-than-spectacular Danny Villanueva, who had little distance and no punting ability. The club's kicking coach, Ben Agajanian, and a brace of assistant coaches were sent out with Brandt in a chartered plane to interview candidates. They auditioned 1,300 kickers in 29 states, including a bus driver who left a busful of passengers to run onto the field in his cap and uniform and kick three field goals. The quest produced ten candidates, a sum soon narrowed to two. One, Harold Deters, was invited to summer camp, but was released early in the season after hitting only 1 of 4 attempts. The other was Mac Percival, a high school coach who was ironically discovered at the first stop—in Dallas. His wife had entered him in the trials. The Cowboys signed him, then traded him to Chicago just before the season opener. (He kicked 13 of 26 field goals for the Bears, including 4 of 7 from beyond the 40, and had 7 productive years for Chicago. In his last year as a pro, he kicked 2 of 8 field goals and 4 of 5 extra points for the Cowboys in 1974 before yielding to Efren Herrera.) In the end, the job was still Villanueva's. He kicked 8 of 19 field goals and missed 2 extra points, and was gone after the season. The next year saw the final Kicking Karavan, a scaled-down version that visited eight cities and produced zilch.

KILLIAN, GENE
Offensive guard, 6'4", 250 lbs., b. 9/22/52

Killian was a sixteenth-round draft pick out of Tennessee in 1974. He saw some action filling in for All-Pros Blaine Nye and John Niland, who was in his last year. In the final game of the year, Killian raced across the field to catch Raiders linebacker Phil Villiapiano from behind, after a 27-yard run with a Dallas fumble. It was his only year in the NFL.

KINER, STEVE
Linebacker, 6'1", 220 lbs., b. 6/12/47

Kiner was a free spirit (once, when the Cowboys practice field parking lot was full, he parked in Coach Tom Landry's spot during a rainstorm). A third-round draft pick from Tennessee in 1970, Kiner was known chiefly for the fact that he roomed with Duane Thomas. He saw limited action his rookie season. He was impatient with his playing time, and during training camp in 1971, at his own request, he was traded to New England. He had an excellent year there, then finished out his career with five years (1974–78) in Houston.

KING, ANGELO
Linebacker, 6'1", 220 lbs., b. 2/10/58

A free agent find in 1981, King fit the mold of the small, quick linebacker needed

to combat the modern pass-oriented offense. King was cut in late August, but was recalled when Mike Hegman fractured his arm in the 1981 opener.

King showed a flair for special teams early in the season, and when Hegman returned to health, King was retained. Coach Tom Landry considered King a candidate to eventually replace aging outside linebacker D.D. Lewis, sometimes comparing him to Doomsday Defense backer Dave Edwards. But King, a teammate of Dextor Clinkscale at South Carolina State, lost out to Anthony Dickerson and was traded to the Detroit Lions for a draft pick. King played for the Lions from 1984–87 before retiring.

KITSON, SYD
Offensive guard, 6'5", 272 lbs., b. 9/27/58

The Cowboys signed Kitson in November 1984, a month after he was released by the Green Bay Packers. A third-round draft pick of the Packers in 1980, Kitson played four years for the Packers, but appeared in only one game for the Cowboys in 1984, his last year in the NFL.

KLEIN, DICK
Offensive tackle, 6'4", 255 lbs., b. 2/11/34

Klein had spent two years with Chicago and then was traded to the Cowboys before their 1960 maiden season. The Iowa ex was good enough to start at tackle for Dallas that year, but traveled to Pittsburgh, Boston, and Oakland in the next four years. He retired after the 1964 season.

KOSAR, BERNIE
Quarterback, 6'5", 210 lbs., b. 11/25/63

Almost ten years of loyal service to the Cleveland Browns didn't seem to mean much by the fall of 1993. Kosar, the team's epicenter for almost a decade, was expendable in the eyes of new coach Bill Belichick. So when the Cowboys were in the market for

Cowboys All-Time Interception Leaders

	No.	Yards	Avg.	Long	TD
1. Mel Renfro (1964–77)	52	626	12.0	90	3
2. Everson Walls (1981–89)	44	391	8.9	37	0
3. Charlie Waters (1970–78, 80–81)	41	584	14.2	56t	2
4. Dennis Thurman (1978–85)	36	562	15.6	96	4
5. Michael Downs (1981–88)	34	433	12.7	31	1
6. Cornell Green (1962–74)	34	553	16.2	59	2
7. Lee Roy Jordan (1963–76)	32	472	14.8	49	3
8. Cliff Harris (1970–79)	29	281	9.7	60	1
9. Chuck Howley (1961–73)	24	395	16.5	58	2
10. Don Bishop (1960–65)	22	364	16.5	57	0

a short-term quarterback after Troy Aikman was shelved with a strained left hamstring, Dallas acquired the veteran Kosar. The first of his two Cowboy starts came against Phoenix. Kosar completed 13 of 21 passes for 199 yards and 1 touchdown in a 20–15 Dallas victory. The following week in Atlanta, Kosar was forced to the air more frequently after the Falcons built a 20–0 lead early in the second half. He completed 22 of 39 passes for 186 yards and 2 touchdowns, but the Cowboys lost, 27–14. The rest of Kosar's Cowboy career consisted of mop-up duty, thanks to Aikman's return the following game, though that did include time in the 30–13 victory over Buffalo in Super Bowl XXVIII in Atlanta.

KOWALCZYK, WALT
Running back, 6′0″, 205 lbs., b. 4/17/35

A light fullback from Michigan State, Kowalczyk was traded to the Cowboys in 1960 by the Detroit Lions, after two years with the Philadelphia Eagles. He was an all-purpose back that first year, carrying 50 times for 156 yards, and catching 14 passes for 143 yards. He was picked up by the Oakland Raiders the next year and saw little action in his last year before retiring.

KUPP, CRAIG
Quarterback, 6′4″, 215 lbs., b. 4/14/67

Kupp was drafted out of Pacific Lutheran by the Giants in 1991, but spent time in Phoenix and was waived late in the season. Dallas picked him up to back up Steve Beuerlein, who started the last four games of the season after Troy Aikman was hurt. When Aikman came back, Kupp was released and never played again in the NFL.

KUPP, JAKE
Offensive guard, 6′3″, 230 lbs., b. 3/12/41

Kupp, a ninth-round draft pick out of Washington in 1964, played two years on the Dallas offensive line (1964–65), primarily at guard. He was traded after the '65 season to Washington, where he played one year before being traded to Atlanta and then New Orleans in 1967. He spent eight more years with the Saints before retiring after the 1975 season.

KYLE, AARON
Cornerback, 5′11″, 185 lbs., b. 4/6/54

Kyle was the Cowboys' first-round draft pick in 1976. He was wiry and tough, with 4.6 speed in the 40-yard dash, and was known as a hitter. The Wyoming ex played on specialty teams and on passing downs in his first year, and made some big plays. He became a starter at right cornerback his second year when Mel Renfro finally started to slow down, but he missed four midseason games with a fractured wrist. He returned for the playoffs and performed well. In Super Bowl XII against Denver, he had three tackles, an interception, and a fumble recovery. In 1978 he shared the club lead in fumble recoveries with 2, intercepted 3 passes in the regular season, and got another in the playoffs against Atlanta. But in the Super Bowl against Pittsburgh, John Stallworth caught a short pass, broke Kyle's tackle, and raced 75 yards for the Steelers' first TD. Bone spurs that developed in training camp 1979 gave him trouble, but he started every game that year and performed ably, but at less than 100 percent; he intercepted 2 passes the first game of the season and didn't get another one all year. Kyle was traded the next season to Denver, where he played well until retiring after the 1982 season.

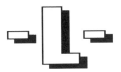

LAIDLAW, SCOTT
Running back, 6'0", 205 lbs., b. 2/17/53

Drafted by the Cowboys in the fourteenth round of the 1975 draft, the Stanford ex had only 3 catches and 11 receptions his rookie year. But in 1976, replacing an injured Robert Newhouse as the season started, he had 94 carries for 424 yards and 38 catches for 325 yards. But hamstring problems hampered him in 1977, and he finished with only 9 carries and 5 catches. The next two years a mostly healthy Laidlaw subbed ably for Newhouse, running 75 times for 312 yards and catching 6 passes in 1978; he had strong starts down the stretch of that season (1978) and in the first two playoff games, but a healthy Newhouse returned to start in the Super Bowl against Pittsburgh. A thigh injury in training camp gave Laidlaw problems in 1979, and he only rushed 69 times for 236 yards, with just 12 passes. He was traded to the New York Giants before the 1980 season and retired halfway through the year.

LANDRY, TOM
Head coach

The Only Coach The Cowboys Have Ever Had—until the Jones Gang roared into town—was a native Texan and a Pro Bowl cornerback for the New York Giants from 1950 through 1955. Thomas Wade Landry's college career at the University of Texas was interrupted by WWII; he enlisted in the Air Force and flew thirty missions as a bomber pilot with the Eighth Air Force. In 1946, he resumed his college career and played with Bobby Layne on some excellent Texas teams.

Four years later, after a year with the New York Yankees of the All-America Football Conference, he joined the Giants. The former Mission, TX all-regional fullback had only average speed, but to gain an edge, he studied opposing offenses day and night. In 1954, he was made player-coach, and a full-time member of the Giant staff 2 years later. He was constantly refining the 4-3 defense, and under his guidance, the Giants became the best defensive unit in the league. When Clint Murchison Jr. brought an NFL team to Dallas in 1960, he decided he needed "the thinking man of pro football" for his coach. Though Landry was the obvious successor to Jim Howell in New York, he wasn't convinced his future was in football. He had lived in Dallas for several years during the

Tom Landry

111

off-season and had started a successful insurance business, which he planned on making a full-time career. But the challenge of forming a new team in Dallas proved too strong, and on December 28, 1959, General Manager Tex Schramm called a press conference to announce the hiring of the Cowboys' head coach, Thomas Wade Landry. His five-year contract called for $34,500 per annum.

The Cowboys had not been permitted to participate in the December 1959 draft. The following March, Landry and Schramm were given twenty-four hours to pick three players from each of the twelve NFL teams. (Each team was allowed to protect twenty-five players.) They selected their thirty-six castoffs and went to camp in Pacific Grove, Oregon in July. Almost 200 players were invited to camp; some stayed only a day, some a night. The team that emerged from that first camp was a group of old, injured, or ineffective castoffs—culled from the worst draft pool in the history of the NFL—and a handful of free agents, among them 5'7" Eddie LeBaron, the veteran Washington Redskins quarterback. LeBaron was thinking of retiring and practicing law in Washington, D.C. He cost a first-round choice in the next draft, but the Cowboys would have an experienced field general in charge of the offense.

That first year they lost every game except one, a 31–31 tie with the New York Giants, Landry's old team. They shared the Cotton Bowl with Lamar Hunt's AFL Dallas Texans, who were starting their first year; they also had to compete with tremendously popular high school and college (SMU) football games played at the same time. About 30,000 people attended that first game, but the remainder of the season saw crowds ranging from 10,000 or 15,000 down to 5,000. In the cavernous Cotton Bowl, the stands seemed empty. It took five years before the stands averaged half-full. The next season the Cowboys won five games, then four, then five again. After the 1963 season, there were public rumblings about

Landry and his lack of success; Murchison responded by signing Landry to an unprecedented ten-year contract extension in February 1964 (when the longest extension at the time was three years). The 1965 season was the breakthrough year: a strong rookie crop, the maturing process, and the refinement of Landry's strategies resulted in a 7–7 record. From there it was all downhill.

Landry, more than anyone, ushered in the modern age of pro football with his complex defenses (which evolved into the Flex) and his multiple-offense formations; they soon became SOP for every team. When he dusted off the shotgun (initially designed by Red Hickey for his San Francisco 49ers in 1960) and dubbed it the Spread, it revolutionized third-down and two-minute offenses forever.

After five straight years of losing the big one, the Cowboys' triumph in Super Bowl VI was a vindication of sorts for Landry and his system. Then, throughout the seventies, Dallas battled Pittsburgh for the Team of the Decade (Dallas was 2 for 5 in Super Bowl appearances while Pittsburgh won all 4 of theirs). Nineteen eighty-five saw the Cowboys' 20th straight winning season, a record for an NFL team, but the next few years were the rockiest since the early sixties. So many years of success had resulted in low draft choices, and even the Cowboy computer couldn't produce enough stars to replace the team's aging nucleus. The rest of the NFL had caught up to Dallas in more ways than one. Amid heavy criticism for Landry's playcalling (even owner H.R. "Bum" Bright called his coach's choices "horrendous," and Schramm admitted, "some of the things we're doing are frankly mystifying"), the team slipped to 3–13 in 1988, and when Arkansas oilman Jerry Jones bought the team from Bright the next year, Landry was fired in shoddy fashion. (Although Jones took the fall, the blame in this case belonged to Bright and Schramm.) Tex Schramm and Gil Brandt departed in short order. Despite more than one peace offering from the Jones regime, it wasn't until his

Ring of Honor induction in 1994 that Landry publicly made up with Jones.

Landry's public persona was that of a cold, efficient, emotionless machine. In truth, he was an emotional man; he just felt that masking those emotions got the job done better by allowing him to concentrate on the situation at hand. Landry may have taken that logic to an extreme; he could be cold and businesslike when releasing men who had played more than a decade for him. But more than once he broke into tears in one-on-one and team meetings, and many of his players knew Mount Landry was, for the most part, a facade. The man who ranked his priorities as "faith, family, and football" inspired an unbelievable devotion in his players, who frequently cited Landry as the man they respected and cared for more than any other. The sight of the cool, dignified Landry roaming the sideline in his fedora is one that won't be forgotten by Cowboy fans for a long, long time.

LANG, DAVID
Running back, 5'11", 210 lbs., b. 3/28/68

Following four years as a backup, special teamster, and kick returner with the Los Angeles Rams, Lang signed with the Cowboys as a free agent in 1995. The Northern Arizona University product had 1 carry for 7 yards and led the special teams with 30 tackles, an unofficial club record.

LASSIC, DERRICK
Running back, 5'10", 188 lbs., b. 1/26/70

The Cowboys sought an effective backup runner to spell Emmitt Smith when they selected Lassic with one of their fourth-round picks in 1993. But when Smith staged a holdout and missed the first two games of the season, the rookie from Alabama suddenly found himself at the center of Dallas' title defense. He ran for 75 yards in the opener at Washington, a 35–16 Redskins victory, and 52 yards the following week when Buffalo left Texas Stadium with a

13–10 win. Smith returned the following week, and the Cowboys' march to a second consecutive Super Bowl title was on. As for Lassic, he finished the season as the club's second-leading rusher with 269 yards on 75 carries. He was sidelined all of the following season with a knee injury, and was picked up by the Carolina Panthers in the 1995 expansion draft.

LAUFENBERG, BABE
Quarterback, 6'3", 203 lbs., b. 12/5/59

The man who can claim roommate status with both John Elway and Troy Aikman spent two seasons in a Cowboys uniform. He was thrust into the starting role early in the 15th game of the 1990 season, when Aikman was lost with an injured right shoulder and Dallas sported a 7–7 record. The Babe completed 13 of 36 passes to the Cowboys and 4 to the opposing Philadelphia Eagles in a 17–3 loss. With a playoff bid still a long shot, the following week in Atlanta the Falcons loaded their defense to stop the running game of Emmitt Smith and dared Dallas to pass. The result was that Smith was held to 34 yards, Laufenberg threw for 129 (1 touchdown and 2 interceptions), and the Cowboys lost, 26–7 in Babe's lone Cowboys start at quarterback. It turned out to be his last NFL game, ending a colorful eight-year stint that also featured stops in Washington, New Orleans, and San Diego. Laufenberg has enjoyed his retirement years in Dallas, becoming a radio sportscaster and joining the Cowboys' game-day broadcasts in addition to writing a sports column.

LAVAN, AL
Assistant coach

Lavan was an NFL defensive back in the late sixties for the Philadelphia Eagles and Atlanta Falcons before joining the staff of his alma mater, Colorado State, in 1972 as receivers coach. He held several college assistant jobs and handled defensive backs and special teams for the Falcons from 1975–76.

He joined the Cowboys as their running backs coach in 1980, and until 1988, coached NFL Hall of Famer Tony Dorsett and Herschel Walker before Tom Landry's coaching staff was swept out in 1989 with the arrival of Jimmy Johnson. Lavan joined the San Francisco 49ers staff, and later coached at the University of Washington.

LAVETTE, ROBERT
Running back, 5'11", 190 lbs., b. 8/8/63

A fourth-round draft pick from Georgia Tech in 1985, Lavette was a naturally gifted runner who rushed for nearly 10,000 yards in high school and college. His daunting task with the Cowboys was to somehow beat out the two stars in front of him, Tony Dorsett and Herschel Walker.

Lavette averaged 5.2 yards per carry in his first two preseasons, but his primary contributions during the regular season came on special teams, returning 70 kickoffs for a 19.7-yard average in 1985–86. Lavette moved on to the the Philadelphia Eagles in 1987, his last season in the NFL.

LAWLESS, BURTON
Offensive guard, 6'4", 255 lbs., b. 11/1/53

Lawless was the Cowboys' second-round draft choice in 1975, one of the Dirty Dozen rookies to make the team that year. He was the only one to win a starting job that season, and the first rookie since Ralph Neely in 1965 to start on the Dallas offensive line. Herb Scott challenged him and won his starting spot the next year, but Lawless later alternated with Scott as a play messenger. An ankle injury in 1977 limited him to a backup role, although he started six games due to injuries to Scott and John Fitzgerald. During his final year with Dallas, in 1979, he was again a play messenger, alternating with an improving Tom Rafferty, who started at right guard. He was traded to Detroit the following year and then Miami the next, before retiring.

LeBARON, EDDIE
Quarterback, 5'7", 160 lbs., b. 1/7/30

Eddie LeBaron was a pinpoint passer, a savvy onfield leader, and probably the best ball handler and faker—with a football, that is—in the NFL, the league's "midget magician." He had been a steady performer during the fifties at Washington (except for a year in the Canadian Football League in 1954) after an outstanding career at College of the Pacific. And he was smart—he led his law class at George Washington University while with the Redskins. He had retired to Midland, TX after the 1959 season to practice law full-time, but the chance to play for Tom Landry—and an opportunity to work for a top Dallas law firm—persuaded him to leave retirement and head to Texas. Dallas had given up a number-one choice in the next year's draft for LeBaron, but it was a wise move; rookie Don Meredith needed seasoning, so the diminutive lawyer started

Eddie LeBaron trots off the field in a 1962 road game against Washington; replacing him is Don Meredith (17). *(From the collection of the Texas/Dallas History and Archive Division, Dallas Public Library)*

all but one game that first year. The next two years the two shared the reins almost equally, and midway through his final year, Meredith was made the permanent starter. Two days after LeBaron announced his retirement, Landry started LeBaron in his last home game, against Pittsburgh. He completed his first pass, then didn't connect on another. After the season, LeBaron moved to Reno, NV to practice law, then worked with a Las Vegas firm. Thirteen years after he left football, he was lured back to it by the Atlanta Falcons, where he became general manager. He is still regarded as one of the top businessmen in the game.

LETT, LEON
Defensive tackle, 6′6″, 288 lbs., b. 10/12/68

Lett's penchant for disaster early in his career has been balanced by his development into one of the NFL's top interior linemen. How else could a quiet kid out of Emporia (KS) State be forgiven for two memorable gaffes?

In the first, his showboating allowed Buffalo's Don Beebe to knock the ball from his grasp just short of the goal line in Super Bowl XXVII. Beebe picked up the ball and raced virtually the length of the Rose Bowl field after Lett had held the ball low to begin what turned out to be a premature touchdown celebration just a few strides from the end zone after a fumble recovery.

The second mistake reinforced the notion that Lett was prone to brainlock under the national glare. On Thanksgiving Day in 1993, Lett's mistake gave the Miami Dolphins a nationally televised victory on Texas Stadium turf that had been covered with a glaze of ice from a freak storm. A Miami field goal attempt had been blocked and Lett inexplicably slid into the loose ball, making it a live ball that the Dolphins would recover for a second shot at the game-winning chip shot. Pete Stoyanovich would not miss a second time, and the 19-yarder gave Miami a 16–14 decision. For weeks

Leon Lett

thereafter, anyone who pulled a "Lett" was accused of doing something stupid.

But coach Jimmy Johnson, known for emphasizing discipline first and foremost, surprised most of the assembled media that day by not making Lett a public subject of his wrath. And, as Johnson probably knew that frigid day, Lett would go on to a become a Cowboys stalwart on the defensive line.

Lett arrived at 1991 training camp in Austin as a lightly regarded seventh-round draft pick. After making the 47-man roster, he was placed on injured reserve with a back problem before the season opener, and there he stayed for the first eleven weeks of the regular season. That allowed Lett to increase his strength and add some weight. Lett showed a glimmer of his future greatness in the final five games of the regular season.

Nicknamed "Big Cat" by teammates for his agility, Lett started slowly in 1992, but he picked up the pace as Dallas faced a string of teams from the AFC West. In an October matchup with Seattle, Lett had 2 tackles, 2 quarterback pressures, and he knocked down a pass. The next week he recorded his first career sack and had two tackles against Kansas City. On October 25, against the Los Angeles Raiders, Lett recovered a fumble, and later added his ill-fated 64-yard fumble return in the Super Bowl.

In 1993 Lett continued his improvement, the foul-up against Miami notwithstanding. Lett saw action in only eleven games due to a broken ankle, but he was fast becoming a force off the bench, leading all defensive linemen by batting down 4 passes. Lett filled in at all four spots on the defensive line and got his first NFL start in the season opener against Washington, subbing at right tackle for the injured Tony Casillas. Lett also started against Washington in the December rematch, filling in for Charles Haley at right end.

Lett came up big in the 1993 postseason, starting all three playoff games at right tackle for the injured Russell Maryland. Playing in his second straight Super Bowl, Lett was involved in another big play, this time making a contribution that did not end in ridicule. He forced Buffalo's Thurman Thomas to fumble early in the third quarter, setting up teammate James Washington's recovery and 46-yard touchdown return, tying the game at 13–13 and swinging the momentum back to Dallas. Lett had 6 tackles during the game and 17 for the playoffs.

Casillas departed the Cowboys via free agency and Maryland was moved from the right to the left side, opening the way for Lett to become a full-time starter at right tackle for the 1994 season. He responded with a flourish, contributing 68 tackles, 4 sacks, 26 quarterback pressures, and 7 tackles for losses.

For Lett, 1995 was a bittersweet season. He was slapped with a four-game suspension for violating the league's antidrug policies and failed to repeat as a Pro Bowler. But he was also a member of another championship team, collecting his third Super Bowl ring in four seasons. Despite the missed time, Lett had 53 tackles, 3 sacks, 6 tackles for losses, 19 quarterback pressures, and he knocked down 3 passes.

Lett has made his share of mistakes, but few question his status as one of the NFL's elite players.

LEWIS, CARL
Wide receiver, 6'3", 187 lbs., b. 7/1/61

The Cowboys have always prided themselves on their draft-day creativity, and their ability to turn athletes from other sports into football players. Team president Tex Schramm gambled a twelfth-round pick on Lewis in 1984, but the Olympic superstar sprinter and long jumper could never be coaxed into joining the Cowboys and attempting to direct his speed into an NFL career as a receiver. He joins other "what if" draft picks such as Merv Rettenmund (no. 20, 1965), who went on to a long career in baseball; Lou Hudson (no. 20, 1966) a star basketball guard for many years; and Pat Riley (no. 11, 1967), who was an overachieving forward in the NBA before becoming one of the most successful coaches of the modern era.

LEWIS, D. D.
Linebacker, 6'1", 210 lbs., b. 10/16/45

Dwight Douglas Lewis was the Cowboys' third-round draft pick out of Mississippi State in 1968. He was a find; other NFL teams thought him too small for linebacking. He was a hard hitter with good speed and he played on all specialty teams his rookie year. The next year was spent in the military; when he came back for 1970, he backed up the superior linebacker corps of Chuck Howley, Lee Roy Jordan, and Dave Edwards. It wasn't until 1973 that he became the Cowboys' starting weakside linebacker, taking over Howley's spot. He remained there for the next seven years, starting in three Super Bowls. Lewis was not flashy, but a solid, dependable linebacker who brought a ferocious intensity to his job. He rarely gambled as his predecessor had; "he was always the one who would turn the run in so the great play could be made by someone else," said teammate Charlie Waters.

D. D. Lewis (50) drags down a Houston Oiler. *(From the collection of the Texas/Dallas History and Archive Division, Dallas Public Library)*

Though he was never recognized as All-Pro or invited to the Pro Bowl, Landry called him Dallas' most underrated player. He retired after the 1981 season.

LEWIS, WOODLEY
Wide receiver, 6'0", 195 lbs., b. 6/14/27

In his six years with the Los Angeles Rams and four years with the Chicago Cardinals, Lewis was a valuable defensive back and receiver. He came to the Cowboys in 1960 for one last year as a backup receiver; he caught one pass for 19 yards, and then retired after the season.

LILJA, GEORGE
See Replacement Games

LILLY, BOB
Defensive tackle, 6'5", 255 lbs., b. 7/26/39

The first number-one draft pick in Cowboys history (in 1961) became one of the greatest defensive linemen ever to toss aside blockers, and the first Cowboy elected to the Pro Football Hall of Fame.

Although initially drafted by Lamar Hunt's Dallas Texans of the AFL, the farmboy from Throckmorton, TX, who developed his tremendous strength hauling hay (his father owned a hay-baling business) went with the Cowboys after talking with Schramm. A unanimous All-American out of Texas Christian (he was known as the Purple Cloud), where he gained notoriety by lifting Volkswagen Beetles, one end at a time, onto campus sidewalks, Lily made the NFL All-Rookie team in 1961 as a defensive end. But midway into his third year he made the switch to tackle and began earning his nickname—Mr. Cowboy. ("Abner" was a nickname his teammates used.) He was extremely quick and frighteningly fast. No one in the league drew more double and triple teams, but he would claw and rip through three blockers quickly enough to tip a pass, catch it in midair, then run it in for a touchdown. And he missed only one game in fourteen years—the NFC Championship Game against Minnesota in 1973, a year in

Bob Lilly *(From the collection of the Texas/ Dallas History and Archive Division, Dallas Public Library)*

which Lilly was constantly hobbled by back and leg injuries.

He was the anchor of the original Doomsday Defense in the late sixties, and the five years from 1966 through 1970 when Dallas couldn't win the big one ate at him. No one took losing harder than Lilly; after losing Super Bowl V to Baltimore, he threw his helmet almost half the length of the field. The 24–3 victory over Miami in Super Bowl VI was sweet vindication. He was named All-Pro seven times, played in eleven Pro Bowls, and was the first player inducted into Texas Stadium's Ring of Honor, in 1975. Induction into the Pro Football Hall of Fame came in 1980. He was also an astute businessman, and at various times owned an accounting firm, a motel chain, a nightclub (The Other Place), and lots of real estate. A longtime shutterbug, Lilly also published a collection of his Cowboy photographs in 1983 entitled *Bob Lilly: Reflections.*

LILLY, KEVIN
Defensive tackle, 6'4", 265 lbs., b. 5/14/63

Tulsa ex Lilly played the 1988 season with San Francisco as a backup defensive

lineman. The next year he was brought in by the Cowboys for the first Washington game and then released the following week. San Francisco picked him up again, then released him at season's end, his last in the NFL.

LISCIO, TONY
Offensive tackle, 6'5", 255 lbs., b. 7/2/40

Liscio was the first great offensive lineman for the Cowboys. He was signed out of Tulsa by Green Bay in the third round of the 1963 draft, but he was the final Packer cut that year. The Cowboys picked him up the week of the season opener, and he won the starting job late in the season. He played some that year, and the next year emerged as one of the best pass blockers in the league. But with four games left in 1964 he injured his knee, and sat out a year and a half—after the operation, he was hit with jaundice and a staph infection. He came back strong in 1966, and started at guard. When John Niland became a regular in 1967, he moved to tackle, and started through the next three years. In 1970 he was sent to the San Diego Chargers as part of the trade that brought

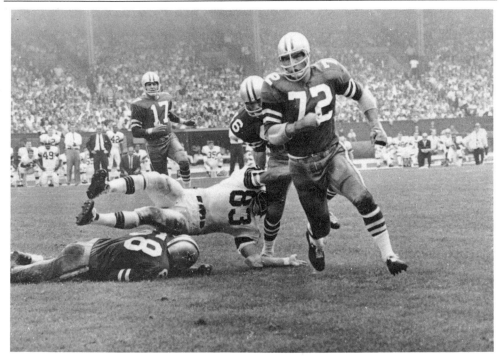

Tony Liscio (*From the collection of the Texas/Dallas History and Archive Division, Dallas Public Library*)

Lance Alworth to Dallas. But bad hamstrings limited his playing time, and he was about to be traded to the Miami Dolphins when he retired. Then, ten games into the 1971 season, tackle Ralph Neely broke his leg in a motorcycle accident. Tom Landry called Liscio, who was involved in real estate in Dallas. Liscio knew the system; would he consider coming in to shore up the offensive line? He said he'd give it a try. He started the next game, against Washington, and every game after that. Dallas won every one, including a 24–3 whipping of the Dolphins in Super Bowl VI in which they set a new team rushing record. Then he retired for good, and went back to his real-estate business.

LIVINGSTON, BRUCE
See Replacement Games

LIVINGSTON, WARREN
Cornerback, 5'10", 185 lbs., b. 7/5/38

As a rookie free agent out of Arizona in 1961, Livingston earned the starting nod at cornerback. Livingston was one of the best open field tacklers in the NFL, and he had good speed. But eight games into the season, he fractured an arm and was out for the rest of the year. The next year an injury to the same arm slowed him. He was replaced by rookie Mike Gaechter, and later moved to safety. In 1963 they traded positions, and Livingston remained at cornerback for several years, splitting time there with Don Bishop through 1965. He was released before the 1967 season, and then retired.

LOCKETT, J. W.
Running back, 6'2", 230 lbs., b. 3/23/37

Lockett was a rookie tight end out of Central Oklahoma who was signed by San Francisco in 1961. They traded him to Dallas during the season, and he was immediately made a fullback. He was a strong runner who was tough to take down, and he saw plenty of action on that talent-starved team, alternating with Amos Marsh and carrying 77 times for 298 yards and a 3.9

average; he also had 19 catches for 149 yards and returned a few kickoffs. The next year he had only 8 carries for 24 yards and 7 receptions, and he led the team in punt returns. In 1963 he was traded to Baltimore, then Washington the next year, and then retired.

LOCKHART, EUGENE
Linebacker, 6'2", 233 lbs., b. 3/8/61

Lightly regarded in the 1984 draft, Lockhart was a sixth-round pick from the University of Houston who developed into one of the Cowboys' defensive stars of the late eighties. Lockhart's bone-rattling hits made him the sensation of 1984 training camp, and when incumbent middle linebacker Bob Breunig was struck down by a back injury, "Gene, the Hitting Machine" became the first rookie in franchise history to start in the middle.

At the time, Lockhart was only the fourth man to start at middle linebacker for the Cowboys, following Jerry Tubbs, Lee Roy Jordan, and Breunig. Lockhart rewarded defensive coordinator Ernie Stautner's confidence by contributing 86 total tackles and 2.5 sacks his rookie season.

By 1985, Lockhart was entrenched as a starter, leading the team in tackles (128), fumble recoveries (4), and forced fumbles (3). He also returned an interception 19 yards against Pittsburgh for his first career touchdown. The following season was more of the same as Lockhart registered 121 tackles and a career-high 5 sacks.

Lockhart was off to his best start in 1987 when he broke a bone in his leg against Atlanta in early December; he still finished with 80 total tackles. He regained his health for the 1988 season and, operating under the personal motto "No Pity," Lockhart had another outstanding season with 121 more tackles.

That set up a bittersweet 1989 season for Lockhart. While the Cowboys went an abysmal 1–15 in Jimmy Johnson's first year, Lockhart had a season to remember. The middle linebacker in Johnson's system was supposed to make the bulk of the tackles, and that was the case for Lockhart, who set a club record with 222 tackles, 55 more than Breunig's previous team record; his 154 solo tackles were also a record. Lockhart had at least 10 tackles in every game, became the first Cowboy to earn All-Pro recognition since 1985, and also shattered the team record for solo tackles in a game with 16 against the Phoenix Cardinals.

Johnson's defensive style favored more mobile linebackers, however, and he traded Lockhart to the New England Patriots in 1991. He went on to play two years for the Patriots. Lockhart was released after the 1992 season, and he later decided he wanted to retire as a Cowboy. Management was accommodating, and Lockhart signed a quickie contract in August of 1994, then held a retirement press conference.

Lockhart remained a Dallas-area resident, sharing ownership in a popular sports cafe among other business enterprises.

LOGAN, OBERT
Safety, 5'10", 180 lbs., b. 12/6/41

"Little O," a rookie free agent out of Trinity, became a starter at safety in the 1965 season and produced several big plays. Against Philadelphia, he picked off a goal-line pass with two minutes left to preserve a 21–19 Dallas win. In the last game of the year, he grabbed a blocked New York Giant field goal and returned it 60 yards for his first and only touchdown as a professional. He had fair speed, but he was an aggressive, sure tackler. In the 1967 expansion draft he was signed by New Orleans. In no time, he was placed on waivers and picked back up by the Cowboys, who needed help in their secondary due to injuries to Mel Renfro and Dickie Daniels. He is the only player who has left the Cowboys, played with another team, and come back to the Cowboys. He played backup safety and wide receiver for the rest of the year. After the season, when Landry told him he'd be traded, he decided to retire.

He later became the coach of the semipro San Antonio Toros.

LONG, BOB
Linebacker, 6'3", 235 lbs., b. 2/24/34

Long had spent five years with Detroit and two with Los Angeles before coming to the Cowboys in 1962 for a future draft choice. He spent the year as a backup and retired after the season.

LONGLEY, CLINT
Quarterback, 6'1", 195 lbs., b. 7/28/52

"The Mad Bomber" (a nickname given to Longley for wild tosses in training camp) was Roger Staubach's understudy for two years. He was acquired out of Abilene Christian by the Cincinnati Bengals in the 1974 supplemental draft, then was traded to the Cowboys for a fifth-round draft choice. He didn't play a single regular-season down until Roger Staubach suffered a concussion in the Thanksgiving Day game against the Redskins. When Longley entered the game in the third quarter, the Cowboys were down 16–3. A national TV audience watched him complete 11 of 20 passes and a last-minute 50-yard TD pass to Drew Pearson that was all the more amazing because Washington had seven defensive backs on the field. It was his second TD throw of the game, won by Dallas 24–23. Offensive lineman Blaine Nye put it best: "a triumph of the uncluttered mind."

The following year, Longley started against the New York Jets in the season finale and again guided the team to a victory, 31–21. But during training camp the following year, he and Staubach exchanged blows twice; after the second time, a sucker punch delivered by Longley on the last day of camp, he was traded to the San Diego Chargers. He backed up Dan Fouts there for a year, and then hit the road again, eventually landing with Hamilton of the Canadian Football League. His last stop in football was with the Shreveport Steamers of the American Football Association.

Clint Longley

LOTHRIDGE, BILLY
Kicker, 6'1", 195 lbs., b. 1/1/42

Lothridge, the runner-up to Roger Staubach for the 1963 Heisman Trophy, was an All-American kicker/quarterback out of Georgia Tech drafted by the Cowboys in the sixth round of the 1964 draft. During the subsequent season, he was the third-string signal-caller behind Don Meredith and John Roach; he threw 9 passes and completed 2, caught a couple of passes (one for a touchdown), and was the starting punter, averaging 40.3 yards on 62 punts. He was traded to Los Angeles the next year, and then spent six good years in Atlanta as their regular punter. Lothridge finished his career in 1972 as a backup punter for Miami; he was forced to retire due to kidney problems.

LOWRY, ALAN
Assistant coach

Lowry spent five seasons as defensive backfield coach for his alma mater, the

Cowboys All-Time Longest Forward Passes

95	Don Meredith to Bob Hayes	@ Washington, November 13, 1966 (TD)
91	Roger Staubach to Tony Dorsett	vs. Baltimore, September 4, 1978 (TD)
90	Troy Aikman to Alvin Harper	@ San Francisco, November 13, 1994
89	Craig Morton to Bob Hayes	@ Kansas City, October 25, 1970 (TD)
87	Troy Aikman to Michael Irvin	vs. Phoenix, September 20, 1992 (TD)
86	Craig Morton to Lance Rentzel	vs. Philadelphia, November 1, 1970 (TD)
86	Bernie Kosar to Emmitt Smith	vs. Phoenix, November 14, 1993
85	Eddie LeBaron to Amos Marsh	@ LA Rams, September 30, 1962 (TD)
85	Roger Staubach to Bob Hayes	@ NY Giants, December 12, 1971 (TD)
84	Don Meredith to Pete Gent	vs. Pittsburgh, October 30, 1966 (TD)
84	Steve Pelleur to Herschel Walker	vs. Philadelphia, December 14, 1986 (TD)

University of Texas, and five more as the Cowboys special teams coach before he was named Cowboys receivers coach in 1987.

As a native of Irving, Lowry certainly knew the directions to Texas Stadium. At the University of Texas, Lowry was one of the few players in Southwest Conference history to win All-SWC honors on both offense and defense. He was a defensive back at UT in 1970 and 1971 as the Longhorns won two conference titles and a national championship. Lowry was switched to offense in 1972 when he quarterbacked the Longhorns to a 10–1 season and a come-from-behind victory over Bear Bryant's University of Alabama team in the Cotton Bowl.

After working for the Cowboys, Lowry coached special teams for the Tampa Bay Buccaneers, San Francisco 49ers, and, most recently, for the Houston Oilers.

MACKOVIC, JOHN
Assistant coach

Tom Landry always worked with quarterbacks himself, but in 1981 he hired Mackovic, a bright young head coach at Wake Forest, to handle those duties. Mackovic brought an impressive resume that included assistant coaching stops at Purdue, Arizona, Army, and San Jose State, and he was eager to move to the NFL.

Kansas City Chiefs owner Lamar Hunt, a Dallas resident, was impressed by Mackovic, and hired him as the Chiefs' head coach in 1983. Mackovic was fired after the 1986 season and later became head coach of the University of Texas, winning the final Southwest Conference championship in 1995.

MAEGLE, DICKIE
Safety, 6'1", 195 lbs., b. 9/14/34

Former Rice All-American Maegle was the number-one draft pick of the San Francisco 49ers in 1955; he led the team in interceptions each of his five years there. After a year with Pittsburgh, where he also led the team in interceptions, he came to Dallas as a player-coach in 1961. Despite a knee injury only half-healed, he started the entire season at free safety, directing the movements of the younger backs around him. He had surgery on a bad foot after the season, and decided to retire during next year's training camp when it was clear that he couldn't perform adequately.

MANDERS, DAVE
Center, 6'2", 240 lbs., b. 2/20/41

A center from Michigan State, Manders was signed as a free agent by the Cowboys in 1962. He was quick and strong, with huge legs, and he looked like the real thing; but he packed up and left training camp, then played two years for Toledo in the United League.

He came back to the Cowboys in 1964 and almost immediately began pressuring Mike Connelly for the starting job at center. The next year he was a starter, and in 1966 he was voted to the Pro Bowl. But in the 1967 preseason, he injured his knee and was out for the year. "Dog" was one of the hardest-working Cowboys, and the next year he came back strong. He regained his position, and was the starting center in Super Bowl V and VI. In his last couple of years,

Dave Manders (*From the collection of the Texas Dallas History and Archive Division, Dallas Public Library*)

he began to split time with John Fitzgerald. He retired before the 1975 season after ten strong seasons with the Cowboys.

MANNING, WADE
Cornerback, 5'11", 190 lbs., b. 7/25/55

Manning was an interesting story: a backup cornerback signed by the Cowboys as a free agent, in 1979, who never played in college. He had been a Big Ten centerfielder for Ohio State; his last football experience was in high school as a 5'1" safety. He made the Cowboys as a kick return specialist and backup corner. In 1979, he returned 7 kickoffs for 145 yards, and 10 punts for 55 yards, but missed seven games in the middle of the season with a bad knee. Manning was traded to Buffalo in September 1980, but returned to Dallas when he failed the Buffalo physical; he then had cartilage surgery on his knee. He spent all of the following season on injured reserve. He was traded to the Denver Broncos in 1981, and saw two years as a backup wide receiver (3 catches each year) and kick returner before retiring.

MARION, BROCK
Safety, 5'11", 189 lbs., b. 6/11/70

A three-year starter in college at cornerback, Marion was the Cowboys' seventh pick in the 1993 draft. During his first two years in Dallas, he was a standout on the special teams units and a capable fill-in on the nickel and dime defenses. In his rookie year, he was third on the team with 19 special teams tackles, and in 1994 was again third, with 23 tackles. He had only one start in his first two years, but he stepped up and responded with flying colors in 1995.

In his third season as a Cowboy in 1995, Marion successfully filled the void left when James Washington signed as a free agent with Washington. The Nevada-Reno product was the team's third-leading tackler in the 27–17 victory over Pittsburgh in Super Bowl XXX, and he led the team for the year in interceptions with six, passes

defensed with 13, and was second in tackles with 114. All in all, it was an excellent year for the third-year Marion.

At least one member of Marion's immediate family may have had mixed feelings about the outcome of Super Bowl XXX in Arizona. His father, Jerry, played for the Steelers back in the not-so-glory days of 1967. There is more NFL blood in the family tree: cousin Brent McClanahan was a running back with Minnesota for eight seasons.

MARSH, AMOS
Running back, 6'1", 220 lbs., b. 5/7/39

"Moose" was a nationally ranked sprinter at Oregon State who also played some football; he was one of Gil Brandt's early finds, and was signed as a free agent in 1961. He began at wide receiver but quickly won the vacant starting fullback job; he was big and fast, and became a reliable receiver out of the backfield. For four years (1961–64) he combined with Don Perkins to give the Cowboys a respected running game; his first two years he was the team's primary kickoff returner, and he also returned his share of punts. In 1962, his second and best year, he led the league in yards per carry with 5.6 (and 802 yards); he also ran back a kickoff 101 yards for a touchdown and had pass receptions of 85 and 70 yards. But his play was erratic over the next two years, and he alternated as a starter with Jim Stiger. In 1965 he was traded to Detroit, where he finished out his career three years later.

MARTIN, HARVEY
Defensive end, 6'5", 250 lbs., b. 11/16/50

Martin, the Cowboys' third-round choice in the 1973 draft, had been a defensive tackle at tiny East Texas State. But the Cowboys quickly converted him to defensive end, and he became the best of his era. He led the Cowboys in quarterback sacks seven of his eleven years, and finished with a club-record 113. His 20 sacks in 1977 set a team record; that year he was named co-MVP

Amos Marsh dragged down by Redskins, 1962. *(From the collection of the Texas/Dallas History and Archive Division, Dallas Public Library)*

Harvey Martin

(with Randy White) in Super Bowl XII. He teamed with Ed "Too Tall" Jones to give the Cowboys the best end tandem for a decade, and he was named to the Pro Bowl four times (1976, 1977, 1978, 1979) and the All-Pro team once (1976). Jones got more of the press, but many thought Martin the better end; said Fran Tarkenton, who had good reason to know, "Everybody talks about Too Tall Jones, but that Martin is about as good a pass rusher as I've seen." He earned a reputation as a clean but extremely tough and intimidating rusher, and for a while the press tried to use a "Too Mean" sobriquet on him to match his partner's (it didn't stick). Said Martin in defense of his style, "It's more fun to take someone's head off than to have them take yours off." He was known for the fastest, toughest outside speed rush in the NFL; when opponents concentrated on taking that away, he developed a fierce inside rush. Martin was a clutch performer who made big plays in the playoffs: in Super Bowl XIII, he broke through the Steeler line in the first period and sacked Terry Bradshaw, jarring the ball loose. Too Tall Jones recovered, and the Cowboys scored. His 1977 season was one of the greatest ever by an NFL defensive player—85 tackles, a league-leading 23 traps (an early version of the sack), 2 fumble recoveries in the NFC title game, the co-MVP award in the Super Bowl, All-Pro, and NFL Defensive Player of the Year. He retired after the 1983 season.

MARTIN, KELVIN
Wide receiver, 5'9", 162 lbs., b. 5/14/65

A fourth-round draft pick from Boston College in 1987, the small but speedy Martin took advantage of the Cowboys' depleted receiver corps in the late eighties to put up some impressive numbers from 1988-90, catching 45 or more passes all three years. That put Martin in exclusive company, joining Bob Hayes, Tony Hill, and Drew Pearson as the only Cowboys receivers at that time with 45 or more receptions in three straight seasons.

Like many NFL rookies, Martin made his first contributions on special teams. He missed the first eight games due to injuries, then averaged 9.8 yards in 22 punt returns (the best in club history at that time), and 19.8 yards in 12 kickoff returns.

"K-Mart" established himself as an NFL receiver in 1988 when he caught 8 passes for 95 yards and 2 touchdowns in an October Monday nighter against New Orleans. Three weeks later, Martin had another eight-catch performance for 97 yards against Philadelphia, and finished the season with 49 catches for 622 yards and 3 touchdowns.

Martin was off to a blockbuster year in 1989 with 46 catches for 644 yards when he suffered a season-ending knee injury on November 19 against Miami. At that point, Martin was 10th in the league in receptions and yardage.

In his first start since the injury, Martin opened the 1990 season against San

Kelvin Martin

Diego with 2 catches for 78 yards. Over the second half of that season, Martin caught 38 passes, leading or tying for the team lead in six of eight games, and he finished the season with 64 catches for 732 yards.

In 1991, the Cowboys' talent level through Johnson's aggressive drafting had produced Alvin Harper to team with Michael Irvin, and Martin was relegated to the role of third receiver, and he had only 16 receptions for 243 yards. Martin remained a heavy contributor as the Cowboys drove to the playoffs, however, returning 21 punts for an 11.6-yard average, the fifth-highest in club history.

In a critical game in December against Philadelphia, Dallas trailed, 13–11, when Martin returned a punt 85 yards for the winning touchdown. It was the longest punt return of the 1991 season, the third-longest in club history, and the longest since Dennis Morgan's 98-yarder against St. Louis in 1974.

The Cowboys were on the verge of greatness in 1992. Martin, now a clutch possession receiver, again made key plays, catching 32 passes for 359 yards and three touchdowns, and averaging 12.7 yards in 42 punt returns and 21 yards in 24 kickoff returns. In the postseason, Martin added four catches for 33 yards and a touchdown, and averaged 9.6 yards in 5 punt returns and 22.3 yards in 9 kickoff returns as the Cowboys marched to the first of back-to-back Super Bowls with a resounding 52–17 victory over the Buffalo Bills.

Newly liberalized free agency rules began to gnaw away at the Cowboys' talented roster, however, and Martin took the money and an opportunity to start when he signed during the off-season with the Seattle Seahawks, with whom he had some strong seasons.

MARYLAND, RUSSELL
Defensive tackle, 6'1", 279 lbs., b. 3/22/69

The most recent Cowboy to be selected first in the draft almost wasn't. Dallas coach Jimmy Johnson had put together a series of trades to move to the top of the draft board, and Johnson gave serious consideration to drafting Notre Dame Heisman Trophy–winning wide receiver "Rocket" Ismail away from the Toronto Argonauts of the Canadian Football League. But the Cowboys could not match the incredible offer from the Argos, and Ismail signed with the Los Angeles Raiders a few years later.

It's doubtful there were many complaints from Cowboy fans over the selection of Maryland, who was a valuable contributor

Russell Maryland

to the Dallas defense for five years before agreeing to a free agent offer from the Oakland Raiders following the '95 season (to the tune of $19 million over six years).

Maryland was a high school player in Chicago who almost escaped the eye of big-time college recruiters. He was close to heading to the Ivy League before Johnson, then boss at the University of Miami, used one of his last available scholarships for Maryland. The result was two All-America awards and the 1990 Outland Trophy given to the nation's best lineman, all the while starring for Hurricane teams that went a combined 44-4.

Maryland arrived in the NFL in 1991 with the fanfare expected of the top pick in the draft. Then fans got a close look at him. Maryland was a roly-poly guy, listed generously at 6'1". Critics wondered if the real Russell Maryland had been kidnapped. They expected the second coming of Ed "Too Tall" Jones, or a rangy Bob Lilly-type. Maryland's feet also became a public issue. He'd inherited flat feet from his mother's side of the family, and the condition gave him considerable pain.

Maryland may have lacked physical stature, but he compensated with a heart as big as Texas, the quality that Johnson most respected in him. Maryland could be blocked out of a play, but the rotund tackle kept on coming. He also became a respected locker room leader, just as he had been at Miami.

As a 1991 rookie, Maryland saw spot duty during the first half of the season, but his relentless attitude forced Johnson to insert him into the starting lineup for a game in early November against Houston. He finished his first pro start with 5 tackles, a sack, a quarterback pressure, and a tackle behind the line of scrimmage.

Over the final seven regular-season games, no Cowboys player had more sacks or quarterback pressures than Maryland, who finished the season with 4.5 sacks to lead all NFL rookie linemen. Maryland also helped

the Cowboys back into the playoffs, with great things on the horizon.

In 1992, Maryland started the final thirteen games and all three post-season games as a run-stopping force, on a team bound for the Super Bowl. Maryland played almost the entire season with a dislocated toe that required postseason surgery, yet he contributed heavily to a unit that was best in the league against the rush, allowing only 77.8 yards per game on the ground. He finished the season with 49 tackles, 5 for losses, forced 1 fumble, and recovered 2 others. The second fumble recovery came in the final regular season game of the year, against his hometown Chicago Bears.

Maryland's hard work and determination paid off in 1993 when he was selected for his first Pro Bowl, becoming the first defender drafted by Dallas to be selected to the Pro Bowl while a member of the Cowboys since Randy White in 1985. On the way to Hawaii, Maryland also picked up his fourth championship ring in seven years, adding his second Super Bowl ring to two national championships at the University of Miami.

Hampered again by foot problems, Maryland missed four regular-season starts, then sat out the divisional playoff victory over Green Bay due to an ankle problem. But Maryland remained productive with 56 tackles, 2.5 sacks, 6 tackles for losses, and 12 quarterback pressures, as the Cowboys rolled to their second straight Super Bowl title.

For the first time in his career, Maryland, in 1994, was able to fight off nagging injuries and start all sixteen regular-season games to help the Cowboys to the number-one overall defensive ranking in the league. The Cowboys missed out on a third straight Super Bowl, but Maryland had 47 tackles, 3 sacks, and a career-high 21 quarterback pressures.

In 1995, Maryland marked his fourth season as a full-time starter with 34 tackles, 2 sacks, 3 tackles for losses, and 16 quarterback pressures. Then, in Super Bowl XXX,

Maryland turned in one of his strongest games of the season with 3 tackles and 4 quarterback pressures as the Cowboys beat the Pittsburgh Steelers, 27–17.

Salary cap problems hamstrung the Cowboys in the off-season, however. Maryland didn't want to leave, but when Raiders owner Al Davis came through with a tempting offer, he had to accept.

MATTHEWS, RAY
Wide receiver, 6'0", 195 lbs.

Clemson ex Matthews had spent nine years with the Pittsburgh Steelers as an all-purpose back when he was picked up by the Cowboys in the expansion draft of 1960. He played on that first Dallas team, starting one of the last games of the season and catching 3 passes for 44 yards, and then he retired.

MAVERICK LINE

In 1962, second-year end Bob Lilly was joined on the defensive line by rookies George Andrie at the other end, and Guy Reese and John Meyers at tackles. It was a large line—they ranged from 6'4" to 6'7", and all four tipped the scales between 250 and 260. The Maverick Line, as they were dubbed by the press, is believed to be the youngest starting defensive front in NFL history. Reese and Meyers didn't stick around for long—they both were gone after the 1963 season—but Andrie and Lilly went on to comprise half of the Doomsday Defense's front four almost a decade later.

McCORMACK, HURVIN
Defensive tackle, 6'5", 274 lbs., b. 4/6/72

The former sports management major from Indiana University had the opportunity to manage tremendous improvement in his pro career heading into the 1996 season. The subtraction of Russell Maryland provided McCormack the chance to move into Dallas' rotation of defensive linemen.

He came to the Cowboys as a free agent before the 1994 season, and in his two years logged time at both tackle and end. He possesses particularly fine speed for his size (running the 40-yard dash in about 4.8 seconds) and is explosive off the ball.

McCREARY, BOB
Offensive tackle, 6'5", 255 lbs.

This rookie free agent out of Wake Forest joined the Cowboys a week before their 1961 season opener. He saw limited action as a backup on the offensive line and was released after the season, his only one in the NFL.

McDANIELS, DAVID
Wide receiver, 6'4", 200 lbs., b. 3/9/45

When the Cowboys' second-round draft pick in 1968, a rangy receiver out of Mississippi Valley College, reported to training camp, there was some embarrassment on the part of the scouting department. He was significantly smaller and slower than their reports showed. McDaniels was a washout; he made the team, but he didn't catch a pass in the regular season. He was traded in 1969 to Philadelphia for Mike Ditka. This time he didn't make the team, and he retired from pro football.

McDONALD, PAUL
Quarterback, 6'2", 185 lbs., b. 2/23/58

When Danny White went down for the season with a wrist injury in 1986, the Cowboys needed a veteran backup behind young quarterbacks Steve Pelluer and Reggie Collier. In mid-season the Cowboys signed McDonald, a six-year veteran with the Cleveland Browns who had worked with Dallas offensive coordinator Paul Hackett at Southern Cal and in Cleveland. While at USC, McDonald led the Trojans to two Rose Bowl victories and a national championship.

McDonald started all sixteen games for Cleveland in 1984, enduring an alarming 53 sacks, but was still able to complete 55 percent of his passes for 3,472 yards. His best passing day came in 1984 against New England when he had a career-high 320 yards and completed 62 percent of his throws. That same season, he completed 75 percent of his passes against New Orleans and clicked on 10 straight attempts against Houston. McDonald also led the Browns to the playoffs in 1982, after Brian Sipe was injured.

When the Browns released him following the 1985 season, McDonald signed with the Seattle Seahawks for 1986, but Seattle also waived him before the regular season. The lefthanded McDonald led the Cowboys in passing in the 1987 preseason with a quarterback rating of 92, but he never attempted a regular-season pass for Dallas.

McDONALD, TOMMY
Wide receiver, 5'10", 170 lbs., b. 7/26/34

Eight years with the Philadelphia Eagles had been good to the Oklahoma All-American: six straight trips to the Pro Bowl, and miles of yardage on the receiving end of Norm Van Brocklin and Sonny Jurgensen tosses. But Philadelphia cleaned house in 1964, and he was traded to Dallas for three players to beef up the Cowboys receiving corps. His arrival generated much excitement, but McDonald had a disappointing year with only 612 yards and 2 touchdowns. He asked to be traded in 1965 and was, to the Los Angeles Rams, where he reverted back to his old form with 1,036 yards and 9 TDs. He played one more year for the Rams and then retired.

McILHENNY, DON
Running back, 6'0", 205 lbs., b. 11/22/34

When McIlhenny was chosen by the Cowboys in the 1960 expansion draft, it was a homecoming of sorts—he had been a star running back at SMU in the mid-fifties.

After one year with Detroit, he had spent three with the Green Bay Packers, before they were the Packers of legend. As a fullback for the Cowboys, he had 321 yards on 96 carries behind a nonexistent front line, then was traded to San Francisco, where he carried 10 times all year and then retired.

McINTOSH, TODDRICK
Defensive tackle, 6'3", 277 lbs., b. 1/22/72

The graduate of Berkner High School in the Dallas suburb of Richardson spent less than a season with the Cowboys after being selected in the seventh round of the 1994 draft. McIntosh was one of many talented Texas high school football players during the 1990s who played their college ball in the state of Florida. In McIntosh's case, it was Florida State University. He was a key figure in the Seminoles' victory over Nebraska in the Orange Bowl to claim the 1993 national championship. He saw little action for the Cowboys, and was put on waivers during the season and picked up by the Tampa Bay Buccaneers.

McKINNON, DENNIS
Wide receiver, 6'1", 185 lbs., b. 8/22/61

Talented, but sometimes untamed, McKinnon arrived in Dallas via Plan B in 1990 after seven years with the Bears, and played with the team into late October. He scored the Cowboys' first touchdown of the season on a 28-yard pass from Troy Aikman in a season-opening 17–14 victory over San Diego that matched Dallas' win total for all of 1989. The Cowboys had a 3–4 record in the games that McKinnon played. He finished with 14 catches for 172 yards but couldn't break up the starting combination of Kelvin Martin and Michael Irvin. He finished the year in Miami, and then retired. A member of Chicago's 1985 Super Bowl team, McKinnon's best season was the 1988 campaign that saw him grab 45 balls for 704 yards. The Florida State University product grew up in South Florida and patterned his play after the Miami Dolphins' star receiver of the early seventies, Paul Warfield.

McLean, Scott
Linebacker, 6'4", 233 lbs., b. 12/16/60

Free agent McLean, out of Florida State, was a backup linebacker and special-teams player for the Cowboys in 1983, before a knee injury ended his career.

McSwain, Chuck
Running back, 6'0", 191 lbs., b. 2/21/61

A fifth-round pick from Clemson in 1983, McSwain flashed potential with his speed and quickness. In a 1983 preseason game against Miami, McSwain took a swing pass from Gary Hogeboom, cut across the field, and dashed 67 yards for a fourth-quarter touchdown. When the Cowboys got the ball back on an onside kick, they drove for the winning score on a 1-yard touchdown by McSwain with two seconds to play.

But McSwain, who rushed for 2,297 yards and 22 touchdowns for Clemson, tore a tendon in a finger on his first kickoff return in a September game against the New York Giants, and spent the rest of the season on injured reserve.

In 1984 McSwain returned 20 kickoffs for a 20.2-yard average, but he found himself in a difficult spot, backing up future Hall of Famer Tony Dorsett. After he was released by the Cowboys in 1985, he signed with the Los Angeles Raiders, then with the New York Jets, before playing for the New England Patriots in his last NFL season, in 1987. His brother, Rod, was a cornerback for the Patriots.

Meeks, Ron
Assistant coach

After developing Fresno State University's pass defense into the tenth-best in NCAA Division I-A in 1990, Meeks came to Dallas and was reunited with much of the coaching staff that he'd spent time with as a graduate assistant at the University of Miami in 1986–87. His pro playing career consisted of two seasons with the Canadian Football League's Hamilton Tiger-Cats, and a third with the CFL's Ottawa Rough Riders. He spent only one season with the Cowboys, leaving to join Dave Wannstedt's new staff in Chicago.

Memmelaar, Dale
Offensive tackle, 6'2", 255 lbs., b. 1/15/37

Memmelaar was a 28th-round draft choice of the Cardinals in 1959. After three unimpressive years, the former Wyoming star was placed on waivers and picked up by the Cowboys in 1962. He became the starter on the offensive line the next two years, then was released and picked up by a Cleveland team that went on to win the NFL Championship Game over Baltimore.

Meredith, Don
Quarterback, 6'3", 200 lbs., b. 4/10/38

The first player selected out of college by the Cowboys was the team's first great quarterback. Joe Don Meredith from Mount Vernon, TX had a strong arm, a quick release, and a flair for the dramatic. He was a charismatic leader with confidence to spare. (He would sometimes enter the Cowboy huddle singing "I Didn't Know God Made Honky-Tonk Angels," one of his favorites.)

A two-time All-American at hometown SMU, Meredith was romanced by Lamar Hunt's Dallas Texans, but he opted for the NFL franchise. Tex Schramm signed him to a personal services contract before the Cowboys were officially a team—a very impressive $150,000 for five years, all guaranteed. Although veteran Eddie LeBaron started almost every game that first year, Meredith saw some action, and started once. The next two years, Meredith started several games and shared more of the quarterbacking duties with LeBaron in Landry's infamous shuttle system.

Don Meredith receiving a snap from Malcolm Walker, 1968. *(From the collection of the Texas/Dallas History and Archive Division, Dallas Public Library)*

Though LeBaron was a scrambler, Meredith was a pocket passer; he took a brutal beating behind a weak line and received boos from the unreasonable Cotton Bowl crowd. Another problem was his coach. Meredith, an easygoing good ol' boy in the tradition of another great NFL quarterback from Texas, Bobby Layne, was Landry's exact opposite in many ways—the coach was a devout Chistian, the quarterback a devoted partier—and they disagreed on certain fundamental football points. Meredith often ignored Landry's messengered plays, run in by receivers, and their altercations were frequent.

But midway through the 1963 season, Landry announced the team was Meredith's to lead; LeBaron was about to retire, and it was time to see what Meredith was made of. Over the last 8 games Dallas won 3 and lost 5 as he began to show what he could do with a football—in a loss against San Francisco, Dandy hit 30-of-48 for 460 yards (still a Cowboy record), and the next week, he was

25-of-32 for 302. He was beginning to come around to Landry's way of thinking.

The next year, the team was his to lead. Though they won only five games, Meredith was emerging as an inspiring leader, constantly playing with pain and injuries. Even Landry praised his bravery, saying, "He quarterbacked for us when no other quarterback could have stood on the field." Meredith started out 1965 struggling, though, and Landry alternated him with rookies Craig Morton and Jerry Rhome. But neither replacement established himself, and after a five-game losing streak and a 2–5 record, Landry made it official: Meredith was the permanent starter. Dandy Don responded with a strong second half, and Dallas won 5 of their last 7. He was significantly aided by a strong rookie draft that yielded Bullet Bob Hayes, Dan Reeves, Ralph Neely, and Jethro Pugh. Dallas finished 7–7 and Meredith threw 22 touchdowns, one behind league leader Johnny Unitas. The next year, 1966, was even better—Dallas' breakthrough year. The Dallas offense was the NFL's most versatile and explosive, and the defense led the league in sacks. Meredith remained remarkably healthy on the way to 24 touchdown passes and a 54 percent completion average. Dallas' record of 10–3–1 landed them in the NFL Championship Game against the mighty Packers.

It was the first of many big ones that the Cowboys couldn't win. Meredith's passing was mediocre throughout most of the game, but after a 68-yard TD toss to Frank Clarke, and a defensive stand, he drove them to a first down at the Packer 2-yard line with 1:58 to go and Dallas behind by a TD. But mental mistakes, a perfect pass dropped by Reeves, and a low pass to end Pettis Norman left them still at the 2 on fourth down. Meredith was hurried into a bad pass that was picked off, and Green Bay ran out the clock to win 34-27.

In 1967, Meredith suffered cracked ribs in the preseason and played poorly after his recovery. When he cracked another rib in the fourth game of the season, and then developed pneumonia, third-year man Craig Morton played ably in his place. Meredith left the hospital a week later 20 pounds lighter and much weaker. Three weeks later he was starting, but raggedly. A broken nose and a twisted knee in the last two games left him pulverized for the playoffs. Somehow, he led Dallas to a 52-14 win over Cleveland, and then it was time to travel to Green Bay to once again play for the NFL title against the Packers. Meredith never solved the secret of throwing in the sub-zero weather, and he had a miserable first half. The offense improved in the second half, enough to go up 3 points late in the fourth quarter. Then, the most famous quarterback sneak in history won the Ice Bowl in the last seconds for the Pack, and an emotionally depleted Meredith considered retirement. But he signed a three-year contract and claimed to be excited about the upcoming season.

Nineteen sixty-eight saw the team notch their finest record (12–2) as Meredith had one of his best years, with a completion percentage of 55.3 and an NFL-second-best quarterback rating. They were a heavy favorite when they travelled to Cleveland for the conference playoff, but after a 10–10 halftime score, the Cowboys were never in the game. Meredith threw as many interceptions as completions, three, as they lost 31–20, a shattering blow to a team that was sure it was headed to the Super Bowl.

Meredith had been booed at the Cotton Bowl since his SMU days, when the crowds blamed him for the Mustangs' misfortunes. Now, after the years of frustrations and near-misses, the boos, combined with the constant pain and scarring, had become too much. At the age of 31, Meredith announced his retirement on the eve of training camp 1969 and went to work directing a stock-brokerage office in Dallas. His nine-year totals were 17,199 yards, 135 touchdowns, and a 50.7 percent completion average. It wasn't long before his natural charisma and good looks landed him TV acting parts and commercials, and then an Emmy-Award-winning stint on ABC's *Monday Night Football* opposite Howard Cosell and Frank Gifford. But after a while, even that lost its fascination for Meredith; he quit the show in 1974, then returned in 1977 for seven years. He left for good in 1984, and eased out of show business by the end of the decade. He lives in Santa Fe and keeps a very low profile.

MEYERS, JOHN
Defensive tackle, 6'6", 265 lbs., b. 1/16/40

Meyers was a free agent signed out of Washington in 1962. He was the starting tackle that year on the defensive line known as the Maverick Line for its youth—only sophomore Bob Lilly had any pro experience. When Lilly was moved to tackle, halfway into the 1963 season, Meyers was benched. He played two years with Dallas, then was traded to Philadelphia. He retired after four years with the Eagles.

MICKEY, JOEY
Tight end, 6'5", 275 lbs., b. 11/29/70

The two-year starter at the University of Oklahoma played five games for the Cowboys (with no receptions) during the 1993 season, and was waived the following May. That was his only year in the NFL.

MILLEN, HUGH
Quarterback, 6'5", 216 lbs., b. 11/22/63

The Cowboys thought they were acquiring a valuable insurance policy for star quarterback Troy Aikman when they got six-year veteran Millen from New England during the 1993 NFL draft—he had completed over 60 percent of his passes as a starter there on a mediocre team. It turned out that wide receiver Alvin Harper would throw more passes during the 1993 regular season for the Cowboys than Millen (and Harper only threw one). Millen didn't even retain the number two quarterback slot that was handed to him for the duration of the preseason—he was lapped by rookie Jason Garrett. And by the time Dallas needed a stop-gap starter in October, when Aikman was injured, the club brought in Bernie Kosar from Cleveland. Millen spent time later that year with Miami, then landed in Denver for the 1994 season.

MILLER, JIM
Punter, 5'11", 183 lbs., b. 7/5/57

Miller was the only barefooted punter in the NFL when the Cowboys signed him on November 18, 1983 to replace rookie John Warren, who was placed on injured reserve after suffering a knee injury. Miller became comfortable kicking without a shoe as a child roaming barefoot on the family farm in Mississippi.

The San Francisco 49ers punter the previous three seasons, Miller split the punting duties with Danny White down the stretch in 1983. Miller's job was to punt inside the opponent's 50-yard line, and he

averaged 35.6 yards in 5 opportunities. Warren returned to health in 1984, reclaiming his job, and Miller was released. He served as a backup with the New York Giants in 1987, his last year in the NFL.

MITCHELL, AARON
Cornerback, 6'1", 196 lbs., b. 12/15/56

Mitchell arrived at the Cowboys' 1979 training camp in Thousand Oaks, CA as a second-round draft pick from Nevada–Las Vegas with a reputation as a hard hitter. Teammate Charlie Waters nicknamed him "A.M.-P.M."—"They're wide awake when he hits 'em, and their lights are out when he walks away," Waters said. Somewhat overlooked in college because he played for a low-profile program, Mitchell also had blazing speed, running a 4.5 40-yard dash.

Mitchell saw action his rookie year on special teams and as the backup to Bennie Barnes at left cornerback. With Barnes sidelined by a sore foot, Mitchell drew his only start as a rookie against Cincinnati, and he made an impression with a 36-yard interception return that helped clinch the victory over the Bengals. He was named to the All-Rookie team by UPI and *Pro Football Weekly*.

But Mitchell's coverage technique was raw and undisciplined, and he wasn't able to break into the starting lineup his second season. Mitchell played for the Tampa Bay Buccaneers in 1981, then moved on to the USFL in 1983–84.

MONDAY NIGHT FOOTBALL

ABC premiered the longest-lasting show in TV history in 1970 with Howard Cosell, Don Meredith, and Keith Jackson behind the mikes. CBS had tried Monday night football five times in the previous four years, but with lukewarm response. Commissioner Pete Rozelle kept pushing for it though, and his instincts were right. It wasn't long before the show in the booth was more important than the game on the field. The caustic interplay between Cosell, the

Cowboys All-Time Longest Punts

84	Ron Widby	@ New Orleans, November 3, 1968
75	Sam Baker	@ LA Rams, September 30, 1962
75	Billy Lothridge	vs. NY Giants, October 11, 1964
73	Danny White	vs. LA Rams, October 14, 1979
71	Sam Baker	@ NY Giants, December 16, 1962
71	Billy Lothridge	vs. St. Louis, September 12, 1964
67	Dave Sherer	@ St. Louis, October 23, 1960
64	Sam Baker	vs. NY Giants, December 1, 1963
64	Mike Saxon	vs. Atlanta, December 22, 1991
63	Mike Saxon	@ St. Louis, September 13, 1987

logorrheic ex-labor lawyer, and Dandy Don, the ex-Cowboys quarterback who combined down-on-the-farm charm and knowledgeable analysis, was irresistible. (Meredith won an Emmy that year for his work.) Jackson concentrated on play-by-play and was replaced after the season by the phlegmatic Frank Gifford, who continued in the straight man role.

The show became a longstanding success. The Cowboys first played on *MNF* on November 16, 1970, against the St. Louis Cardinals. It was an inauspicious debut; the Super Bowl-bound Cowboys lost 38–0—the first regular or postseason shutout ever for Dallas. Ironically, the hometown Cotton Bowl fans began chanting "We want Meredith" in the fourth quarter. Dandy Don, the recipient of more than his share of Cotton Bowl boos, found it highly amusing. Through 1995, the Cowboys have amassed a record of 27–20 on ABC's *Monday Night Football*.

MONTGOMERY, MIKE
Running back, 6'2", 210 lbs., b. 7/10/49

Montgomery was one of the players traded to Dallas for Duane Thomas in 1972. He had spent one solid year in San Diego, and in his first year with the Cowboys, had 35 carries for 83 yards and 8 catches for 131 yards. He was converted to wide receiver the next year and, replacing the injured Otto Stowe halfway through the season, totalled 164 yards on 14 catches; he also led the team with 6 kick returns for a 29-yard average. But an injury in the ninth game of the season finished him for the year. When Drew Pearson came on and began to look All-World, Montgomery's days were numbered. He was traded in 1974 to Houston, where he had similar reception numbers. That was his last year in the NFL.

MOOTY, JIM
Defensive back, 5'11", 175 lbs., b. 6/15/38

In 1960, his only year in the NFL, this free agent from Arkansas was a backup in the defensive secondary, and a second-line punt and kick returner.

MORGAN, DENNIS
Running back, 5'11", 200 lbs., b. 6/26/52

The Cowboys' tenth-round draft pick in 1974 could only do one thing, but he did it well. The quick redhead from Western Illinois (nicknamed "Strawberry") had an

NFL-record-tying 98-yard punt return against St. Louis in the fourth game of the season, and went on to lead the team in punt and kickoff returns. He had 35 kick returns for 823 yards, and 19 punt returns for 287 yards. He was traded to Philadelphia in 1975; he played one year there and retired from the NFL.

MORTON, CRAIG
Quarterback, 6'4", 215 lbs., b. 2/5/43

Morton was the number-one pick in the 1965 Cowboy draft, a big, strong kid who could throw the ball a mile. He'd had an all-star career at California, but he sat the bench for four years behind Don Meredith. The first two years he shared backup duty with Jerry Rhome, another 1965 pick. During the first half of 1965, they each got a chance or two to take over the starting job in place of a struggling Meredith. But when neither proved worthy of the job, Landry made Meredith the permanent starter after the seventh game of the season. That year and the next, the two received little more than mopup duty, except for the odd start when Meredith was injured. Two years later, in the fourth game of 1967, Meredith cracked a rib (he'd injured another in the preseason) and developed pneumonia. Morton started the next three games and played well. Against Pittsburgh, he completed 12 of 16 attempts for 256 yards and 3 touchdowns. But Meredith came back and started, though he was shaky; Morton saw plenty of action the last half of the season and played well, finishing with 10 touchdowns and a 50 percent completion average.

The next year was Meredith's last. He suffered the usual rash of injuries—a knee injury here, a concussion there—enough to give Morton a few starts, and solidify his position as the next in line for the job. It was also the year that the refrain of "We want Morton" echoed down from the Cotton Bowl crowd more than ever, even though Dandy Don was having a good season. When Meredith announced his retirement

Craig Morton

the next July, Morton seemed the logical replacement. But a 27-year-old rookie just out of the service would complicate things. Roger Staubach, a Dallas draft pick four years earlier, had decided he'd like to give football a shot—with the Cowboys.

Jerry Rhome had been traded at his own request, so the duel was between Morton and Staubach. Morton had the experience, but Staubach impressed everyone with his leadership and physical abilities, and he looked very impressive in a preseason game against Los Angeles. Staubach started the first game, due mostly to a dislocated finger of Morton's, and did a good job. But "Curley" (Morton's nickname) was back the next week and started the remainder of the year as the Cowboys went 11–2–1; he had 21 touchdowns and a 54 percent completion average. But he was miserable in a 38–14 playoff loss to Cleveland, hitting only 8 of 24 passes and was benched in the fourth quarter. The next year began with Staubach starting the first game (Morton's shoulder had been bothering him the entire preseason); he won that one and next, but when he stumbled in his third start, Landry pulled him and sent in Morton. He wasn't much better, as the Cowboys suffered their first loss. But Morton started the rest of the season. Dallas split its next six games, but the Doomsday Defense stiffened down the stretch, and enabled the Cowboys to win their last five. Morton's year wasn't spectacular—only 15 touchdowns and a 49 percent completion rate—but his arm had bothered him all year. It didn't get any better in the playoffs. In a 5–0 win over Detroit, a sore-armed Morton completed only 4 of 18 attempts, and 7 of 22 the next week against San Francisco. He threw three interceptions in the Super Bowl; one of them was a fluke off the hands of Walt Garrison, but he threw another with 1:09 left in the game that enabled Baltimore to kick the winning field goal.

The next year, Landry alternated Morton and Staubach—sometimes on successive series—with varying results. But before the eighth game, with the Cowboys 4–3, he named Staubach his starting quarterback for the rest of the season. The Dodger responded in stirring fashion, leading the Pokes to a win in the Super Bowl. Morton finished with 7 touchdowns and a 55 percent completion rate, but saw no postseason action. Staubach injured his shoulder in the 1972 preseason and was out for most of the season. Morton directed the offense the entire year, although Staubach saw some action in the second half. Morton finished the year with 15 TDs and a completion average of 55 percent, but in the playoff game against San Francisco he faltered. Landry yanked him and put in Staubach, who rallied the team to a last-second win. In the NFC Championship Game loss to Washington, Morton didn't even play. Staubach was the starter the entire '73 season, and Morton had only 13 completions in 32 attempts in mopup duty.

In 1974 he signed a contract to play in 1975 for the Houston Texans of the upstart World Football League, and after the first regular-season game, he was traded to the New York Giants for a first-round choice in the '75 draft—which turned out to be Hall of Famer Randy White. Morton started for three years in New York (he never defected to the WFL) and then was sent to Denver in the offseason. After three miserable years on a bad Giants team, he thrived in head coach Red Miller's system (he was named the NFL's Comeback Player of the Year), and led the team to the Super Bowl—against the Cowboys. He had a forgettable showing against an overwhelming Dallas defense, throwing as many interceptions (4) as completions. He was replaced in the third quarter. As one sportswriter put it, it took thirteen years, but Morton finally helped the Cowboys win a Super Bowl.

He fell off next year and shared some time with his backups, and in 1979 lost his starting job to Norris Weese. But after six weeks of erratic offense, he got his job back and performed well. Virtually the same scenario was enacted the next year with Matt Robinson; after six games, Morton became the starter for the rest of the season, hitting 61 percent of his passes. But it was in 1981, under new coach and former teammate Dan Reeves, that he had his best year ever: 3,195 yards and 21 touchdowns on 60 percent passing. But a last-game defeat sent them home before the postseason. In his final year, 1982, he started and played well for two weeks, until the strike; then he lost his job to Steve DeBerg and saw no more action. He retired after the season, never having won the big one—despite, some would say, many chances to do it.

MURCHISON, CLINT JR.
Owner

Clint Murchison Jr. was a smart businessman—smart enough to know that you "hire the best possible people you can find to run your business, then step back and let them run it. And unless you have evidence they aren't getting the job done, you leave

Clint Murchison (*Courtesy Burk Murchison*)

them alone." A former 125-pound running back for the Massachusetts Institute of Technology (where he earned an M.S. in math), the football-crazy millionaire even bought twenty season tickets to the ill-destined 1952 Dallas Texans, a team so bad and unpopular the syndicate of Dallas businessmen that owned the team relinquished ownership seven games into the season. Murchison was interested in taking over the team, but the syndicate refused to allow the cautious entrepreneur to look over the books. Two years later, he came close to buying the San Francisco 49ers and moving them to Dallas, but the deal fell through. He made inquiries about the Washington Redskins, then the Chicago Cardinals. No luck.

When word spread that the NFL would add two new teams in 1960, Murchison was the first in line. After much lobbying and behind-the-scenes negotiations, the NFL owners voted on January 28, 1960 to create two new franchises. One would be in Dallas.

Murchison and his brother John D. (the two brothers shared 95 percent of the team equally) led a group of investors in paying $600,000 over the next two years: $50,000 for the franchise, and $550,000 as payment for the veteran players drafted from the existing teams. Murchison had earlier hired Tex Schramm as general manager; for their on-field manager the two decided to go after the smartest coach in the NFL—Tom Landry, an assistant with the New York Giants. When he came aboard, the brain trust was set. It took a bit more than a decade, but when the Cowboys beat the Miami Dolphins in the 1971 Super Bowl, Clint Murchison was the toast of the town. He had brought big-league football to Dallas, he had run the rival AFC Dallas Texans out of town, he had given Tom Landry an unprecedented ten-year contract in 1964 when many were calling for his head, and he had taken his team away from Dallas to Irving, and convinced the fans to follow. His golden touch extended to several other fields—he was an aggressive, shrewd entrepreneur who made fortunes in restaurants, real estate, and several other ventures.

Murchison rarely interfered with Landry and Schramm and how they ran the team. He suggested a play to Landry only once, a reverse to Bob Hayes (the play lost ten yards, although Landry deliberately left out two blocks to make sure the owner never tried it again). After a while, he didn't even attend owners' meetings, preferring that Schramm represent his interests there. He was, by his own admission, more fan than owner, although he took full advantage of owning the world's most popular football team.

His generous sense of humor was legendary, and he was a world-class prankster and practical joker. (*Classic Clint* by Dick Hitt goes a long way toward capturing the true essence of his puckish wit.) There's no better example of his mischievous ways than the story of the Chicago bear. When Dallas visited Chicago to play the Bears in 1960,

Murchison dreamed up an unusual idea to publicize the fact that the oldest NFL team was playing the newest. He arranged for a trained bear to be waiting in the lobby when the Cowboys arrived at their hotel. As the players arrived they witnessed a unique scene: the bear in mock battle with a man dressed in wild west cowboy attire. The event was a great success—so great that Murchison invited the bear and his trainer to the Cowboys' hospitality suite. Soon they had both blended in with the crowd and were drinking beer to celebrate the occasion. Later that evening, the trainer staggered off into the night, leaving the bear behind. It wasn't until the wee hours of the morning that the few hardy souls remaining noticed the trainer's absence, and wrestled with the problem of what to do with the bear. Murchison walked him to the elevator, pushed LOBBY, helped the bear in, and waved goodbye as the doors closed. The bear was never seen again.

Murchison continued as unobtrusive owner and number-one fan until the team was acquired in the spring of 1984, by a limited partnership headed by H.R. "Bum" Bright, a Texas A&M booster who made his millions in the oil business. The price was $20 million for the stadium and $60 million for the franchise—the largest amount ever paid for a sports team. By this time, Clint Murchison had been suffering from a degenerative nerve disease since the late seventies. On March 30, 1987, the founder of the Dallas Cowboys died at the age of sixty-three.

MURCHISON, OLA LEE
Wide receiver, 6'3", 220 lbs.

Murchison was a wide receiver and sprinter at the University of the Pacific with 9.4 speed in the hundred. He was drafted by the 49ers in 1960, but a knee injury had kept him out of any action. The undermanned Cowboys picked him up a year later, and he

saw spot time on specialty teams. He left football after that 1961 season to become a music teacher.

MURRAY, EDDIE
Kicker, 5'11", 195 lbs., b. 8/29/56

Thirteen-year veteran NFL kicker Murray joined the Cowboys in 1993 after Lin Elliott fell out of favor with coach Jimmy Johnson. The club was off to an 0–2 start. Less than five months later, the Cowboys were world champions for a second consecutive year. Of course, the end of Emmitt Smith's holdout, two games into the season, had a little more to do with the Dallas turnaround than the signing of Murray. But the veteran NFL kicker did play an important role in the title season. When the Cowboys faced San Francisco in a big mid-October showdown, Murray kicked 3 field goals to account for the 9-point winning margin. Field goals of 44 and 43 yards were the difference in a 5-point win over Phoenix in mid-November. He hit 3 in a 23–17 win over Philadelphia. His biggest kick of the year was the 41-yarder in overtime to win the season finale against the New York Giants at the Meadowlands to clinch the NFC East crown. Murray had a sensational year for the Cowboys, hitting every extra point and 28 of 33 field goal attempts for an 85 percent completion rate. He left the Cowboys after the season to join the Eagles, where he had another excellent year.

MYERS, JIM
Assistant coach

Myers had been a longtime coach in the collegiate ranks before he signed on with the Cowboys as their offensive line coach in 1962. Under his eye, the Dallas offense consistently ranked at the top of the NFL, and he coached several All-Pro and Pro Bowl linemen. He was named assistant head coach in 1977, and remained with the Cowboys until his retirement following the 1986 season.

MYLES, GODFREY
Linebacker, 6'1", 242 lbs., b. 9/22/68

Those weren't misprints on the Cowboys' defensive depth chart for Super Bowl XXX. Myles was the backup for Robert Jones at middle linebacker...and for Darrin Smith at weakside linebacker...and for Dixon Edwards at strongside linebacker. He has size, speed, and quickness, and is good against the run and covering receivers out of the backfield. He will head into the 1996 season with the chance to dent the starting lineup, with Jones and Edwards having left the squad via free agency after helping bring the Lombardi Trophy back to Valley Ranch from the Valley of the Sun—provided the torn anterior cruciate ligament in his left knee he suffered in the first half of the Super Bowl heals properly. He'll also have to compete with newly signed veterans Fred Strickland and Broderick Thomas.

Myles was a third-round draft pick of the Cowboys in 1991 and developed slowly through the years, playing on special teams and subbing mostly for Jones in the middle. But in 1995, he started the first seven games at weakside linebacker for contract holdout Smith, then started four of the last five games for an injured Jones. He played well, tying for the lead among linebackers with 5 passes defensed, and he collected 99 tackles. His position at the University of Florida was called Gatorback, which meant he was a hybrid of outside linebacker and strong safety.

NEELY, RALPH
Offensive tackle, 6'6", 265 lbs., b. 9/12/43

An All-American at Oklahoma, Neely, in 1965, became a hotly contested pawn in the NFL-AFL war. He signed an agreement with the Houston Oilers before finishing his college career, but a judge ruled the contract void. Neely then signed with the Cowboys; they had negotiated a trade with the NFL team who had made him their second-round pick, the Baltimore Colts. Dallas also had to give up several future draft choices, but it was worth it. He had excellent speed, quickness, and he exploded off the line; Green Bay defensive end Willie Davis called him "the finest offensive tackle I've ever played against."

Ralph Neely

Nicknamed "Rotten" by his teammates, he started the first game of his rookie season and soon became the anchor of the offensive line. He played most of the 1967 season on an injured knee, though it didn't keep him from All-Pro and Pro Bowl honors. "He is so good," said Bob Lilly, "that he's the only player I ever knew who was never a rookie." He was named to two Pro Bowls and to four All-Pro teams during his thirteen-year career. And in 1971, after six years at right tackle, Neely moved to a new position, left tackle, to make room for Rayfield Wright. But seven games into the season, he broke his right leg walking his off-road motorcycle up a hill. He would be out for the season. (Landry asked recently retired Tony Liscio to come back and fill in for the rest of the year. Dallas didn't lose another game that year, beating Miami in the Super Bowl.) Neely came back the next year, but frequently played through constant pain, exacerbated by several knee operations and a season-long broken hand. He retired after the 1977 season and the victory over Denver in Super Bowl XII.

NEWHOUSE, ROBERT
Fullback, 5'10", 215 lbs., b. 1/5/50

"House" was the second-round draft pick of the Cowboys in the 1972 draft, and for a decade was a dependable, tough fullback who fought for every extra inch he could get. The all-time leading rusher at Houston, he backed up Walt Garrison his first year, gaining 116 yards on 28 rushes. The next year, he backed up both Garrison and Calvin Hill and gained 436 yards on 84 carries for a healthy 5.2-yard average. He

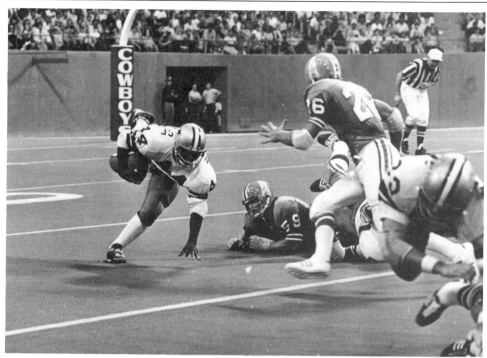

Robert Newhouse *(From the collection of the Texas Dallas History and Archive Division, Dallas Public Library)*

was the team's second-leading rusher in 1974, filling in when Hill was hurt, with 501 yards on 124 carries. He rushed for 97 yards against the Eagles despite breaking a rib early in the first quarter.

Garrison retired after a rodeo injury, and Newhouse became the starter at fullback in 1975. He responded with 930 yards on 209 carries, and 34 catches for 275 yards, and he had 56 yards in the Super Bowl loss to Pittsburgh. The next year his numbers dropped off—only 450 yards on 116 carries—but in 1977, playing next to Tony Dorsett, he had a fine year with 721 yards on 180 carries. He had rushing games of 80 and 81 yards in the playoffs, then capped it off with a 29-yard TD pass to Golden Richards in the Super Bowl against Denver.

In 1978, a broken bone in his right leg that struck him down with four games left limited him to 584 yards on 140 carries, and 20 receptions. The next year, a stress fracture of the lower left leg in the season opener limited him to 124 carries for 449 yards. He

lost his starting job to Ron Springs in 1980 but regained it a month into the season and kept it, gaining 451 yards on 118 carries. But he was strictly a backup in the last three years of his career, totaling just 33, 79, and 34 yards on the ground in that span. Newhouse was a punishing runner; he stayed low to the ground and was extremely hard to take down, and he had a tremendous second effort. Said teammate Dave Edwards, "tackling him is like tackling a shot put."

NEWSOME, TIMMY
Running back, 6'1", 236 lbs., b. 5/17/58

The little-known Newsome's size and speed intrigued the Cowboys and, in keeping with their history of tapping small college talent, they invested a 1980 sixth-round pick on the athlete from Winston-Salem State.

Newsome remained more suspect than prospect over his first five seasons, however, starting only five games over that span. He had the size to play fullback, but Robert

Newhouse was better at the blocking chores required by the position.

In training camp 1982, the Cowboys switched Newsome to tailback, and he initially balked at the move, leaving camp because a guy named Tony Dorsett owned the tailback job. But he finally gave in and demonstrated a knack for making plays when given the opportunity.

In a victory over Washington in December 1982, Newsome broke several tackles en route to an 18-yard touchdown. The following week against Houston, he caught one pass for a 43-yard gain and another for a 46-yard touchdown in which he slipped one tackle and broke three others. Then, in a playoff victory over Green Bay, Newsome caught a career-high 7 passes for 70 yards and also scored on a 2-yard run, while splitting fullback duties with Newhouse in place of the injured Ron Springs.

In 1983, Newsome turned a short pass into a 52-yard touchdown with 47 seconds left against Tampa Bay to force overtime in a game the Cowboys eventually won. Newsome set three career highs in 1983, rushing for 185 yards, catching 250 yards in passes, and scoring 6 touchdowns.

Springs had blocked his path to a starting job, but that situation changed when coach Tom Landry tired of Springs' locker room lawyering and disruptive influence, and released him in 1985.

Nicknamed "Tippin' Timmy" by former teammate Butch Johnson, Newsome started fourteen games, missing two with injuries. Newsome caught 46 passes for 361 yards, both career highs, but his rushing left much to be desired as he averaged only 2.9 yards in 88 carries. "I know we need more production at fullback," Landry said prior to the 1986 season. "We need a strong fullback, Timmy or someone else, who can pick up the tough yards, catch the football and produce six to seven hundred yards."

Newsome was out of the starting lineup again in 1986, when Landry attempted to use both Dorsett and newly arrived Herschel Walker in the same backfield, with Walker playing fullback. Newsome then figured in an ill-fated Landry experiment in which Newsome, Dorsett, and Walker played together in a full-house backfield. Newsome again set career highs with 48 catches and 421 receiving yards and also served as the third tight end.

Newsome started eight games during the strike year of 1987, rushing for 2 touchdowns in a loss to Detroit, and catching 2 touchdown passes in another defeat to Miami. In 1988, Newsome's season ended with a calf injury suffered in practice following the ninth game; at the time, he was on pace for a career high in catches. His 30 receptions that year moved him into ninth place on the franchise's all-time list.

Jimmy Johnson arrived in 1989, and Johnson was determined to remake the team in his style. Injuries and age pushed Newsome into retirement prior to the '89 season; he turned an off-season career in computer programming into a full-time occupation.

NEWTON, NATE
Offensive lineman, 6'3", 320 lbs.,
b. 12/20/61

The only championships predicted for Newton when he arrived as a free agent in 1986 involved a knife and fork. But Newton's fat-man act fooled every critic, and he developed into a Pro Bowl guard and a top contributor to three Super Bowl teams.

Newton, whose brother, Tim, played defensive line for the Minnesota Vikings and Tampa Bay Buccaneers, was signed by the Washington Redskins as a rookie free agent in 1983, but was released on the final cut. The setback may have worked in Newton's favor, since he was free to sign with the USFL Tampa Bay Bandits, and he improved as a player in his two seasons for the Bandits.

With the demise of the USFL, Newton was a free agent again, only now a more marketable one, and he joined the Cowboys for the 1986 season. Although his weight

Nate Newton

was an ongoing problem, the Cowboys' coaching staff saw more than a fat guy. Newton was an all-around athlete at Jones High School in Orlando, and he played both offensive and defensive line at Florida A&M, where he won four letters. He was agile, quick, and strong. Newton played in eleven of sixteen games as a backup in his first year in Dallas.

Nathaniel Newton Jr.'s career was on the rise, and in 1987 he started the opener at left guard and stayed there for all eleven of the games he played in during the strike-shortened season. A change was in store for Newton: after remaining a starting guard in 1988 and 1989, new coach Jimmy Johnson shuffled the line in 1990 and installed Newton as the starting right tackle.

Newton showed his versatility by playing so well, he was named the Cowboys' Most Valuable Offensive Player by *Pro Football Weekly*. He was also the only Dallas offensive lineman to earn All-Pro votes from the Associated Press, gaining recognition when he held Philadelphia Eagles All-Pro defensive end Reggie White to 3 tackles and no sacks in 2 meetings.

Weight continued to be a concern, however, and each off-season Newton and the coaching staff warred over the numbers on the scales, earning him the nickname "The Kitchen." He would at times balloon to nearly 400 pounds, pay the appropriate fines during training camp, drop some of the weight, and then turn in another outstanding performance during the season. Newton also worked with a nutritionist during off-seasons when his weight got out of hand.

In 1992, the emergence of young offensive tackle Erik Williams prompted the coaches to shift Newton back to left guard. Newton and center Mark Stepnoski became the first Cowboys offensive linemen voted to the Pro Bowl since 1982. Behind Newton and Company, Emmitt Smith won his second straight rushing title, and the Cowboys won their first Super Bowl since the 1977 season.

The funniest and most outspoken figure in the Cowboys locker room, Newton remains among the league's premier guards; since 1992 he has been to three more Pro Bowls. Meanwhile, the Cowboys captured three Super Bowls in four seasons, the first time that feat had been accomplished in league history. Much of the credit must go to Newton and an offensive line considered the league's best.

NILAND, JOHN
Offensive guard, 6'4", 247 lbs., b. 2/29/44

An All-American at Iowa, Niland played nine strong years (1966–74) for Dallas before finishing his career with Philadelphia. He started four games at right guard as a rookie, when Jim Boeke was injured and

Tony Liscio moved into Boeke's spot, then became a regular in his sophomore season. His nickname was "Gorgo" because he ate everything in sight, and he was a terror as a pulling guard. He was very fast for a lineman (he had been an all-state fullback in high school), and helped make the Cowboys' power sweep the most feared since that of the champion Green Bay Packers. Against the Dolphins in Super Bowl VI he was spectacular, opening gaping holes for Duane Thomas and Walt Garrison to run through.

Niland was a six-time Pro Bowler and a three-time All-Pro, and a man who off the field gave much of his time and money to underprivileged children. (He had been an abandoned child himself.) But early in the 1973 season, psychological problems led to a confrontation with police who had been summoned to corral a "partly incoherent" Niland running wild through the streets; as the police physically restrained him, his elbow was damaged, and nerve damage was

John Niland (76) and Walt Garrison (32) lead-blocking for Les Shy, 1970. *(From the collection of the Texas/Dallas History and Archive Division, Dallas Public Library)*

done to his left hand, leaving it partially paralyzed.

Niland recovered psychologically, but his injuries placed him on the injured reserve list midway through the season. He was traded to the Philadelphia Eagles before the 1975 season; he injured his knee in 1976, and never played again.

NOLAN, DICK
Defensive back/assistant coach, 6'1", 185 lbs., b. 3/26/32

Nolan had played with Tom Landry in the mid-fifties in the New York Giants' defensive secondary, and for him in the late fifties when Landry was New York's defensive coach. In 1962, he retired at the age of thirty, and was hired by his old friend as an assistant coach. But injuries to the defensive backfield forced him to suit up and play the entire season—which was, apparently, Landry's plan all along.

After the season, he permanently retired and continued as the defensive backfield coach, contributing his expertise to the original Doomsday Defense of the late sixties and developing All-Pros Cornell Green and Mel Renfro. He left to become head coach of the San Francisco 49ers from 1968–75, then was head coach at New Orleans from 1978–80. After a year as defensive coordinator in Houston, he returned to Dallas in 1982, first to coach the receivers for four years, and then to coach the defensive secondary once again. He left Dallas after the 1990 season.

NOONAN, DANNY
Defensive lineman, 6'4", 275 lbs., b. 7/14/65

Noonan was another success story from the University of Nebraska when he arrived as a number-one Cowboys draft pick, and the twelfth player taken in 1987. A native of Lincoln, NE who grew up six miles from the Nebraska campus, Noonan was an undersized 220-pounder when he joined the Cornhuskers' program. He hit the weight room, and when he departed Noonan

weighed 282 pounds, boasted a bench press of 500 pounds, and was a consensus All-America selection at nose tackle. When the Cowboys called Noonan to inform him he was their number-one pick, he was working out at the Nebraska weight-training facility.

After beginning his rookie year as a reserve end, he was moved to right tackle. Over the second half of his first season, he shared the job with future Hall of Famer Randy White, who was struggling with injuries. Playing in run situations, Noonan completed his rookie year with 27 total tackles as the heir apparent to White.

Noonan took over the job full-time in 1988, and although he started all sixteen games, injuries limited his effectiveness. Even so, he tied for the team lead with 7.5 sacks and paced all of the club's defensive linemen with 84 tackles. In 1989, after missing most of the first ten weeks of the season with a groin injury suffered in training camp, Noonan appeared in only seven games, starting five, and he finished with only 23 tackles and 1 sack. But Noonan was determined to show the Cowboys that he wasn't another in a series of first-round busts of the eighties, and he started fifteen of sixteen games in 1990, contributing 85 tackles and 4.5 sacks.

Johnson was continually upgrading his defensive personnel, and by 1991 Tony Casillas, Tony Tolbert, Jimmie Jones, Russell Maryland, and Leon Lett had all been added to the line rotation. Noonan was the starting right tackle in the first three games of the 1991 season, then went to the bench as a backup end and tackle. When Casillas was injured, Noonan was back among the starters for three games.

But Noonan's string of injuries frustrated Johnson, who traded Noonan to the Green Bay Packers for the 1992 season, his last in the NFL.

NORMAN, PETTIS
Tight end, 6'3", 220 lbs., b. 1/4/39

Norman, a free agent out of Johnson C. Smith College in North Carolina, played

Pettis Norman

nine years (1962–70) for the Cowboys. His first two years he played behind Lee Folkins, but was a standout on specialty teams. He took over the tight end spot in 1964 and caught 24 passes for 311 yards, his best year. But he wasn't a starter for his receiving ability. He didn't have tremendous hands, but he was one of the best blocking tight ends in the NFL, and he was a tough competitor who often played hurt.

During most of his Cowboy career, he was often removed on third-down passing situations for more surehanded receivers. During 1966–67 he split time with Frank Clarke, who had moved to tight end from wide receiver, then Pete Gent, a flanker, in 1968. His last two years he battled against the newly acquired Mike Ditka, the Hall-of-Fame-bound tight end, and a fleet of flankers and backs who caught everything in sight and left few scraps; Ditka and Norman, between them, caught only 14 passes all year. He started in Super Bowl V but didn't catch a pass. After the 1970 season, he was traded to San Diego with Ron East and Tony Liscio for All-Pro flanker Lance Alworth.

After his retirement, Norman settled in Dallas, where he became a respected leader in the black community.

NORTH DALLAS FORTY

Pete Gent, Cowboys wide receiver from 1964–68, wrote this thinly disguised roman a clef in 1973. The novel received strong reviews and sold very well, although Tex Schramm called it "a total lie…offensive and malicious." The truth is, it's a well-written, perceptive portrait of Dallas in the late sixties, and the best book on pro football ever written. The 1979 film with Nick Nolte as the wide receiver and Mac Davis as the high-living quarterback—obviously patterned after Gent and his good friend Don Meredith—was also excellent, and probably the best football film ever made. Gent wrote four more sports novels (Texas Celebrity Turkey Trot, The Franchise, North Dallas After Forty, and Conquering Heroes), but none had the impact of his first.

NORTON, JERRY
Safety, 5'11", 195 lbs., b. 5/16/30

Norton, a former star running back at SMU, had decided to retire after eight years with the Eagles and the Cardinals. But Tex Schramm talked him into a Dallas uniform for the 1962 season. In December, he ran back a St. Louis field goal attempt 94 yards for a TD, still a Dallas record. He was traded to Green Bay just before the 1963 season and played for the Packers two more years (as their regular punter) before retiring with 35 career interceptions.

NORTON, KEN JR.
Linebacker, 6'2", 241 lbs., b. 9/29/66

When the Cowboys selected Norton out of UCLA in the second round of the 1988 draft, he was better known for his famous father, former heavyweight champion Ken Norton Sr., than for any of his own exploits on the football field. Not that Ken

Ken Norton, Jr.

Jr. wasn't a prospect. He was an All-American on a college team that included future Cowboys teammates Troy Aikman and James Washington; Norton was the highest-selected Bruins linebacker since Jerry Robinson was taken by the Philadelphia Eagles in the first round in 1979.

Personnel director Gil Brandt took some heat after Norton contributed little his rookie season. The Los Angeles native broke his thumb in the preseason and played only three games his first year. But in 1989, Norton began to emerge as a force on an awful Cowboys defense, although injuries again limited his production. Norton played the equivalent of nine games because he missed three with a knee injury and played only the first and third quarters the last half of the season. He still finished sixth on the team with 87 tackles.

Starting on the weak side in 1990, Norton led the team in solo tackles (79) and total tackles (119). He also paced Cowboys linebackers in sacks and tied for second on the club in fumbles recovered and forced fumbles, despite missing most of the last two games with torn knee cartilage.

Norton spent most of the off-season rehabilitating the injury, then was able to start all sixteen games in 1991 for the rapidly improving Cowboys. Now playing on the strong side, his 13 tackles for losses led the team, and Norton made an even bigger impact in the playoffs, pacing the defense with 17 tackles in the two post-season games.

The Cowboys were ready to take the next step, and Norton would be among the movers and shakers. Jimmy Johnson was dissatisfied with Robert Jones' work in the middle, and Norton was shifted to middle linebacker. When Bill Bates went down with a season-ending knee injury, Norton also played linebacker in the nickel defense and was a special teams contributor. Few in the league were better at their jobs in 1992, although Norton somehow missed Pro Bowl selection despite leading the Super Bowl champs with a career-high 120 tackles. Norton reached double-digits in tackles in three games, recovered a fumble against Philadelphia in the playoffs, and intercepted a pass against San Francisco in the NFC title game.

In the Super Bowl, Norton was outstanding. He had 10 tackles to lead the team, was involved in a quarterback pressure that forced Buffalo's Jim Kelly out of the game in the second quarter, then scooped up a fumble and raced 9 yards for a fourth quarter touchdown, the first of his career, to cap Dallas' scoring in a 52–17 rout. Norton also made 2 tackles during a key goal-line stand to preserve the Cowboys 14–7 second-quarter advantage.

By 1993, Norton had developed into one of the game's most respected linebackers as he led the Cowboys to a second Super Bowl title. He finished with a team-leading 159 tackles, had 2 sacks, a team-leading 10 tackles for losses, and an interception. He then capped his best season as a Cowboy with a Pro Bowl berth.

Norton was a hot commodity after the 1993 season. He was not only an all-star player, but was also a leader with two Super Bowl rings. Free agency was now the law of the league and Norton was in a position to capitalize. The league's salary cap hamstrung the Cowboys, and Norton had little choice but to jump at a lucrative offer from the arch-rival 49ers, who followed Norton's lead and went on to win a Super Bowl of their own the following season.

NOVACEK, JAY
Tight end, 6'4", 234 lbs., b. 10/24/62

An honest-to-goodness cowboy from Wyoming, Novacek proved to be one of Dallas' most savvy acquisitions of the 1990s. He was signed away from Phoenix in 1990 as a Plan B free agent at the same time that the Cowboys traded for the Cardinals' other tight end, Rob Awalt. Not only did Novacek win the starting tight end job in Dallas, but no other tight end in the NFL has been as productive during his six seasons with the Cowboys. He has been selected to five Pro Bowls (1991–95), the most ever by a Dallas tight end, and he has caught more passes,

339, than any other tight end in Cowboys history.

After five years as a dependable tight end for the Cardinals, Novacek blossomed in his first year in Dallas. He was second on the team with 59 catches for 657 yards and 4 touchdowns. His next year was a virtual carbon copy—59 catches for 664 yards, and 4 touchdowns. His 11 receptions against Green Bay were the most in the NFC in a single game that year. A sprained left knee kept him out of two full games and part of another, but he came back healthy and was named All-Pro. Against Chicago in the playoffs, he hauled in the game-winning touchdown catch on third-and-goal from the Bears' 3-yard line in the third quarter, his only catch of the day. The following season in 1993 he had 68 receptions (a new season high for Dallas tight ends) for 630 yards and 6 touchdowns, good for another All-Pro selection. In Super Bowl XXVII against the Bills, Novacek scored the Cowboys' first touchdown, a 23-yarder, and went on to lead the team in receptions with 7.

His totals dropped off the next two years—44 catches for 445 yards and 1 touchdown in 1993, 47 for 475 and 2 TDs in

Jay Novacek

1994—but he made up for it in the postseason. The following year, against Green Bay in 1993 he had 6 catches for 59 yards and a TD, and 4 catches for 57 yards and a touchdown against San Francisco in the NFC Championship Game. He had another 5 grabs in Super Bowl XXVII against the Bills. The following year against Green Bay, he set a Dallas playoff record with 11 catches (for 104 yards), then grabbed 5 passes for 72 yards in the Championship Game loss to San Francisco.

His 1995 season was superlative. Despite a pulled abdominal muscle that kept him out of two games and arthroscopic surgery that sidelined him for the last game of the season, he had 62 catches for a career-high 702 yards; five went for touchdowns. But he was healthy by the time the playoffs rolled around. He had 5 receptions against Green Bay and 5 more in the Super Bowl against Pittsburgh, including a 3-yard TD grab. He also earned his fifth consecutive Pro Bowl nod, and a first-team All-NFC selection by UPI. Novacek may keep a low profile off the field, but he didn't leave his cowboy background back in Wyoming. Throughout his Cowboy playing days, he often takes part in cutting horse competitions in the Dallas area.

NUTTING, ED
Offensive tackle, 6'4", 245 lbs., b. 2/8/39

The Cleveland Browns' second-round draft choice in 1961 was traded to Dallas in 1962, but a knee injury in the preseason sidelined him the entire year. He came back the next year and started at right tackle most of the season, then retired.

NYE, BLAINE
Offensive guard, 6'4", 255 lbs., b. 3/29/46

The fifth-round pick from Stanford in 1968 was a defensive lineman in college. He

Blaine Nye

was converted to offense by the Cowboys, and was a starter at right guard by 1970. He started that year's Super Bowl and two others, and in his nine years with the Cowboys (1968–76) he was an All-Pro once and a Pro Bowler once.

In his last few years, Nye developed an odd habit of retiring just before training camp; ostensibly he was holding out, but it never took much (usually the end of camp) before he was in the fold again. "Never carve what I say in stone," he said. Nye may have hated two-a-days, but he was a stable, dependable lineman; said Tom Landry, "He just never has a bad football game." He was a member of the infamous Zero Club along with Pat Toomay and Larry Cole, and is the only ex-Cowboy to own a Master's Degree in Physics.

OSWALD, PAUL
Center, 6'4", 275 lbs., b. 4/9/64

A reserve lineman out of Kansas who saw brief action with Dallas in 1988, Oswald also played for the Pittsburgh Steelers in 1987, and the Atlanta Falcons after the Cowboys released him in 1988.

OTTO, BOB
Defensive lineman, 6'6", 251 lbs., b. 12/16/62

Otto joined the Cowboys in 1986 after he was released on the final cut by the Seattle Seahawks, but he played only briefly for Dallas. The Idaho State ex also played for the Houston Oilers in 1987.

OVERTON, JERRY
Safety, 6'2", 190 lbs., b. 1/24/41

The Cowboys' fifteenth-round draft pick in 1963, Overton had been an excellent defensive back at Utah; he ran the 100-yard dash in 9.8. It wasn't until the seventh game of the season that he was made the starting free safety, over Jim Ridlon. He gave up a long touchdown pass that won the game for Pittsburgh, but he remained the starter for the remainder of the year. He improved steadily, and also returned five punts, but a badly broken bone suffered while skiing in the offseason ended his career.

OWENS, BILLY
Defensive back/linebacker, 6'1", 207 lbs., b. 12/2/65

As a tenth-round pick out of Pittsburgh in 1988, Owens earned rookie playing time with the nickel package by quickly picking up Tom Landry's defense. Owens also played linebacker in the nickel, but he wasn't around for the 1989 season when Jimmy Johnson and his coaching staff undertook a massive housecleaning, and 1988 proved to be his only year in the NFL.

Cowboys All-Time Longest Punt Returns

98	Dennis Morgan	@ St. Louis, October 13, 1974 (TD)
90	Bob Hayes	vs. Pittsburgh, December 8, 1968 (TD)
85	Kelvin Martin	@ Philadelphia, December 15, 1991 (TD)
83	Kevin Williams	vs. Washington, November 20, 1994 (TD)
79	Kelvin Martin	vs. Washington, September 7, 1992 (TD)
74	Kelvin Martin	vs. LA Rams, November 15, 1992 (TD)
69	Bob Hayes	vs. St. Louis, November 23, 1967 (TD)
69	Mel Renfro	vs. Green Bay, November 29, 1964 (TD)
68	Gary Allen	vs. Kansas City, November 20, 1983 (TD)
64	Kevin Williams	vs. Miami, November 25, 1993 (TD)

PALMER, PAUL
Running back, 5'9", 181 lbs., b. 10/14/64

The Cowboys found themselves in need of immediate help at running back following the blockbuster trade of Herschel Walker to Minnesota, midway through the 1989 season, especially since Vikings running back Darrin Nelson never made it to Dallas in the trade. Enter Palmer, whose running nearly won him the Heisman Trophy at Temple University. He had debuted with Kansas City in 1987, and in 1988 had been the busiest man in the NFL with 134 carries, 53 receptions, and 23 kick returns.

After a brief stop in Detroit, early in the 1989 season, he made his Cowboys debut on October 22 at Kansas City and rushed for a team-high 85 yards in a 36–28 Chiefs victory. He ended up the team's top rusher for the season with 446 yards on 112 carries—a far cry from the 1,514 yards from Walker that led the club the previous season. Palmer's best day coincided with the Cowboys' only victory of the season, when he gained 110 yards in Dallas' 13–3 triumph at Washington. He also had 17 catches for 93 yards. But his future with the Cowboys, or lack thereof, was evident when Palmer, despite being the team's top ground gainer, didn't dress out for the final game of the year. The rationale: Palmer didn't fit into the Cowboys' game plan that day. He left the Cowboys via Plan B free agency and signed with Cincinnati, though he never played in the NFL again. Before his football career was over, he was chugging into end zones for the Barcelona Dragons of the World League of American Football.

PARKS, BILLY
Wide receiver, 6'1", 185 lbs., b. 1/1/48

Parks had a fine rookie year with San Diego in 1971, then was traded to Dallas for the 1972 season. With Lance Alworth in his final year and Bob Hayes having an off year, Parks and Ron Sellers led the flanker corps in receptions; Parks had 18 catches for 298 yards. He had a spectacular playoff game against San Francisco with 7 receptions for 125 yards and a touchdown. But "Harpo," as he was nicknamed by teammates for his frizzy blond hairdo, was a moody nonconformist who didn't always toe the Landry line, and he was traded to Houston the next year with defensive end Tody Smith. He had two good years and one mediocre one there before retiring.

PARRISH, JAMES
Offensive tackle, 6'6", 310 lbs., b. 5/19/68

Parrish signed on with the Cowboys' practice squad on December 7, 1993 and was activated five days later, when starting center Mark Stepnoski was lost with a season-ending knee injury. The journey to the Dallas roster wasn't a simple one. The Temple University product spent time with Miami (who signed him as a rookie free agent in 1991), San Diego, the World League of American Football's London Monarchs and Barcelona Dragons, San Francisco, and Indianapolis before landing a spot, albeit a brief one, with the Cowboys. Parrish was an infrequently used backup, and was released after the 1994 season. He was signed by the Steelers in February 1995.

PATERA, JACK
Linebacker/assistant coach, 6'1", 240 lbs., b. 8/1/33

After three years with the Baltimore Colts, who had drafted him out of Oregon in the fourth round, and two with the Chicago Cardinals, Patera was picked up by Dallas in the expansion draft of 1960. The first starting middle linebacker for the Cowboys played sparingly due to knee injuries—in 1960 he went down with torn knee cartilage in the fourth game and missed the rest of the season, and in his second year, he played only in the last two games of the season— but he was a hard hitter when healthy and a dedicated student of the game. He put his knowledge to work when he retired after the 1961 season to be a defensive line coach; he tutored the Rams' Fearsome Foursome and the Vikings' Purple People Eaters before becoming the head coach of the expansion Seattle Seahawks from 1976–82.

PATTERSON, ELVIS
Cornerback, 5'11", 195 lbs., b. 10/21/60

The former Giants, Chargers, and Raiders back didn't lack for confidence, even when his days as a Cowboy were limited to one season for that very reason. He was signed by Dallas early in 1993. Having been relegated to mostly special-teams duty late in his career, Patterson followed the 1993 season by asking for a raise from $450,000 to $733,333. That would have made Patterson the NFL's highest-paid special-teams performer alongside Buffalo's Steve Tasker— would have. The Cowboys instead released him, and he retired after the season, his tenth in the NFL.

PEARSON, DREW
Wide receiver, 6'0", 175 lbs., b. 1/12/51

Pearson was a dual-sport athlete at Tulsa, playing both football and baseball; he played quarterback, wide receiver, and center field. Tulsa wasn't very good, and there was no one who could throw to him, so he was generally ignored in the 1973 college draft. But the Dallas computer knew who he was, and he was signed as a free agent.

He moved to Dallas in early June and began working out every morning with Roger Staubach; they immediately clicked as a passer-receiver combination. In training camp, he made the team as a backup wide receiver and punt/kickoff returner; then, when flanker Otto Stowe broke an ankle in midseason, and Mike Montgomery was injured two games after that, Pearson stepped in and caught everything thrown his way. He finished with 22 catches for 388 yards, and in the conference playoff against Los Angeles he made 2 receptions for 87 yards— both of them touchdowns, and the second one an 83-yarder.

The following year he led the league with 1,087 yards, then followed with outstanding years of 822, 806, 870, 714, and 1,026-yard totals. The next four years saw his numbers decrease as Tony Hill became the favorite receiver of Staubach and then Danny White. But Pearson still delivered in the clutch. He had a knack for last-gasp catches, many of which were game-winners. He became known as Mr. January for his dramatic playoff heroics, such as the 1973 playoff game against Los Angeles when Pearson went up between two defenders for a long Staubach pass at midfield—and came down with it, and raced 50 yards for an 83-yard TD play that destroyed any hope the Rams had that day.

But the most thrilling was the Hail Mary touchdown pass against Minnesota on December 28, 1975. With less than two minutes remaining, the Cowboys were down 14–10 against an indomitable Viking defense. From their own nine-yard line, Staubach threw 5 passes—all to Pearson. The final one was a 50-yard desperation pass with 24 seconds remaining on the clock that

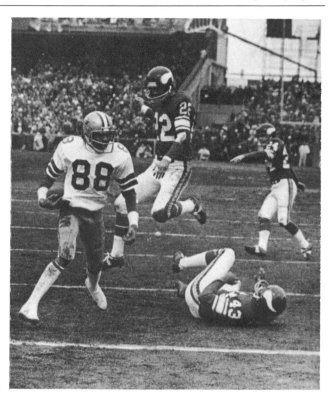

Drew Pearson

was actually underthrown. A pump fake had frozen safety Paul Krause; Pearson, racing downfield with cornerback Nate Wright, screened Wright out as he slowed for the falling ball. There was contact, and Wright went down; Pearson juggled the ball, then caught it between his elbow and hip and jumped into the end zone. Another catch to remember was the Thanksgiving Day 1974 game-winner from The Mad Bomber, Clint Longley, who was subbing for a dazed Staubach. That was also a 50-yarder, and with the Efren Herrera kick put the Cowboys ahead to stay by one point.

In March 1984, an early-morning auto accident left Pearson with serious internal injuries—particularly a lacerated liver—and his younger brother dead. Pearson's injuries healed, but his doctors told him that football was too dangerous: an internal hemmorhage could be fatal. He flirted with a comeback, then retired, settling for a trial stint on the Cowboy coaching staff. He finished his ca-

reer with 489 receptions, 7,822 yards, and 48 touchdowns. In 22 playoff games, Pearson had 67 catches, 1,105 yards, and 8 touchdowns, and he was named to three Pro Bowls and three All-Pro teams. He has gone on to become one of the most successful black businessmen in the country.

PEARSON, PRESTON
Running back, 6'1", 210 lbs., b. 1/17/45

Pearson was another Cowboy who hadn't played a down of college football. He'd been a tenacious guard on Illinois' basketball team—and perhaps the only man who ever blocked a Lew Alcindor shot in college. But he'd been drafted by Don Shula and the Colts. After eight solid years with Baltimore and then Pittsburgh, Pearson was put on waivers near the end of the 1975 preseason. Nobody claimed him except Dallas, a squad badly in need of a dependable running back. He became the final

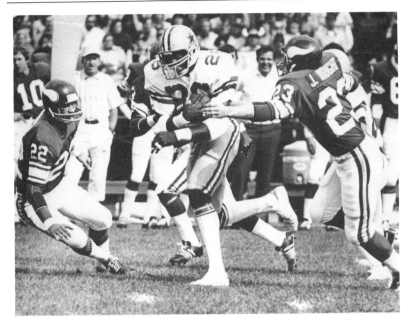

Preston Pearson

piece in the puzzle team that would go to the Super Bowl with thirteen rookies on the roster.

Pearson missed the first game of the season, saw spot action the next three games, then won a starting job. He became more valuable as the year wore on—Tom Landry called him "the key to our season." Pearson rushed for 509 yards on 133 carries, and had 27 receptions for 351 yards and a 13-yard average (he also led the team with 16 kick returns for a 24-yard average). He capped it off in the playoff game against Los Angeles with 7 passes for 123 yards and 3 touchdowns. He was used perfectly. He wasn't a big running back, but he ran exact routes and was an excellent receiver—and he was unbeatable in the open field where he had room to maneuver. Landry ran him about ten times a game, often on screens away from congestion. The result was beautiful; Pearson's skills were used better than they ever had been.

In 1976 a knee injury requiring surgery hampered Pearson, and he missed a good portion of the season; he managed to start just two games late in the year. He finished with only 68 carries for 233 yards and 23

catches for 316 yards. He also led Dallas in rushes and receptions in the 14–12 playoff loss to Los Angeles. The next year, a rookie sensation from Pitt named Tony Dorsett helped lead the Cowboys to the Super Bowl. Pearson was the starter for the first nine games of the season, but Dorsett started from then on. Pearson played on obvious passing downs, and he was incredibly successful. He caught 46 passes (then a Cowboy record for a running back) for 535 yards, floating out of the backfield, and he rushed 89 times for 341 yards. He missed the first playoff game because of injury, but against the Vikings in the NFC Championship Game, he had 3 catches for 48 yards and delivered a key block in a Dorsett TD run. In the Super Bowl win over Denver, he led the team with 5 catches (for 37 yards).

The next year Pearson was one catch better: 47 receptions for 526 yards, to go with 25 runs for 104 yards. The next two years, Pearson's last, looked on paper like a winding-down period: only 26 receptions for 333 yards in 1979. But 23 of those catches were for first downs or touchdowns, some kind of clutch-receiving record. In January 1979, he played in his fifth Super Bowl, a record he shares with only a handful of others. He had only a couple of catches in the loss to the Steelers. In 1980, he had 20 catches for 213 yards, and 5 catches in two playoff games. He retired after the season. His 1985 autobiography, *Hearing the Noise,* is one of the better insider's books on pro football.

PEETE, RODNEY
Quarterback, 6'0", 193 lbs., b. 3/16/66

In 1994, the revolving door for backups for quarterback Troy Aikman swung open for Peete. He came to Valley Ranch following five seasons with Detroit, during which he passed for more than 1,000 yards each year, and was in and out of the starting lineup. In the season before he came to the Cowboys, his record as a starter was 6–4. He started twice for Dallas in 1994, with Aikman shelved by injuries. On October 23 in Phoenix, he led the Cowboys to a 28–21 victory by hitting 12 of 19 passes for 186 yards and no interceptions. On December 4, in Philadelphia, Peete led the Cowboys past the Eagles, 31–19, with 172 yards on 10 for 17 passing. In his limited play, he actually finished with a better quarterback rating than Aikman (102.5 to Aikman's 84.9). Following the NFC Championship Game loss in San Francisco, Peete signed with the Eagles.

PELLUER, STEVE
Quarterback, 6'4", 212 lbs., b. 7/29/62

Pelluer witnessed the Danny White-Gary Hogeboom quarterback controversy, then saw the arrival of Troy Aikman. In between, he had a few fleeting moments of glory, but the soft-spoken, polite Pelluer experienced an otherwise frustrating career.

His brother, Scott, had preceded him to the Cowboys as a fourth-round draft pick in 1981. A fifth-round pick from the University of Washington in 1984, Steve Pelluer was selected with an eye toward the future. White and Hogeboom were vying for the

Steve Pelluer

starting job and there were few opportunities for Pelluer, even in practices. He was active for only one game as a rookie and he didn't play, nor did he play his second season until he made a dramatic Cowboys debut in a key game in December 1985, against the New York Giants.

With White and Hogeboom both knocked out of action by injuries, Pelluer took charge with the NFC East title on the line. Pelluer entered the game with the Cowboys clinging to a flimsy 21–14 fourth-quarter lead, and he led the Cowboys on a 72-yard drive for what would prove to be the winning touchdown in a 28–21 decision.

Hogeboom was traded following the 1985 season, elevating Pelluer to the backup role. White suffered a broken wrist in a mid-season loss to the Giants and suddenly, Pelluer was the man. Although there were those who questioned his ability as a leader, he started six of the last seven games in the 1986 season. Dallas lost six of those seven to miss the playoffs, and the inexperienced Pelluer took his share of the heat. In a shocking loss to Seattle, Pelluer completed

14 straight passes to set a club record, but there were few other highlights for Pelluer.

White regained the number one nod for the strike-marred 1987 season, but he still hadn't fully recovered from his wrist injury. Pelluer wasn't the answer either in his four starts, as the Cowboys limped to a 7–8 mark, in a season highlighted by Herschel Walker's running and pass receiving.

By 1988, the Cowboys were clearly headed toward mediocrity. Age and injuries tore apart the offensive line, and Pelluer, the starter in fourteen of sixteen games, struggled with the rest of the unit. Pelluer had some big statistical days, including 300-yard outings against Philadelphia and Washington, but he also was prone to make killer mistakes.

Jimmy Johnson's arrival in 1989 coincided with the drafting of Aikman and Steve Walsh. The Cowboys were committed to the future, and Pelluer was dealt to the Kansas City Chiefs, where he ended his NFL career with two years as a backup. He attempted a comeback in 1996 with Frankfurt of the World League of American Football.

PENN, JESSE
Linebacker, 6′3″, 218 lbs., b. 9/6/62

Penn arrived as a second-round pick in 1985 with plenty of promise. A two-year starter at Virginia Tech as a stand-up defensive end, Penn faced a difficult adjustment to the pros, however.

Penn showed flashes of the big-play linebacker Tom Landry was seeking when, starting a game as a rookie in place of the injured Jeff Rohrer, he turned in 5 tackles and returned a blocked punt 49 yards for a touchdown against Cincinnati. In a preseason game against Green Bay, Penn returned an interception 77 yards for a touchdown.

In 1986, he started another game for the injured Rohrer, making six tackles, forcing a fumble, and recovering two fumbles against Detroit. He also had 2.5 sacks in 1986, playing on the nickel defense. But

Penn never was able to deliver consistently on his enormous potential, and 1986 was his final season in the NFL.

PEOPLES, GEORGE
Running back, 6′0″, 211 lbs., b. 8/25/61

Peoples was an eighth-round pick from Auburn in the 1982 draft who made the team as a rookie. A backup fullback and special teamer, Peoples was primarily a blocker who had 7 carries for 22 yards in his only season for the Cowboys. He spent a year with New England and two years with Tampa Bay as a reserve (one carry in three years) before retiring.

PERCIVAL, MAC
Kicker, 6′4″, 219 lbs., b. 2/26/40

The infamous Kicking Karavan of 1967, in which the Cowboys "interviewed" 1,300 aspiring kickers during a 23-city tour, produced only two players of any promise. Percival, out of Texas Tech, was one of them. Ironically, he was found in Dallas, where he was teaching high school; his wife entered him in the competition. He was signed by Dallas, but was traded to Chicago before the season opener. Over the space of seven years in the Windy City he became the Bears' all-time leading scorer. In 1974, his last in the NFL, he signed with Dallas when Toni Fritsch went down with a bad knee. He kicked 2 of 8 field goals and 4 of 5 extra points before giving way to Efren Herrera.

PERKINS, DON
Running back, 5′10″, 200 lbs., b. 3/4/38

Along with Don Meredith, Perkins signed a personal services contract with Tex Schramm in 1960, before the Cowboys were officially a team. He was a highly touted All-American halfback out of New Mexico. Although he was drafted by the Baltimore Colts, he signed with Dallas, and Baltimore received a ninth-round draft choice in 1962 as compensation. He reported to camp

Don Perkins *(From the collection of the Texas/Dallas History and Archive Division, Dallas Public Library)*

twenty pounds heavy; when it came time to do the Landry Mile, he couldn't finish it. Then he broke his foot playing for the College All-Stars and was lost for the season. There were some questions about his attitude.

But the next year, he came to camp ready to play; he gained 815 yards behind a nonexistent offensive line. Over the next seven years he was as steady a fullback as there was in the NFL, gaining 6,217 yards for a 4.1-yard average. He wasn't exceptionally fast, but he had acceleration; he could cover ten yards faster than Bullet Bob Hayes, and he was an excellent blocker. He was tough and aggressive—he once played an entire quarter with a broken arm—but off the field, he was a family man, a perfect gentleman, and almost devoid of ego. He gave the young team instant credibility in the running game, and for his efforts, he was named All-Pro once and participated in five Pro Bowls. In the 1966 NFL Championship Game against Green Bay, perhaps his finest moment, he gained 108 yards on 17 carries.

He walked away from the game at the age of thirty (he had originally wanted to retire two years before, but was talked out of it by Schramm) after the 1968 season, one of his most productive ever. The main reason? He wanted to spend more time with his wife and four children. He was the second player selected to the Cowboy Ring of Honor, in 1976.

PERKINS, RAY
See Replacement Games

PERRYMAN, ROBERT
Fullback, 6'2", 233 lbs., b. 10/16/64

Perryman's NFL notoriety was forged after he left the Cowboys. He played for Dallas for a short while late in the 1990 season after four years with the Patriots. He was one of the New England players named in a 1991 sexual harrassment suit filed by sportswriter Lisa Olsen of the *Boston Herald* for his actions with the Patriots before he became a Cowboy. He took advantage of Plan B to leave the Cowboys for Denver in 1991; after the 1992 season he was out of the league.

PETERSEN, KURT
Offensive lineman, 6'4", 278 lbs., b. 6/17/57

Petersen had the size, strength, quickness, and smarts to be a starting guard in five of his first six seasons with the Cowboys.

Petersen was a linebacker and defensive lineman at Missouri before the Cowboys took him in the fourth round in 1980. Petersen played special teams as a rookie, then was thrust into the starting lineup his second season when a knee injury to center Robert Shaw, in the second game, forced the Cowboys to move guard Tom Rafferty to center and Petersen into Rafferty's spot on the right side.

Injuries slowed Petersen in 1983 and 1984, keeping him out of the starting lineup

Cowboys All-Time Longest Kickoff Returns

102	Alexander Wright	vs. Atlanta, December 22, 1991 (TD)
101	Amos Marsh	vs. Philadelphia, October 14, 1962 (TD)
101	Ike Thomas	vs. NY Jets, December 4, 1971 (TD)
100	Mel Renfro	vs. San Francisco, November 7, 1965 (TD)
100	Mark Washington	@ Washington, November 22, 1970 (TD)
97	Thomas Henderson	vs. St. Louis, September 28, 1975 (TD)
97	James Dixon	@ Kansas City, October 22, 1989 (TD)
90	James Dixon	@ Green Bay, October 8, 1989
90	Alexander Wright	vs. NY Giants, September 16, 1990 (TD)
89	Ike Thomas	vs. LA Rams, November 25, 1971 (TD)

for five games. Petersen started the other fourteen games in 1983, thirteen in 1984, then started all sixteen games in 1985. "Pete" received a game ball for his performance against New Orleans in 1983, and another in 1984 for a game against St. Louis. Considered the strongest member of the team, Petersen played so well in 1982 that he was named second-team All-Pro by the Newspaper Enterprise Association.

But Petersen spent the 1986 season on injured reserve following summer knee surgery, and the nagging knee problem ended his career in 1987. Petersen remained in the Dallas area after retirement, pursuing a business career.

PETERSON, CAL
Linebacker, 6'3", 220 lbs., b. 10/6/52

The Cowboys' third-round draft choice in 1974, Peterson had been a defensive end at UCLA. He was big and fast, and the Cowboys converted him to a linebacker. He played well on special teams that year and the next, and saw some action his second year behind Edwards, Jordan, and Lewis. He went to the expansion Tampa Bay Buccaneers in 1976, then played three years in Kansas City and one with the Raiders before retiring.

PHILLIPS, KIRK
Wide receiver, 6'1", 202 lbs., b. 7/31/60

A rash of injuries to the Cowboys receivers in 1984 opened a roster spot for the rookie free agent from Tulsa. After Tony Hill hurt his shoulder in the season opener against the Los Angeles Rams, Phillips caught his first NFL pass and was involved in two fourth-quarter interference calls as the Cowboys came from behind for a 20–13 victory over the Rams.

Originally signed in 1983, Phillips injured his thumb in training camp and spent the season on injured reserve. He clinched a roster spot in the 1984 preseason with an 18-yard touchdown catch in the fourth quarter against Pittsburgh.

The cousin of former NFL linebacker Rod Shoate, Phillips was released by the Cowboys after the 1984 season and never played another regular-season down in the NFL.

PINDER, CYRIL
Running back, 6'2", 218 lbs., b. 11/13/46

Pinder spent five years with Philadelphia (where he led the team in rushing) and Chicago before signing with the Cowboys in 1973. He had 12 carries for only 15 yards, then played in the World Football League during the two years of its existence.

PLOEGER, KURT
Defensive lineman, 6'5", 259 lbs.,
b. 5/14/62

Drafted in the sixth round in 1985 out of tiny Gustavus Adolphus in St. Peter, MN, Ploeger spent his rookie season on injured reserve. Ploeger was a reserve in 1986 and later that year played for Green Bay. He went to Minnesota for one last year in the NFL in 1987.

POIMBEOUF, LANCE
Offensive guard, 6'3", 245 lbs., b. 10/11/40

Poimbeouf was a standout kicker out of Southwestern Louisiana who was signed as a free agent in 1963 for his strong leg, but Sam Baker handled every kick and punt during the year. Poimbeouf saw limited action as an offensive guard and then retired when he was released at season's end.

PONDER, DAVID
Defensive tackle, 6'3", 250 lbs., b. 6/27/62

Released on the final cut of the 1984 preseason, the Florida State free agent re-signed with the Cowboys for the 1985 season. Ponder played a reserve role in 1985, his lone Cowboys (and NFL) season.

PORTERFIELD, GARRY
Defensive end, 6'3", 225 lbs., b. 8/4/43

Porterfield was a 14th-round pick by Dallas in the 1965 draft. The Tulsa ex was a terror in preseason, splitting three helmets in as many weeks. But he was very slow, and he was released in mid-October and never played again.

POWE, KARL
Wide receiver, 6'2", 178 lbs., b. 1/17/62

Powe was more track star than football prospect when the Cowboys drafted him out

of Alabama State in the seventh round in 1985. He showed flashes of brilliance as a rookie, catching a critical 28-yard pass from third-string quarterback Steve Pelluer on a 3-and-15 in the fourth quarter. The catch kept alive what proved to be the winning touchdown drive, in a key game in December against the New York Giants that clinched the NFC East crown.

The following week, against San Francisco, Powe started for the injured Tony Hill and caught 7 passes for 127 yards, at that time the biggest numbers for a rookie Cowboys receiver since Drew Pearson in 1973.

Powe's 14 catches in 1985 were also the most by a Dallas first-year receiver since Pearson's 22 in 1973.

Powe's 1986 season was brief; he hurt his neck in the opener against the Giants and spent the rest of the season on injured reserve. Powe never played again in the NFL.

POZDERAC, PHIL
Offensive tackle, 6'9", 283 lbs.,
b. 12/19/59

A gawky rookie in 1982 training camp, Pozderac gained the attention of the Cowboys' veteran defensive linemen when he refused to back down in practice altercations. The fifth-round pick from Notre Dame made the roster as a rookie, then started two games his second season. By 1984, Pozderac was the starting right tackle and was also the tallest player in the league (one-half inch taller than teammate Ed "Too Tall" Jones).

"Poz" was physical and hard to intimidate, but in 1986 he became perhaps the best-known offensive lineman in the league, and for all the wrong reasons. Pozderac was flagged for a series of holding penalties in nationally televised games, and the Monday morning call of "Number 75...holding ...repeat third down" was heard around many an office water cooler that season.

Nevertheless, Pozderac opened the 1987 season as the starting right tackle, but he soured on football during the '87 players strike, and quit the game for a business career when the regular players returned to action.

PRICE, JIM
Tight end, 6'4", 247 lbs., b. 10/2/66

A three-year NFL veteran with the Los Angeles Rams drafted out of Stanford University, Price's cup of coffee with Dallas came about in 1993 when he was acquired from the Los Angeles Rams in the search for a backup for Jay Novacek. Give him credit for one catch for four yards in his last season in the NFL.

PRO BOWL

The All-Pro teams are selected by various press organizations; the Pro Bowl, on the other hand, is generally considered the truer judge of quality, since Pro Bowl players are selected by other players. Except for two years, 1986 and 1989, the Cowboys have had at least one player voted to the Pro Bowl since their very first season. (See back of book for complete Cowboys Pro Bowl selections.)

PRUITT, MICKEY
Linebacker, 6'1", 218 lbs., b. 1/10/65

The former University of Colorado star was claimed off waivers from Chicago before the 1991 season, becoming the only veteran reserve linebacker on a roster loaded with rookies. He filled in for the balance of the 1991 season, replacing an injured Ken Norton for one game, and spent the bulk of his two-year Dallas stay as a substitute and special-teams player. He was released after the 1992 season, his last in the NFL.

PUGH, JETHRO
Defensive tackle, 6'6", 255 lbs., b. 7/3/44

Jethro Pugh was one of super scout Gil Brandt's greatest finds—an eleventh-round draft pick in 1965 from an obscure little school in North Carolina called Elizabeth City State College. Over most of the next

Jethro Pugh

fourteen years, he would anchor the left side of the Dallas defensive line. He was a member of the Doomsday Defense, which was named by sportswriter Gary Cartwright in 1970, though most of the group had actually been together for several years before that—"Willie, Lilly, George, and Jethro" was a mnemonic some Cowboys fans used to remember the front four of the mid-sixties Cowboys.

Pugh played some at defensive end his first couple of years, but in 1967 he settled into the spot he'd secure through 1978—left tackle. Pugh was, like Dave Edwards, an unsung hero of the Doomsday Defense; although, amazingly, he was never an All-Pro or selected to the Pro Bowl, he was highly respected by his teammates and peers. (Sportswriter Jim Murray said that he was the greatest defensive lineman in the NFL never selected to the Pro Bowl.) Pugh led the team in sacks five consecutive years (1968–72).

He was quiet off the field, but a fierce competitor and a rock-solid, stabilizing presence in the defense. He played in the shadow of fellow tackle Bob Lilly, a perennial All-Pro, who received a great deal of attention from the media. Pugh, nicknamed "Buzz" (short for "Buzzard") by his teammates, made an amazing number of big plays in his fourteen years as a Cowboy, from blocked passes and caused fumbles to quarterback sacks and hurries.

But he's probably remembered more than anything else for his role in the infamous 1967 Ice Bowl: it was Pugh who Jerry Kramer blocked to open a slight hole through which quarterback Bart Starr slipped to score the winning touchdown. For the record, Packer center Ken Bowman made just as good a block on Pugh, who otherwise had an excellent game against Green Bay—and Kramer was probably offsides.

PUTNAM, DUANE
Offensive guard, 6'0", 230 lbs., b. 9/5/28

Three-time All-Pro Putnam had spent eight years with the Los Angeles Rams when he was acquired by the Cowboys in the 1960 expansion draft. He started at left guard that first year, then was traded to Cleveland for a draft choice. He spent a year there and another year in Los Angeles before retiring.

QUREISHI, SALAM

Not long after the Dallas Cowboys entered the NFL in 1960, Tex Schramm decided that the Cowboys needed a more scientific method of evaluating players and collating the wealth of material the Cowboys scouting department was beginning to collect. He contacted Service Bureau Corporation, a subsidiary of IBM, and asked them to develop a way to apply computer science to the problem. SBC sent Qureishi, a native of India, to Dallas to discuss the project with Schramm. Qureishi was ignorant of American football, but he was a computer genius. After some discussion, SBC entered into a contract with the Cowboys to develop a program that would provide analysis of the qualities of a good football player. The program, it was hoped, would eliminate emotions and other non-quantifiable prejudices that contributed to inaccurate evaluations.

After three years of long talks between Qureishi and Schramm, Landry, his coaches, and player personnel director Gil Brandt, the intellectual Indian learned about pro football and the qualities that made up a good football player—not only easily measurable qualities such as speed, height, and weight, but important intangibles such as quickness, body control, mental alertness, competitiveness, agility, balance, and explosiveness. It was then necessary to establish accurate measures of each one; this was done using the Cowboys' scouting questionnaire, which was filled out by their scouts, and college coaches around the country. The system even took into consideration evaluations of the scouts and coaches. An SMU psychologist, Dr. Robert Stoltz, was also consulted to assist in the task of determining clearer and more concise meanings for the descriptions the scouts were giving.

The Cowboy computer rankings were first used extensively in the 1965 draft—the year they picked a player from a small college named Jethro Pugh in the eleventh round. Soon after the project began, Los Angeles and San Francisco joined it, and the New Orleans Saints were included when they entered the NFL in 1967. (Schramm figured that the Cowboys needed more information to reduce the margin of error. Each club, however, shared only 40 percent of its information with the others.) The IBM investment was soon paying off, as draft after draft saw the Cowboys scoop up unheralded athletes and turn them into NFL stars. Soon other clubs (and sometimes Dallas) were joining draft information networks such as Blesto, Sepo, and the National Scouting Combine. Today, of course, every pro football program to some extent utilizes information bought from at least one combine in its scouting operation and draft decisions—a process started by Schramm and Qureishi.

RAFFERTY, TOM
Guard/center, 6'3", 250 lbs., b. 8/2/54

The Penn State ex was drafted in the fourth round of the 1976 draft, because the Dallas scouts rated him the best pulling guard available. He lived up to that reputation, earning a starting job in his second season, and keeping it for many years. He spent most of his rookie year on specialty teams, then replaced retired All-Pro Blaine Nye at right guard during the 1977 training camp. He also subbed for injured center John Fitzgerald for two games. But a pulled calf muscle slowed him early in 1978, and he alternated with Burton Lawless as play messenger for Landry most of the season.

Rafferty won the job outright the next year, and played well. He continued at right guard until the second game of 1981, when center Robert Shaw was injured. He replaced Shaw and started at center for the next several years (he had been the deep snapper for several years already). He teamed with guard Herb Scott on the block that cleared the way for Tony Dorsett's record 99-yard TD run at Minnesota, on January 3, 1983. He didn't miss a game in his career, and beginning with his second season, was a starter for all but the last few games of his 14-year career, when rookie Mark Stepnoski started at center the last four games of 1989. He retired after the 1989 season.

RANDALL, TOM
Offensive guard, 6'5", 245 lbs., b. 8/3/56

Randall, a defensive tackle at Iowa State, was selected by the Cowboys in the seventh round of the 1978 draft. He was converted to the offensive line and backed up Burton Lawless, Tom Rafferty, and Herb Scott during the season, including the Super Bowl loss against Pittsburgh. He was released before the next season, with the arrival of highly touted offensive lineman Robert Shaw.

RANDLE, SONNY
Wide receiver, 6'2", 190 lbs., b. 1/6/36

Ulmo "Sonny" Randle Jr. was an eleven-year veteran when he was picked up by the Cowboys just before the 1968 season. He caught four passes for 56 yards, then retired after the season.

Tom Rafferty

REECE, BEASLEY
Defensive back, 6'1", 195 lbs., b. 3/18/54

Reece was the Cowboys' ninth-round draft pick in 1976. He had been a cornerback at North Texas State, but he also saw some action at wide receiver in his rookie season in Dallas. Reece was very fast, but couldn't make the catches in a game; he had only 1 catch for 6 yards. He was sent to the Giants before the next season and spent seven solid years there, leading the team in interceptions twice (he had 8 in 1983). Near the end of 1983 he was traded to Tampa Bay. He retired after the 1984 season.

REESE, GUY
Defensive tackle, 6'5", 240 lbs., b. 9/22/39

Reese was a college star at SMU who had played high school ball in Dallas—the team's first homegrown Cowboy. He was a 15th-round draft choice in 1962. He and fellow rookies John Meyers and George Andrie teamed with sophomore Bob Lilly to form what was probably the most inexperienced defensive front four in NFL history—dubbed the Maverick Line by the local press. Two years later, he was traded to Baltimore for Jim Colvin, then in the expansion draft went to Atlanta for one year before retiring.

REEVES, DAN
Halfback/assistant coach, 6'1", 205 lbs., b. 1/9/44

Farmboy Dan Reeves had been a rollout quarterback at South Carolina, but fancy passers like Craig Morton and Jerry Rhome (both drafted by the Cowboys) were the pro preference in the 1965 college draft. Reeves wasn't drafted, so when Dallas signed him as a free agent, he knew he'd have to make it somewhere else. In training camp he was tried at several skill positions, but it was at running back that he stuck. He had only average speed, but he had a nose for the goal

Dan Reeves

line, great vision, and football smarts. He made the team and spent most of his first year on special teams, but the following year he led the team in rushing and was second to Bob Hayes in receiving. The next year his numbers were almost as good. "Frog," as his teammates called him, even threw an option pass occasionally (he would be listed as the Cowboys third quarterback one year). In 1968, after a great start, he tore ligaments in his knee in the fourth game of the year. He was out for the season, and he would never be the same runner; a series of operations would rob him of his running skills.

He played effectively in spots through the 1972 season—he caught a key pass in the 1970 NFL Championship Game against San Francisco—but primarily as a backup. In 1970, he was made an assistant coach, the youngest in the NFL; he coached the offensive backfield while he was still a part of it. He remained a coach under Landry until 1981 (he quit for one year, 1973), when he was named the head coach of the Denver Broncos, a team he led to three Super Bowls in the second half of the decade. He was hired in 1993 as head coach of the New York Giants.

RENFRO, MEL
Safety/cornerback, 6'0", 190 lbs.,
b. 12/30/41

The only man on those late-sixties Cowboys teams who gave Bob Hayes a run for his money, Renfro was a kickoff and punt returner par excellence. He had been a running back (and a sprinter, long jumper, and hurdler) at the University of Oregon, and it was clear from his first day he knew where to go with a football. (He also rushed 8 times for 52 yards in 1966.) Renfro was picked in the second round of the 1964 draft, and due to a logjam at receiver and running back, the Cowboys put him on defense.

He soon made his presence felt: he led the league in kickoff and punt return yardage, and for good measure, snagged 7 interceptions. Six years later he made the rare transition from free safety to cornerback,

Mel Renfro

the quickest position on the defense; two years later, he was voted to the Pro Bowl. Renfro was Deion Sanders before Deion, forcing opposing quarterbacks to throw away from him; sometimes he'd go an entire game without defending a pass. He was voted to the Pro Bowl his first ten years in the league, and was a five-time All-Pro. During his fourteen-year career (1964–77) he set many club records: 52 interceptions, a 26.4-yard career average on kickoff returns, and several others. Renfro gained 168 yards on 4 kickoff returns in a game against Washington in 1964, had a 90-yard interception return TD against St. Louis in 1965, a club-record 10 interceptions in 1969 (since surpassed by Everson Walls in 1981 with eleven), and a 110-yard kickoff return against San Francisco in 1965. The most controversial play in his career occurred in Super Bowl V; his tip of a Johnny Unitas pass resulted in a 75-yard TD by John Mackey. Renfro swore he never touched it, and films of the play are inconclusive. He was inducted into the Ring of Honor in 1981, and finally was elected to the Pro Football Hall of Fame in 1995.

RENFRO, MIKE
Wide receiver, 6'0", 187 lbs., b. 6/19/55

The Cowboys weren't known as big traders under Tex Schramm, Tom Landry, and Gil Brandt, but they did pull the trigger on a significant deal in 1984 when they acquired Renfro from the Houston Oilers for Butch Johnson, in what turned out to be a steal for Dallas.

The Oilers soon dumped Johnson, while Renfro remained a productive player through the 1987 season. "Fro" seemed destined to play for the Cowboys at some point in his career. He was born and raised in Fort Worth, where he starred at Arlington Heights High School. His father, Ray, a former All-Pro wide receiver with Cleveland from 1952–63, had been a Cowboys assistant coach from 1968–72. As a kid, Mike served as a Cowboys ball boy, and later starred for

Cowboys All-Time Longest Interception Returns

100	Mike Gaechter	vs. Philadelphia, October 14, 1962 (TD)
96	Dennis Thurman	@ Washington, September 6, 1981
94	Darren Woodson	@ Philadelphia, December 4, 1994 (TD)
90	Mel Renfro	@ St. Louis, October 4, 1965 (TD)
86	Mike Gaechter	vs. Washington, November 3, 1963
79	Thomas Henderson	vs. Tampa Bay, October 2, 1977 (TD)
78	Dennis Thurman	@ St. Louis, November 2, 1980 (TD)
74	Jim Ridlon	@ NY Giants, November 8, 1964 (TD)
68	Randy Hughes	vs. Cincinnati, September 30, 1979
68	Dextor Clinkscale	vs. NY Giants, September 18, 1983 (TD)

an awful TCU team in Fort Worth, setting school records for receptions, yards, and touchdowns.

Renfro wasn't the fastest, tallest, or best leaper among NFL receivers, but he was a precise route-runner with good hands who served as the Cowboys' possession receiver for four seasons.

During his six seasons with the Oilers (1978–83), Renfro had registered career highs for receptions (39) in 1981, and yardage (459) in 1980. In 1984, his first season for the Cowboys, Renfro grabbed 35 passes for 583 yards, and also threw a 49-yard touchdown pass to Doug Donley on a gadget play in a game against Philadelphia.

The following season, Renfro enjoyed a career year, catching 60 passes for 955 yards and 8 touchdowns. In his first seven seasons in the NFL, Renfro never had a 100-yard receiving day. But he had three 100-yard games in 1985, including a 164-yard effort against San Francisco, and another 100-yarder against Minnesota in 1987. Coach Tom Landry was a big fan of Renfro, in 1985 calling him "as valuable a player as we had" as the Cowboys captured another NFC East title.

Mike Renfro

Renfro was slowed by a preseason shoulder injury in 1986 and started only six of the 12 games for which he was activated, finishing with a disappointing 22 catches for 325 yards. But he was productive again in 1987 with 46 receptions for 662 yards and 4 touchdowns. He came up with a clutch 43-yard catch on a fourth-and-13 situation with 1:06 remaining to set up a tying field goal against New England in a game the Cowboys would go on to win in overtime, 23–17. Two weeks later on Thanksgiving Day against Minnesota, he caught 3 second-half touchdown passes, 2 in the final six minutes, to bring the Cowboys back from a 38–24 deficit. The game went into overtime, and the Cowboys eventually lost.

Renfro's career ended following the 1987 season. He finished only 337 receiving yards short of the 5,000-yard plateau, and 846 yards short of his dad's NFL totals. Renfro went on to a real estate career in Fort Worth and also owned several successful thoroughbred race horses.

Lance Rentzel

RENFRO, RAY
Assistant coach

Renfro, father of Cowboys receiver Mike Renfro, was a six-time All-Pro receiver at Cleveland, then an assistant coach at Detroit and Washington before coming to the Cowboys as their pass offense coach in 1968. He remained with Dallas through 1972.

RENTZEL, LANCE
Wide receiver, 6'2", 200 lbs., b. 10/14/43

The son of wealthy parents, Rentzel was a star running back at Oklahoma when he was drafted by Minnesota in 1965. For two years, he was often injured; he returned kickoffs and punts, and caught only two passes. His trade to Dallas was a result of a Minnesota disorderly conduct conviction (reduced from an indecent exposure charge)

and a suspended sentence. He blossomed as a flankerback for the Cowboys, leading the team in receptions three straight years, and gaining 1,009 yards in 1968.

Rentzel was a clutch receiver. In the 1967 Ice Bowl, he caught a 50-yard option pass from Dan Reeves that put Dallas temporarily ahead of Green Bay, and he had 13 receptions in one game (still a Dallas record), against Washington in 1970. Intelligent, good-looking, a talented musician, and married to actress Joey Heatherton, he seemed to have everything. But then, just days before the Thanksgiving Day game against Green Bay in 1970, he was charged with indecent exposure to a minor child, a felony. He quit the team immediately. In April 1971, after pleading guilty, he received a five-year probated sentence. He was traded in May 1971 to the Los Angeles Rams for tight end Billy Truax; he had several productive years there, until he retired after the 1974 season.

REPLACEMENT GAMES

The strike of 1987 was one of the most divisive episodes in Cowboys history. Dallas, perhaps more than any other NFL team, experienced inner turmoil as pro- and anti-NFL Players Association factions tore away at the guts of the team. Fading Cowboys stars Randy White, Danny White, and Tony Dorsett crossed the picket lines at various times during the strike and played with the strikebreakers, much to the displeasure of union leadership.

Even before Dorsett and the two Whites decided to play, the Cowboys had already lined up one of the strongest replacement teams in the league. Team president and general manager Tex Schramm knew a strike was coming, and he was in favor of letting the games go on, with or without the league's stars. Schramm had his scouts working overtime during training camp, identifying fringe players for a potential scab team. Meanwhile, franchises like the New York Giants were barely prepared for stocking a strike team, and when the league shut down in late September, all the decent players had been signed, leaving the Giants and their ilk to scour the sandlots for truck drivers and substitute teachers.

In the first two strike games, seventh-round draft choice Kevin Sweeney quarterbacked the Cowboys to smashing victories over the New York Jets (38–24) and the Philadelphia Eagles (41–22). Kelvin Edwards and Cornell Burbage were talented wide receivers, at least in relation to the defensive backs they faced. Ninth-round draft choice Alvin Blount supplied an adequate running attack behind a decent offensive line.

While pro-union fans in the Rust Belt turned their backs on the replacements, Dallas embraced them. A crowd of 40,622 turned out at Texas Stadium for the game against Philadelphia. On October 19, 60,612 showed up in Irving for a game against Washington.

The fans would go home disappointed from the third and final replacement game. The Redskins, under workaholic coach Joe Gibbs, had also put together a competitive strike team and Washington got by Dallas, 13–7, even though Danny White completed 21 of 36 passes for 262 yards and Dorsett rushed for 81 yards.

The regular players were back the following week, but the Cowboys' team unity had been destroyed. Dallas lost five of its last nine games to finish 7–8 and out of the playoffs.

The Replacement Players (Cowboys who played only in replacement games):

Adams, David	RB, Arizona
Armstrong, Jimmy	DB, Appalachian State
Blount, Alvin	RB, Maryland
Borreson, Rich	TE, Northwestern
Brady, Kerry	K, Hawaii
Burnette, Dave	OT, Central Arkansas
Cesario, Sal	G, Cal. Poly-SLO
Cisowski, Steve	DT, Santa Clara
Coleman, Anthony	DB, Baylor
Courville, Vince	WR, Rice
Duliban, Chris	LB, Texas
Dwyer, Mike	DT, Massachusetts
Flaherty, Harry	LB, Holy Cross
Green, Alex	CB, Indiana
Haynes, Tommy	S, Southern California
Hendrix, Tim	TE, Tennsesee
Hill, Bill	CB, Rutgers
Johnson, Walter	DT, Pittsburgh
Jones, Dale	LB, Tennessee State
Jones, E. J.	RB, Kansas
Lilja, George	C, Michigan
Livingston, Bruce	DB, Arkansas Tech
Perkins, Ray	DE, Virginia
Sawyer, Buzz	P, Baylor
Scott, Chuck	WR, Vanderbilt
Shearin, Joe	C, Texas
Shields, Joe	OL, Portland State
Simmons, Victor	LB, Central State-Ohio

Snyder, Loren	QB, Northern Colorado
Spivey, Sebron	WR, Southern Illinois
Swan, Russ	LB, Virginia
Timmer, Kirk	LB, Montana State
Walker, Gary	OL, Boston University
Watts, Randy	DE, Catawba
Westberry, Gary	C, Hampton
White, Gerald	FB, Michigan
Zentic, Mike	C, Oklahoma State

REYNOLDS, JERRY
Offensive tackle, 6'6", 315 lbs., b. 4/2/70

Reynolds spent what amounted to a red-shirt year with the Cowboys in 1994, activated but never getting into a game. He was a walk-on at the University of Nevada-Las Vegas and developed into an honorable mention All-Big West Conference in only his sophomore year. The Cowboys signed him off the Cincinnati Bengals practice squad in November 1994 after Erik Williams suffered his season-ending auto injury. He was activated but didn't play in the Washington game on November 20. He went to camp with the Cowboys in 1995 and was with them during the season, though he saw no action. He was waived by Dallas after the season and picked up by the Giants.

RHOME, JERRY
Quarterback assistant coach, 6'0", 185 lbs., b. 3/6/42

Rhome was a highly touted college passer at Tulsa, an accurate thrower who thrived on the rollout game. The Cowboys made him a future pick at number 13 in the 1964 draft. He signed with the team in 1965 along with that year's quarterback pick, Craig Morton, and saw plenty of action in the preseason. Meredith was struggling, and Rhome started a few games in the first half of the season. But neither he nor Morton showed the savvy necessary to take over as permanent starter, and at the season's mid-

point, Landry named Meredith the starter for the rest of the year. Rhome hit on 50 percent of his passes as a rookie.

The next year Meredith stayed relatively healthy, and the only extended action Rhome saw was in the last two games of the season, when he and Morton shared the reins as Meredith took a breather. He threw only 36 passes but completed 21 of them for a 58 percent completion rate. The next year, he saw even less action as Morton moved ahead of him on the depth chart; Rhome threw 9 completions in 18 attempts. He spent the next year on the taxi squad, then was traded at his request; Cleveland picked him up for a few future draft picks. He worked a year there as a backup, then was traded to Houston, where he saw the most action of his career subbing for an injured Charley Johnson; he passed for more than 1,000 yards. The next year he was dealt to the Rams, where he backed up Roman Gabriel and threw only 18 passes. He retired after the end of the season. He went into coaching, serving as an assistant at San Diego, Washington, and Seattle, and joined the Cowboys as quarterbacks coach in 1989.

RICHARDS, CURVIN
Running back, 5'9", 200 lbs., b. 12/26/68

A fourth-round Cowboys draft pick in 1991, Richards' elevator with the Cowboys crashed quickly. He was actually the team's number two rusher in 1992, his 176 yards not quite matching Emmitt Smith's 1,713. But the LaPorte, TX, product became the poster boy for just how easy it was to get on the bad side of coach Jimmy Johnson. With the Cowboys steaming along in 1992 toward their second consecutive playoff berth under Johnson, Richards suffered two ill-timed fumbles in Dallas' final game of the regular season, against Chicago. Richards was cut the next day, before the Cowboys' first playoff game scheduled for two weeks later. He played a year as a little-used backup for Denver in 1993, then was out of the NFL.

RICHARDS, GOLDEN
Wide receiver, 6'0", 172 lbs., b. 12/31/50

As the Cowboys' second-round draft pick in 1973, Richards showed an immediate return. The speedster out of Hawaii led the team in punt returns and, backing up Bob Hayes, caught 6 passes for 91 yards, including a 53-yard TD. He capped off the season with a 63-yard touchdown punt return against the Vikings in the NFC Championship Game. The next year, he won the starting split end job from Bob Hayes and responded with 26 catches for 467 yards and 5 touchdowns. In 1975 he had five fewer catches (21) but his 451 yards went for a 22-yard average and 4 TDs; he also led the team again in punt returns. He had a touchdown in the Championship Game win over Los Angeles, but in the Super Bowl, the Pittsburgh defense laid some vicious hits on him; he didn't have a single catch, and broken ribs finally finished him for the afternoon.

A hamstring injury the next year slowed Richards down, and finally forced him out of the lineup late in the season. He finished with 19 catches for 414 yards, another 22-yard average. (He gave up punt return duties to Butch Johnson.) In 1977 his regular-season numbers (17 catches, 225 yards) were down—throws to rookie Tony Dorsett and veteran Preston Pearson saw to that—but he had a 32-yard TD pass in the NFC Championship Game victory over Minnesota, and a 29-yard scoring catch in the Super Bowl win against Denver.

The following year was his final as a Cowboy; Richards' fragile body had taken a terrible beating during his five years in Dallas, and he wasn't the receiver he'd once been. In preseason, a sensational Tony Hill beat Richards and Butch Johnson out for the starting position. Richards didn't catch a pass for Dallas that year; a few weeks into the season he was traded to the Chicago Bears for a third-round draft choice. He had a good year there with 28 receptions for 381 yards, then played a backup role in 1979, his

Golden Richards (*From the collection of the Texas/Dallas History and Archive Division, Dallas Public Library*)

final season, catching only 5 passes and then going on the injured reserve list with a tear in his right knee. He later learned that he had played the season with a broken arm. The Bears released Richards in April 1980. He had a tryout with the Denver Broncos but he hurt his hand and was cut. He retired from football at the age of 29.

RICHARDS, HOWARD
Offensive lineman, 6'6", 262 lbs., b. 8/7/59

The Cowboys had big plans for Richards when they grabbed the second-team All-American from Missouri in the first round of the 1981 draft. Richards was big, strong, and agile, a finalist for the 1980 Lombardi Award given to the top college lineman in the country. But a series of injuries prevented Richards from delivering on those high expectations.

Richards was a prospect at tackle and guard his rookie year, but he was relegated to special teams because of the veteran stars ahead of him on the depth chart. In 1982, Richards started eight games at left guard, after Herb Scott injured a knee in preseason. When Scott came back in 1983, Richards and Scott were used for most of the season as play messengers while splitting time at left guard, although Richards also shuttled plays at right guard for two games and also started one game at left tackle.

When former Pro Bowler Pat Donovan retired prior to the 1984 season, the Cowboys looked to Richards as the replacement. But a training camp groin injury left him in a backup role behind Phil Pozderac. Richards became the starting left tackle midway through the 1984 season, after Pozderac moved to right tackle to replace the injured Jim Cooper. But after four games, Richards tore a tendon above his knee in a game against the Cardinals in his hometown of St. Louis. Richards, whose uncle, Ernie McMillan, was a Pro Bowl offensive tackle for the Cardinals, underwent knee surgery, and his 1984 season was finished.

Richards' knee did not heal as fast as he wanted, and he sat out the first seven games in 1985. Richards came back to play in 1985, and also served as a backup in 1986, but his knee never fully recovered, and his career was finished after the season.

RICHARDSON, GLOSTER
Wide receiver, 6'0", 200 lbs., b. 7/18/42

Richardson spent four years with Kansas City as a sometime starter before coming to the Cowboys in 1971, for receiver Dennis Homan. He had 8 catches for 170 yards that year, then spent three years with the Cleveland Browns before retiring in 1975.

RIDGWAY, COLIN
Punter, 6'5", 211 lbs., b. 2/19/39

In 1956, in Melbourne, Australia, 16-year-old Ridgway was the youngest track and field athlete to participate in a modern Olympics, finishing sixth in the high jump at 6'7¾". A few years later "the Boomer" highjumped over seven feet for Lamar Tech. He signed with the Cowboys in 1965 and spent most of the year on the taxi squad, although he punted 13 times for a 39-yard average. (It was in that 1965 preseason, in a game in San Francisco's Kezar Stadium, that a booming punt by Ridgway fell to the ground for a 3-yard gain.) The next year, he had a bad exhibition season and was released. He stayed in Dallas to work for a travel wholesale company. In 1994, he was murdered in his Highland Park house; in Spring 1996, an out-of-town suspect was arrested in an alleged murder-for-hire plot.

RIDLON, JIM
Safety, 6'1", 175 lbs., b. 7/11/34

After six steady years with the San Francisco 49ers, the former Syracuse standout was traded to Dallas in 1963. He started at safety for most of the next two years, earning All-Pro status in 1964 when he had 4 interceptions, one of them for a 74-yard TD. He retired after that season. Years later he wrote a 40-page text entitled *Keying Defenses* when he began a career as a professor at his alma mater.

RING OF HONOR

Cowboys president and general manager Tex Schramm came up with the idea to honor individuals who had made outstanding contributions to the organization. Schramm decided that the group, first known as the Court of Honor, would be very select, and that the honorees would have their names and years of service prominently displayed in silver letters on the wall at Texas Stadium. Inductees were originally chosen by Schramm, who was a one-man committee. Jerry Jones, who became owner in 1989, took over those duties when Schramm left the organization.

Cowboys All-Time Longest Fumble Returns

97	Chuck Howley	@ Atlanta, October 2, 1966 (TD)
86	Michael Downs	@ Houston, December 13, 1982 (TD)
84	Don Bishop	vs. St. Louis, October 28, 1962 (TD)
77	Jim Jeffcoat	vs. Washington, September 24, 1989 (TD)
72	Benny Barnes	@ San Francisco, October 11, 1981 (TD)
63	Jim Ridlon	vs. Philadelphia, December 6, 1964 (TD)
58	Chuck Howley	vs. San Francisco, November 7, 1965
54	Mike Montgomery	vs. Detroit, October 30, 1972 (TD)
42	Bob Lilly	@ St. Louis, December 15, 1963 (TD)
41	Bob Lilly	@ Washington, November 28, 1965

Bob Lilly was the first inductee in 1975, followed by Don Meredith and Don Perkins in 1976. Chuck Howley entered in 1977, then Mel Renfro received the honor in 1981, and Roger Staubach in 1983.

In 1989, Lee Roy Jordan became the first Ring of Honor member selected by Jones, followed by an originally reluctant Tom Landry in 1993. Randy White and Tony Dorsett entered the Pro Football Hall of Fame in 1994, and received Ring of Honor inductions together that same year.

ROACH, JOHN
Quarterback, 6'4", 195 lbs., b. 3/26/34

The former third-round draft pick from SMU had spent six years as a capable backup quarterback (first for the Cardinals, then behind Bart Starr at Green Bay) when he retired after the 1963 season to Dallas. But Eddie LeBaron had just quit the Cowboys, leaving Don Meredith as the lone signal-caller. When Tex Schramm called, Roach took the offer, and joined the team twelve days before the season opener. He saw a decent amount of action behind the injury-prone Meredith and even started a few games, hitting 32 of 68 passes for 1 touch-

down and 6 interceptions. He retired, this time for good, after the season.

ROBERTS, ALFREDO
Tight end, 6'3", 252 lbs., b. 3/17/65

Unfortunately for the popular tight end from the University of Miami, the spotlight he attracted in two seasons playing with the Cowboys didn't come close to matching the attention he received when he and former teammate Michael Irvin were confronted by Irving, TX, police along with two "self-employed models" at a Residence Inn during the spring of 1996. Though illegal drugs were found in the room, no charges were filed against Roberts.

He came to Dallas via Plan B free agency from Kansas City to be Jay Novacek's backup. While not the same quality receiver as Novacek, Roberts was a valuable blocker who made significant contributions to the Emmitt Smith Express. He caught 16 passes for 136 yards in 1991, but a foot injury limited him to 3 receptions for 36 yards the next year, his last in the NFL. He owns two homes back in his native South Florida that are used for a family-owned project called

Home Sweet Home that helps handicapped children.

ROBINSON, LARRY
Running back, 6'4", 210 lbs., b. 4/6/51

Robinson was another Cowboy computer special—a good athlete who hadn't played a down of college football. He had been a basketball player at Tennessee, and was signed as a free agent in 1973. He made the club as a running back and appeared in four games as a kick returner (4 for 86 yards), and on special teams, and he had 2 rushes for 17 yards. He was released after the season.

ROE, BILL
Linebacker, 6'3", 232 lbs., b. 2/6/58

The Cowboys' fortunes were fading by the mid-eighties because of a series of bad draft picks and poor luck with players like Roe. Roe was a third-round pick out of Colorado in 1980, the team's highest pick because a trade for veteran defensive lineman John Dutton had sent first- and second-round selections to the Baltimore Colts.

Roe was a special-teams standout as a rookie, then spent the 1981 season on injured reserve following a sprained ankle in training camp. The South Bend, IN native never was able to challenge for a starting job. He spent 1983–85 in the USFL, then finished his NFL career in 1987 with the New Orleans Saints.

ROHRER, JEFF
Linebacker, 6'2", 222 lbs., b. 12/25/58

The Cowboys selected Rohrer in the second round of the 1982 draft, making him the highest NFL draft pick from Yale since Dallas chose Calvin Hill in the first round in 1969.

Rohrer developed into a solid starter at outside linebacker from 1985–87 after spending his first three seasons as a backup

on the outside and in the middle, and as a special teamer.

The native of Manhattan Beach, CA took over the right linebacker spot from Anthony Dickerson in 1985, finishing with 54 total tackles. Rohrer enjoyed his best season in 1986 with 111 tackles, second on the team to middle linebacker Eugene Lockhart. He led the team in tackles in 4 of 16 games and caused a team-high 4 fumbles.

In 1987, Rohrer went to the bench on passing downs, but he still led all Cowboys linebackers with four sacks, more than his first five seasons combined. In Dallas' upset victory over the defending Super Bowl champion New York Giants at Texas Stadium, Rohrer had a sack and a team-high 8 tackles. Against Miami, he had 9 tackles and a sack, and then followed that performance four days later, on Thanksgiving Day, with a season-high 10 tackles against Minnesota.

A serious back injury sidelined him the entire 1988 season. He tried to come back in training camp the following year but was cut. Intelligent and articulate, Rohrer retired and moved on to a business career.

ROPER, JOHN
Linebacker, 6'1", 228 lbs., b. 10/4/65

Some Cowboy fans expected big things from Roper when he was acquired from Chicago, before the 1993 season. After all, he was a familiar name from the great Texas A&M Wrecking Crew defense of the late eighties. And he had made a dent in the Bears defense over four years, though he was considered moody and unpopular among his peers. What Coach Jimmy Johnson expected was at least someone who could stay awake during team meetings. But Roper was discovered dozing during a special-teams meeting. Three days later, his club-high two sacks through five games didn't mean much to Johnson, and he was released. He caught on with Philadelphia for the rest of the 1993 season, his last in the NFL.

Cowboys Biggest Playoff Days——Rushing

160	Tony Dorsett	vs. LA Rams, December 28, 1980
150	Emmitt Smith	vs. Green Bay, January 14, 1996
143	Duane Thomas	@ San Francisco, January 3, 1971
135	Duane Thomas	vs. Detroit, December 26, 1970
132	Emmitt Smith	vs. Buffalo, January 30, 1994
125	Calvin Hill	@ San Francisco, December 23, 1972
114	Emmitt Smith	vs. Philadelphia, January 10, 1993
114	Emmitt Smith	@ San Francisco, January 17, 1993
110	Tony Dorsett	vs. Tampa Bay, January 9, 1983
108	Don Perkins	vs. Green Bay, January 1, 1967

ROSS, DOMINIQUE
Fullback, 6'0", 203 lbs., b. 1/12/72

Ross left college early to get into the NFL in 1995, but not the conventional way. He finished his course work at Valdosta (GA) State with a year's eligibility remaining. He became the first player in school history to rush for more than 1,000 yards, which he did as a sophomore. He signed with Dallas as a free agent and spent almost the entire 1995 season on the practice squad; although he was activated December 21, his only action was on December 25 against Arizona, with two special teams tackles.

ROY, ALVIN
Assistant coach

Roy joined Landry's staff in 1973 as a strength and conditioning coach, after earlier stints with the Chargers and the Chiefs. His background was in weightlifting and strength conditioning (he had trained the winning American weightlifting team in the 1952 Olympics), and his impact on the Cowboys was dramatic. In the next few years, Landry credited him with helping Dallas to dramatically outscore opponents

(by more than two to one) late in the game. He left the Cowboys in early 1975.

RUCKER, REGGIE
Wide receiver, 6'2", 190 lbs., b. 9/21/47

Rucker was a free agent signed by the Cowboys in 1969. He spent the year on the taxi squad, but was activated early in 1970 when Lance Alworth cracked some ribs in the preseason. He performed well, catching nine passes for 200 yards, but was traded early in the 1971 season to the Giants, and then the Patriots. In the next ten years (the last seven with Cleveland) he blossomed as a receiver; he retired with 447 catches for 7,065 yards.

RUZEK, ROGER
Kicker, 6'1", 195 lbs., b. 12/17/60

Ruzek gained a reputation as a solid kicker in the USFL when he converted 70.8 percent of his field goal attempts for the New Jersey Generals in 1984–85.

In 1987, his first season in Dallas, Ruzek established several firsts for a Cowboys player. He kicked 5 field goals in a game against the Rams, he tied an NFL record by making 4 field goals in a quarter against the Rams, and he was successful on 88 percent (22 for 25) of his field goal attempts.

His most amazing feat, however, was that he became the first Cowboys player to be released, re-signed in the same training camp, and then make the final roster. An ankle injury forced Ruzek to revamp his kicking style in 1987 training camp and he was the first kicker released. When he was re-signed two weeks later, Ruzek reverted to his old style, and he went on to finish second in the NFL and first in the NFC in field goal percentage. His 92 points tied for fourth-best among the league's kickers.

Coach Tom Landry liked Ruzek's consistency, but in 1988, Ruzek's career took a sour turn. He missed training camp and the first two regular-season games due to a contract holdout, and when he returned, Ruzek struggled, raising the ire of fans disgusted with highly paid athletes who didn't perform.

Ruzek got himself straightened out on October 23, when he made all 3 attempts against Philadelphia. That ignited a streak of 7 straight field goals, including a 50-yarder against Minnesota in mid-November. But Ruzek finished the season 12-for-22 and lost his job to Luis Zendejas, who had handled the kicking chores during Ruzek's holdout, midway through the 1989 season.

The roundabout paths taken by Zendejas and Ruzek underscore the nomadic life of a kicker. Zendejas had been waived by the Philadelphia Eagles in 1989, and Ruzek signed with the Eagles that same year, following his release by the Cowboys, and remained Philadelphia's kicker until 1993.

St. Edward's University

After 25 years in Thousand Oaks, CA, new owner Jerry Jones moved summer training camp to Austin, TX, and the campus of St. Edward's University in 1990. Just 200 miles down I-35 from Dallas, St. Ed's is a convenient location for Cowboys fans in Texas. During the training camp, held from mid-July to mid-August, the team draws an average of almost 100,000 fans to the free-of-charge practice sessions and annual scrimmages with other NFL teams.

Saldi, Jay
Tight end, 6'3", 225 lbs., b. 10/8/54

Saldi was the only free agent rookie to make the Cowboys in 1976. He worked hard in training camp and was thrust into the position of Billy Joe DuPree's backup after Jean Fugett signed with the Redskins and Percy Howard injured a knee in preseason. He had only 1 catch for 19 yards, but he occasionally spotted a healthy DuPree and played especially well on specialty teams. In 1977 he was named special-teams captain, a duty he filled until he suffered a broken right forearm early in 1978 against St. Louis. He had 11 receptions for 108 yards in 1977, and had a key fumble recovery on a punt in the NFC Championship Game against Minnesota. In his aborted 1978 season he had only 3 catches, but he came back strong the next year and served as a second tight end and sometime third wide receiver. He caught 14 passes that year for 181 yards, and he had 2 catches and a TD (Roger Staubach's last) in a playoff loss to Los Angeles. Saldi didn't have the greatest hands in the league, but he had good speed and ran tight routes, and he blocked well.

In 1980 he had his best year as a Cowboy. The Cowboys used a two-tight-end setup more than ever before, and Saldi also alternated as a play messenger with DuPree. The result was 25 catches for 311 yards, 1 less than DuPree; his 37-yard grab and run to the 3 to set up the go-ahead TD in the NFC wild-card victory over Los Angeles was his biggest. But the next year he had only 8 receptions for 82 yards as a third-year Doug Cosbie began alternating with DuPree. He had only 1 catch for 8 yards in his last year with Dallas; he was traded to Chicago in 1983, where, as a backup, he caught 12 passes for 119 yards. The next year, his final in the NFL, he had 9 catches for 90 yards.

Salonen, Brian
Tight end/linebacker, 6'3", 226 lbs., b. 7/29/61

The 1984 tenth-round pick from Montana made the team as a rookie tight end and played all sixteen games on special teams. He was moved to linebacker, a position he hadn't played since high school, prior to 1985 training camp.

That set up a busy year for Salonen. On Wednesdays and Thursdays during the season, he went to meetings and practiced with the defense as the backup to outside linebacker Mike Hegman. On Fridays he worked with the offense as the third tight end. And since he was on every special team, he also had to attend those meetings and practices. Salonen played the second half of a 1985 game at St. Louis when Hegman was injured, his only extended game action for the Cowboys. A serious groin injury kept him on injured reserve for the next two years, after which he retired.

SANDEMAN, BILL
Defensive tackle, 6'6", 255 lbs., b. 11/30/42

Sandeman was signed as a free agent in 1965, but he injured a knee and missed the entire season. He played a backup role on the defensive line in 1966, then was picked up by New Orleans for a year. He spent the next seven years with the Atlanta Falcons, retiring after the 1973 season.

SANDERS, DEION
Cornerback, 6'1", 185 lbs., b. 8/9/67

Dallas' ultimate football villain became one of its favorite heroes in 1995. After having rented his services to the San Fran-

cisco 49ers for their Super season of 1994, "Prime Time" brought his act to Valley Ranch. Joining the Cowboys in October, following a media-driven courting and arthroscopic surgery, Sanders became an offensive and defensive threat.

It took a while before he was integrated fully into the Dallas defense, but toward the end of the season and in the playoffs, he made a major contribution to the Cowboys' drive toward Super Bowl XXX. Sanders finished his half-season with two interceptions and 10 passes defensed. His 47-yard catch down the middle of the Pittsburgh defense was one the game's most electric plays, and set up the Troy Aikman to Jay Novacek pass that gave Dallas an early 10–0 lead. He made his Cowboy debut in Atlanta, against his first NFL team—underscoring the fact that he chose to sign with the Cowboys at least in part for the opportunity to play regularly on offense in addition to defense.

Deion Sanders

Sanders has been called the best cornerback ever to play the game, and it may be true. He has tremendous speed and instincts, and despite his flamboyant media image, is an observant student of the game. He can take away one entire side of the field for an opposing quarterback.

He called his Cowboy Super Bowl win more thrilling than his 'Niners Super win. "I didn't even get to touch the trophy last year," he said. As for baseball—he has played with the Atlanta Braves, New York Yankees, Cincinnati Reds, and San Francisco Giants—he said he would become a full-time football player in 1996.

SARGENT, BRODERICK
Fullback, 5'11", 215 lbs., b. 9/16/62

After two years with the Cardinals, Baylor ex Sargent signed with the Cowboys in 1989. Starting three of the first four games at fullback, he had 20 carries for 87 yards and 6 catches for 50 yards, and also saw special-teams action. He was cut before the 1990 season. "Sarge" headed north of the border to play for the World League's Montreal Machine in 1991.

SATURDAY NIGHT MASSACRE

Arkansas oilman Jerry Jones was hungry to join the club of NFL owners, and when Dallas businessman "Bum" Bright decided to sell the team following the 1988 season, Jones was soon at his door. Jones had the resources, and Bright had grown disenchanted with a deteriorating team.

On the night of February 24, Jones and his University of Arkansas football teammate and college roommate, Jimmy Johnson, went to dinner at a popular Mexican restaurant near downtown Dallas. A newspaper reporter happened to be at the restaurant, a photographer was notified, and the resulting photo decorating the sports page the following morning captured the images of two men who were celebrating. Clearly, there was more to this than just rumors.

Jones had reached an agreement with Bright to buy the team and Texas Stadium lease for an estimated $150 million. Johnson, the highly successful coach of the University of Miami, would take over for coach Tom Landry. Jones flew to Austin that morning to notify Landry, who had an off-season home in the state capital.

Back in Dallas, Jones held a press conference on that Saturday night, February 25. The event was carried live on local TV, before an audience of horrified fans who knew things would never be the same. Jones had experienced little contact with the media in his hometown of Little Rock, and he came off as "Jethro" Jones, at one point telling the world that he would have complete control of the team, down to the "jocks and socks."

Even those who had suggested that Landry was over the hill expressed their outrage. But four years later, most of those same fans were toasting Jones and Johnson as the Cowboys captured the first of three Super Bowls in four seasons.

SAWYER, BUZZ
See Replacement Games

SAXON, MIKE
Punter, 6'3", 200 lbs., b. 7/10/62

Saxon's eight-year run as the Cowboys' punter was the second-longest in team history, behind Danny White's nine years. Saxon took over for White in 1985, and the former San Diego State walk-on became one of the league's best.

An eleventh-round pick by Detroit in 1984, Saxon was released by the Lions on the final cut, after averaging 43.5 yards per attempt in preseason. The Cowboys signed Saxon as a free agent in 1985, and the rookie soon demonstrated he could handle the pressure when his first punt against Washington, in a nationally televised Monday night opener, sailed 57 yards. Saxon averaged 41.9

yards per punt in 1985, the highest ever by a Dallas rookie.

In 1986, he set a team record for punts with 86, shattering White's previous mark of 82 in 1984. Each summer, the Cowboys brought other punters to training camp, but by the start of the regular season, Saxon was still their man. His specialty was the pooch kick, dropping the ball inside an opponent's 20-yard line, and he got that job done 16 or more times per year from 1987–92, best in the league. He also excelled at getting the ball off ahead of the rush, going 190 straight kicks without a block from 1986–89.

At the end of the 1992 season, Saxon had the longest tenure of any punter with an NFC team, and second-longest in the NFL. He also had gone 53 straight games and 220 consecutive punts without having one blocked until the Buffalo Bills got to one in the first quarter of the Cowboys' lopsided victory in Super Bowl XXVII.

Coach Jimmy Johnson had little patience with punters or kickers, however, and he felt Saxon was slipping, so he released him prior to the 1993 season. Saxon didn't go long without a job, however, continuing his career with the New England Patriots in 1993, before signing with the Minnesota Vikings for the 1994 season.

SCHAUM, GREG
Defensive end, 6'4", 250 lbs., b. 1/1/54

Schaum, the Cowboys' seventh-round pick in the 1976 college draft, had been a tackle and guard at Michigan State. But in his one year in Dallas, he was the only backup for defensive ends Ed Jones and Harvey Martin. He was primarily a special-teams player. A knee injury forced him to miss the entire 1977 season; the next year, he was traded to New England, where he played for one year before retiring.

SCHOENKE, RAY
Offensive tackle, 6'3", 225 lbs., b. 9/10/41

Schoenke was an eleventh-round pick from SMU in Dallas' 1963 draft. A center in college, he played two years for the Cowboys as a backup offensive tackle. He sat out a year with an injury, and then played ten years on the offensive line of the Washington Redskins.

SCHRAMM, TEX
General manager/president

The man christened Texas E. Schramm was born in California to two native Texans who were determined that their son would attend a Texas college. When he graduated with a journalism degree from the University of Texas in 1947 (his college years, like Tom Landry's, were interrupted by WWII; he spent four years with the Air Transport Command, rising to the rank of captain), he went to work for the *Austin American* on their sports staff. His father, a Los Angeles stockbroker, helped him land the job of publicity director for the fresh-from-Cleveland Rams. At a salary of $100 per week, he began learning how a football organization worked. The Rams became successful, and so did Schramm; by the time they won the 1951 championship he was general manager. (Future NFL Commissioner Pete Rozelle was his PR man.)

Six years later, he left the Rams to work for CBS television in New York as assistant to Bill MacPhail, the network's vice president of sports. In 1959, when Clint Murchison Jr. was looking for someone with front-office experience to organize his new NFL franchise in Dallas, his friend, Chicago owner George Halas, suggested Schramm. Murchison called and found Schramm eager to return to the NFL. He was hired as general manager and vice-president of the club at $36,500 a year, along with some enticing stock options. When Murchison expressed his interest in New York assistant coach Tom Landry to head the Dallas coaching staff, Schramm went after him. After Schramm convinced his fellow UT alum that he would have absolute authority over the team on the field, Landry agreed to take the job.

Murchison didn't meddle with the

running of the team, so Schramm had virtually complete control over the operation. More than anything, Schramm was a marketing genius. He grafted a Hollywood glamour onto the Cowboys operation that coincided with the rise in popularity of the NFL, and it was largely due to his work that the Cowboys became known as America's Team. He realized the importance of a good scouting system, and was instrumental in designing the Cowboys' famed computer evaluation system. Schramm, Landry, and two first-year hires—scout and former NFL coach Hampton Pool, and part-time scout Gil Brandt—soon had a scouting organization that became the envy of the league. When they hired an IBM statistical expert to devise a computerized rating system, it revolutionized pro football scouting and drafting.

In 1967 Schramm was made president of the Cowboys, and the stock options which he exercised made him part owner and a wealthy man. He was instrumental in working with NFL Commissioner Pete Rozelle on the merger in 1970 between the NFL and the AFL. For the next twenty years he worked tirelessly to solidify, through good seasons and bad, the Cowboys' position at the top of the NFL marketing heap. When the organization was bought by H.R. "Bum" Bright in March 1984, he stayed on as president and general manager. He left the organization less than two months after Tom Landry was fired in 1989; his authorized biography, *Tex*, written with Bob St. John, was published in 1988.

SCHULTZ, CHRIS
Offensive tackle, 6'8", 288 lbs., b. 2/16/60

The Cowboys drafted Schultz, a native of Hamilton, Ontario, in the seventh round of the 1983 draft purely on potential. Schultz had played defensive line at the University of Arizona until he was switched to offensive tackle as a senior, and the Cowboys had enjoyed some success with several of these defense-to-offense changes in postion.

Schultz had the size and quick feet

necessary to excel at the position, but he played sparingly as a rookie, primarily on special teams. He spent 1984 on injured reserve with a bad knee suffered in training camp.

Schultz built himself up from 265 to 288 pounds while on injured reserve, and in 1985, he worked himself into the starting lineup for nine games at both left and right tackle. He was called the most improved player on the team by line coach Jim Myers, but Schultz could never overcome the knee problems, and 1985 was his final NFL season. Schultz went on to a career in the Canadian Football League.

SCHWANTZ, JIM
Linebacker, 6'2", 232 lbs., b. 1/23/70

The Purdue ex learned the Cowboys' defensive scheme...with the Chicago Bears, of all teams. He signed with the Bears as a free agent in 1992 and spent two years on Chicago's practice squad. Part of that term included a stint under head coach Dave Wannstedt, who went to the Bears after serving as Jimmy Johnson's defensive coordinator, both with the Cowboys and at the University of Miami. Mostly contributing on Dallas special teams in 1994, his glory day came in the November 20 game against Washington when he recorded 3 solo tackles in the fourth quarter. In the 1995 season he was third on the team with 23 special-teams tackles, and he led the team with 10 in three post-season games; he also saw action at linebacker several times throughout the year.

SCOTT, CHUCK
See Replacement Games

SCOTT, HERB
Offensive guard, 6'2", 250 lbs., b. 1/18/53

Scott was one of the Dirty Dozen rookies who made the team from the draft of 1975. He was drafted out of obscure Virginia Union in the thirteenth round and barely made the Cowboys. He learned the offensive

Herb Scott

line and made a few starts for Burton Lawless when Lawless was hurt. The following year, he won the starting job at left guard—a job he kept for seven years and two Super Bowls.

Scott suffered from hamstring problems early in his career—during the second half of the 1976 season he alternated with Burton Lawless as a play messenger, and in 1977 injuries cost him four starts. He was Dallas' best open-field blocker, and he was also an excellent pass blocker; he and guard Tom Rafferty teamed on the block that cleared the way for Tony Dorsett's record 99-yard TD run at Minnesota on January 3, 1983. "Pooch" was voted to the Pro Bowl three times (1979, 1980, 1981) and the All-Pro team twice (1980, 1981). He retired after the 1984 season.

SCOTT, KEVIN
Running back, 5'9", 177 lbs., b. 10/24/63

Scott came to the Cowboys in 1989 after playing two seasons with San Diego. He was actually second on the team in receptions with nine when he tore the anterior cruciate ligament in his left knee in the fourth quarter of the season opener against Washington. So much for his status as the backup tailback behind Herschel Walker and as an extra fullback to block on passing downs. That was the end of his NFL career.

SCOTT, SEAN
Linebacker, 6'1", 190 lbs., b. 4/10/60

Scott was a hard-hitting free agent from Maryland who made the squad in 1988 as a reserve linebacker and special-teams player. He was released after the season, his only one in the NFL.

SCOTT, VICTOR
Defensive back, 6'0", 203 lbs., b. 6/1/62

Another in the series of high draft picks of the eighties that didn't pan out for the Cowboys, the speedy Scott came with much promise in the second round of the 1984 draft.

A two-time Big Eight All-Conference selection and a 1983 second-team All-American at Colorado, Scott arrived at training camp in 1984 competing with Ron Fellows and Rod Hill for the starting right cornerback position. Scott was raised in a tough neighborhood in East St. Louis, IL, and he used athletics as his ticket out of the ghetto.

Scott debuted as an extra defensive back on passing downs, and he turned in 19 tackles and an interception as a rookie. The Cowboys considered him a better bet as a safety, but played him at cornerback because that was a need area in the mid-eighties, especially after defensive coordinator Ernie Stautner switched cornerback Dennis Thurman to safety in 1984.

In 1985, Scott took some steps toward his goal of starting, coming up with one of the big plays of the season. He intercepted a Phil Simms pass with 46 seconds left to preserve the Cowboys 28–21 victory over the Giants that clinched another NFC East title for Dallas. Scott filled in for the injured Fellows for three games at cornerback; he led the secondary with 3 sacks on blitzes; he earned 4 game balls for his special teams plays; and he returned an interception 26 yards for a touchdown against Washington.

Hamstring problems and a broken wrist ruined Scott's 1986 season, as he played in only five games. Big things were expected in 1987, but a strained chest muscle incurred in training camp limited him to five games and no starts. Injuries again reduced Scott's playing time in 1988, his final season in the NFL.

SECULES, SCOTT
Quarterback, 6'3", 219 lbs., b. 11/8/64

The Cowboys thought so much of Secules's potential that they kept the 1988 sixth-round draft pick from Virginia on the roster as a fourth quarterback, even though he didn't take a snap in a preseason or regular-season game his rookie year.

Secules was so impressive in 1989 spring mini-camps that new coach Jimmy Johnson predicted a bright future. But with Troy Aikman and Steve Walsh ahead of him on the depth chart, there was no possibility of playing time for Secules, who was traded to the Miami Dolphins. He played three years there as a little-used backup to Dan Marino. After sitting out 1992 with a shoulder injury, he was traded to New England, where he had the busiest season of his career subbing occasionally for Drew Bledsoe: 75 completions on 134 attempts. He retired after the season.

SELLERS, RON
Wide receiver, 6'4", 195 lbs., b. 2/5/47

Sellers played three productive years with New England before coming to the Cowboys in 1972. He had a fine year with 31 receptions for 653 yards, capping it off with the winning touchdown in the final seconds of a dramatic come-from-behind win over San Francisco in the playoffs. He was traded to Miami in 1973, where he played one season before retiring from the NFL.

SEPTIEN, RAFAEL
Kicker, 5'10", 179 lbs., b. 12/12/53

Septien is the greatest placekicker in Cowboys history, holding the job from 1978–86. In the mid-nineties, Septien was still the franchise's all-time scoring leader with 874 points and topped the field goal list with 162.

Born in Mexico City, Jose Rafael Septien Michel was the son of a two-time member of Mexico's World Cup soccer team. Rafael could also kick a football, and he went on to Southwest Louisiana, where he booted 9 field goals of more than 50 yards.

Septien was selected by New Orleans in the tenth round of the 1977 draft, was released in training camp, then was signed by the Los Angeles Rams. Septien caught on as the Rams' kicker, and he led all rookies in 1977 with 86 points and 18-of-30 field goals. When Septien was released by Los Angeles after the final preseason game of 1978, the Cowboys immediately signed him.

Septien scored at least 90 points and hit at least 15 field goals in seven of his nine years with the Cowboys. Septien seemed to save his best for pressure situations, converting 18-of-21 post-season field goal attempts, including 15 in a row from Super Bowl XIII through the 1982 NFC title game. He converted all 3 career field goal attempts in overtime. He was also consistent, scoring in 128 straight games from the second game of his rookie year through the eleventh game of the 1985 season.

A back injury limited his effectiveness in a roller-coaster 1985 season. Septien converted all 3 field goal tries in the season opener against Washington, made only 3 of 10 attempts in the next three games, in-

Rafael Septien

cluding a one-for-five disaster against Houston, but finished by making 13 of his last 15. He then pulled a muscle in his kicking leg during warmups for a playoff game against the Rams and was unable to play.

Septien bounced back with 15 field goals in 21 tries and 88 points in 1986, but he was beset by personal problems and the Cowboys released him following that season. Septien later pleaded guilty to charges of indecency with a child. He never played again in the NFL.

SHANNON, RANDY
Linebacker, 6'1", 221 lbs., b. 2/24/66

It's a rare feat for an eleventh-round draft pick to make an NFL roster. (In fact, it can't be done anymore, since the draft no longer lasts eleven rounds.) But here was an eleventh-rounder who was a starter three weeks into his rookie season. Shannon was picked late out of the University of Miami in Jimmy Johnson's first Cowboy draft. When Shannon made the starting unit for the game against Washington, he proved it was no fluke by recording 11 tackles. For the record, Shannon was the first Cowboy rookie to start at outside linebacker since Dave Edwards in 1963. He ended up starting four games that season and finished second in special-teams tackles. The downside for Shannon was that he could start four games because the 1989 Cowboys were only good enough to win one game. As Johnson and Company added better quality players at a rapid rate, Shannon lasted only one more season as a backup in Dallas, and was released after 1990, his last year in the NFL.

SHARK DANCE

The Shark Dance was the name of special teamster Kenny Gant's anticipatory dance, which he would perform before each

Dallas kickoff for a few years in the early 1990s; the Texas Stadium band obliged by playing the familiar *Jaws* movie theme. Gant also performed the dance when he turned in a big play on defense.

SHAW, ROBERT
Center, 6'4", 261 lbs., b. 10/15/56

The Cowboys had great expectations for Shaw when they drafted him out of Tennessee in the first round in 1979. Dallas had never invested a first-round pick on a center in their history, and the quick, strong, and brainy Shaw seemed ideal to anchor their line through the eighties. The Cowboys hadn't taken an offensive lineman in the first round since John Niland in 1966.

Shaw struggled as a rookie in 1979, starting only one game and contributing mainly on special teams. But he worked hard in the weight room in 1980 and reported to training camp 20 pounds heavier, and with a much better idea of what it took to excel in the NFL.

When veteran starter John Fitzgerald went down with an injury late in the season, Shaw moved in to start the last two games of the regular season and all three playoff games. He received a game ball for his performance in a wild card victory over the Los Angeles Rams, earning the praise of the coaching staff for his blocking against linebacker Jack "Hacksaw" Reynolds.

Shaw was on the verge of establishing himself as one of the NFL's elite centers in 1981 when he injured a knee in the second game against St. Louis. He tried rehabilitating the knee without surgery and started a game against San Francisco a month later, but the knee failed to hold up, and he underwent surgery the following week. A budding career was over.

Shaw's career in the business world proved to be much more impressive than his contributions on the football field. After retiring from the Cowboys, Shaw worked with Roger Staubach's real estate firm and became a well-respected executive in Dallas.

SHEARIN, JOE
See Replacement Games

SHEPARD, DERRICK
Wide receiver, 5'10", 181 lbs., b. 1/22/64

After two years with the Redskins, and a month of the 1989 season with New Orleans, the former Odessa (TX) High School and University of Oklahoma wideout was the Cowboys' top punt returner in 1989 and 1990 while also serving as a backup receiver. He had 31 punt returns for 251 yards, and 27 kick returns for 529 yards in 1989, and added 20 catches for 304 yards his first year with Dallas. In 1990 he had only 20 punt returns and two kick returns, and he didn't have a single reception; his 1991 numbers were even weaker, since the Cowboys were turning to veteran receiver Kelvin Martin for punt returns (Martin placed third in the NFL in that category in 1991). Shepard, a teammate of Troy Aikman's at Oklahoma in 1984–85, was released after the 1991 season, his last in the NFL.

SHERER, DAVE
Punter, 6'3", 225 lbs., b. 2/14/37

Former SMU end and punter (he led the nation in punting), Sherer was the second-round draft choice of the Baltimore Colts in 1959. He was left unprotected in the 1960 expansion draft and picked up by the Cowboys. He punted 57 times for an above-average 42.5-yard per kick. But the next year, Dallas was looking for someone to handle both placekicking and punting chores. When he was replaced by Allen Green and let go, he retired.

SHERRARD, MIKE
Wide receiver, 6'2", 187 lbs., b. 6/21/63

The Cowboys had been searching for a game-breaking wide receiver to fill the void left by the retirements of Tony Hill and Drew Pearson, and they thought they'd found him when they drafted Sherrard in the first round in 1986.

Sherrard offered a glimpse of what the Cowboys hoped would be a bright future in the third game of his rookie season against Atlanta. Sherrard caught a 22-yard pass from Danny White, faked a defender out of his path, and reached the end zone untouched. The Cowboys lost the game, 37–35, but they liked what they saw from the former UCLA star.

The following week against St. Louis, Sherrard turned an underthrown pass into a 27-yard touchdown; two weeks later against Washington, Sherrard took the ball away from cornerback Darrell Green while both were falling in the end zone for another 27-yard TD.

He completed the 1986 season with a team-high five touchdowns, all from 20 yards or more, and a team-leading per-catch average of 18.2 yards. Sherrard, second in fan voting for NFL Rookie of the Year, cracked the starting lineup by the 13th week of the season, and his 41 catches were the most by a Cowboys rookie receiver since Bob Hayes had 46 in 1965. "Mike Sherrard should be a Pro Bowl player," Coach Tom Landry said. "He's got that kind of ability. Our deep passing attack will be built around him."

But the franchise's incredible run of bad luck with high draft picks in the eighties continued. In 1987 training camp, Sherrard accidently kicked himself during a passing drill and sustained a compound fracture of both bones in his right leg. Sherrard spent the 1987 season on injured reserve, then suffered another major setback in March 1988 when he re-fractured the leg while jogging on the beach in Los Angeles. The second break wasn't as serious as the first, but it guaranteed that Sherrard would also miss the 1988 season.

A new coaching staff was in place in 1989, and Coach Jimmy Johnson decided that Sherrard's leg would never heal sufficiently for him to be a productive player. After Dallas released him, Sherrard signed

with the San Francisco 49ers and after sitting out the 1989 season, he played for the 'Niners from 1990–92 as a backup to Jerry Rice and John Taylor. Sherrard's best season for the 49ers came in 1992 when he caught 38 passes for 607 yards.

He joined the New York Giants as a free agent in 1994, catching 53 passes for 825 yards and 6 touchdowns. Sherrard never became the superstar that had been predicted, but he bounced back to salvage a more than respectable career.

SHIELDS, JOE
See Replacement Games

SHOFNER, JIM
Assistant coach

Shofner celebrated a homecoming when he was hired by Tom Landry in 1983 as the Cowboys' quarterbacks coach. Shofner was from the Dallas suburb of Grapevine, had starred in football at TCU in Fort Worth in the mid-fifties, and had served as head coach at TCU from 1974–76.

A defensive back for the Cleveland Browns from 1958–63, Shofner had also held NFL assistant coaching assignments with Houston, Cleveland, and San Francisco. He left the Cowboys following the 1985 season, then in 1988 was offensive coordinator for the St. Louis-Phoenix Cardinals. He returned to Cleveland in 1990, where he was offensive coordinator, then interim head coach for the final seven games.

In 1991 Shofner was the Browns' player personnel director, then joined the staff of the Buffalo Bills in 1992 as quarterbacks coach, matching wits against the Cowboys' staff in two Super Bowls.

THE SHOTGUN

Tom Landry needed some help in 1975. It was to be a rebuilding year; the Cowboys had slipped the previous season to 8–6 and failed to make the playoffs for the first time in nine years. This season didn't look to be much better—the Cowboys were heading into the season with no less than 13 rookies on their roster. Landry's only two proven runners, Calvin Hill and Walt Garrison, were gone, one to the WFL and the other to pasture, and the only dependable receiver was a less-than-speedy free agent from Tulsa, Drew Pearson. What to do?

In 1960, to revive a similarly weak offense, San Francisco head coach Red Hickey had devised a formation in which the quarterback dropped back on obvious passing downs and took the snap ten yards back. The theory was that it gave the quarterback an extra second, and also eliminated the step-back and improved his view of the field. The new shotgun offense was a roaring success, especially the following season, when the team won four of its first five games handily. But the Chicago Bears constantly blitzed their middle linebacker past the center and destroyed the 'Niners 31–0. The Shotgun was never again successful, and in 1963, when the team lost their first three games and Hickey resigned, new coach Jack Christiansen scrapped the formation.

So when assistant coach Mike Ditka suggested the scheme to Landry, he was skeptical. But he realized that defenses had begun to bring in an extra defensive back on obvious passing situations, and when assistant coach Dan Reeves supported Ditka, Landry agreed to give it a try—not that he had many other options.

The Shotgun, or the Spread, as Landry called it for the three wide receivers spread out on the flanks, was almost immediately effective. The wet-behind-the-ears 'Boys finished 10–4; in the playoffs they beat the Minnesota Vikings with a last-second Hail Mary TD pass from Roger Staubach to Pearson. Staubach threw it out of the Shotgun, which the team was using in third down passing situations and their two-minute hurry-up offense.

The formation wasn't picked up by other teams until the early eighties, but it's now a staple in similar situations for almost every team in the league, including the Cowboys.

SHULA, DAVE
Assistant coach

Maybe it was the familiar last name that attracted such scrutiny and criticism, but Shula's two seasons in charge of the Jimmy Johnson offense were filled with public scorn over the results of the unit. In retrospect maybe it wasn't fair; even a young Troy Aikman (drafted in 1989) and a young Emmitt Smith (drafted in 1990) needed time to develop. But Shula didn't get time. He was demoted after the 1990 season when Johnson brought in Norv Turner from the Los Angeles Rams, and Shula took the hint, landing a job as the receivers coach in Cincinnati. For Shula, whose NFL coaching career began under father Don with the Miami Dolphins in the early eighties, the consolation prize was becoming the NFL's youngest head coach, with the Bengals, a year later.

SHY, LES
Running back, 6'0", 205 lbs., b. 4/5/44

An honorable mention Little All-American at Long Beach State, Shy was a twelfth-round pick by the Cowboys in the 1966 draft. He was a talented runner with speed and moves, but he played behind some solid runners. Backing up a healthy Dan Reeves and Don Perkins, he had 17 carries for 118 yards that year; the next season was a virtual repeat, with another 17 rushes, this time for 59 yards, exactly half of the previous year's gains. He ran a few kickoffs back and caught a few passes too. The next two years he saw more action—64 carries for 179 yards in 1968 along with 10 receptions, and 42 for 155 in 1969 with 8 catches—but a couple of backs named Hill and Garrison were at the top of the chart. In 1970, he was traded to the New York Giants; he saw almost no action there, and retired after the season.

SIMMONS, CLEO
Tight end, 6'2", 225 lbs., b. 10/21/60

Simmons was a free agent find in 1983 who started training camp as a long-shot but beat out fourth-round pick Chris Faulkner as the third tight end behind Doug Cosbie and Billy Joe DuPree. He was among the top special-teams players for the Cowboys in 1983, but he failed to make the team the following year after Dallas drafted tight end Fred Cornwell in the fourth round. He never played in the NFL again.

SIMMONS, DAVE
Linebacker, 6'4", 245 lbs., b. 8/3/43

Simmons had played three years in St. Louis and New Orleans when he was acquired for a future draft pick by the Cowboys in 1968. He played sparingly behind some great linebackers—Chuck Howley, Lee Roy Jordan, Dave Edwards—and then retired after the season.

SIMMONS, VICTOR
See Replacement Games

SLATON, TONY
Center/guard, 6'3", 280 lbs., b. 4/12/61

It took the former University of Southern California standout six years to earn a regular starting job with the Los Angeles Rams. Having accomplished that in 1989, Slaton promptly turned around and signed as a free agent with the Cowboys for the 1990 season. He almost made it six playoff appearances in six seasons until the Cowboys lost their last two games of the 1990 season to fail to make the playoffs. He backed up at center and on the offensive line during the season, then retired from the NFL.

SLOWIK, BOB
Assistant coach

The pride of the Fighting Blue Hens (he was a two-year starter for the University of Delaware), Slowik spent the 1992 season in Dallas as a defensive assistant. He had previously coached at East Carolina University, which developed a reputation as a little-known NCAA Division I-A program that could put a scare into a more high-profile program. When Cowboys defensive coordinator Dave Wannstedt became coach of the Chicago Bears in 1993, Slowik followed him north to become the Bears' defensive coordinator.

SMAGALA, STAN
Defensive back, 5'10", 184 lbs., b. 4/6/68

Smagala never doubted his ability, despite having a body build that could be confused with your favorite grocery checkout boy. Despite his build, he had excellent speed. During his three seasons as a cornerback with the Fighting Irish, Smagala had to cover the likes of Miami's Michael Irvin, Michigan State's Andre Rison, and West Virginia's Reggie Rembert. He was drafted out of Notre Dame in the fifth round in 1990, and his rookie season was cut short in late September when he broke an arm helping to force a fumble on a second-half kickoff. He played sparingly during the 1991 season, then was released and gone from the NFL.

SMEREK, DON
Defensive lineman, 6'7", 266 lbs., b. 12/20/57

The Cowboys always invited an army of rookie free agents to training camp, and Smerek was one that made the team in 1980. The Nevada-Reno product got off to a shaky start, however, spending his rookie year on injured reserve following knee surgery, then played in only two games in 1981 before suffering broken ribs.

Smerek battled his way back onto the roster in 1982 and proved valuable down the stretch and in the playoffs, filling in at tackle for the injured John Dutton. Dutton was back in 1983, but Smerek continued to make his mark, replacing Dutton on passing downs and finishing fourth on the team with 6 sacks.

When Harvey Martin retired prior to the 1984 season, Smerek was due to battle Jim Jeffcoat for Martin's right end position. But when All-Pro tackle Randy White held out of training camp in a contract dispute, Smerek filled in at tackle. Meanwhile, Jeffcoat won the job at end, and when White returned, Smerek was back on the bench as a reserve.

A shoulder injury cost Smerek six games in 1985. A knee problem knocked him out of five more in 1986 but in ten games, he ranked behind only the four starting linemen with 4.5 sacks.

In 1987, Smerek crossed the picket line during the players' strike after coming back from another training camp injury. He started all three replacement games, but when the regular players returned, Smerek was back on the bench again for what proved to be his final season in the NFL.

SMITH, DARRIN
Linebacker, 6'1", 230 lbs., b. 4/15/70

Smith demonstrated a knack for good timing in 1995 when he missed the bulk of the season while holding out, yet was there in Tempe, AZ, to share in the glory of the Super Bowl XXX victory. He regained his starting position at weakside linebacker shortly after his return and blitzed his way into Neil O'Donnell's memory during the Cowboys 27–17 victory over the Pittsburgh Steelers.

A player known for combining intelligence and speed, Smith was picked out of the University of Miami in the second round in 1993. He had started all but three games he suited up for through 1995.

As a rookie, he barged into the starting lineup for thirteen regular-season games and all three in the postseason, earning consensus All-Rookie status after leading all NFL rookies with 93 tackles. Thrust into the first unit when Ken Norton was shifted to the middle, Smith overcame a relative size disadvantage to become a playmaking force,

turning in 11 playoff tackles, 4 in the victory over Buffalo in Super Bowl XXVIII.

Smith had an even better season in 1994 with 103 tackles, 4 sacks, 6 tackles for losses, and 10 passes defensed for the league's top-rated unit.

With a galaxy of stars waiting at the pay window, the Cowboys were in a bind as far as compensating younger players, and Smith, a restricted free agent, was unhappy with owner Jerry Jones' offer. He sat out the first seven games before agreeing to terms on October 14.

Although the layoff reduced his effectiveness, Smith still finished seventh on the team with 65 tackles and paced linebackers with 3 sacks despite playing only nine regular-season games. He was also a contributor in Super Bowl XXX, finishing with 6 tackles in the decision over the Steelers.

SMITH, DARYLE
Offensive tackle, 6'5", 276 lbs., b. 1/18/64

Smith was cut by the Seattle Seahawks in 1987 training camp, then joined the Cowboys as a replacement during the players' strike. He was so impressive at left tackle that the Tennessee ex was retained after the strike was settled.

When left tackle Mark Tuinei injured a knee on Thanksgiving Day, Smith found himself in the starting lineup with the real players for the final month of the season. Tuinei's knee problems opened the way for Smith again at the beginning of the 1988 season, and he started four games before he was sidelined due to broken ribs. Dave Widell took over for Smith in early October, and by the time Smith returned, he received little playing time. He played a year in Cleveland and then two in Philadelphia before retiring.

SMITH, DONALD
Safety, 5'11", 186 lbs., b. 2/21/68

Smith was picked by Minnesota in the tenth round of the 1990 draft out of Liberty University, Jerry Falwell's college in Virginia, but was released before the season began. He made the Cowboys a year later and saw minimal duty in his one season in a Cowboy uniform, accounting for two tackles on special teams. He was released after the season, his only one in the NFL. He seemed to miss his calling as a return man, having averaged 27.3 yards per kickoff return as a senior at Liberty.

SMITH, EMMITT
Running back, 5'9", 209 lbs., b. 5/15/69

Emmitt Smith is arguably the most celebrated player in Dallas' storied football history. In six seasons since leaving the University of Florida with a year's eligibility remaining, Smith has amassed 8,956 yards

rushing, 13th on the NFL's career list, and smashed the record for touchdowns in a season with 25 in 1995. He has a Super Bowl ring for every other year he has played in the NFL.

Cowboys coach Jimmy Johnson had already invested his number-one pick in the 1990 draft to select University of Miami quarterback Steve Walsh, leaving Dallas without the first overall pick in the draft that the Cowboys deserved for a 1–15 season in 1989. But Johnson used one of the draft picks obtained in the blockbuster Herschel Walker deal as part of a deal to move into the first round.

Some scouts weren't sold on Smith, contending he didn't have blinding breakaway speed, downgrading his 3,928 yards and

Emmitt Smith

56 school records during his three seasons at Florida. The NFL has no test to measure a player's heart, however, and Smith has demonstrated his grit on a regular basis throughout his career.

What makes Smith such a special player? He has uncanny vision and balance, the ability to accelerate into and through a hole, run to daylight, and break tackles. There are others with greater speed, but seldom is Smith hauled down from behind in the open field. Ask him how he does what he does, and he simply shrugs. Some talents can't be explained.

After missing training camp and the preseason in a bitter rookie contract dispute, Smith signed right before the regular-season opener. In spot duty, he carried only twice in the opener before drawing his first pro start the following week against the New York Giants. Some critics still wondered what all the fuss was about, as Smith picked up only 11 yards against the Giants, 63 against Washington, and 28 in a September 30 rematch with the Giants.

Smith was biding his time, and in the next game he exploded for 121 yards in 23 carries as the Cowboys snapped a three-game losing streak. He was on his way, finishing fifth in the NFC and tenth in the league with 937 rushing yards, tops among rookies. His 241 carries shattered Tony Dorsett's Cowboys rookie record, and his 3 100-yard games were the second-most ever by a Dallas rookie.

In 1991, Smith emerged as a bona fide star, earning his initial rushing title with 1,563 yards to become the first Cowboy to pace the league in rushing. At 22 years and seven months, Smith became the youngest player in league history, and 28th overall, to rush for more than 1,500 yards, earning him a starting berth in the Pro Bowl.

He also paced the NFL in carries with 365, becoming the 19th player with more than 350 attempts, and his eight 100-yard games were the second-most in club history. Not coincidentally, the Cowboys returned to the playoffs for the first time since 1985 and

Smith rushed for 105 yards in a first-round victory over Chicago. The Bears had never allowed a running back to surpass the century mark in post-season play, a record that dated to 1932 and spanned 27 games.

Smith was only warming up, however. In 1992 he set franchise records with 1,713 rushing yards, 18 touchdowns on the ground, and 19 TDs overall. Team goals have always been foremost on Smith's checklist, and the Cowboys' 52–17 victory over the Buffalo Bills in Super Bowl XXVII (he rushed for 108 yards against Buffalo) was more important to Smith than his consensus All-Pro and Pro Bowl honors.

Of all Smith's tremendous accomplishments, the greatest may have been what he achieved on a blustery early January afternoon at the New Jersey Meadowlands to close out the 1993 season. With the Cowboys needing a victory over the New York Giants to retain the NFC East crown, Smith collected the bulk of 168 yards after separating his right shoulder late in the second quarter. He was the catalyst for the Cowboys' dramatic overtime victory, wrapping up his third straight rushing title with 1,486 yards. Smith then capped another highlight reel season by rushing for 132 yards to win the Super Bowl MVP, as the Cowboys claimed their second straight league crown over the Bills. Further testament to his ability was the beginning of the '93 season, when the Cowboys struggled to an 0–2 start before Smith ended a contract holdout.

Smith's hallmark is consistency. In 1994, he lost the rushing title to Detroit's Barry Sanders, but Smith still racked up 1,484 yards. More importantly, Smith accumulated a team-record 22 touchdowns, tying for second in the league in scoring (a club-record 132 points) and becoming the first non-kicker to lead the Cowboys in scoring since Bob Hayes and Dan Reeves scored 66 points apiece in 1967. The Cowboys offense felt comfortable putting the ball in Smith's hands, because he didn't fumble in the 449 times he handled the ball on runs and passes. Dallas failed in its bid for three straight Super Bowls, but nobody was blaming Smith.

He was back in the big game following the 1995 season after establishing a fistful of new team records: touchdowns (a league-record 25), rushing yards (1,773), 100-yard rushing games (11), points (150), consecutive games with a touchdown (11), rushing attempts (377), and rushing/receiving yards (2,148). Smith's numbers weren't eye-opening in Super Bowl XXX (49 rushing yards, 2 touchdowns) but he didn't care because the Cowboys won their third title in four years with a 27–17 decision.

When not diving into the end zone, or slipping through enemy lines, Smith likes a good game of dominoes in the Cowboys' player lounge. His autobiography, *The Emmitt Zone,* was published in 1994. He's also an astute businessman, and he operates a sports collectibles store bearing his name (and most of his touchdown footballs) in his hometown of Pensacola, FL, where he scared the locals on national signing day following a spectacular career at Escambia High. The rumors were that Smith would attend the University of Florida, but that the University of Nebraska was a close second. Smith walked into the news conference wearing a bright red football jersey, the Cornhuskers' color. Fooled 'em, just like he has been doing to NFL defensive coaches for six years.

With continued health and productivity, an eventual run at all-time rushing leader Walter Payton's 16,726 yards is entirely possible for the amazing Emmitt.

SMITH, J. D.
Running back, 6'1", 200 lbs., b. 7/19/32

A fast North Carolina A&T running back, Smith was an outstanding player for the San Francisco 49ers for eight years, after breaking in as a free agent with the Chicago Bears in 1956. The Cowboys picked him up in 1965. He'd been a two-time Pro Bowler and a one-time All-Pro with the 49ers, but his best years were behind him. He was Don Perkins's backup at fullback, and saw spot duty (86 rushes for 295 yards) the first year, then almost none the second. He retired after the 1966 season.

SMITH, JACKIE
Tight end, 6'4", 225 lbs., b. 6/1/41

It is the cruel fate of Hall of Famer Jackie Smith to be forever remembered for one of the few passes in his illustrious career he did not catch.

In fifteen years with St. Louis, Smith proved himself one of the greatest receiving tight ends in the history of the NFL. He caught 480 passes for a 16.5-yard average, better than wide receiver Lynn Swann's or Charlie Joiner's. He retired after the 1977 season with a serious neck injury, but when Jay Saldi was injured four games into the following season, he was enticed out of his rocking chair by Tom Landry. The 37-year-old backed up a healthy Billy Joe DuPree and didn't have a catch in the regular season, but he had three receptions, including a clutch TD catch from Danny White, in a come-from-behind victory over Atlanta in the playoffs.

The scene was set. In Super Bowl XII, a rematch with the Pittsburgh Steelers, the defending champion Cowboys were driving for a tying touchdown at the end of the third quarter. From the Steeler 10-yard line, quarterback Roger Staubach found Smith all alone in the end zone, no Steeler within 10 yards of him. Staubach lobbed the ball. The pass was a bit short and behind Smith, and he turned to receive the pass. But he stumbled, and somehow the pass went right through his hands and bounced off his body and fell to the ground. Smith fell back onto the AstroTurf, frozen in anguish. The Cowboys had to settle for a field goal, and eventually lost by four points. The irony was painful: Smith was one of the surest-handed receivers in NFL history.

The sight of a distraught Smith thrashing in the end zone is an image seared into the memories of a generation of Cowboy fans. And it was an image many fans would

Jackie Smith

not let Smith forget. Like Bill Buckner, the Boston Red Sox first baseman whose egregious error handed the New York Mets the 1986 World Series, Jackie Smith became a symbol of defeat and a perfect whipping boy. By 1996, with the Cowboys in Super Bowl XXX, the bitter 55-year-old Smith had had enough questions: "I think seventeen years is enough to be nice and I don't want to be nice about it anymore."

A businessman today, Smith lives in St. Louis and devotes much of his time to fundraising for charitable organizations.

SMITH, JIM RAY
Offensive guard/tackle, 6′3″, 245 lbs., b. 2/27/32

Smith was one of many former NFL greats discarded by other teams and snapped up by a new team desperate for experience. After seven superb years at Cleveland— including four All-Pro selections and five

Pro Bowls—the Baylor ex was traded to Dallas. He decided to retire, but was talked into playing by Tex Schramm and Tom Landry. He played two seasons in Dallas; each year, a knee injury and operation early on limited his playing time. He retired after the 1964 season.

SMITH, JIMMY
Wide receiver, 6′1″, 205 lbs., b. 2/9/69

Smith's stay with the Cowboys wasn't a pleasant one. He was drafted out of Jackson State with a second-round pick in 1992 with the hopes of providing depth behind the likes of Michael Irvin, Kelvin Martin, and Alvin Harper. But he missed the '92 season after suffering a broken leg. When Martin left for Seattle before the 1993 season, there appeared to be a greater chance for Smith making the team. But while battling with rookie Kevin Williams for Martin's vacancy as the number-three receiver, and leading the club in receiving during preseason, Smith underwent an emergency appendectomy before the last preseason game. So much for his chances of making the Cowboys. Afterward, he and his agent sought compensation from the Cowboys for what they believed was inappropriate action taken by the team's medical staff regarding his 1993 illness.

SMITH, KEVIN
Cornerback, 5'11", 184 lbs., b. 4/7/70

One of the few downers of the 1995 championship season for Cowboy fans was the loss of Smith during the season opener against the New York Giants. He suffered a partially ruptured right Achilles tendon early in the game, and was lost for the season. Before that, he had started 46 straight regular-season and playoff games at cornerback. The Cowboys managed, with Larry Brown putting together a solid season and the ownership bringing in Deion Sanders midway through the season. But Smith, the Cowboys' first pick in 1992 out of Texas A&M, was on the brink of becoming a Pro Bowl player, having started in Super Bowl XXVII as a 22-year-old rookie. He earned a starting position late in his rookie season and had made 39 consecutive regular-season starts until his streak ended with him hobbling into the Giants Stadium end zone. He combines steady reliability as a cover man with the ability to come up with the big play when needed. Over the 1994–95 seasons he averaged 80 tackles, 15 passes defensed, and 4 interceptions a year.

SMITH, SEAN
Defensive tackle, 6'4", 280 lbs., b. 3/27/65

Smith racked up plenty of frequent flyer miles in 1989, his only year with the Cowboys. He spent 1987–88 with the Chicago Bears and was picked up by Dallas for the 1989 season. He spent just a short time with the Cowboys, as a backup on the defensive line, before he was gone to Tampa

Bay, and he wasn't there very long before he was sent to the Rams. The next two years, his last in the NFL, he spent with the New England Patriots.

SMITH, TIMMY
Running back, 5'11", 222 lbs., b. 1/21/64

While Smith's time with the Cowboys was far from glamorous (6 carries for 6 yards in one game in 1990), he owns a storied place in NFL history. After gaining only 126 yards as a rookie with Washington in 1987, he was forced into his first starting role in Super Bowl XXII against Denver in San Diego. All he did was gain a Super-record 204 yards, as the Redskins rallied to destroy the Broncos 42–10. He must have figured it was the turf at Jack Murphy Stadium, because he left the Redskins after that game to sign, through Plan B, with the San Diego Chargers. He was released before the season began, didn't play at all, and carried the ball for the Cowboys only in their 1990 season opener against, of course, San Diego. He was out of the NFL after the season.

SMITH, TODY
Defensive end, 6'5", 250 lbs., b. 12/24/48

Bubba Smith's little brother Tody was the Cowboys' first-round draft choice in 1971. The Cowboys had high hopes for him, but he held out for most of training camp, and he spent the first half of the year on the taxi squad. When he was activated, he showed plenty of potential, but offseason surgery on a bad knee (hurt in a pickup basketball game) hampered his development. The next year he saw some backup action, but he was traded to Houston before the 1973 season. He spent three years there and one with Buffalo before retiring.

SMITH, WADDELL
Wide receiver, 6'2", 180 lbs., b. 8/24/55

The free agent from Kansas played only the 1984 season, contributing on spe-

Cowboys Biggest Playoff Days——Receiving

192	Michael Irvin	@ San Francisco, January 15, 1995
144	Bob Hayes	vs. Cleveland, December 24, 1967
142	Tony Hill	vs. Green Bay, January 16, 1983
136	Billy Parks	@ San Francisco, December 23, 1972
126	Michael Irvin	vs. Green Bay, January 16, 1994
124	Kevin Williams	vs. Philadelphia, January 7, 1996
123	Preston Pearson	@ LA Rams, January 4, 1976
117	Alvin Harper	@ San Francisco, January 17, 1993
115	Tony Hill	vs. LA Rams, December 26, 1983
114	Michael Irvin	vs. Buffalo, January 31, 1993

cial teams; he also had 1 catch for 7 yards. That was his only season in the NFL.

SMITH, VINSON
Linebacker, 6'2", 231 lbs., b. 7/3/65

Smith went from free-agent signee in 1990 to Super Bowl starter at the January 1993 game in Pasadena. He was a hard-nosed hitter who was especially tough against the run; he was often pulled in passing situations. Smith, for the most part, saw special-teams action until he got his chance when Ken Norton was shelved by injury in the final game of the 1990 season, opening a spot at weakside linebacker. He recorded a team-high 11 tackles and also recovered a fumble. That was the starting slot that Smith then filled the following season, and he was the team's sixth-leading tackler until a bout with hepatitis sidelined him for three games in November. In 1992, Smith moved over as the starter at strongside linebacker, finishing fifth on the team with 69 tackles, and he was a key element in the Cowboys' surge toward the number-one over-all defensive ranking in the NFL. So it came as a shock to many—Smith included—when he was traded to the Chicago Bears before the 1993 season, having been replaced

in the Dallas starting lineup by Dixon Edwards. Smith got a measure of immediate revenge when the Bears beat the Cowboys in a preseason game. His biggest dent in NFL annals came as a Bear, when he was fined $12,000 for what the league deemed was an inappropriate hit on Rams quarterback Chris Miller.

SNYDER, LOREN
See Replacement Games

SOLARI, MIKE
Assistant coach

Solari came to the Cowboys as their special-teams coach in 1987 from the University of Pittsburgh, where he was offensive line coach and offensive coodinator. In addition to coordinating special teams for the Cowboys, Solari also helped Jim Erkenbeck coach the offensive line during his stay from 1987–88.

SOLOMON, JESSE
Linebacker, 6'0", 235 lbs., b. 11/4/63

Solomon's bizarre stay with the Cowboys was best highlighted by his snub of owner Jerry Jones on the practice field, refusing to shake his boss's hand. Not the way to move up in the organization. But it was his moving down in the organization, without his prior notification, that ignited his volatile exit from Valley Ranch. He came to Dallas as part of the haul in the Herschel Walker "steal" in October 1989. For the balance of that season, he split time at weakside linebacker with Ken Norton. He figured himself a starter for 1990. Coach Jimmy Johnson thought otherwise, and Solomon promptly declared himself a holdout. He missed the first seven games of the 1990 season and, upon his return, was mostly relegated to playing only on passing downs. He was later traded to New England, though he was Patriots property for only two days before being dealt on to Tampa Bay. He later played with Atlanta and Miami.

SOLOMON, ROLAND
Safety, 6'0", 196 lbs., b. 2/6/56

Solomon made the roster in 1980 as a rookie free agent from Utah, but he was waived during the season and played for the Buffalo Bills later that year. Solomon also played for the Denver Broncos in 1981.

SPIVEY, SEBRON
See Replacement Games

SPRADLIN, DANNY
Linebacker, 6'1", 221 lbs., b. 3/3/59

The Cowboys valued Spradlin's ability as a big hitter when they selected him from Tennessee, in the fifth round of the 1980 draft. They liked Spradlin so much that they traded veteran backup middle linebacker Bruce Huther to the Cleveland Browns during 1980 training camp to make room for Spradlin.

But "Spur" Spradlin had veteran Bob Breunig ahead of him and the overaggressive Spradlin had problems grasping the read-and-react flex defense. Spradlin played well on special teams, but Breunig was a fixture

on the Cowboys defense. Spradlin was traded to Tampa Bay in 1983 for a fifth-round pick, and he played for the Buccaneers from 1983–84 before finishing his career with the St. Louis Cardinals in 1985.

SPRINGS, RON
Running back, 6'1", 216 lbs., b. 11/4/56

When Springs arrived at his first Cowboys training camp in 1979 as a fifth-round draft choice, he knew there was little chance he'd be starting at his college position of tailback as long as he remained in Dallas. The Cowboys already had Tony Dorsett at the position Springs played at Ohio State.

As a rookie, Springs served as Dorsett's backup, and he filled in well. Springs even started two games for the injured Dorsett. In the season opener at St. Louis, Springs threw a 30-yard fourth-quarter touchdown pass to Tony Hill in a 22–21 victory. In a comeback victory over Washington in December, Springs rushed for 79 yards and caught 6 passes for 58 yards, including a 26-yard touchdown late in the fourth quarter as the Cowboys wrapped up the NFC East title with a 35–34 decision. Springs also led the team in kickoff returns in 1979.

But if the Cowboys were to get Springs on the field consistently, he'd have to change positions, so he was shifted to fullback for the 1980 season. Springs gained ten pounds during the off-season, then won the job from Robert Newhouse in training camp. He twisted an ankle in the third game, however, and didn't take the position back from Newhouse until 1981. Nonetheless, Springs was again an effective fill-in at tailback, rushing for 326 yards in his second season and catching 15 passes for 213 yards, including a 56-yard touchdown.

Springs had a breakthrough season in 1981, holding the fullback job for the entire year. He combined for 984 yards rushing and receiving, scored a team-high 12 touchdowns, and tied Tony Hill for the club lead with 46 receptions, one short of Preston Pearson's Cowboys record for a back. Springs

Ron Springs

had 11 catches in a September game against New England, a team record, and he turned in three games of better than 100 yards rushing and receiving. In a 28–27 victory over Miami, Springs caught a 32-yard touchdown late in the fourth quarter for the decisive points.

In the strike-shortened 1982 season, Springs rushed for 243 yards and caught 163 yards in passes over the nine-game schedule. He led the league's running backs and set a club record for a back with 73 catches for 589 yards in 1983, when he also rushed for 541 yards and scored 8 touchdowns.

Springs had outstanding speed and hands for a fullback, and he became an improved blocker. He was also among the team's leading locker-room humorists. Teammates called him "Idi Amin," a reference to the pistol-waving dictator. Springs acquired the nickname as the ringleader of a fishing trip during which he decided it was easier to shoot the fish than reel them in.

Springs also wasn't shy with his opinions about how the club was being run, and after rushing for only 197 yards (a 2.9-yard average) and catching 454 yards in passes in 1984, the Cowboys released Springs just before the 1985 season. Springs signed with the Tampa Bay Buccaneers and also played for the Bucs in 1986, his final NFL season. He later served as an assistant football coach at Howard University under head coach and former teammate Steve Wilson.

STALLINGS, GENE
Assistant coach

After six years as head coach at Texas A&M, Stallings joined Landry's staff in 1972 as the defensive backfield coach and remained through 1985. He oversaw the development of Pro Bowlers Charlie Waters, Cliff Harris, Everson Walls and Michael Downs. He left the Cowboys to become the head coach of the Phoenix Cardinals, and after seasons of 4–11–1, 7–8, and 7–9, he was fired with five games to go in the 1989 season. He later went on to win a national championship as head coach at Alabama.

STALLS, DAVE
Defensive end, 6'4", 255 lbs., b. 9/19/55

When Stalls joined the Cowboys in 1977 as a seventh-round pick from Northern Colorado, he weighed 235 pounds, not the ideal size for a designated pass rusher. But Stalls compensated with extraordinary effort, and by 1978 he surprised skeptics by emerging as a third down pass-rusher, spelling Jethro Pugh or Larry Cole at left tackle.

He was an even more interesting story off the field. Stalls studied marine biology during the off-season, and his specialty was shark behavioral research.

Stalls used his quickness to register 4 sacks and an assist on another in 1978, then added a sack in the NFC Championship Game against the Los Angeles Rams. Weight-room diligence added 20 pounds of muscle to his frame, and in 1979 he surprised everyone by winning the left tackle position in the preseason, going on to start the first 12 games.

Stalls was back in a reserve role when John Dutton took over at left end and Cole moved back to left tackle. Stalls finished 1979 with 5 sacks and assists on two others, but that didn't change the fact that he was undersized; he was traded to Tampa Bay prior to the 1980 season. He played for the Bucs until 1982, then finished his career with the Raiders in 1983.

STAUBACH, ROGER
Quarterback, 6'3", 197 lbs., b. 2/5/42

In the early sixties, the Cowboys took more chances on players than any other NFL team. Their 1964 tenth-round draft choice was the previous year's Heisman Trophy winner—a Naval Academy junior named Roger Staubach. Everyone knew he was a born leader and an excellent quarterback; the

Roger Staubach

problem was, he would have a four-year commitment to the Navy after graduating. And who knew if he'd want to—or be able to—play football then?

After he graduated, he did a tour of duty in Vietnam as a supply officer, at a base just south of Da Nang; for two years he played no football. During the next two years, he made appearances at the Cowboys' summer training camps, and by the time his tour of duty was up, he decided he'd give fifth-year man Craig Morton a run for his money. Don Meredith had just retired, and Staubach was a 27-year-old rookie. He showed some promise in that 1969 preseason (rushing for more than 100 yards in his first start), and he started the first game of the season due to a Morton dislocated finger. It

Cowboys 300-Yard Passing Games—Playoffs

380	Troy Aikman	@ San Francisco, January 15, 1995
337	Troy Aikman	vs. Green Bay, January 8, 1995
330	Danny White	vs. LA Rams, December 26, 1983
322	Danny White	@ Atlanta, January 4, 1981
322	Troy Aikman	@ San Francisco, January 17, 1993
312	Danny White	vs. Tampa Bay, January 9, 1983
302	Troy Aikman	vs. Green Bay, January 16, 1994

was an easy 24–3 win over St. Louis, but the following week, Morton was back as the starter. Staubach still had a lot to learn about the NFL game; he saw only infrequent mop-up duty the rest of the year.

Staubach got a bit more action the next season, again starting and winning the first game due to a Morton injury. He started and won the second game, then faltered with two interceptions in the next. He played little the rest of the year, and none at all in the postseason as the Cowboys ultimately lost to the Colts 16–13 in the Super Bowl. But the 1971 season was different; Landry decided he had two starting quarterbacks, and that they would alternate much as Meredith and LeBaron had in the early years. Then, with the team struggling halfway through the season, Staubach replaced Morton as the starter. Staubach was superb, passing and rushing and guiding the team brilliantly, and the Cowboys didn't lose another game that year, finally winning the big one handily in the Super Bowl against Miami. It was Staubach's coming-out party.

A badly separated shoulder sustained while trying to run through a linebacker during the very next preseason sidelined Staubach for most of the 1972 season. Dallas squeezed into the playoffs as a wild card, and faced a San Francisco team that had already beaten them badly once. Morton was inef-

fective, and with the Cowboys down 28–13 near the end of the third quarter, Landry sent in Staubach, who hadn't thrown a touchdown all season. He started badly, enduring several sacks, incompletions, and a fumble; but the 49ers missed a field goal, Calvin Hill broke away for 45 yards, and Dallas kicked for three. With two minutes to go, they were still down twelve. But then Staubach caught fire; he hit wideout Billy Parks on a post pattern with a 20-yard TD pass, and Dallas recovered the onside kick at midfield. Two big plays later—a Staubach run for 21, a pass to Parks for 19—the Cowboys were on the ten. The 49ers blitzed on the next play, and Staubach barely got off a pass that landed in the hands of wide receiver Ron Sellers in the end zone. The extra point made it 30–28. Though Dallas was dominated the next week by Washington, Staubach was beginning to earn his nickname of "Captain Comeback."

Barring injury, he would be the Cowboys' starting quarterback until he retired. Staubach wasn't always perfect; he had a few horrendous games, like the 1973 NFC Championship Game against Minnesota, a 27–10 loss in which he fumbled once and threw four interceptions. (He had led the league that year in passing with a 63 percent completion rate.) In 1974 he had a less than stellar season, hitting only 52.8 percent of his passes for only 11 touchdowns (and 15 interceptions). Craig Morton was gone, traded to the New York Giants after the first game, and Clint Longley was Staubach's backup. (The rookie from Abilene Christian was unneeded during the season, save for one shining moment, his wild come-from-behind victory after Washington on Thanksgiving Day.) But an 8–6 record didn't earn a playoff berth.

Nineteen seventy-five was an extraordinary year; although a slew of great players would leave or retire, the Dirty Dozen rookie picks would help the 'Pokes make it to the Super Bowl. Landry spread out the offense and used the shotgun more than ever before, and Staubach had a fine year; only Fran Tarkenton at Minnesota had a better one percentagewise in the NFC, and Staubach led in yards per attempt. After a midseason slump, Dallas finished strong, and faced Minnesota as the wild-card team. With less than two minutes left in the fourth quarter, the Cowboys were down 14–10 and near their own goal line. But Staubach engineered a gutsy drive down the field, throwing 5 passes, all to Drew Pearson—the last one an underthrown 50-yarder that Pearson cradled against his hip near the goal line and carried into the end zone to win it for Dallas. The Hail Mary propelled them past Los Angeles into the Super Bowl against Pittsburgh. Staubach threw two TDs in the Super Bowl, but also three interceptions in the 21–17 loss. The next year he started strong, completing close to 70 percent of his passes in the first seven games, but in the next game his right hand was stepped on as he ran for a touchdown. Not only was his hand bruised, but a bone was chipped. As the season wore on, his passing average dropped drastically. His regular-season totals were virtually the same, and Dallas finished 11–3, but the lack of a serious running threat was part of the reason they lost in the first round of the playoffs against Los Angeles. Staubach had 3 interceptions and hit only 15 of 37 passes.

Dallas' first pick in the draft, Tony Dorsett, solved the running problems in 1977. The Cowboys were dominant in every phase of the game that year, and Staubach led in virtually every passing category; again it was only Tarkenton ahead of him in completion percentage. The team breezed through the playoffs and the Super Bowl, where they crushed Denver's Orange Crush 27–10. Staubach was in fine form in the first two victories, but nothing less than superb against the Broncos, completing 17 of 25 attempts with no interceptions. His only touchdown pass was a long bomb from the Denver 45, which a broken-fingered Butch Johnson lunged for and barely caught in time to fall into the end zone. Staubach's old rival, Craig Morton, completed as many passes to the Cowboys (4, all in the first half) as he did to his teammates.

The next year, 1978, would be one of Roger the Dodger's best. He had an incredible regular season, leading the league in touchdowns (25) and yards-per-attempt (7.7), and was the NFL's top-ranked quarterback, the third time he won that distinction. The Cowboys steamed into the playoffs on a six-game win streak after their habitual midseason slump. Against wild-card Atlanta, Staubach left the field late in the second quarter with a concussion after a so-so start, and White directed two second-half touchdown drives to win 27–20. The next game, against Los Angeles, was scoreless at the half, but 28–0 Dallas when it was over; 7 LA turnovers led to 4 Dallas scores, two of them on Staubach passes to Scott Laidlaw and Billy Joe Dupree. That set the table for a rematch of the best Super Bowl ever—Pittsburgh-Dallas. With less than a quarter to play, Dallas found themselves down 35–17; they had outplayed the Steelers straight up, but miscues and a bad call had tripped them up. Staubach drove down the field, scrambling and passing, and found Billy Joe Dupree at the seven-yard line. The big tight end broke two tackles and staggered into the end zone for the score. The Cowboys recovered the obvious onside kick with little time left on the clock. A few plays later, a 25-yard pass to Pearson got the 'Pokes to the Pittsburgh four, and a bullet to Butch Johnson in the end zone made it 35–31. With only 22 seconds left, the Steelers recovered Efren Herrera's onside kick and ran the clock out on another great Super Bowl.

Staubach's final year was another excellent showing. Again he led the league in touchdowns (27) and yards-per-attempt (7.8), and he completed 58 percent of his passes. Dallas swooned in November, losing four of their next five games, but ended the season on a three-game win streak and a personal high note for Staubach. A playoff berth was at stake on the final Sunday against Washington, and the Skins led 34–21 with less than seven minutes left when Captain America went to work. A touchdown strike to Ron Springs with only three minutes left, a scoring pass to Tony Hill with 39 seconds on the clock, and a Rafael Septien extra point won it in classic come-from-behind fashion for the Cowboys. It was Staubach's last hurrah; Los Angeles beat them 21–19 in the playoffs two weeks later (his final pass was an unintentional and illegal one to offensive lineman Herb Scott). He was 13 of 28 for 150 yards and 1 touchdown in his last NFL game. Three months later he retired. As he walked out of Landry's office after telling him, he said, half in jest, "Coach, what if I come back this year? Will you let me call the plays?" Landry only smiled and said, "No, we have a system going here."

Throughout his career, Staubach chafed under Landry's tight reins. Landry insisted on all the playcalling save for the first eleven games of 1973. Dallas was leading the league in offense at the time, but a Thanksgiving Day loss to Miami changed Landry's mind, and he called the offensive plays from then on. But some of Staubach's greatest triumphs came when he modified or scrapped Landry's messengered calls, par-

ticularly when the Cowboys were in their two-minute offense and Staubach was forced to call his own plays.

He was a tough on- and off-field leader who simply refused to lose, and his attitude influenced the team—so much that they, their fans, and the opposing team began to believe that if there was any time left on the clock the Cowboys could win. He led enough last-minute comebacks to warrant that kind of irrational belief, and to cement his reputation as one of the greatest quarterbacks the NFL has ever seen. He has published two autobiographies: *First Down, Lifetime to Go* (1974) and *Time Enough to Win* (1980).

STAUTNER, ERNIE
Assistant coach

One of the NFL's all-time great defensive linemen (voted to nine Pro Bowls), Stautner joined the Cowboys as their defensive line coach in 1966, after a season as an assistant with the Washington Redskins (he had also been a player-coach the previous two years with Pittsburgh). He later became Dallas' defensive coordinator while still retaining his duties to the defensive line. He stayed with Dallas until Jerry Jones bought the Cowboys in 1989, then went on to coach Arena Football and in the World League of American Football.

STEELE, ROBERT
Wide receiver, 6'4", 196 lbs., b. 8/2/56

Steele was a reserve and special teamster for Dallas in 1978, then played for the Minnesota Vikings in 1979. The Northern Alabama ex had one catch before retiring from the NFL.

STEPHENS, LARRY
Defensive end, 6'3", 255 lbs., b. 9/24/38

Stephens, a charter member of the Fearsome Foursome, was traded from the Los

Angeles Rams to Dallas just days before the first game of the 1963 season, primarily to fill in for the injured George Andrie. He was the regular at end for two years. He wasn't particularly fast, but he was a smart football player, and he started some and filled in at every defensive line position. The former Texas standout had begun his career three years before as a defensive tackle at Cleveland. He played five strong years for the Cowboys (1963–67), then was released on waivers and retired.

STEPNOSKI, MARK
Center, 6'2", 271 lbs., b. 1/20/67

One of the quiet success stories of the Jimmy Johnson era, this third-round pick in 1989 out of the University of Pittsburgh developed into one of the NFL's finest centers. He earned Pro Bowl trips for the 1992–94 seasons, winning the starting position late in his rookie year and keeping it until his departure to Houston as a free agent following the 1994 season.

Mark Stepnoski

Stepnoski was the first Cowboy rookie to start at center since Robert Shaw in 1979. He was the smallest member of Dallas' mammoth offensive line, but his smarts and speed made him one of the best centers in the game, and he was a key player in Emmitt Smith's prolific 1991–94 seasons. Stepnoski started 68 consecutive games until being hobbled by a knee injury in December 1994.

STEWART, CURTIS
Running back, 5'11", 208 lbs., b. 6/4/63

Stewart was signed as a free agent out of Auburn in 1989. He saw only limited special-teams action, then was released after the season, his only one in the NFL.

STIGER, JIM
Running back, 5'11", 195 lbs., b. 1/7/41

A 19th-round draft selection of the Cowboys in 1963 out of Washington, Stiger saw occasional action his first year backing up fullback Amos Marsh, gaining 140 yards on 31 carries. He had 13 receptions for 131 yards, and was the team's number-one punt returner and a good kick returner. Halfway through the '64 season Amos Marsh was injured, and Stiger stepped in and started; he finished the year with 68 carries for 280 yards and 9 catches for 85 yards. The addition of rookie sensation Mel Renfro excused him from return duty. Early in the 1965 season, he was traded to the Los Angeles Rams, where he played three years as a backup and then retired.

STINCIC, TOM
Linebacker, 6'2", 225 lbs., b. 11/24/46

This third-round choice out of Michigan in the 1969 draft played three years for the Cowboys. He didn't see much action backing up Chuck Howley, Bob Edwards, and Lee Roy Jordan, but when he did, it was usually in the middle for Jordan. He saw some action in both Super Bowls V and VI, then was traded to the New Orleans Saints before the 1972 season. He played one year there and then retired.

STOKES, SIMS
Wide receiver, 6'1", 195 lbs., b. 4/18/44

The sixth-round draft pick from Northern Arizona played only one year (1967) in the NFL. He was extremely quick, and ran a few kickoffs back during the regular season. He went to Baltimore the next season, where he was cut just days before the season opener. He is the answer to this trivia question: To whom did Don Meredith throw a long incomplete pass on the last play of the game in the Ice Bowl?

STONE, RON
Offensive guard/tackle, 6'5", 309 lbs., b. 7/20/71

Sometimes a big man is worth a big contract, but most of the NFL was shocked when Stone left the Cowboys after three seasons to sign a five-year, $10-million deal with the New York Giants shortly after Super Bowl XXX. True, Stone was the backup at four of the Cowboys' offensive line positions at the end of the 1995 season. But the key word there was backup; Stone had only one regular-season start in his three years with the Cowboys. Stone was a latecomer to football, playing for the first time during his junior year in West Roxbury, MA, and was a fourth-round draft pick out of Boston College for the Cowboys in 1993.

STOUDT, CLIFF
Quarterback, 6'4", 222 lbs., b. 3/27/55

Stoudt, who broke into pro football in 1977 with the Pittsburgh Steelers, spent the final week of the 1990 season as the Cowboys' emergency backup quarterback. Not that the veteran from Youngstown State University had much more to do the previous season with Miami; he was a roster member for seven games and spent three of those as a holder. Stoudt, who once passed for more

than 2,000 yards for Pittsburgh and spent two seasons in the USFL, was also with the Cowboys in 1991, after which he retired from football.

STOWE, OTTO
Wide receiver, 6'2", 190 lbs., b. 2/25/49

Stowe was traded to the Cowboys in 1973 to shore up the receiving corps. He had backed up Paul Warfield for two years in Miami without seeing much action, although he had excellent speed and was an outstanding blocker. The Iowa State ex got off to a great start—he was leading the team in receiving yards and touchdowns—when he broke his ankle in the seventh game of the season. That sidelined him for the rest of the year; rookie Drew Pearson filled in for him admirably, and Stowe was traded to Denver in 1974. He spent one year there, and caught only two passes, before retiring.

STRAYHORN, LES
Running back, 5'10", 205 lbs., b. 9/1/51

Strayhorn was the last player drafted by the Cowboys in 1973 (seventeenth round, out of East Carolina), but he appeared in eleven games. He had 11 carries for 62 yards and a touchdown and handled two kickoff returns. The next year he again carried 11 times, this time for 66 yards, and had two more kickoff returns. He was released and retired from the NFL after the season.

STUBBS, DANIEL
Defensive end, 6'4", 264 lbs., b. 1/3/65

The former University of Miami All-American came to Valley Ranch thanks to a trade with San Francisco. His mission was specific: to bolster Dallas' pass rush. No problem; he started fifteen games and tied for the team lead in sacks with 5.5. But with the addition of talented defensive linemen like Leon Lett in 1991, Stubbs made no starts that year, and played in only seven games, moving on to Cincinnati before the season was over. He played through the 1993 season, then saw action with the Eagles in 1995.

STUDSTILL, DARREN
Safety, 6'1", 186 lbs., b. 8/9/70

The University of West Virginia's seventh-leading passer all time was drafted in the sixth round in 1994 with the intention of moving him to safety. After all, it had worked for the likes of Nolan Cromwell and the Cowboys' own Charlie Waters. It didn't really work with Studstill, who was gone after one season. He spent most of the season inactive, getting into only the New Orleans game on December 19. The following year, he played for the expansion-team Jacksonville Jaguars on special teams.

STURGIS, OSCAR
Defensive end, 6'5", 280 lbs., b. 1/12/71

A seventh-round draft pick in 1995 out of the University of North Carolina, Sturgis was one of the pleasant surprises of training camp, and he stuck with the team. He was inactive for the first thirteen games of the season, then saw limited backup action in the last several games and against Philadelphia in the playoffs. He was expected to get a shot at moving into the Cowboys' regular rotation of defensive linemen following the defection of Russell Maryland to Oakland after the season. Sturgis only moved to defense during his junior year at Carolina after playing tight end.

STYNCHULA, ANDY
Defensive end, 6'3", 250 lbs., b. 1/7/39

Stynchula had spent eight years in the NFL with Washington, New York, and Baltimore before the Cowboys obtained him in 1968 for a future draft choice. He backed up the defensive line, primarily at end, then retired after the season.

SULLIVAN, MIKE
Offensive guard, 6'3", 278 lbs., b. 12/22/67

Toughness was never a question with Sullivan; he started a school-record 48 games for University of Miami that posted a record of 44–4 despite the removal of a benign tumor behind his left ear, a sprained right ankle that put him on crutches, and painful back problems. But toughness couldn't keep Sullivan at Valley Ranch for more than the 1991 season, during which he primarily saw special-teams action. He went on to play several years with Tampa Bay.

SUPER BOWL

Of the thirty Super Bowls played through the 1995 season, the Dallas Cowboys have participated in eight of them. No other team can claim that kind of success. (However, San Francisco, 5–0, and Pittsburgh, 5–0, have better winning percentages.) The Cowboys' Super Bowl rundown:

Super Bowl/ Year	Opponent	Result/Score
VI, 1971	Baltimore	L, 16–13
VII, 1972	Miami	W, 24–3
X, 1976	Pittsburgh	L, 21–17
XII, 1978	Denver	W, 27–10
XIII, 1979	Pittsburgh	L, 35–31
XXVII, 1993	Buffalo	W, 52–17
XXVIII, 1994	Buffalo	W, 30–13
XXX, 1996	Pittsburgh	W, 27–17

(See also "Cowboys Super Bowl Roundup," page 258)

SWAN, RUSS
See Replacement Games

SWEENEY, KEVIN
Quarterback, 6'0", 193 lbs., b. 11/16/63

The Cowboys released their seventh-round pick from Fresno State on the final cut

Kevin Sweeney

in 1987. About a month later, Sweeney was the toast of Dallas.

Sweeney was re-signed for the Cowboys strike team, and he led the replacements to two victories. His strong arm produced 4 touchdowns and 20.8 yards per completion, including a 77-yard TD pass to Cornell Burbage, Dallas' longest completion of the season, in a victory over Philadelphia. Fans loved his story: how he played for his head-coach father, Jim, at Fresno State and finished his career as the most prolific passer in NCAA history with 10,623 yards. As a kid, Sweeney accompanied his father to Cowboys training camp in California, where ten-year-old Kevin fielded punts for Danny White.

When the regular players returned, Sweeney was retained as a reserve, creating ill feelings in the locker room. But he was brought back for 1988, finishing with 33 completions in 78 attempts for 314 yards, 3 touchdowns, and 5 interceptions.

Sweeney, who was about two inches shorter than his program listing, simply wasn't tall enough to be an NFL starter, and his career was over following the 1988 season.

SWITZER, BARRY
Head coach

The former head coach of the Oklahoma Sooners—and for sixteen years one of the most disliked men in Texas—had been a couch potato for five years when he received a call the morning of March 22, 1994 from old friend Jerry Jones, owner of the Dallas Cowboys. Jones was attending the NFL winter owners' meeting in Orlando and had just made a decision. Was Switzer interested in coaching the Cowboys? Switzer's affirmative answer didn't take long, and a week later he found himself driving down to Dallas from Norman, OK, for a press conference announcing his hiring. It was a move that left Dallas Cowboys fans aghast—and

Barry Switzer

another step on a long journey for the bootlegger's boy from Crossett, AR.

Switzer has been surprising people for a long time. After three years as a center and linebacker for the Arkansas Razorbacks (he was elected captain as a senior in 1959), he spent two years in the Army upon completing his bachelor's degree in business administration in 1960. Two years later, he served as the scout team coach for the Razorbacks under Frank Broyles. In 1964–65 he coached the team's offensive ends; he coached both Jerry Jones and future Cowboys coach Jimmy Johnson as Arkansas claimed the national championship in 1964.

Switzer moved to Oklahoma in 1966 as the offensive line coach under Jim Mackenzie. Chuck Fairbanks succeeded Mackenzie upon the latter's death in 1967, and he named Switzer his offensive coordinator. Three years later, Switzer took on the duties of assistant head coach. When he was named head coach in 1973, his success with the Sooners was quick and tremendous. He guided the team to 28 consecutive wins from 1973 to 1975 and went 37 straight games without a loss. Oklahoma won back-to-back national championships in 1974 and 1975, then won another in 1985. During his sixteen-year tenure at Oklahoma, he won 12 Big Eight titles and 8 of 13 bowl games.

But Switzer resigned in the midst of player scandals in 1989 and half-heartedly pursued business ventures in Norman. He didn't need the money, but he did need a challenge—and Jones's offer was that and then some.

Switzer hadn't coached an offense besides the outmoded wishbone in many years, and he had never coached in the NFL. He had a lot to learn, and he admitted it freely. But he wasn't prepared for the criticism he would receive—from the public, the media, and even his players.

Switzer's laid-back attitude was light years from control-freak Jimmy Johnson's tough, put-the-fear-of-God-in-'em approach. He allowed players to skip an occasional

practice, a taboo with Johnson regardless of the reason. He talked to players before doing things. He went to their houses. He told jokes in the locker room and in team meetings. It was a radical adjustment for many players, especially Troy Aikman, who had played for Switzer at Oklahoma before transferring to UCLA: Aikman had gown to like Johnson's approach.

He also had to fight the public perception that he was just a figurehead coach, that his experienced assistants did all the coaching—or at least the parts that owner Jones didn't handle. It got worse when Jones began dressing and acting like a coach during training camp. Former San Francisco coach Bill Walsh called him a "ceremonial coach." And as the 1994 season wore on, things got worse, until Switzer snapped just before the first playoff game. In a closed meeting he made it clear that he was the boss in loud, unSwitzerlike fashion. The outburst helped, at least with the players, but when the Cowboys lost to the 49ers in the NFC Championship Game the criticism increased. Switzer wasn't tough enough on his players, unlike Johnson, who had won two Super Bowls with essentially the same team and a drill-instructor attitude. Even some of the players claimed to miss the crack of the Johnson whip.

Things changed as the 1995 season took shape. Switzer had watched for a year; now he began to take charge more openly. His easygoing style of motivation began to take. Switzer had always been good with players, relating to them and motivating with a carrot, not a stick. As the Cowboys marched toward another Super Bowl, the criticism lessened; it didn't disappear, but no one could argue with a team that went 13–3 and eventually won the Super Bowl in the face of severe pressures, on and off the field.

One of the hardest things to do in the NFL to is win when everyone expects you to. Switzer wasn't perfect during the season—there was plenty of second-guessing after a questionable call by the Dallas coach allowed the Eagles to get the ball back and move for a game-winning field goal in the 14th game of the season. But it became clearer as the playoffs neared that this was Barry Switzer's team, and he was the one making the decisions. The 27–17 Super Bowl XXX triumph in February 1996 was a vindication for Switzer, who silenced his critics and proved he could do it his way.

Switzer's autobiography, *Bootlegger's Boy*, was published in 1990.

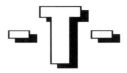

TALBERT, DON
Offensive tackle, 6'5", 220 lbs., b. 3/1/39

All-American Talbert was an eighth-round draft pick from Texas (as a future) in 1961. He joined the team as a rookie in 1962, and then spent two years with the Army in Vietnam. He rejoined the Cowboys in 1965 and started at right tackle until rookie Ralph Neely took over. He went to Atlanta in the next year's expansion draft; three years later he went to New Orleans in their expansion draft. "Varmint," as he was nicknamed for his wild and woolly ways, became a Cowboy again in 1971, his last year in the NFL, backing up the offensive line.

Talbert's brother, Diron, was a defensive lineman with the Redskins during the seventies who conducted a decade-long verbal battle with Roger Staubach. The week before every Washington-Dallas game he kept sportswriters busy with his taunts and insults, most of which were aimed at the Dodger.

TAUTALATASI, JUNIOR
Running back, 5'11", 208 lbs., b. 3/24/62

For the record, his first name was actually Taivale. He was a backup running back in Philadelphia (1986–88) before signing with the Cowboys as a free agent. He played thirteen games for Dallas that season without a start, carrying 6 times for 15 yards, and grabbed 17 passes for 157 yards. And that duty occurred only because fellow running back Kevin Scott suffered a season-ending knee injury. It was a surprising flame-out for a player who, as a rookie, rushed for 163 yards and caught 41 passes out of the backfield for 325 yards. He retired from the NFL after the season.

TENNELL, DEREK
Tight end, 6'5", 270 lbs., b. 2/12/64

Tennell, signed by the Cowboys only five days before their first playoff game against Philadelphia following the 1992 season, was surprised to hear his number called in the huddle with Dallas lurking at the Eagles' 1-yard line in the first quarter. "I was thinking, 'Don't drop the darn thing.'" He didn't. The touchdown pass turned out to be Tennell's only reception as a Cowboy. It was 50 percent of his regular-season total, those two passes being caught as a member of the Minnesota Vikings after starting the season on Detroit's roster. Tennell returned to Minnesota as a free agent for the 1993 season, then retired from the NFL.

TEXAS STADIUM
The glittering showcase of Cowboys football, Texas Stadium opened on October 24, 1971 with all the proper fanfare and an appropriate result: a 44–21 Dallas victory over the New England Patriots. The first touchdown was scored by that legendary malcontent, Duane "Sphinx" Thomas, on a 56-yard run just two minutes into the game. That successful beginning carried through the season, which ended with the team's first world championship, a 24–3 victory over the Miami Dolphins in Super Bowl VI.

Located in the Dallas suburb of Irving, Texas Stadium's seating capacity was 66,024 in the mid-nineties, although owner Jerry Jones had unveiled expansion plans that would boost the facility's capacity to more than 100,000. Texas Stadium's most distinctive feature is its partial roof, which covers fans from inclement weather but keeps the game outdoors where it belongs. Jones' expansion plans also included a retractable roof and installation of a grass field.

Even after 25 years, Texas Stadium remained one of the finest football facilities in the country, featuring two DiamondVision color replay screens, 296 luxury suites, 52 concession stands, 85 rest rooms, 115 drinking fountains, and a Lone-Star-state-sized 130 acres of parking. Texas Stadium replaced the revered but aging Cotton Bowl, home to the team from its inception in 1960.

Tours of Texas Stadium are available throughout the year, including weekends and holidays when no events are scheduled.

Texas Stadium, 2401 Airport Freeway, Irving, TX 75062; (214) 438-7676.

THOMAS, BILL
Running back, 6'2", 225 lbs., b. 8/7/49

Thomas was a big back with good speed out of Boston College whom Dallas made their first-round draft pick in 1972. In training camp that year, he aggravated an old shoulder injury, underwent surgery, and didn't join the active roster until the eighth game. He had no rushes but ran back two kickoffs; the next year he was traded to Houston. He spent one year there as a backup, and one year in Kansas City before retiring from the NFL.

THOMAS, BLAIR
Running back, 5'10", 195 lbs., b. 10/7/67

The Cowboys' top rusher in their play-off opener following the 1994 season was *not* Emmitt Smith, who gained only 44 yards on seven carries. The hoss that day, in a 35–9 whipping of Green Bay, was Thomas, with 70 yards on 23 carries. But Thomas, the New York Jets' first-round pick of 1990, was

merely a spaceholder while Smith recovered from a hamstring injury that sidelined him for the season finale against the New York Giants. In that game at the Meadowlands, Thomas gained 63 yards. But after the Packers game, he was nowhere to be found—with Smith back at full strength—when the Cowboys beat San Francisco in the NFC Championship Game at Candlestick Park. He finished the regular season with 43 carries for 137 yards and 2 touchdowns, and added four receptions and three kick returns. Thomas signed as a free agent with Tampa Bay in 1995.

THOMAS, DAVE
Cornerback, 6'2", 205 lbs., b. 8/25/68

Credit the sharp memory of Cowboys scouting director Larry Lacewell for Thomas's presence on the 1993–94 Dallas rosters. Thomas's final season of college football was the 1990 campaign at the University of Tennessee. He didn't play football in 1991 or 1992. But on draft day 1993, Lacewell—new to the Cowboys with the incoming Barry Switzer regime—recalled Thomas from Lacewell's days on the Tennessee staff. Thomas earned a roster spot, with the help of an interception in the final preseason game, and spent two seasons helping out on special teams. He was selected by the new Jacksonville Jaguars in the 1995 expansion draft.

THOMAS, DUANE
Running back, 6'1", 200 lbs., b. 6/21/47

A quiet, intense halfback from West Texas State who grew up on the streets of South Dallas, Thomas was the Cowboys' first-round draft pick in 1970 and one of the more fascinating individuals the NFL has ever seen. When starter Calvin Hill left the sixth game, against the Chiefs, with a bad back, Thomas rushed for 134 yards on just 20 carries, including a 47-yard touchdown

Duane Thomas returns a 1970 kickoff. *(From the collection of the Texas/Dallas History and Archive Division, Dallas Public Library)*

that brought the Kansas City crowd to their feet. He gained 803 yards that year, on 5.3 yards a carry, best in the NFL, and was named Rookie of the Year. Against Detroit and San Francisco in the playoffs, he gained 135 and 143 yards, but in the Super Bowl against Baltimore he was held to 35 yards on 18 carries; he caught a short pass for a TD, but fumbled on the Baltimore goal line early in the second half of what would be a 16–13 Dallas loss. (Although center Dave Manders recovered, Baltimore claimed possession and was awarded the ball.)

The following year, dissatisfied with his low-dollar contract, and under financial pressures, he held out. In July, while training camp was in progress, he held a Dallas press conference to explain his situation. He called Tom Landry a "plastic man, actually no man at all," Tex Schramm "sick, demented, and completely dishonest," and Gil Brandt "a liar." After an aborted trade to New England that was quickly cancelled "for

moral and ethical reasons"—Thomas didn't get along with New England management, and they thought he was on drugs—he was back in uniform a few games into the season.

On the field it looked like he'd never been away, but off the field his comments to the press and teammates were few and far in-between; Bob Hayes dubbed him "Othello" for his brooding countenance. Still, most of his teammates claimed to like him, although there were few who could understand him; even other black players confessed bewilderment. But Dallas roared to an 11–3 record, bolstered by Thomas's league-leading 11 touchdowns. He gained 95 yards on 19 carries to help the Cowboys win their first Super Bowl 24–3 over Miami. In the locker room, with actor-adviser Jim Brown at his side, he rattled interviewer Tom Brookshier in a classic exchange: "Are you really that fast?" "Evidently."

During training camp the following year, Thomas increasingly marched to a different drummer, talking to no one, practicing when he felt like it. (Much later, in his 1988 autobiography *Duane Thomas and the Fall of America's Team*, Thomas berated the Schramm-Landry-Brandt triumvirate as hypocritical, racist, and greedy.) Landry had bent the rules for him plenty, but there was a limit. Before camp was over, he was traded to San Diego for Billy Parks and Mike Montgomery.

He sat out the entire year in a contract dispute. He landed in Washington next, and worked hard to regain his 1971 form, but he couldn't break into the starting lineup; he spelled Larry Brown with occasional success. The next year was somewhat better—he led the team in rushing touchdowns, and in his last game in the NFL he carried 8 times for 102 yards, all in the second half. In 1975 he played for Hawaii in the World Football League; he pulled a muscle the second week and played only in five games, rushing 34 times for 92 yards. By this time, Thomas's vegetarian diet and his penchant for running long distances as practice had slimmed him down—he was in good shape, but he didn't have the explosion or power he once had. The WFL folded after eleven weeks.

Thomas returned to Dallas and asked Landry to give him a chance to play in 1976. But he missed much of training camp with a pulled hamstring and failed to show the speed he once had. He was cut at the end of preseason. In 1978 he talked Green Bay into a tryout; he pulled a muscle and was released. A year later, the Packers gave him another tryout. He worked out two days and was released again. That was his last attempt at professional football.

THOMAS, IKE
Cornerback, 6'2", 190 lbs., b. 11/4/47

The highest-picked football player in the history of Dallas' Bishop College (he was a seventh-rounder in 1971), Thomas had 4.5 speed in the forty. He started the year on the taxi squad, but when veteran Herb Adderley

was injured (colliding with a TV camera) he started the next game against St. Louis at left cornerback. He was burned deep several times, and didn't play much defense the rest of the season. He also ran back 7 kickoffs for an amazing 42-yard average, including one for 89 yards against the Los Angeles Rams, and another for 101 yards (a record that stood for twenty years) against the New York Jets. He was traded to Green Bay in 1972, and later played with the Buffalo Bills and in the Canadian Football League.

THOMPSON, BRODERICK
Guard, 6'5", 280 lbs., b. 8/14/60

Like Herschel Walker, Nate Newton, and Todd Fowler, Thompson was a USFL graduate who went on to a career in the NFL. Thompson played for five USFL teams before signing with the Cowboys in August 1985.

A defensive tackle at Kansas, Thompson originally joined the Cowboys as a rookie free agent in the summer of 1983. The Cowboys released him, but Thompson's mother told him the Cowboys would be calling again in two years. After making a name for himself in the USFL, the call came.

Thompson would become an NFL contributor elsewhere, however. He was released by Dallas at the end of 1986 training camp, signed with San Diego in 1987, and played for the Chargers until 1992. Thompson was traded to the Philadelphia Eagles in 1993, played for the Eagles until 1994, then signed a free agent contract with the Denver Broncos in March 1995.

THORNTON, BRUCE
Defensive lineman, 6'5", 266 lbs., b. 2/14/58

Thornton was a long-shot eighth-round draft pick in 1979 when he made the team by beating out two defensive linemen drafted higher. He had 32 career sacks during his college career at Illinois, and he was a good student, twice earning Academic All-Big 10. Thornton was also a talented musician, turning down several scholarships for his saxophone playing to accept an athletic free ride.

Thornton turned in a strong rookie campaign, taking advantage of Ed Jones's retirement when Jones attempted a boxing career. He finished second on the team to Harvey Martin with 6 sacks. Against the Chicago Bears in September, Thornton enjoyed a homecoming when he registered 2 sacks, knocked down a pass, and blocked an extra point. Two weeks later against Cincinnati, he intercepted a Jack Thompson pass caused by Martin's pressure.

Jones' return in 1980 reduced Thornton's playing time, but he came up with a big game in the wild card round against the Los Angeles Rams with 3 sacks. But Thornton was never able to crack the Cowboys talented foursome of Randy White, John Dutton, Jones, and Martin. He was waived by the Cowboys and claimed by the St. Louis Cardinals in 1982, then played in the USFL in 1984–85.

THOUSAND OAKS

After four training camp sites in the three previous years (Pacific University in Forest Grove, OR; St. John's Military Academy in Delafield, WI; St. Olaf College in Northfield, MN; and Northern Michigan College, Marquette, MI, near Lake Superior), the campus of California Lutheran College in Thousand Oaks, CA (about 45 miles north of Los Angeles) was chosen to be the Cowboys' new summer home in 1963. Located in the Conejo Valley, "The Oaks" offered a cool breeze and dependably near-perfect weather. The area grew with the Cowboys; what was once just a few residential areas, a bowling alley, and the campus now boasts movie theaters, several restaurants and shopping malls, and the population has grown from 10,000 to over 100,000 residents. It would remain the Cowboys'

training camp until 1990, when new owner Jerry Jones moved summer camp to St. Edward's University in Austin, TX, just 200 miles down I–35 from Dallas.

THURMAN, DENNIS
Defensive back, 5'11", 179 lbs., b. 4/14/56

Thurman lacked size and speed, which was why the University of Southern California star wasn't selected until the eleventh round of the 1978 draft. But Thurman was the thinking man's defensive back, a future coach who gave the Cowboys nine seasons of intelligent, play-making coverage. Said ex-linebackers coach Jerry Tubbs of Thurman, "As a leader and a winner you didn't find 'em any better."

At USC, Thurman intercepted passes in seven straight games and led the nation in interception return yardage in 1976. He made the Dallas roster as a long-shot cornerback, even though he supposedly was short on the speed required for the position.

Dennis Thurman

The Cowboys were immediately impressed. Former teammate Charlie Waters probably summed up Thurman best: "Dennis really studied our system and he wanted to know why we did this or that. He asked such interesting questions that I thought, 'Hey, he's a player.' He just has this great feel for split-second analysis, that innate knack for being where the ball is."

As a rookie, he excelled on special teams but also saw more action than expected at cornerback due to injuries to Benny Barnes and Mark Washington, intercepting two passes there. He was voted Dallas' top special teams performer in the playoffs, recovering an onside kick that led to the Cowboys final touchdown in Super Bowl XIII, a 35–31 loss to the Pittsburgh Steelers in what was considered one of the greatest Super Bowls of all time.

Thurman continued to be a contributor off the bench in 1979, playing in the nickel defense, starting a game at cornerback, and filling in for the injured Randy Hughes at safety.

Shoulder injuries to Hughes opened the door for Thurman to take over the starting free safety job in 1980. Defensive coordinator Ernie Stautner was looking for more turnovers, and Thurman was the perfect solution, coming up with 5 interceptions and 2 fumble recoveries, and finishing second on the team with 101 tackles. Thurman also served as special teams captain in 1980.

Although Thurman was better suited to safety, the Cowboys needed a cornerback in 1981, and he turned in one of the finest seasons ever by a Dallas defensive back with 9 interceptions, third-best in the NFL, and at that time, the third-highest total in club history. It was a year of surprises for the Cowboys secondary. In addition to Thurman's excellent season, the Cowboys also uncovered two free agent gems in Everson Walls and Michael Downs. Thurman's biggest game came in December against the Philadelphia Eagles when he tied a franchise record with 3 interceptions as the Cowboys clinched another NFC East title.

Waters had been the leader of the secondary, but when he retired prior to the 1982 season, Thurman inherited the role. He remained the starting right cornerback in 1982 and 1983, picking off 9 more passes in those two seasons and extending his streak to 57 consecutive starts. In a 1982 playoff win over Green Bay, Thurman matched an NFC playoff record with 3 interceptions, including a 39-yard touchdown return.

As the years went by, however, Thurman's lack of speed became more of a liability at cornerback, and in 1984 the Cowboys switched him to reserve free safety. But with extended use of the 4–0 nickel defense, Thurman played as much as ever, finishing with 5 interceptions and serving as the on-the-field coordinator of the various passing down packages.

In 1985, the Cowboys' defensive backs—including Everson Walls, Dextor Clinkscale, Michael Downs, Ron Fellows, Bill Bates, Victor Scott, and Ricky Easmon—were dubbed Thurman's Thieves as they combined for 33 interceptions, one behind the league-leading Chicago Bears. (Thurman chipped in with 5.) The secondary was a major factor in the Cowboys' 10–6 record. They also made possible, through excellent coverage, and well-timed secondary blitzes, a team-record 62 sacks. (A staged photo of the eight in classic 1930s-gangster suits and fedoras that appeared in *The Dallas Morning News* irritated some fans and teammates who thought the whole thing was too flashy.)

By this time, Thurman was only a backup and passing-down back. Despite his leadership and football intuition, Thurman was waived prior to the 1986 season. He immediately signed with the St. Louis Cardinals. There he was reunited with former Cowboys secondary coach Gene Stallings, who had been named the Cardinals head coach. Thurman went on to become a defensive backfield coach for the Cardinals, then accepted a college assistant's job at his alma mater.

Cowboys All-Time Records Vs....

Arizona Cardinals	44–22–1
Atlanta Falcons	12–6
Buffalo Bills	5–2
Chicago Bears	10–6
Cincinnati Bengals	4–2
Cleveland Browns	10–17
Denver Broncos	5–2
Detroit Lions	8–7
Green Bay Packers	12–10
Houston Oilers	5–3
Indianapolis Colts	7–3
Kansas City Chiefs	4–2
Miami Dolphins	2–6
Minnesota Vikings	12–7
New England Patriots	6–0
New Orleans Saints	14–3
New York Giants	43–22–2
New York Jets	5–1
Oakland Raiders	3–3
Philadelphia Eagles	45–28
Pittsburgh Steelers	14–13
St. Louis Rams	12–13
San Diego Chargers	5–1
San Francisco 49ers	11–13–1
Seattle Seahawks	4–1
Tampa Bay Buccaneers	8–0
Washington Redskins	39–31–2

THURMAN'S THIEVES
See Thurman, Dennis

TIMMER, KIRK
See Replacement Games

TIPPINS, KEN
Linebacker, 6'1", 226 lbs., b. 7/22/66

Signed as a free agent out of Middle Tennessee State University, Tippins was part of Jimmy Johnson's first Cowboys team in 1989. His statistical contributions were 4 tackles from scrimmage and 4 on special teams. He signed with Atlanta before the 1990 season and played several years there.

TITENSOR, GLEN
Offensive guard, 6'4", 275 lbs., b. 2/21/58

A defensive lineman at Brigham Young after starting his college career at UCLA, Glen Watson Titensor was another in a long line of players converted by the Cowboys into offensive linemen, following in the footsteps of Blaine Nye, John Fitzgerald, Pat Donovan, and Kurt Petersen.

The third-round pick in the 1981 draft went through the typical learning process that such a radical change in position requires, serving as a backup center and guard before securing the job at starting left guard, five games into the 1984 season.

A solid if unspectacular blocker, Titensor started 44 consecutive games until a knee injury sent him to injured reserve for the 1987 season. Titensor came back to play as a reserve in 1988, but knee problems forced him to retire.

TOLBERT, TONY
Defensive end, 6'6", 263 lbs., b. 12/29/67

Was it the genius of Jimmy Johnson, or did the Cowboys simply stumble into the good fortune of Tolbert's development into a star defensive lineman? After all, Tolbert was selected in the fourth round of the 1989 draft out of Texas–El Paso as a 226-pound outside linebacker.

Then again, Tolbert was part of a Miners team that won ten games—usually a three-year total at UTEP—and played in a

Tony Tolbert drags down San Diego running back Ronnie Harmon.

bowl. Moved up to the line, he was an almost immediate hit, and earned five starts as a rookie. The Cowboys didn't rush him. They brought him off the bench most of the time in 1990, giving him only four more starts before turning over the defensive end postion to him in 1991.

Tolbert made an impact in 1991 at left end, leading the team with 7 sacks and 25 quarterback pressures while playing the run effectively, and turning in 73 tackles.

The Cowboys were emerging as one of the forces in the league, and so was Tolbert, who had slowly built himself into more than 260 pounds, on a frame more suited to basketball power forward than NFL lineman. Tolbert paced Cowboys defensive linemen in 1992 with 87 tackles and was a key figure in helping Dallas to the league's number-one ranking in rushing defense. Tolbert added a sack in the Super Bowl XXVII victory over Buffalo.

In 1993 Tolbert again led the Cowboys in sacks with 7.5 and had 23 quarterback pressures despite coming out on certain pass-

ing downs. Teaming with Charles Haley at the other end, Tolbert had his most consistent season with at least 6 tackles in half of the Cowboys regular-season games, then had one sack in each of Dallas's playoff games as the team rolled to a second straight Super Bowl championship.

Tolbert's 1994 season was more of the same as he registered career highs for solo tackles (57), total tackles (89), and tackles for lost yardage (7). In the last six games of the regular season, Tolbert had 48 tackles, 3 sacks, 5 tackles for lost yardage, 8 quarterback pressures, 4 passes knocked down, and he even threw in his first career interception.

The Cowboys won their third Super Bowl in four seasons in 1995, and Tolbert was again a key contributor, despite two aching knees that would require offseason surgery and jeopardize his career. Tolbert again established a career high with 99 tackles, tied for second on the team with 5.5 sacks, led the Cowboys with 41 quarterback pressures, and forced 2 fumbles. Tolbert's never been to a Pro Bowl, but with 96 straight starts entering the 1996 season, and a team-high 45 sacks since 1990, few Cowboys defenders have been more productive.

TOOMAY, PAT
Defensive end, 6'5", 240 lbs., b. 5/17/48

A sixth-round draft choice in 1970, Toomay was another classic Gil Brandt catch—a high-school basketball star who was recruited by Vanderbilt as a quarterback. In college he switched from safety, in his senior year, to linebacker and then defensive end. He played five solid years with the Cowboys, becoming one of their top pass rushers. Nicknamed "Ropes" because the

Pat Toomay

savvy Toomay always seemed to know them, he logged plenty of time backing up such greats as George Andrie and Larry Cole, and later Harvey Martin and Ed "Too Tall" Jones, but he was more than a mere backup. His rookie year he started the last three games of the season for an injured Cole, and the next year he split time with Andrie. In 1975 he was traded to the Buffalo Bills; a year later he was a member of the expansion Tampa Bay Buccaneers. He finished his career with three years in Oakland, where he saw limited duty due to knee problems.

Toomay was one of the more interesting Cowboys on and off the field. Tom Landry was stunned when he and other coaches realized one preseason that Toomay, who had been named a starter one game, had recruited other players to take his place on the various special teams so he could fully concentrate on his starting duties. (They only found out watching game film the next Tuesday.) In his spare time he managed the career of Ray Wylie Hubbard, one of the mid-seventies outlaw country singers. He was a charter member of the infamous Zero Club with Blaine Nye and Larry Cole, and the author of *The Crunch*, a 1975 account of his stay with the Cowboys. He also wrote a novel about game fixing in football, *On Any Given Sunday.*

TOWNES, WILLIE
Defensive end, 6'5", 260 lbs., b. 7/21/43

Townes was a second-round draft pick out of Tulsa in the 1966 draft. He was big, fast, and aggressive; he made spectacular plays, and it wasn't long before he worked his way into the starting lineup. His rookie season he moved ahead of Larry Stephens once he got his weight down. In the 1967 Ice Bowl his hit on Bart Starr resulted in a fumble that end George Andrie ran in for a score.

He was exceptionally fast for a man his size—he had run hurdles in college—but

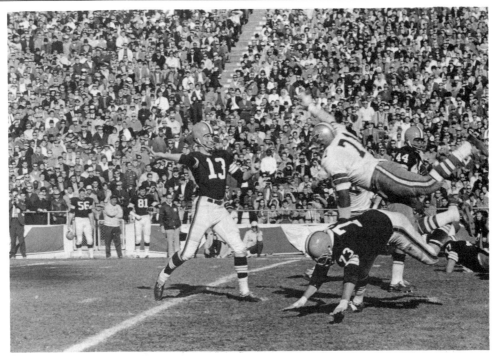

Willie Townes (71) pressures Cleveland quarterback Frank Ryan, 1967. *(From the collection of the Texas/Dallas History and Archive Division, Dallas Public Library)*

"Baby Cakes" had a weight problem. He always reported to camp too big, and spent more time at the Fat Man's Table than anyone. It didn't help when he went down with a knee injury midway through the 1968 season; after a year on the sidelines recovering, he came back the next year overweight and out of shape, and was traded to the New Orleans before the season. He played one year as a backup there before retiring.

TREMBLE, GREG
Safety, 5'11", 190 lbs., b. 4/16/72

Tremble spent the 1994 training camp with the Cleveland Browns and was released before the season opener. The Georgia ex signed with the Cowboys and made the team in training camp. Tremble played on special teams and nickel defense situations, rec-

ording 6 tackles, before being released on waivers in mid-October.

TRUAX, BILLY
Tight end, 6'5", 240 lbs., b. 7/15/43

This LSU ex had started at tight end for most of his seven years with the Los Angeles Rams as Roman Gabriel's favorite receiver; he was also an excellent blocker. Truax was traded to the Cowboys in 1971. He backed up Mike Ditka, the front-line tight end, on injured legs, but between the occasional start and shuttling plays into the huddle, he caught 15 passes for 232 yards that year, and 4 for 49 yards the next. In 1973, his final year in the NFL, he backed up rookie sensation Billy Joe DuPree, but didn't catch a pass.

TUBBS, JERRY
Linebacker/assistant coach, 6'3", 220 lbs., b. 1/23/35

Tubbs was an All-American at Oklahoma, and the Walter Camp Award winner as the nation's outstanding player in 1956; he was so good, he finished fourth in the Heisman Trophy voting. He was drafted in the first round by the Chicago Cardinals the next year and played a season and a half there. After a trade to the 49ers and two years there, he decided to call it quits; he had a good job lined up with Coca-Cola. But when that fell through, and he was selected by the Cowboys in the expansion draft of 1960, their first year, he was back in football.

He was a bit light for linebacker, but he had excellent lateral movement, and he was very fast, maybe the fastest linebacker in the NFL. After finally convincing Tom Landry that he was better suited to play middle instead of outside linebacker—and after an injury to Jack Patera—he became the leader of the early Dallas defenses. He was All-Pro and a Pro Bowler in 1962, and known as one of the most aggressive players in the game. He started at middle linebacker six straight years. Playing for losing teams all those early years was tough on Tubbs; he'd never lost a game at Oklahoma. After the 1964 season he announced his retirement, but Landry persuaded him to come back for another year as a player-coach. He retired again a year later, confident that third-year linebacker Lee Roy Jordan was ready to take over his spot. But he came back one more year as a backup; halfway through the year he injured his back and watched from the sidelines the rest of the season. He was even activated for the next season, 1967, but never played a down, and continued to coach the linebackers. He continued in that position for more than twenty years, and four Cowboy linebackers were named to the Pro Bowl under his tutelage: Lee Roy Jordan, Bob Breunig, Chuck Howley, and Thomas Henderson. He left the Cowboys when Jimmy Johnson took over as coach and cleaned house in 1989.

TUINEI, MARK
Offensive tackle, 6'5", 305 lbs., b. 3/31/60

In 1983 training camp, Tuinei was one of 85 rookie free agents attempting to catch the eye of Tom Landry and his coaching staff. Fourteen years later, Tuinei was entering his 11th camp as the Cowboys starting left tackle, the longest tenure among any current Cowboys starter, and a two-time Pro Bowler.

Now the team's elder statesman with fellow 1983 free agent Bill Bates, Tuinei certainly has come a long way since his rookie orientation when he hooked on as a defensive tackle. His college career could only be described as checkered, playing his first two years at UCLA before transferring to Hawaii, where injuries limited him to seven games as a senior.

Tuinei's physical play in camp impressed defensive coordinator Ernie Stautner and Tuinei got into ten games as a reserve his rookie season. He played in sixteen games his second season, seeing action as a backup at all four line positions.

In 1985, the Cowboys experienced a depth crunch on the offensive line and Tuinei was switched to center, backing up starter Tom Rafferty. The following season was the most confusing of his brief career, as injuries to other players forced him to split time between the offensive and defensive tackle. Subbing for injured defensive tackle Randy White, Tuinei had 6 tackles in an October game against Denver. The following week, Tuinei started at left offensive tackle and he remained there for the rest of the season.

In 1987, Tuinei concentrated on offense, where he has spent the rest of his career. He started the first eight non-strike games on the left side before injuring his left knee on Thanksgiving Day. Resulting sur-

Mark Tuinei

gery landed him on injured reserve for the rest of the season, then he re-injured the knee during the 1988 season after seeing action in only five games, sending him back to injured reserve.

Tuinei finally emerged in 1989, remaining healthy and starting all sixteen games at left tackle. He didn't miss a practice or a snap during games; in a matchup against Pro Bowl linebacker Lawrence Taylor of the New York Giants, Tuinei did such a good job he earned player of the game honors.

He missed three games with a sprained right knee, but started the other thirteen in 1990 with an emerging front five that was developing into one of the league's best. By 1995, he had started 73 of 75 games, including playoffs, and had played in more Cowboys games (189 including the post-season) than any other Dallas offensive player.

In addition to his three starts in Super Bowl victories, Tuinei's career highlights include the back-to-back trips to the Pro Bowl following the 1994 and 1995 seasons. While some players treat the Pro Bowl as a chore, Tuinei delighted in the opportunity to play before family and friends in his native Hawaii.

TURNER, JIMMIE
Linebacker, 6'1", 214 lbs., b. 2/16//62

A rookie free agent from little Presbyterian College in Suwannee, GA, Turner was released on the final cut prior to the 1984 season, then was re-signed with five games left to bolster a linebacking corps depleted by injuries. Turner played exclusively on special teams in his limited action and was unable to make the roster the following summer.

TURNER, NORV
Assistant coach

The right place at the right time? Suffice to say the Cowboys' rise to a playoff team in 1991, then a Super Bowl power the next two seasons, had something to do with Turner's arrival as offensive coordinator in 1991. Coach Jimmy Johnson had just demoted David Shula to create the vacancy. The choice for a replacement was Turner, a Los Angeles Rams offensive assistant who was a particular favorite of Rams offensive coordinator Ernie Zampese. The Dallas offenses he built in 1992 and 1993 frustrated defenses with their tremendous balance. Stopping Emmitt Smith could take all day. And if that was accomplished, what about Troy Aikman passing to the likes of Michael Irvin and Alvin Harper... and a tight end as talented as Jay Novacek? Turner was rewarded for his efforts by being named coach of the Washington Redskins before the 1994 season. Imitation being the highest form of flattery, Turner had his Redskins playing like the Cowboys in sweeping the two-game series from Dallas during the 1995 season.

Cowboys All-Time Leaders— Most Seasons

15	Ed Jones	1974–78, 1980–89
14	Bob Lilly	1961–74
14	Lee Roy Jordan	1963–76
14	Jethro Pugh	1965–78
14	Randy White	1975–88
14	Tom Rafferty	1976–89
13	Chuck Howley	1961–73
13	Cornell Green	1962–74
13	Dave Edwards	1963–75
13	Ralph Neely	1965–77
13	Rayfield Wright	1967–79
13	Larry Cole	1968–80
13	Mike Hegman	1976–88
13	Danny White	1976–88
13	Bill Bates	1983–
13	Mark Tuinei	1983–

VAN RAAPHORST, DICK
Kicker, 5'11", 215 lbs., b. 12/10/42

Van Raaphorst was a free agent kicker out of Ohio State signed by the Cowboys in 1964. He was 28 of 29 on extra points, but only 14 of 29 on field goals. He was released before the next season when Danny Villanueva was signed. He sat out a year and played two years with San Diego (both years were virtual carbon copies of his Dallas season) before retiring from the NFL.

VANDERBEEK, MATT
Linebacker, 6'3", 243 lbs., b. 8/16/67

The former Michigan State University teammate of fellow Cowboy Dixon Edwards established himself as a force on Dallas' special teams in 1993–94. He entered the NFL as a free agent with Indianapolis in 1990, starting seven games for the Colts at inside linebacker. He returned to the starting lineup only once in the next two seasons in Indianapolis, and was waived in 1993. His special-teams play for the Cowboys earned him a nomination from that spot for the Pro Bowl team. He left Dallas via free agency for the Washington Redskins in 1995.

VEINGRAD, ALAN
Offensive tackle, 6'5", 280 lbs., b. 7/24/63

Such was Veingrad's globe-hopping route to Valley Ranch: he was born in Brooklyn, graduated from high school in Miami, and played college football at East Texas State University. As a rookie in 1986, he started all sixteen games for Green Bay—in front of highly touted draftee Tony Mandarich at right tackle—after failing to catch on with Tampa Bay or Houston. The rest of

his Packer days weren't as rewarding, in part because of a hip injury that forced him to miss the entire 1988 season. He signed with the Cowboys through Plan B free agency in 1991 and started four games at left tackle in place of the injured Mark Tuinei. The 1992 season brought more of the same, a backup role with the exception of one game in which Tuinei was hurt. He was released after the season, his last in the NFL.

VILLANUEVA, DANNY
Punter/kicker, 5'11", 200 lbs., b. 12/5/37

Villanueva was a five-year veteran with the Los Angeles Rams when he was traded to the Cowboys for receiver Tommy McDonald in 1965. He remained in Dallas for three years, his best coming in 1967 when he led the NFL in extra-point kicks (56 of 56) and the Cowboys with 107 points. The New Mexico State product was a good but not great kicker, but there were some highlights; in 1966 he kicked a 30-yard field goal with 11 seconds left to beat the Redskins 31–30 and put Dallas into their first playoffs. In the 1966 Championship Game loss to the Packers he kicked 2 field goals, and he kicked 1 in the Ice Bowl loss the next year. But his punting average never approached his strong Los Angeles numbers, and the Cowboys were not completely happy with him; in 1967 they initiated a Kicking Karavan traveling circus that visited cities all over the country and tried out 1,300 aspiring kickers. When all the dust settled, only one kicker, Harold Deters, was signed; he stayed through a few games and was released, having connected on only 1 of 4 field goals. Villanueva remained the kicker and punter for the season, then retired to become a successful Spanish-language television personality and businessman.

221

WALEN, MARK
Defensive tackle, 6'5", 267 lbs., b. 3/10/63

Retirements and injuries had depleted the Cowboys' defensive line in the mid-to-late-eighties, creating an opening for Walen, a 1986 third-round draft pick from UCLA.

Walen was on injured reserve his rookie year with a broken ankle, giving him plenty of time for his hobby of restoring classic cars, but he made a smashing debut in 1987, recording a sack in the season opener against St. Louis. In 1988 he played primarily in passing situations at end or tackle, finishing with 4 sacks and 25 tackles. He also started two games, including a 9-tackle, 2-sack performance against Phoenix when he stepped in for the injured Kevin Brooks.

In 1989, there was a new coaching staff aboard, and Walen was one of only four returning defensive linemen. He was impressive enough in training camp to earn the starting job at left tackle, and he had a sack and a tackle for a loss in the first five minutes of the second preseason game against the Raiders. But Walen suffered a season-ending injury to his left knee in a meaningless exhibition, marking the end of his pro football career.

WALKER, GARY
See Replacement Games

WALKER, HERSCHEL
Running back, 6'1", 226 lbs., b. 3/3/62

The Cowboys were never afraid to gamble on draft day, and they made one of the wisest picks in their history when they invested a fifth-round choice in 1985 on Walker, the 1982 Heisman Trophy winner from the University of Georgia who, at the time, was the marquee player of the USFL.

Walker was the star of the New Jersey Generals, the spring league's glamour team, and in three seasons Walker rushed for 5,562 yards, caught 1,484 yards in passes and scored a mind-boggling 61 touchdowns. His 2,411 yards rushing in 1985 remains a pro football record.

Walker had a long-term contract with the Generals, but the USFL suspended play in 1986. That made the Cowboys' investment of a draft pick they had acquired from the Houston Oilers (in a trade that only cost them Butch Johnson) seem like pure genius. Walker's signing on August 13, 1986 drew as much media interest as any Cowboys-related event of the decade, with the exception of Jerry Jones' arrival as the team's new owner and the firing of Tom Landry in 1989.

Now that Landry had Walker, he had to decide how to use him. That was easier said than done. Already set at tailback was Tony Dorsett, at that time the greatest runner in club history.

Some considered Walker to be odd. Others said he simply marched to a different drummer. He claimed he ate only one meal a day; he referred to himself in the third person; he was a martial arts devotee; he danced with the Fort Worth Ballet; and he dreamed of being an FBI agent. He was also an extraordinary talent.

Landry decided to deploy Walker as a fullback and pass receiver, and Walker responded. He rushed for 737 yards, caught 76 passes for 837 yards, and scored 14 touch-

Herschel Walker hurtles the Giants' goal-line defense for a touchdown.

downs. Walker became the first player in NFL history with more than 700 yards both on the ground and through the air, while Dorsett was rushing for 748 yards and accounting for 267 more yards in receptions. For the long term, however, there wouldn't be room for two superstars in the same backfield.

Walker was entering the prime of his career, while Dorsett's star was fading. Walker had another terrific season in 1987, leading the league with 1,606 combined yards (891 rushing, 715 receiving). Meanwhile, Dorsett rushed for 456 yards while growing increasingly more resentful as his role diminished.

The Cowboys sent Dorsett to the Denver Broncos for a draft choice prior to the 1988 season. Herschel Junior Walker had the job to himself, and he put up more impressive numbers: 1,514 yards rushing and 505 yards in receptions, to become only the 10th player in league history to gain more than 2,000 yards in a season. Walker also was voted to the Pro Bowl for the second straight season and won All-Pro honors. All those accomplishments were bittersweet,

however, as the Cowboys trudged to a 3–13 record.

A new coach, Jimmy Johnson, was aboard the following February, and he was soon hatching plans to rebuild the franchise. Walker was his most marketable commodity, and on October 12, 1989, Johnson pulled off one of the biggest heists in NFL history.

Walker was sent to the Minnesota Vikings for five players and six draft picks. The players weren't terribly significant, but the draft choices helped transform the Cowboys from jokes into champions. Emmitt Smith, Kevin Smith, and Russell Maryland were only three of the players the Cowboys landed through the Walker deal.

While the Cowboys would go on to win three Super Bowls in four seasons with the help of players from the deal, Walker's career nosedived with the Vikings, whose coaching staff didn't seem to have a clue how to use him. Walker was released by the Vikings in June 1992, and he soon signed with the Philadelphia Eagles. After three years in Philadelphia, he accepted a free agent deal with the New York Giants in 1995.

WALKER, LOUIE
Linebacker, 6'1", 215 lbs., b. 7/23/52

A free agent signed out of Colorado State in 1974, Walker was one of the last players cut by Dallas before the season opener. He rejoined the team for the last eight games of the season and played well on special teams. He was released before the next season and never played in the NFL again.

WALKER, MALCOLM
Offensive tackle/center, 6'4", 255 lbs., b. 5/24/43

The number-two draft choice of the Cowboys in 1965 was a top-notch linebacker from Rice. He was extremely quick, and Dallas decided to convert him into an offensive lineman. Before he even got to training camp that summer, he badly twisted a knee practicing for the College All-Star Game. After surgery, he spent his entire rookie year mending on the sidelines. He wasn't activated until late the following year, and the next year he backed up the center and tackle positions. In 1968, after an intense regimen of strength and conditioning in the off-season, he gained the starting center spot when Mike Connelly was traded and Dave Manders was also returning from knee surgery. He tore up his knee again the next year, then was traded to the Green Bay Packers, before the 1970 season, for cornerback Herb Adderley. More knee surgery after the season forced him to retire.

WALLACE, RODNEY
Offensive guard/tackle, 6'5", 260 lbs., b. 2/10/49

Wallace was a tenth-round draft choice from New Mexico in 1971. Toward the end of the season he was asked to take the injured Blaine Nye's starting position at right guard in a pivotal late-season game against Los Angeles. His man, Merlin Olsen, never got to quarterback Roger Staubach. He subbed at tackle and guard on the offensive line for the next three years (1971–73), and nursed a back injury during the 1974 season. He tried to come back the next season but was unsuccessful and retired.

WALLS, EVERSON
Cornerback, 6'1", 193 lbs., b. 12/28/59

The improbable story seemed perfect for a made-for-TV movie: Walls, raised two miles from the Cowboys' North Dallas practice facility, won a roster spot as a 1981 rookie free agent and barged into the starting lineup in the fifth game of his rookie year.

Walls led the nation as a Grambling senior with 11 interceptions in as many games, but scouts said he was a step too slow to play cornerback in the NFL. He had an incredible knack for the big play, however, intercepting 3 passes, recovering a fumble, and scoring a touchdown with a blocked punt in the preseason to secure a position on the 1981 Cowboys. "I look at it as a challenge that nobody drafted me," Walls said. "From the first day, I wanted to prove they were wrong."

Walls continued his spectacular play during the season, finishing with an NFL-high 11 interceptions to break Mel Renfro's team record and becoming the first rookie to lead the league since Detroit's Lem Barney in 1967.

Walls picked off 2 more passes and recovered a fumble in the NFC Championship Game, during which he was involved in one of the key plays in club history when San Francico's Dwight Clark made a leaping late-fourth quarter touchdown catch behind him to give the 49ers a 28–27 decision. Walls continued his amazing run when he was chosen for a Pro Bowl berth, and he made two more interceptions in that game.

Nicknamed "Cubby" by his mother as a baby for his resemblance to a bear cub,

Everson Walls makes an interception against the Cardinals.

Walls maintained his high profile, intercepting 14 more passes over the next three years and earning more Pro Bowl and All-Pro honors in 1982, 1983, and 1985. Walls had 9 more interceptions in 1985 and remained a starter through the 1989 season.

New coach Jimmy Johnson was shaking up the roster, however, and Walls was released after the 1989 season. He departed with 44 career interceptions, second on the Cowboys all-time list behind Mel Renfro's 52.

He signed as a free agent with the New York Giants and went on to win his first Super Bowl in 1990. Walls was traded to Cleveland during the 1992 season and played two years there before retiring.

WALSH, STEVE
Quarterback, 6'2", 200 lbs., b. 12/1/66

And to think there was a time when debate raged among Cowboy fans over whether Walsh should be starting ahead of Troy Aikman. Three Super Bowl rings have justified Aikman's status—not that Walsh hasn't put together a solid career. It was,

though, difficult to come in as the second million-dollar rookie quarterback, which Walsh did when coach Jimmy Johnson

Steve Walsh

picked up his bags at the airport in the summer of 1989. That first season together, Walsh threw for 1,371 yards compared to Aikman's 1,749. Most of those yards came in the five starts Walsh made with Aikman out injured; and he did account for the team's lone victory, the 13–3 shocker at Washington, complete with an on-side kick. By 1990, Walsh was no factor, and he was traded during the season to New Orleans. He guided the Saints into the postseason both of the next two years, a feat he also accomplished with Chicago in 1994, for former Cowboys assistant Dave Wannstedt.

WALTER, MIKE
Linebacker, 6'3", 238 lbs., b. 11/30/60

The Cowboys struck out on another second-round draft pick when they released 1983 second-rounder Mike Walter before the 1984 season. But Walter was claimed in waivers by the San Francisco 49ers, and the 'Niners had a bargain when they shifted him from outside linebacker to the inside. Walter became a starter during 1985 training camp and was one of San Francisco's leading tacklers as the 'Niners won three Super Bowls to become the team of the eighties.

WALTON, BRUCE
Offensive tackle, 6'6", 250 lbs., b. 6/14/51

Walton, the older brother of basketball great Bill Walton, was the Cowboys' fifth-round draft pick in 1973. The UCLA ex saw action in seven games his first year, backing up at both guard and tackle, and playing on special teams. In 1974 he played on special teams and started one game for the injured Rayfield Wright. The next year was his last in the NFL; he saw plenty of action on special teams and backed up Wright infrequently.

WANNSTEDT, DAVE
Assistant coach

The first of the Jimmy Johnson disciples to colonize the NFL after the new era

Cowboys hit it big was Wannstedt, when he left Dallas to become coach of the Chicago Bears for the 1993 season. With the Bears, he quickly built a playoff team, reaching the postseason in just his second year as head coach. He first hooked up with Johnson in 1977, when Wannstedt was already an assistant coach at the University of Pittsburgh and Johnson joined the staff as defensive coordinator. When Johnson took over the Oklahoma State University program in 1979, he brought along Wannstedt as defensive line coach. He was promoted to defensive coordinator in 1981 and left Johnson temporarily to join the staff at the University of Southern California, 1983–85. Wannstedt rejoined Johnson at the University of Miami in 1986, again as defensive coordinator, and came to Dallas in 1989. At Valley Ranch, he was responsible for taking the dregs of that 1–15 team in 1989 and building the league's best defense.

WARD, BOB
Assistant coach

Ward replaced Alvin Roy as the Cowboys' strength and conditioning coach in the spring of 1975. He remained with the Cowboys through the '89 season.

WARREN, JOHN
Punter, 5'11", 205 lbs., b. 11/8/60

Coach Tom Landry had gone with Danny White as his punter for seven seasons, but in 1983, he decided not to expose his starting quarterback to further risk of injury as a punter. Warren, a free agent from Tennessee, won the job and averaged 39.8 yards in 39 punts.

Warren experienced a wild 1984 season, however, shuttling between jobs as a punter in Dallas and produce truck driver in his hometown of Knoxville, TN. Warren was beaten out for the job by Jim Miller in training camp, and Warren was released. Miller was found lacking, and White was handed his former role. But Warren was re-signed on October 27 so that White could concentrate on quarterbacking the team. Two weeks later, Warren was released again to open a roster spot; but the Cowboys recalled Warren on November 21 as punting insurance for White. Warren stayed with the Cowboys for the rest of the season, but was soon back behind the wheel of a truck and never punted again in the NFL.

WASHINGTON, JAMES
Safety, 6'1", 200 lbs., b. 1/10/65

Many fans think the real MVP of Super Bowl XXVIII should have been this UCLA product, who helped account for 17 points against the Bills. (He narrowly lost the award to Emmitt Smith.) In the first quarter, Washington's hit on Thurman Thomas caused a fumble that led to an Eddie Murray field goal. Early in the second half, Washington scooped up another Thomas fumble and zigzagged his way 46 yards for a touchdown; the extra point tied the score at 13. But his most lasting contribution to Cowboys' lore is likely the interception on the first play of the fourth quarter that solidified Dallas' triumph at the Georgia Dome. The Cowboys only led 20–13 at the time but when the Bills' Jim Kelly found Washington near midfield, the subsequent 34-yard touchdown drive gave Dallas a two-touchdown lead that was never threatened.

Washington, a trash-talker from the mean streets of Los Angeles, was drafted out of UCLA by the Rams in the fifth round in 1988, and he brought a reputation as a hard-hitting, aggressive safety to Dallas as a Plan B pickup in 1990. He started at safety for most of his five years with the Cowboys. In his first year as a Cowboy, he tied for the team lead in interceptions with 3 and led the team in forced fumbles. The following season, his second full year as a starter, he finished second on the team in tackles with 113, tops among defensive backs. In 1992 he again tied for the team lead in interceptions with 3, and added 2 in the playoffs. A sprained knee early in 1993 sidelined him for two games, and when he returned, he saw action primarily in the nickel defense and on

special teams; he led nonstarters in tackles with 42. His last year with the Cowboys, he again tied for the team lead in interceptions with 5, and made 101 tackles, fifth on the team. He signed with the Redskins (and former Cowboys assistant coach Norv Turner) after the 1994 season.

WASHINGTON, MARK
Defensive back, 5'10", 185 lbs., b. 12/28/47

A thirteenth-round draft pick out of Morgan State in 1970, Washington saw limited duty that year, although he did run a bobbled kickoff back 100 yards for a touchdown. A knee injury kept him out of most of the 1971 season; the next two years he was restricted to subbing for the starters. In midseason 1974 he settled in as the starting left corner until hobbled by an ankle injury the last two games. "Strip" started at left corner again in 1975, but in 1976 lost his starting job to Benny Barnes, although he later started at right corner after an injury to Mel Renfro. Both years he had 5 interceptions. The next season, Aaron Kyle and

Mark Washington

Barnes emerged as the starting corners. In 1978, his final year, he was strictly a substitute in the secondary.

WATERS, CHARLIE
Safety, 6'1", 195 lbs., b. 9/10/48

Charles Tutan Waters came to the Cowboys as their third-round pick in the 1970 draft. He had been a receiver in Clemson, but he took over the starting job at free safety his rookie year after Cliff Harris left during the year for the military. He led the team with 5 interceptions and started in the Super Bowl loss to Baltimore. But Harris recaptured the job in 1971, forcing Waters to fill in, and perform on specialty teams. Although he wasn't really fast enough for the position, he earned a cornerback job and kept it the next three years (1972–74). But when longtime strong safety Cornell Green retired, just prior to the 1975 season, the position was his.

Strong safety was his natural position, and Waters made that clear very quickly; he earned the first of three Pro Bowl appearances in 1976, and he was twice an All-Pro. He was known for his bone-jarring hits, and he was a big-game performer. He raised his play even higher in the playoffs; he holds the NFL playoff record for most career interceptions with 9, the single-game record with 3, and he was a starter in 5 Super Bowls.

But in a 1979 preseason game against Seattle, Waters went down untouched with a torn ligament in his right knee. He was out for the year. A rigorous rehab regimen only partially rehabilitated the knee, but in 1980 he returned—with a bulky knee brace that slowed him considerably. He still shared the club interception lead with 5. Additional surgery in the offseason gave him one final year, and he used it to field-coach a young secondary nicknamed Charlie's Angels that included free agent rookies Everson Walls and Michael Downs. He retired after the 1981 season with 41 career interceptions.

WATKINS, KENDELL
Tight end, 6'1", 305 lbs., b. 3/8/73

This second-round draft choice from Mississippi State University in 1995 is the latest attempt to place someone in the understudy role for Jay Novacek at tight end. Used almost exclusively as a blocking tight end in running situations, Watkins caught 1 ball for 8 yards during the season. He also saw special-teams action, recovering a squib kick against Washington. The rarity of a 300-pound tight end could make him a different kind of weapon, for blocking as well as receiving. In college, he caught only 11 passes during his career while collecting 80 knockdown blocks.

WATTS, RANDY
See Replacement Games

WAYT, RUSSELL
Linebacker, 6'4", 235 lbs., b. 10/6/42

The Cowboys' eighth-round pick out of Rice in the 1965 draft saw limited action as a backup during the season and was released.

WELCH, CLAXTON
Running back, 5'11", 200 lbs., b. 7/3/47

Welch was the Cowboys' ninth-round pick in the 1969 college draft. The Oregon ex saw little action in his three years in Dallas, rushing 25 times for 85 yards behind Walt Garrison. He had 27 yards on 5 carries in the NFC Championship Game against San Francisco. He sat out a year, and then played the 1973 season with New England before retiring.

WELLS, NORM
Guard, 6'5", 261 lbs., b. 9/8/57

Wells was a long-shot twelfth-round pick from Northwestern who survived a mid-camp switch from defensive to offensive line and made the roster in 1980. Wells injured his knee in the third game while playing on special teams and spent the rest of the season on injured reserve. He returned for a playoff game against Atlanta, but injured the knee again while on special teams, and underwent surgery in the offseason. Although Wells attempted comebacks the next two seasons, he never played again.

WESTBERRY, GARY
See Replacement Games

WHITE, BOB
Offensive lineman, 6'5", 273 lbs., b. 4/9/63

A seventh-round pick of the New York Jets in 1986, White was signed by the Cowboys in 1987 but was released on the final roster cutdown after making the switch from guard to center. White was re-signed for the replacement team during the players strike and was kept after the strike was settled. In 1988, White started three games for injured center Tom Rafferty, but his career ended following the 1989 season.

WHITE, DANNY
Quarterback/punter, 6'2", 180 lbs., b. 2/9/52

White was a third-round draft pick out of Arizona State for the Cowboys in the 1974 draft. (His father, Wilford "Wizzer" White, was a halfback with the Chicago Bears in 1951–52.) But instead of sitting on the Dallas bench as the third-stringer behind Staubach and Morton, he opted to play for Memphis in the World Football League for two years, gaining valuable experience throwing to Paul Warfield and handing off to Larry Csonka. The WFL went under after two years, and Dallas signed him in 1976. His punting skills made him doubly valuable.

Danny White

As a punter he wasn't long, but he was consistent, with good hang time, and he was accurate; he could drop a kick into the coffin corners when necessary. (Staubach dubbed him "America's Punter.") And every so often he'd run out of punt formation for a big gain, if he saw the return team dropping back too much. The next four years he saw limited duty filling in at quarterback for Staubach; in 1978 he subbed for an injured Staubach in a playoff game against Atlanta, and brought the team from behind to win. That was the year they lost to Pittsburgh in a Super Bowl rubber match.

The next year, Staubach retired and the team was White's. In his first year as a starter, he broke the Dodger's record for touchdowns with 28, and hit 59.6 percent of his passes, but he threw 4 interceptions in two postseason games. In 1981 he had another stellar season, 22 touchdowns and 57 percent, and a great postseason. But that was the year of The Catch; after White (having a fine 16-of-24 passing day) brought his team from behind to go ahead of San Francisco, a last-minute Dwight Clark TD reception won the game for the 49ers. White's late fumble allowed San Francisco to run out the clock and go to the Super Bowl. He had another excellent season in strike-shortened 1982—63 percent, 16 TDs, a league-leading 8.42 completion average—but a concussion in the NFC Championship Game loss against Washington was another season-ending downer. In the 1983 season opener against Washington, he threw 3 TDs in the second half to overcome a 20-point deficit and win 31–30. It was another superb year statistically—29 touchdowns, 63 percent passing—but the team staggered into the playoffs and immediately lost to the Rams. White passed for 330 yards, but he also threw 3 interceptions.

The next year, fifth-year man Gary Hogeboom got the starting nod. He started off strong but got progressively worse. When he sprained his ankle in a late October game against the Saints, White came in facing the short end of a 27–6 score. He completed 15 of 25 passes for 2 TDs, and a late third-down scramble enabled Dallas to win in overtime, 30–27. A few weeks later, White was again the starter. But the Cowboys finished 9–7 and missed the playoffs for the first time since 1976.

The next year was a turning point for Dallas. White had another good year, starting most of the games and hitting 59 percent and 21 touchdowns, and Dallas was 7–3 heading into a showdown with undefeated Chicago. The Bears destroyed the Cowboys 44–0, knocking White out of the game twice. Dallas never completely recovered, and lost to the Rams 20–0 in the playoffs. White threw 3 interceptions.

Almost halfway through the next season, Dallas sported a 6–2 record, but a 17–14 loss to the Giants, in which White broke his wrist, was the turning point. The team won only one of its last eight games under Steve Pelluer. White's short season

included 12 touchdowns and a 62 percent completion average. The next year he hadn't completely recovered; he hit 59 percent of his passes, but threw more interceptions than TDs, and the Cowboys had another losing season. It was his last full year; 1988 saw him throw only 42 passes as a backup to Pelluer and second-year man Kevin Sweeney, and the Cowboys had their worst record (3–13) since their inaugural 0–11–1 season.

White retired after the season with impressive career numbers: 21,959 yards on 59.7 percent passing, 155 touchdowns. He was named to the Pro Bowl in 1982. White was an above-average quarterback for a Dallas team that was only Super Bowl-caliber his first few years as a starter. He had a few bad playoff games, but so did Staubach; he also had some excellent ones, and there were other reasons for big-game losses during his tenure. He never seemed to shake the unavoidable ghost of his predecessor. Unfair or not, White is remembered as a quarterback who couldn't win the big one—not unlike another gutsy play-caller by the name of Meredith.

WHITE, GERALD
See Replacement Games

WHITE, RANDY
Defensive tackle, 6'4", 250 lbs., b. 1/15/53

It was Charlie Waters who dubbed him "Manster"—half man, half monster—and if ever a nickname fit, that one did. One of the best defensive lineman to ever play the game, he had the whole package—size, strength, speed, quickness, agility, and especially, tremendous heart. He never let up.

White was the second player selected in the 1975 draft (out of Maryland, where he won the Outland Trophy and the Vince Lombardi Award as college football's top defensive lineman in 1974), but he languished as a backup linebacker—"the next Lee Roy Jordan"—for two years. When he

Randy White

took over the starting right tackle job in 1977, he was an instant force, a gamebreaker—it took at least two blockers just to slow him down. His highlight film would be an extended miniseries, but the one play that epitomized White's relentless style came in December 1980 against Philadelphia, when he overtook wide receiver Scott Fitzkee from behind after a 49-yard pass play. No one had seen a lineman do *that* before.

White was named to the Pro Bowl every year from 1977 to 1985, and he was named All Pro from 1978 through 1985. He was voted NFL defensive lineman of the year in 1978, and shared co-MVP honors (with Harvey Martin) in Super Bowl XII. He wasn't completely ready to retire after the 1989 season, although his neck was giving him some trouble, but when the new regime fired Tom Landry that was the last straw. (White had once said, "I'd probably run in front of a car for that man.") In 1993, five years after he retired, he was named to the Cowboys Ring of Honor and the Pro Football

Hall of Fame; White received both honors with former teammate Tony Dorsett. He lives in Dallas and stays busy making radio and TV commercials, doing promotional work and appearances, and bass fishing.

WHITFIELD, A.D.
Running back, 5'10", 200 lbs., b. 9/2/43

Whitfield was a little-known running back from North Texas State who made the team in 1965 as a free agent. After five weeks on the taxi squad, he was activated and played the rest of the year as a backup running back (he had 1 carry for no gain). He was let go after the season and picked up by Washington, where he became their regular fullback for three years until he retired. He worked for the Cowboys signing free agents for several years in the mid-eighties.

WHITTINGHAM, FRED
Linebacker, 6'1", 240 lbs., b. 2/4/39

Whittingham had been with three teams—Los Angeles, Philadelphia, and New Orleans—in five years before Dallas acquired him to back up their linebacking trio in 1969. He saw duty on special teams but little else. He was traded just before the 1970 season to the Boston Patriots, then spent another year with Philadelphia before retiring.

WIDBY, RON
Punter, 6'4", 210 lbs., b. 3/9/45

As the Cowboys' regular punter for four years (1968–71), Widby was more than adequate; he had only a few outstanding games but he was a model of consistency. He was named to the Pro Bowl in his last year as a Cowboy, 1971, though he only had a 41.6-yard average that year. The Tennessee ex was an excellent all-around athlete; before he signed with the Cowboys in 1968, he had played two years of pro basketball with the ABA New Orleans team, the Buccaneers.

In 1968 Widby rocketed the longest punt in Cowboy history, an 84-yarder against the New Orleans Saints. His best year was 1969, when he averaged 43.3 yards a punt (second in the NFL), and he still owns the record for best average for a game, minimum 4 punts: 53.4 (the same day of the 84-yarder). In the 1971 Super Bowl he punted 9 times for a 41.9-yard average. Following the 1971 season he was traded to the Green Bay Packers and worked there for two years. During a practice toward the end of the season of his second year, he was injured; a ruptured disc and nerve damage to his legs ended his career.

WIDELL, DAVE
Offensive tackle, 6'6", 300 lbs., b. 5/14/65

Widell's career started with promise when the fourth-rounder from Boston College opened the 1988 season at right tackle for the injured Kevin Gogan, becoming the first rookie offensive lineman to start a season opener for Dallas since Burton Lawless in 1975. More injuries later in the season opened the door for Widell to start eight games at left tackle, and Widell also saw action at guard when Crawford Ker and Nate Newton went down with injuries.

Widell, whose brother, Doug, was also an NFL offensive lineman, got two more starts in 1989, and also served as the deep snapper on the punt team. Jimmy Johnson traded Widell to Denver late in training camp of 1990. The Cowboys got back a seventh-round pick that they used in 1991 to select future Pro Bowl defensive tackle Leon Lett.

WILBUR, JOHN
Defensive tackle, 6'4", 250 lbs., b. 5/24/43

Wilbur was a free agent out of Stanford when he was signed by Dallas in 1966. He played well on specialty teams and filled in on the defensive line his rookie year. He was a backup and sometime starter at offensive guard for the next three years. Wilbur was

fast, aggressive, and fiercely competitive; it seemed that every summer camp would find him in a practice-field fight with a leading defensive player—Lee Roy Jordan one year, Jethro Pugh the next. He was traded to the Los Angeles Rams in 1970. He played there for one year, before finishing out his career with two years with the Washington Redskins.

WILLIAMS, CHARLIE
Safety, 6'0", 190 lbs., b. 2/2/72

By the end of the 1995 season, rookie Williams had established himself as the backup to Brock Marion at free safety. The Cowboys' third-round draft pick in 1995, Williams finished fourth on the team with 18 special-teams tackles, and tied for third with 4 special-teams tackles in the playoffs. Williams, who also played receiver at Bowling Green, has excellent speed and leaping ability.

WILLIAMS, ERIK
Offensive tackle, 6'6", 322 lbs., b. 9/7/68

On the field, Williams has established himself as one of the finest offensive linemen in the game. He blossomed from a 1991 third-round draft pick out of Central State in Ohio, the school's third draft choice ever, to become the textbook NFL blocker.

But off the field, Williams' reputation has been pancaked by two incidents. One involved a woman who accused Williams of sexual abuse, an episode that ended with no official charges filed but plenty of embarrassment to the Cowboys' organization. The second had much more of a direct effect on the team. He missed more than half of the 1994 season after crashing his Mercedes at high speed into a wall on a freeway entrance ramp, following some late-night partying after the team returned from a victory in Arizona.

As a rookie, "Big E" started three games, two at right tackle for Nate Newton and one on the left side for Mark Tuinei.

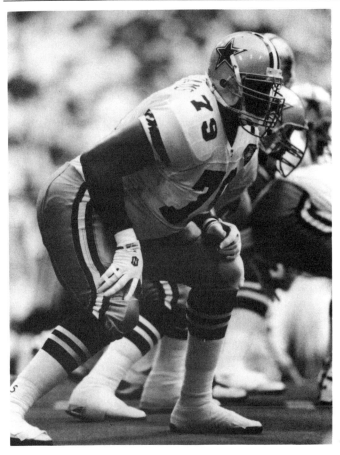

Erik Williams

Line coach Tony Wise knew he had a special player, and in 1992, the Cowboys accommodated Williams, moving him into the starting lineup at right tackle, while shifting Newton to left guard.

He seized the opportunity, starting all sixteen games and three in the playoffs. Williams, a Philadelphia native, drew the attention of opponents when he held Philadelphia Eagles All-Pro defensive end Reggie White without a sack in a 20–10 Dallas win in early November. His blocking skills helped Dallas finish fourth in the league in total offense, and opened the way for Emmitt Smith to nail down his second consecutive league rushing title.

By 1993, Williams had cemented his reputation as one of the NFL's most devastating blockers, earning one of three Pro Bowl invitations for Cowboys offensive linemen. Smith tacked on his third straight rushing crown, and Dallas' front wall gave up the fewest number of sacks in the league, en route to a second straight Super Bowl.

Williams' ride to the Hall of Fame ran into a roadblock with the 1994 car wreck, following the seventh game of the season. Williams began a long, painful rehabilitation from a torn medial collateral ligament, posterior cruciate ligament, and popliteal muscle in his right knee.

Williams was back at workouts by mid-August, beating medical projections, and he opened the season at his usual right tackle spot. When he missed a game due to injury, it was a strained left calf muscle, not the knee, that sidelined him. Williams was not as effective as he was prior to the surgery, but he was good enough to earn first-team All-Pro recognition from *The Sporting News* and *USA Today* as the Cowboys rolled to their third Super Bowl in four seasons.

WILLIAMS, JOE
Running back, 6′0″, 195 lbs., b. 3/30/47

Williams, the Cowboys' twelfth-round draft pick in 1970, spent his first year on the taxi squad. In 1971 the Wyoming ex had 21 carries for 67 yards and 3 catches for 59 yards. The following year he was traded to New Orleans; he played one year as a backup and retired from the NFL.

WILLIAMS, JOHN
Fullback, 5′11″, 213 lbs., b. 10/26/60

Williams played in the USFL from 1983–85, signed with the Cowboys in 1985, and rushed for 40 yards in 13 carries. Dallas released Williams in mid-season and he was signed by the Seattle Seahawks. Williams also played for the New Orleans Saints in 1986 and the Indianapolis Colts in 1987 before retiring.

WILLIAMS, KEVIN
Wide receiver, 5′9″, 195 lbs., b. 1/25/71

The product of Dallas' Roosevelt High School and the Cowboys' second-round draft pick out of Miami in 1993, Williams was content to serve as a return specialist and backup receiver during his first two years with the Cowboys in 1993–94. There was no shame in giving way to Michael Irvin and Alvin Harper, one of the league's most feared receiving combinations.

In his rookie season, Williams, a breakaway threat at any time, touched the ball 27 times on offensive plays—20 catches and 7 carries—and scored 4 touchdowns. He also ranked third in the NFC in punt returns with a 10.5-yard average, and had 31 kick returns for a 22.2-yard average. The following year he was even better, setting a team record for combined kickoff and punt return

yardage with 1,497. He ranked fourth in the NFL with a 26.7-yard kick return average. As a returner, Williams established team records that included becoming the first Cowboy to return a punt and a kickoff for touchdowns in the same season.

But with Harper's departure to Tampa Bay after the 1994 season, Williams took advantage of the opportunity and secured the slot opposite Irvin. He took much of the season before he began producing, but when he did, he was often spectacular. His 38 catches for 613 yards dwarfed his two-year receiving totals to date, and he again led the team in kick and punt returns. In the December 17 thriller against the Giants, he had 5 catches for 85 yards, including 3 during the final drive toward the game-winning field goal (one was a diving third-down sideline grab). A week later he had a career-high 9 receptions for 203 yards and 2 touchdowns vs. Arizona. In the first playoff game he grabbed 6 catches for 124 yards, and had 3 catches the next week against Green Bay; in the Super Bowl he had 2 catches.

WILLIAMS, ROBERT
Cornerback, 5′10″, 184 lbs., b. 10/2/62

Williams played for several bad Dallas teams in the late eighties, then he had to sit and watch when the Cowboys won Super Bowl XXVII following the 1992 season. Williams played in nine games as a nickel back during the 1992 season, but was deactivated for the playoffs, proving once again that life isn't always fair.

A running back and wide receiver at Baylor, Williams failed in his first bid to catch on in the NFL, when he was cut by the Washington Redskins in 1986 training camp. But in 1987, Williams signed with Dallas and won a roster spot after the Cowboys switched him to defensive back. Williams went on to start three games in injury situations his first season, then grabbed the starting job at cornerback in 1988, intercepting 2 passes and finishing second on the team with 19 passes defensed.

Williams started eleven more games in 1989, then spent the rest of his career as a nickel back and a reserve strong and free safety.

Williams experienced a chaotic season in 1992, his final year with the Cowboys. He went on injured reserve in late September with a knee injury. When he returned to practice in late October, the Cowboys put him on waivers, planning on re-signing him because they assumed no other team would claim him. The Phoenix Cardinals did claim him, but he failed their physical. Williams was back with the Cowboys a few days later and played in five straight games before being deactivated for four of the last five games, then for all of the postseason.

WILLIAMS, SHERMAN
Running back, 5'8", 190 lbs., b. 8/13/73

Williams was the first player the Cowboys picked in the 1995 draft, chosen in the second round, as the club sought someone who could give a breather to Emmitt Smith. Williams finished the 1995 season second in club rushing yards with 205 on 48 carries for a fine 4.3-yard average, and he added 3 receptions for 28 yards. Against Arizona on September 24, he broke free in the fourth quarter for a 44-yard touchdown run, his first in the NFL; he finished with his best game of the season with 79 yards. At the University of Alabama, Williams began his career as a backup to another player drafted by the Cowboys to be an Emmitt understudy, Derrick Lassic.

WILLIAMS, TYRONE
Wide receiver, 6'5", 220 lbs., b. 3/26/70

The Cowboys took a reach in 1992—a distant reach to the north—in signing free-agent Williams out of Western Ontario. It probably didn't hurt that he had an uncle who was also a wide receiver for Seattle (Tommy Kane). He spent all of 1992 on the Cowboys' practice squad after being drafted and cut by Phoenix. Williams earned a spot

on the 1993 roster with 11 preseason catches. He played in five games during the season, hauling in a 25-yard pass from Bernie Kosar for his lone NFL reception. He was released after the season, his only one in the NFL.

WILLIS, KEN
Kicker, 5'11", 189 lbs., b. 10/6/66

Since kickers are a somewhat nomadic breed, maybe it shouldn't have been surprising that Willis up and left a building contender like the 1991 Cowboys for—gulp—Tampa Bay. Having owned the number-one kicking job on the team for two years, all he left behind was the opportunity to kick his way into a Super Bowl or two. The free agent out of Kentucky hit 18 of 25 field goal attempts as a rookie, failing on all four attempts from 50 yards or beyond. Willis tied for 11th in NFC scoring among kickers that year. He improved to second the following year, hitting 27 of 39 attempts. The weakest part of Willis's game was kicking off; he was never a threat to force a touchback. And while the 1992 Cowboys marched into the Super Bowl, Willis didn't even last the season with the Buccaneers, finishing with the New York Giants in his last year in the NFL.

WILLIS, MITCH
Defensive tackle, 6'8", 285 lbs., b. 3/16/62

It was homecoming for Willis when he signed with the Cowboys as a free agent in 1989. He attended high school only a few miles from Texas Stadium, in Arlington, TX, and he played his college ball at Texas Stadium, with Southern Methodist University. He was brought to Valley Ranch to add depth to the defensive line. Willis had played three seasons with the Los Angeles Raiders before Dallas signed him, then moved on to Atlanta, one game into the 1988 campaign. His statistical contribution to the 1990 Cowboys was 2 tackles; he was released after the season, his last in the NFL.

WILSON, ROBERT
Fullback, 6'0", 258 lbs., b. 1/13/69

Ranked eighth in career rushing at Texas A&M, Wilson was signed as a free agent in 1994 to battle veteran Tommie Agee for. the reserve fullback role behind Daryl Johnston. He was drafted by Tampa Bay the previous year and started fifteen games, gaining 179 yards while being used primarily for blocking. Although he did make the Dallas roster in 1994, the ball never did make it into his hands; he was released in October and signed by Miami.

WILSON, STEVE
Wide receiver/cornerback, 5'10", 192 lbs., b. 8/24/57

Wilson was another product of the Cowboys' free agent pipeline in 1979 when the Howard University prospect made the club as a backup wide receiver. The Cowboys were deep at receiver, and Wilson contributed mainly as a punt and kickoff returner.

The son of two-time Pro Bowl running back "Touchdown" Tommy Wilson of the Los Angeles Rams, Cleveland Browns, and Minnesota Vikings, Steve Wilson was switched to cornerback in 1980. He wasn't given the luxury of a lengthy period of adjustment, however. Injuries forced Wilson to start eleven games on the corner, and he made some key contributions, intercepting 4 passes during the regular season and 2 more in the playoffs.

Wilson was released in 1982 and signed with the Denver Broncos, for whom he played through 1988. After his retirement as a player, Wilson went on to become head football coach at his alma mater.

WILSON, WADE
Quarterback, 6'3", 206 lbs., b. 2/1/59

The East Texas State University product left New Orleans, and another poten-

tial battle with Jim Everett over the starting job, to accept life as backup to Troy Aikman in 1995. His first "save" situation came when Aikman left the fifth game of the season, at Washington, in the first quarter. Wilson went 21-for-29 for 224 yards as the Cowboys fell short, 27–23. He also followed Aikman in the 38–20 loss against San Francisco at Texas Stadium in mid-November. The closest Wilson had previously been to reaching a Super Bowl was while quarterbacking the 1987 Minnesota Vikings to the NFC Championship Game, a 17–10 loss at Washington. His career record as a starter through 1995 was 35–30.

WISE, TONY
Assistant coach

Wise was ahead of his time in Dallas—at least in terms of his voracious love for hockey. By the time the Minnesota North Stars became the Dallas Stars in 1993, Wise had left Jimmy Johnson's staff to help former Cowboy aide Dave Wannstedt build a new staff with the Chicago Bears. He had coached with and for Johnson at the University of Pittsburgh, Oklahoma State University, and the University of Miami before making the move to Irving in 1989 as the offensive line coach. And the love for hockey wasn't simply vicarious. Wise lettered in hockey, lacrosse, and football at Ithaca (NY) College.

WISENER, GARY
Wide receiver/defensive halfback, 6'1", 205 lbs., b. 8/24/38

A rookie end out of Baylor, Wisener saw limited duty as a wide receiver and defensive back in the Cowboys' first year, 1960. After only a few games in the 1961 season, he was released. He was picked up by the Houston Oilers as a defensive halfback, then retired after the 1962 season to attend law school.

WOICIK, MIKE
Assistant coach

The former Boston College discus thrower (he set a school record of 180 feet, 5 inches) has been the Cowboys' strength and conditioning coach since 1990. Jimmy Johnson hired him away from Syracuse University, where one of his prize pupils was current Cowboys fullback Daryl Johnston. Woicik was voted the NFL's Strength Coach of the Year in 1992, the first year that Johnson took Dallas to the Super Bowl. In a telling statistic, since Woicik's arrival, the Cowboys are 31–9 in games played from Thanksgiving on through to the end of the playoffs.

WOODSON, DARREN
Safety, 6'1", 215 lbs., b. 4/25/69

In only four years, Woodson, the Cowboys' second-round draft pick in 1992, has established himself as one of the game's premier safeties. In four full seasons he has already played in three Super Bowls (starting one), earned two Pro Bowl spots, and established a single-season club record for tackles by a defensive back (155 in 1993).

Woodson's ascent in the Dallas defensive scheme was highlighted by his team-high 10 tackles during the Super Bowl XXX victory over Pittsburgh, in his native Arizona. The former Arizona State University linebacker combines size and speed with terrific instincts and hitting in the secondary. He caught on to the position change extremely quickly, and paid immediate dividends to Dallas' nickel package as a rookie in 1992. While earning two starts, he also picked up a game ball for his special-teams play in a shutout of Seattle. In 1993 he earned a starting job at strong safety in training camp. His 155 tackles were just 4 shy of the team leader, linebacker Ken Norton. He led the team in fumble recoveries

Darren Woodson

with 3. In the regular-season finale at Giants Stadium, on January 2, he made a career-high 19 tackles—the most ever by a Dallas defensive back in a single game. He was also the team's leading tackler in the playoffs. He missed only one start, in the opener at Washington, and only because he was still recovering from a fractured right forearm.

The following year, Woodson had a career season. He was named a consensus All-Pro; he tied for the team lead in interceptions with 5; he was named to the Pro Bowl in only his third year; he was second on the club with 113 tackles; and he tied for third on the team in passes defensed with 12. He also remained on the special teams, tying for third in tackles with 23. Woodson's next year was just as good. He led the team with 144 tackles, intercepted 2 passes, defensed 8 passes, and led the team in the playoffs with 23 tackles, including 11 in the Super Bowl. For his efforts he was again voted a consensus All-Pro and Pro Bowler.

Fast (4.4 in the 40), strong, and smart, Woodson is one of the team's hardest workers off the field. He has a tremendous work ethic; he graduated from high school without the grades needed for an athletic scholarship to Arizona State. So he walked on, and made his name.

WOOLSEY, ROLLY
Defensive back, 6'1", 175 lbs., b. 8/11/53

One of the Dirty Dozen rookie draft picks to make the team in 1975, Woolsey was extremely fast (he ran a 9.6 100-yard dash at Boise State). He saw limited action that year, mostly special-teams work, and ran back 12 kickoffs for 247 yards. The next year he was picked up by the expansion Seattle Seahawks. He had a good year for them, picking off 4 interceptions. He played the next year for Cleveland, then a year for St. Louis, and retired.

WRIGHT, ALEXANDER
Wide receiver, 6'0", 190 lbs., b. 7/19/67

Credit the Cowboys with having the patience to wait for the second coming of Bob Hayes. But Wright's tremendous speed—he was a winner of the NFL's Fastest Man competition—couldn't make up for the fact that he was too slow in learning to become an accomplished receiver. He was chosen in the second round of the 1990 draft out of Auburn, where he had shown flashes of brillance. He didn't help his cause when he held out nearly the entire preseason camp his rookie year. Wright never mastered the art of catching the football. In his two seasons with the Cowboys, he caught only 11 and 10 (none the second half of the season), respectively. He did, however, become a fine kick returner; in 1991, his best year, he had 21 returns for 514 yards and a 24.5 average. In October 1992, Wright was traded to the Los Angeles Raiders for a draft pick, where he became a somewhat busier receiver over the next few years.

WRIGHT, BRAD
Quarterback, 6'2", 209 lbs., b. 5/15/57

Wright was a fourth-round draft choice of the Miami Dolphins in 1981, after producing 39 touchdowns and 4,204 yards of total offense in twenty-two games of an injury-shortened career for the University of New Mexico. Wright made the Cowboys roster in 1982 but didn't attempt a pass in his only NFL season.

WRIGHT, CHARLES
Defensive back, 5'9", 178 lbs., b. 4/5/64

Wright had played for the St. Louis Cardinals in 1987 and the Tampa Bay Buccaneers in 1988, but was waived by the Bucs and signed with the Cowboys during the 1988 season as a special teamster and nickel back. That was his last year in the NFL.

WRIGHT, RAYFIELD
Defensive end, 6'7", 250 lbs., b. 8/23/45

Rayfield Wright

"The Big Cat" was the Cowboys' seventh-round draft pick in 1967, an unknown defensive end from tiny Fort Valley State in Georgia. From those humble beginnings, he became perhaps the greatest pass blocker the NFL has ever seen.

His rookie season the slender Wright was converted to tight end, but he saw little action except for specialty teams. He shifted around from tight end to tackle to defensive end and back to tackle over the next few years. But he got his weight up to 250 and when Ralph Neely moved to left tackle in 1970, after John Wilbur was traded to St. Louis, Wright earned the starting right tackle spot. Two years later he started a string of six straight Pro Bowl selections, and he was named to four All-Pro teams during that time. Said Minnesota defensive great Carl Eller, "Rayfield is pretty much the composite of an All-Pro tackle."

Wright was a quiet giant, but he had confidence in himself from the beginning. The first time he faced All-Pro Deacon Jones (in 1969, filling in for an injured Ralph Neely), before the game a teammate mentioned that he had a tough way to break in. Wright asked why. "Because Deacon is big and he's fast," said the teammate. "Well, I'm big and fast," replied The Big Cat. He went out and overwhelmed Jones.

Throughout most of the seventies he dominated every defensive end he faced. With John Niland, Blaine Nye, Ralph Neely, and Dave Manders, he anchored the strongest offensive line of the decade; in Super Bowl VI they blew away Miami's defensive line on the way to a 24–3 victory. But knee problems in 1976 gave Wright some trouble. He came back strong the next year, but a serious knee injury sidelined him for much of the season. Although the knee continued to bother him in 1978, he still started in the Super Bowl loss against Pitts-burgh. He finished his career after the 1979 season as one of the great tackles in NFL history. He was voted to four All-Pro teams and six Pro Bowls.

WRIGHT, STEVE
Offensive tackle, 6'5", 252 lbs., b. 4/8/59

Wright embarked on a multi-stop pro football career as a rookie free agent with the Cowboys in 1981. The Cowboys were stacked with offensive linemen, and the Northern Iowa ex was waived after the 1982 season.

Wright's stay in the NFL was far from over, however. He signed with the Baltimore Colts in 1983, and stayed with the team through its move to Indianapolis. Wright gradually increased his weight to 280 pounds, and after a year in the USFL, he found a good match for his talents in 1987 when he signed with the Los Angeles Raiders. Wright developed into a dependable backup guard and tackle in six years for the Raiders, but a knee injury ended his career in 1993.

WYNNE, BEDFORD
Minority owner

A friend of Clint Murchison's, Wynne was a minority owner of the early Cowboys along with Toddie Lee Wynne and W.R. "Fritz" Hawn. Clint Murchison and his brother John owned 95 percent of the team, but the high-profile Wynne was the front man for the reclusive Murchison. Wynne got so much ink that it was assumed that he and Clint Murchison were equal owners of the team. He sold his stock in the Cowboys in 1967 to work with the New Orleans Saints.

YOUMANS, MAURY
Defensive end, 6'6", 260 lbs., b. 10/18/36

After three years with the Chicago Bears, including their 1963 championship season, this Syracuse product spent a year recovering from knee surgery before his 1964 trade to the Cowboys. He spent the year backing up Larry Stephens and George Andrie, then became a starter at left end the next year. He was picked up by Atlanta in the expansion draft in 1966 but retired.

YOUNG, CHARLES
Running back, 6'1", 215 lbs., b. 10/13/52

Young was the Cowboys' first-round draft choice (after Ed Jones, originally Houston's pick) in 1974. The North Carolina State ex was a big, strong runner who developed steadily at fullback through the season. He had a 53-yard run against Houston (the club's longest that year) and averaged 6.2 yards on 33 carries; he also had 11 catches for 73 yards and 8 kick returns for a 20.1-yard average. The next year, moving between fullback and halfback, he had 50 carries for 225 yards, and 18 receptions for 184 yards. He also had 3 catches for 31 yards in the Super Bowl loss to Pittsburgh. His final year with the Cowboys, 1976, started out with Young in the starting tailback position, but halfway through the season, he dropped two touchdown passes in a loss to St. Louis and was replaced by Doug Dennison. He rarely left the bench after that, and the final result was more of the same: 48 rushes, 208 yards; 11 receptions, 134 yards. A steady string of minor injuries may have kept him from reaching his full potential, and a serious knee injury sidelined him all of the 1977 season, after which he called it quits.

241

ZAMPESE, ERNIE
Assistant coach

Teacher followed pupil in an odd sequence for the Cowboys' coaching staff before the 1994 season. Zampese, who mentored Norv Turner in their days together with the Los Angeles Rams, became Dallas' new offensive coordinator when Turner left to become coach at Washington. The chain-smoking Californian brought his many colored pens to the Texas Stadium coaching booth and picked up where Turner left off. Of course, with choices like 1) hand the ball to Emmitt Smith or 2) throw the ball to Michael Irvin, the job has its advantages. Zampese was the Southern California high school Player of the Year in 1953 and went on to play tailback for the University of Southern California. His first pro coaching job was with San Diego in 1976.

ZENDEJAS, LUIS
Kicker, 5'9", 179 lbs., b. 10/22/61

For a while in the eighties and early nineties, it seemed every NFL team had a Zendejas as its kicker. Brothers Luis, Joaquin, and Max and cousin Tony all kicked in the NFL, and two more brothers, Allan and Alex, kicked for college teams.

Luis Zendejas was with the Arizona Outlaws of the USFL in 1985, then signed with Dallas for two games in 1987 as a replacement player. When the strike was over, he landed on injured reserve with an ankle injury and was later released. The Cowboys were already familiar with the family. They had drafted Max Zendejas in 1986, but he was unable to beat out Rafael Septien.

The nomadic trek continued for Zendejas in 1988 when he kicked in the first two Cowboys games while Roger Ruzek was returning from a contract holdout. When Ruzek resumed the Cowboys' kicking duties, Zendejas was waived and signed with Philadelphia, making eight straight field goals and 13 in a row from 40 yards or less.

Things got even crazier in 1989, after he had helped the Eagles to the NFC East title the previous year. Philadelphia released him on October 30, and Dallas welcomed him back about a week later. Zendejas converted 5 of 9 field goal attempts for Dallas, which was slogging to a 1-15 record. Zendejas would have been more accurate, but his average attempt was from an NFC-high 38.3 yards.

Zendejas' Cowboy career ended in controversy in 1989 when he was one of the principal figures in the infamous Bounty Bowl. Coach Jimmy Johnson accused Eagles coach Buddy Ryan of offering cash bounties to injure specific Cowboys players. Johnson claimed Zendejas had inside information from a former Philly teammate that such a reward system existed. Eagles special teamer Jessie Small had been flagged for a personal foul after nailing Zendejas with a cheap shot to the head on the second-half kickoff of the Thanksgiving Day game won by Philadelphia, 27-0.

Nothing was ever proven, although Zendejas contended he had a tape recording of a phone conversation proving the existence of a cash-for-KOs system. Zendejas never produced the tape. Ryan wondered aloud why he would want to knock out a kicker who was in the throes of a six-week slump, and the controversy eventually blew over. Zendejas was released after the 1989 season and never played again in the NFL.

ZENTIC, MIKE
See Replacement Games

ZERO CLUB

Blaine Nye, Larry Cole, and Pat Toomay were the charter members of the Zero Club in the early seventies, a kind of Dadaesque gang of three that was, by design, nonfunctional. They were a small group of players who prided themselves on the fact that they didn't get noticed or make headlines. (They were all linemen, of course.) Apathy was the club motto, ennui the goal, and "Thou shalt not seek publicity" the first and only commandment. Of course, anyone who displayed interest in joining the club was vetoed simply for having shown interest.

As Pat Toomay put it in *The Crunch*, his amusing look at life as a Dallas Cowboy: "The Zero Club subscribes to Joseph Heller's Boredom Cultivation Plan. It is universally recognized that when someone is enjoying himself, time passes quickly. Similarly, when someone is not enjoying himself, time drags intolerably; it's one of those unfortunate quirks of nature. However, by actually cultivating boredom, one can slow time down considerably, and Zero Club members are able to add years to their otherwise truncated life experiences." It was only appropriate that the first meeting of the Club included going to see a Don Knotts movie, *How To Frame A Figg*.

ZIMMER, MIKE
Assistant coach

The former Illinois State University quarterback and linebacker joined the Dallas coaching staff in 1994 on the defensive side, primarily responsible for nickel pass

coverage. With Dave Campo's promotion to defensive coordinator in 1995, Zimmer assumed Campo's previous role, running the entire secondary. Before joining the Cowboys' staff, he coached at Washington State University, and before that, Weber State in Utah, where he first worked with Campo in 1981–82.

ZIMMERMAN, JEFF
Offensive lineman, 6′3″, 332 lbs.,
b. 1/10/65

The Cowboys had big plans for Zimmerman in 1987 when the University of Florida prospect was drafted in the third round. The NFL trend had shifted from smaller, quicker linemen to the 300-pound-plus elephants. Zimmerman was a two-time All-American who had outstanding quickness and striking ability for such a large man.

Known to teammates as "Zim" or "Zoom," Zimmerman as a rookie filled in for the injured Nate Newton at left guard, started one game, and got noticed around the league when he knocked New York Giants Pro Bowl linebacker Lawrence Taylor unconscious on a blitz.

A shoulder injury limited Zimmerman to one game in 1988, but he bounced back in 1989, starting one game and seeing action at both guard and tackle. Zimmerman's bad luck with injuries continued in 1990 when a training camp knee problem dragged into the season, knocking him out of most of the first ten games. Zimmerman saw action in the final six, playing at left guard and as the third tight end in short-yardage situations.

Zimmerman came back for 1991 training camp, but his enthusiasm for the game lagged, and he left camp under mysterious circumstances. Teammates said Zimmerman suffered from depression, although he never contacted the Cowboys to explain his situation or announce his retirement.

AMERICA'S TEAM APPENDIX

THE ALL-TIME DALLAS COWBOYS DREAM TEAM

Tom Landry, coach

Defense:

Harvey Martin, end
Bob Lilly, tackle
Randy White, tackle
Charles Haley, end
Chuck Howley, outside linebacker
Lee Roy Jordan, middle linebacker
Ken Norton, outside linebacker
Mel Renfro, cornerback
Everson Walls, cornerback
Darren Woodson, strong safety
Cliff Harris, free safety

Bill Bates, special teams
Bob Hayes, punt returner

Comments: How do you deny Jethro Pugh, one of the greatest defensive tackles ever, a place on this team? With difficulty; but Lilly and White were absolute monsters who required constant double- and triple-teaming—and still made unbelievable plays. Excluding end Too Tall Jones might seem equally blasphemous—Martin made four Pro Bowls, Jones three, and Haley five—but Martin was named co-MVP of Super Bowl XII and NFL Defensive Player of the Year, and Haley's arrival in Dallas in 1992 vaulted the pass defense from 23rd to 5th and was a major factor in that year's Super Bowl victory. (Honorable mention to George Andrie, who went to five Pro Bowls.) Howley and Jordan are nobrainers; Norton led the team two straight years in tackles and was the soul of a team that won two consecutive

Super Bowls. He edges out Bob Breunig (three Pro Bowls) and D.D. Lewis. In the defensive secondary, Renfro and Harris are shoo-ins; Walls vs. Cornell Green is a tossup, but Green played several years at safety. Woodson may seem premature, but he's a franchise player. Deion Sanders may be the best corner ever, but only one year with the 'Boys is too short for our purposes. That leaves Charlie Waters, a great player, odd man out. Bates is Mr. Special Teams, and Hayes averaged an amazing 20.8 yards per punt return in 1968.

Offense:

Drew Pearson, wide receiver
Michael Irvin, wide receiver
Roger Staubach, quarterback
Tony Dorsett, running back
Emmitt Smith, running back
Billy Joe DuPree, tight end
Rayfield Wright, tackle
Nate Newton, guard
John Fitzgerald, center
John Niland, guard
Pat Donovan, tackle

Sam Baker, punter
Rafael Septien, kicker
Mel Renfro, kick returner
Preston Pearson, situation receiver

Comments: Pearson and Irvin beat out Bullet Bob Hayes, who forced the invention of the zone defense; but no one caught more clutch passes than Pearson, and Irvin is right on his tail. The quarterback is a coin flip at

this point; Aikman is more accurate and has yet to lose a Super Bowl, but Staubach threw downfield more and engineered more comebacks. No one challenges Dorsett and Smith, although Don Perkins and Calvin Hill should receive honorable mention. DuPree beats out Doug Cosbie and Jay Novacek, the best pure receiver, by an inch, and Ralph Neely and Herb Scott deserve serious consideration on the line. Erik Williams may very well replace Donovan, if he comes all the way back from surgery, but he hasn't yet. Fitzgerald edges out Mark

Stepnoski and Dave Manders. Baker was only in Dallas for two years (his wild ways didn't mesh with Landry's straight and narrow), but he was one of the best ever, and the position has never been the Cowboys' strong spot. Kicker Septien was both clutch and steady, though Chris Boniol had two strong seasons in 1994–95. Renfro averaged 30 yards per kick return in 1965 and 26.4 for his career. Pearson in 1979 had 26 third down catches—and an astonishing 23 went for first downs or touchdowns.

A Cowboys Chronology—America's Team Year by Year

1959

Former Los Angeles Rams general manager Tex Schramm, now with CBS Sports, contacts Clint Murchison Jr. upon hearing that Murchison is close to receiving an NFL franchise for Dallas. Murchison hires Schramm as his general manager in October.

Since the NFL owners won't meet and approve an expansion team until January 1960, Schramm realizes that the Cowboys won't be able to participate in the NFL draft in November. He convinces Murchison to sign SMU star quarterback Don Meredith and New Mexico fullback Don Perkins to personal services contracts. Unable to acquire NFL contracts, Schramm makes counterfeit copies of the NFL contract and hires part-time NFL talent scout Gil Brandt and Hampton Pool to hire as many free agents as they can. The two sign twenty-eight free agents to a team that technically doesn't exist. Schramm hires New York Giants assistant coach Tom Landry, a Dallas resident, as head coach of the new team.

1960

At the annual league owners meeting in January, Clint Murchison, his brother, and minority owner Bedford Wynne are awarded an expansion franchise—in part due to the players they've already signed. The Cowboys are to play as a "swing" team, playing every other NFL team one time during the first season, although they are listed in the Western Conference standings.

A player pool is set up in a March league meeting in Los Angeles, with each of the twelve NFL teams freezing 25 of 36 names on its roster, the Cowboys are allowed to pick 3 from each team for a total of 36 veterans. Dallas is required to make its choices within 24 hours.

On July 9, training camp starts; rookies report to the first Cowboys training camp at Pacific University in Forest Grove, OR. Almost 200 players will be invited to camp. On August 6, in Seattle, the Cowboys drop their first preseason game 16–10 to San Francisco.

On August 19, the Cowboys make their Dallas debut in the Salesmanship Club Game. They lead the world champion Baltimore Colts into the final minute before a 62-yard pass from Johnny Unitas to Lenny Moore gives the Colts a 14–10 victory. In a preseason game at Louisville, KY, the Cowboys beat the New York Giants 14–3 for their first victory on August 27. Frank Clarke catches 2 touchdown passes, 1 from Eddie LeBaron and 1 from Don Meredith.

In their first league game, Dallas falls to Pittsburgh 35–28 on September 24. Quarterback Bobby Layne leads a fourth-quarter Steeler rally. On December 4, the Cowboys break a ten-game losing streak by tying New York 31–31 at Yankee Stadium. They finish their first season 0–11–1. Wide receiver Jim

Doran is the first Cowboy named to the Pro Bowl.

1961

Training camp begins July 9, at a different site—St. Olaf College in Northfield, MN.

The Cowboys score their first league win by scoring ten points in the final 56 seconds, on September 17, against Pittsburgh, and win 27–24 in their league opener in the Cotton Bowl. A crowd of 23,500 watches Allen Green's 27-yard field goal win it on the final play. They win their next game for their first winning streak ever, and finish 4–9–1 after losing their last four games. Tight end Dick Bielski and fullback Don Perkins are voted to the Pro Bowl.

1962

The team begins summer training at yet another campsite, Northern Michigan College in Marquette, MI.

In a game against Pittsburgh on September 23, for the first time in anyone's memory in an NFL game, points are awarded for a penalty. The Cowboys are called for holding in the end zone on a 99-yard TD pass from LeBaron to Clarke; the touchdown is nullified, and the Steelers are awarded a safety. Pittsburgh wins by that margin, 30–28.

In the fourth quarter of a game against Philadelphia, Cowboy Amos Marsh returns a kickoff 101 yards, and rookie Mike Gaechter returns a pass interception 100 yards, the first time in NFL history that two 100-yard runs have been made in the same game, much less by the same team in the same quarter. The Cowboys win 41–19, and finish the season 5–8–1. Five Cowboys are voted to the Pro Bowl.

1963

The rival Dallas Texans announce that they are moving the franchise to Kansas City. In July, the Cowboys open training camp at a new facility, California Lutheran College in Thousand Oaks, CA.

Receiver Bill Howton breaks Don Hutson's all-time receiving record with a 14-yard catch against Washington on September 29. The Cowboys finish the season with a disappointing 4–10 record. Three Cowboys are named to the Pro Bowl.

1964

With one year to go on his contract, and public rumblings about his disappointing record, Tom Landry is signed to an unprecedented 10–year contract by Clint Murchison.

The Cowboys finish at 5–8–1, another disappointing record. Two Cowboys are named to the Pro Bowl.

1965

The Cowboys notch their first home sellout with the November 21 game against Cleveland, in the Cotton Bowl. Cleveland wins, 24–17. But the Cowboys win 3 of their next 4 games and finish with their first non-losing record, 7–7; they then lose to Baltimore 35–3 in the Playoff Bowl in Miami. A team-record six players are voted to the Pro Bowl.

1966

Tex Schramm, fresh from successful negotiations to merge the NFL and the AFL, is named president of the Dallas Cowboys by owner Clint Murchison, who retains the title of Chairman of the Board.

Dallas and Houston (AFL) reach agreement in the Ralph Neely case. Neely, chosen in the draft by both Dallas and Houston, remains with Dallas for several draft picks and other considerations. The Cowboys win their first championship, capturing the Eastern Conference title with a 10–3–1 record, but lose the NFL Championship Game to Green Bay 34–27 in the

Cotton Bowl. Nine Cowboys are named to the Pro Bowl.

1967

Under the NFL's new format, the Cowboys handily win the Capitol Division with a 9–5 record and defeat Cleveland 52–14 in the Cotton Bowl for the Eastern Conference title. But on December 31 in Green Bay, Dallas loses again to the Packers, 21–17, on the coldest New Year's Eve (20 below) in Green Bay history. Ten Cowboys are named to the Pro Bowl.

1968

For the second straight year, the Cowboys win the Capitol Division, this time with their best record ever, 12–2. But they lose to Cleveland 31–20 on December 21 in the Eastern Championship title game. Dallas wins the Playoff Bowl against Minnesota 17–13. Eight Cowboys are named to the Pro Bowl.

1969

In July, Don Meredith and Don Perkins announce their retirements. The Cowboys again win the Capitol Division, with an 11–2–1 season. Once again they lose to Cleveland, this time 38–14, in the Eastern Championship title game. They defeat Los Angeles 31–0 in the Playoff Bowl Game. Eight Cowboys are named to the Pro Bowl.

1970

The Cowboys win their last five games to finish 10–4, then beat Detroit 5–0 in a divisional playoff, and San Francisco in the NFC Championship Game to advance to the Super Bowl for the first time. They lose 16–13 on a last-minute field goal by Jim O'Brien. Three Cowboys are named to the Pro Bowl.

1971

The Cowboys begin a new era on October 24, when they play their first game in Texas Stadium in Irving, a suburb of Dallas. They win 44–21 over the New England Patriots. Behind quarterback Roger Staubach, they win their last 7 games to finish 11–3 to make the playoffs for the sixth year in a row. The defeat Minnesota 20–12 in the opening round, then beat San Francisco 14–3 to advance to the Super Bowl. They down the Miami Dolphins 24–3 to win Super Bowl VI, as Staubach is named the game's MVP. Eight Cowboys are named to the Pro Bowl.

1972

Calvin Hill becomes the first Dallas player to rush for 1,000 yards in a single season when he gains 111 on December 9, against the Washington Redskins in Texas Stadium. Hill winds up with 1,036 yards on 236 carries.

The Cowboys qualify for the playoffs a record seventh consecutive year, with a 10–4 record. Roger Staubach passes for two touchdowns in the last $1\frac{1}{2}$ minutes to give the Cowboys a 30–28 victory at San Francisco in the first round, but Dallas loses a week later to Washington 26–3. Seven Cowboys are named to the Pro Bowl.

1973

The Cowboys and Coach Tom Landry record their 100th win with a 40–3 victory at Texas Stadium over the New Orleans Saints on September 24. Landry finishes the season with a career mark of 108–80–6 to rank ninth on the list of the NFL's all-time winningest coaches.

The Cowboys regain their NFC Eastern Division title with a 10–4 record to reach the playoffs for the eighth year in a row. Dallas defeats Western Division champion Los Angeles 27–16 in the first round, but falls to Central Division winner Minnesota 27–10 in the NFC Championship Game. Six Cowboys are named to the Pro Bowl.

1974

The Cowboys have the first choice in the NFL college draft for the first time in their history; the number-one pick comes from Houston in exchange for Tody Smith and Billy Parks. Dallas selects Ed "Too Tall" Jones, a 6'9", 260–pound defensive end from Tennessee State. All-Pro linebacker Chuck Howley retires after thirteen years with Dallas.

The Cowboys miss the playoffs for the first time in nine years after going 8–6. Six Cowboys are named to the Pro Bowl.

1975

"Mr. Cowboy," defensive tackle Bob Lilly, retires. He is honored on Bob Lilly Day at Texas Stadium (November 23) and is the first Cowboy inducted into the Ring of Honor. All-Pro defensive back Cornell Green also retires after thirteen years with the Cowboys.

An unprecedented Dirty Dozen rookies make the team. In what is supposed to be a rebuilding year, the Cowboys return to the playoffs with a 10–4 record. After shocking Minnesota in the first round 17–14 on Roger Staubach's Hail Mary pass to Drew Pearson, the Cowboys face Los Angeles for the NFC Championship. In Los Angeles, they defeat the Rams 37–7 as Staubach throws 4 TD passes, 3 to Preston Pearson. But they lose to Pittsburgh in Super Bowl X, 21–17. Three Cowboys are named to the Pro Bowl.

1976

Former Cowboy greats Don Meredith and Don Perkins join Bob Lilly in the Ring of Honor at Texas Stadium, during halftime ceremonies at the Giants game on November 7.

The Cowboys finish with a winning record of 11–3 for their eleventh straight winning year. But a 14–12 playoff loss to Los Angeles ends their season. Eight Cowboys are voted to the Pro Bowl.

1977

Former All-Pro linebacker Chuck Howley becomes the fourth member of the Ring of Honor. He is inducted during halftime ceremonies of the Detroit Lions game on October 30. All-Pro linebacker Lee Roy Jordan retires after fourteen years with Dallas.

The Cowboys roll to an 8–0 start, their best ever, and finish with a 12–2 record, the championship of the Eastern Division, and their twelfth consecutive winning season. They defeat the Chicago Bears 37–7 in a first-round victory at Texas Stadium. A week later, they crush the Minnesota Vikings at home 23–6, for their fourth NFC crown. In Super Bowl XII, against Denver in New Orleans, they overwhelm the Broncos 27–10. Defensive linemen Harvey Martin and Randy White are named co-MVPs of the game. Eight Cowboys are named to the Pro Bowl.

1978

Old pros Ralph Neely and Mel Renfro have retired, and the Cowboys open the season a mediocre 6–4. But with first place in the NFC East on the line, the Cowboys pound the Washington Redskins on Thanksgiving Day, and win their final 6 games to finish 12–4. The Cowboys go on to capture their tenth division title, then advance to the Super Bowl, where they fall to the Pittsburgh Steelers, 35–31. Nine Cowboys are named to the Pro Bowl.

1979

Jethro Pugh's retirement and Ed Jones's decision to quit and become a boxer dominate the off-season headlines, but the Cowboys celebrate their 20th anniversary season with their fourth straight NFC East title. Dallas makes its 13th trip to the post-season in the last 14 seasons, but falls to the Los Angeles Rams in the divisional playoffs in what turns out to be Roger Staubach's final game. Eight Cowboys are voted to the Pro Bowl.

1980

Roger Staubach announces his retirement in March following eleven record-smashing seasons. So does All-Pro offensive lineman Rayfield Wright, who played for the Cowboys thirteen years, and All-Pro safety Cliff Harris, who played ten years in Dallas.

Seven-time All-Pro defensive tackle Bob Lilly becomes the first Cowboy to be inducted into the Pro Football Hall of Fame.

Coach Tom Landry joins George Halas and Curly Lambeau as the only coaches with 200 NFL victories when the Cowboys beat Los Angeles 34–13, on December 28 at Texas Stadium.

Ed Jones bolsters the defensive line when he decides to return from his short-lived boxing career. The Cowboys finish 12–4, beat Los Angeles in the wild card game 34–13, defeat Atlanta 30–27 in a divisional playoff, and lose to the Philadelphia Eagles 20–7 in the NFC Championship Game. Four Cowboys are named to the Pro Bowl.

1981

Former All-Pro defensive back Mel Renfro becomes the fifth member of the Ring of Honor in an October 25 ceremony, during halftime of the Dolphins game at Texas Stadium.

The Cowboys regain the NFC East crown they lost to the Philadelphia Eagles in 1980, capturing their 12th division title since 1966, with their 16th consecutive winning season (12–4). But Dallas drops a 28–27 decision on The Catch to the emerging San Francisco 49ers in the NFC Cham-

pionship Game. Seven Cowboys are named to the Pro Bowl.

1982

More defensive stars retire as Charlie Waters and D.D. Lewis end their careers, then the season takes on a bitter edge as the players go on strike. The Cowboys finish a shortened season at 6–3, and advance to the NFC title game for the third straight season by defeating Tampa Bay 30–17 and then Green Bay 37–26, but the rival Washington Redskins win easily, 31–17. Seven players are named to the Pro Bowl.

1983

Roger Staubach becomes the sixth member of the Ring of Honor in halftime ceremonies of the Tampa Bay game at Texas Stadium, on October 9.

Team officials break ground for a new headquarters and training facility in the Valley Ranch development in Irving.

The Cowboys finish 12–4 but lose in the NFC wild card game to the Los Angeles Rams 24–17. Five players are named to the Pro Bowl.

1984

The team is sold by the Murchison family, owners since the franchise was founded in 1960, to an 11–member limited partnership led by Dallas businessman H.R. "Bum" Bright. All-Pros Harvey Martin and Drew Pearson retire after eleven years with the Cowboys.

The Cowboys kick off their 25th anniversary Silver Season with a 20–13 victory over the Los Angeles Rams behind their new starting quarterback, Gary Hogeboom. Hogeboom looks good early, but later slumps and Danny White retakes the job. The team finishes 9–7 for their nineteenth consecutive winning season, but they miss the playoffs for the first time in ten years. Three Cowboys are named to the Pro Bowl.

1985

Roger Staubach, king of the comebacks in his eleven seasons, is inducted into the Pro Football Hall of Fame. All-Pros Bob Breunig and Herb Scott retire.

Cowboys Center, the team's glittering new headquarters and practice facility, is completed and occupied just before the season opener.

Tony Dorsett becomes the sixth running back in NFL history to surpass 10,000 yards.

The Cowboys beat the Giants on December 15, for their 20th consecutive winning season and thirteenth divisional title in that span with a 10–6 record. They lose to the Rams 20–0 in the playoffs to end their season. Four Cowboys are named to the Pro Bowl.

1986

The Cowboys' international popularity is underscored when they debut in a foreign country, playing an exhibition game in London's Wembley Stadium.

Tony Dorsett, Danny White, and Randy White are all slowed by injuries as the Cowboys begin to show their age, slipping to 7–9, their first under .500 record since 1965. For the first time in the team's history, no Cowboy is voted to the Pro Bowl.

1987

Team founder and first owner Clint Murchison Jr. dies after a long illness at the age of 63.

The Cowboys profit from the demise of the USFL, signing the spring league's marquee player, Herschel Walker. Walker shows he belongs in the NFL, leading the Cowboys in receiving yards, and scoring 14 touchdowns.

Tony Dorsett surpasses 12,000 yards, becoming the fourth rusher in NFL history to do so.

Owner Bum Bright says he is "horrified" at Tom Landry's play-calling, and the Cowboys finish a strike-shortened season at 7–8. For the fans, the season's highlight is the performance of the replacement players, who win 2 of 3 games during the strike. Herschel Walker is the only Cowboy voted to the Pro Bowl.

1988

Tony Dorsett is traded to the Denver Broncos and Herschel Walker asserts himself, rushing for 1,514 yards and catching passes for 505 yards. There are few other bright spots for the aging Cowboys, as a series of failed draft choices leaves the team vulnerable en route to a 3–13 record. Herschel Walker is the only Cowboy voted to the Pro Bowl for the second year in a row.

Owner Bum Bright announces he's selling the team, with an asking price of $150 million.

1989

Arkansas oilman Jerry Jones reaches an agreement to buy the Cowboys and the Texas Stadium lease. Jones also announces that Jimmy Johnson will replace Tom Landry as head coach.

Tex Schramm, the only general manager in the team's 29–year history, resigns and later accepts a position as head of the new World League of American Football. All-Pro defensive tackle Randy White retires after fourteen years with the Cowboys.

The Cowboys begin the rebuilding process by using the number-one overall pick of the draft to select UCLA quarterback Troy Aikman, whom they later sign.

Former All-Pro linebacker Lee Roy Jordan is inducted into the Ring of Honor.

Jimmy Johnson trades his most marketable commodity, running back Herschel Walker, to the Minnesota Vikings for a package of players and draft choices.

Dallas finishes a miserable 1–15 season, the worst in the NFL, and the most defeats in club history. No Cowboy is voted to the Pro Bowl for the second time in the team's history.

1990

"Trader" Jimmy Johnson uses a flurry of deals to maneuver the Cowboys into position to select University of Florida running back Emmitt Smith in the first round.

Jones switches the site of training camp from Thousand Oaks, CA to Austin. The Cowboys draw 100,000 fans to the St. Edward's University campus to view workouts. All-Pro defensive end Ed "Too Tall" Jones retires.

Tom Landry, the Cowboys' head coach for the first 29 years of their history, is enshrined in the Pro Football Hall of Fame.

The Cowboys begin one of the most dramatic turnarounds in recent NFL history, bouncing back from 1–15 to a 7–9 record, missing the playoffs by one game. Emmitt Smith, the NFL rushing leader, is voted Offensive Rookie of the Year and Jimmy Johnson is named Coach of the Year. Smith is the only Cowboy voted to the Pro Bowl.

1991

The rebuilding continues as the Cowboys grab defensive tackle Russell Maryland after Johnson turns a flurry of trades into the first overall pick in the draft. The Cowboys also add Alvin Harper, Dixon Edwards, and Erik Williams in their draft haul.

Tex Schramm, the Cowboys' innovative general manager for 29 years, becomes the fourth member of the Dallas organization to enter the Pro Football Hall of Fame, joining Tom Landry, Bob Lilly, and Roger Staubach.

Dallas wins its last 5 games to finish at 11–5, its best mark since 1983, securing its first playoff berth since 1985. The Cowboys beat the Chicago Bears in the first round, but fall to the Detroit Lions a week later. Four Cowboys are voted to the Pro Bowl.

1992

The Cowboys send six offensive players to the Pro Bowl, the most on offense in club history.

Dallas goes 13–3, the most wins in franchise history.

The Cowboys go on to beat the San Francisco 49ers in the NFC title game and make their first trip to the Super Bowl since following the 1978 season. Dallas then wins its third world championship, 52–17 over the Buffalo Bills in Super Bowl XXVII.

1993

A once-reluctant Tom Landry finally gives in to the man who fired him, Jerry Jones, and becomes the eighth member of the Ring of Honor.

An NFC-record eleven Cowboys are selected to the Pro Bowl. That group includes a club-record eight starters.

Emmitt Smith captures his third straight rushing title, becoming the fourth back in NFL history to do so.

The Cowboys again beat the 49ers in the NFC Championship Game for their NFL-record seventh conference championship. Dallas joins three other NFL teams with four Super Bowl titles, routing the Buffalo Bills, 30–13, in Super Bowl XXVIII.

1994

The deteriorating relationship between Jerry Jones and Jimmy Johnson reaches the breaking point as Jones chafes over the perception that Johnson is the brains behind the Cowboys. Jones buys out Johnson's contract, and the next day, Jones hires longtime friend Barry Switzer as the third coach in team history.

Former Cowboys teammates Randy White and Tony Dorsett are enshrined in the Pro Football Hall of Fame. White and Dorsett are also inducted into the Ring of Honor.

The Cowboys again send eleven representatives to the Pro Bowl.

Dallas falls short in its bid to win a third straight Super Bowl, losing to San Francisco in the NFC Championship Game, 38–28.

1995

The Cowboys sign the NFL's top free agent, cornerback Deion Sanders, to a record $35 million contract.

The relationship between Barry Switzer and Troy Aikman nearly falls apart after assistant coach John Blake, a close friend of Switzer, accuses Aikman of criticizing only black players. Aikman confronts Switzer, and Blake is allowed to leave his post as defensive line coach prior to the playoffs to assume his new job as head coach of the University of Oklahoma. Teammates come to Aikman's defense, and the Cowboys rally to capture another division crown and home field advantage throughout the playoffs.

Jerry Jones says there is no acceptable excuse for the Cowboys to fall short in their bid for an unprecedented third Super Bowl in four seasons, and the team responds to the pressure, beating the Pittsburgh Steelers, 27–17, in Super Bowl XXX.

RING OF HONOR: THE COWBOY HALL OF FAME

The Cowboys honor former players and coaches who made outstanding contributions to the club by inducting them into the Ring of Honor at Texas Stadium. Their names and the years of service are prominently displayed in silver on the wall above the Cowboys' bench at Texas Stadium. Members of the Cowboys' Ring of Honor include:

Bob Lilly, defensive tackle, 1961–1974

Nicknamed "Mr. Cowboy," Bob Lilly was the franchise's first draft choice in 1961, the first name in the Ring of Honor in 1975, and its first inductee into the Pro Football Hall of Fame in 1980. A seven-time All-Pro, Lilly was named to a club-record 11 Pro Bowls. He was a two-time All-SWC pick and an All-American at Texas Christian University before being drafted by Dallas.

Don Meredith, quarterback, 1960–1968

Don Meredith led the Cowboys to their first winning season and their first NFL Championship Game in 1966. Signed by Clint Murchison Jr. before Dallas was granted its NFL franchise, "Dandy Don" played in two Pro Bowls and was named NFL Player of the Year in 1966. A two-time All-American at SMU, Meredith's name was added to the Cowboys' Ring of Honor in 1976.

Don Perkins, running back, 1961–1968

Don Perkins was the first Cowboys player to rush for more than 6,000 yards. A six-time Pro Bowl selection, Perkins finished among the top ten NFL rushers in each of his eight seasons. He was named NFL Rookie of the Year in 1961 and All-Pro in 1962. Perkins was signed before Dallas was granted its NFL franchise. A three-time All-Skyline pick at New Mexico, he was inducted into the Ring of Honor in 1976.

Chuck Howley, linebacker, 1961–1973

When Chuck Howley retired in 1973, Tom Landry said, "I don't know that I've seen anybody better at linebacker than Howley." A six-time All-Pro, Howley was the Most Valuable Player in Super Bowl V. The Cowboys traded for Howley, who was drafted by Chicago in 1958. He was an All-American center at West Virginia. A six-time Pro Bowl selection, Howley was added to the Ring of Honor in 1977.

Lee Roy Jordan, linebacker, 1963–1976

The inspirational leader of the Cowboys' first championship teams was Lee Roy Jordan. The Cowboys' first-round draft choice in 1963 following an All-American career at Alabama, Jordan anchored the Doomsday Defense from his middle linebacker position for 14 years. He was named to the Pro Bowl five times, and the All-Pro team twice. Jordan was inducted into the Ring of Honor in 1989.

Tom Landry, head coach, 1960–1988

The first head coach of the Cowboys, Tom Landry led Dallas to two Super Bowl wins and five NFC titles in his 29 years at the Cowboys' helm. He compiled a career record of 270–178–6, the third-most wins in NFL history, and was elected to the Pro Football Hall of Fame in 1990. Tom Landry was inducted into the Ring of Honor in 1993.

Tony Dorsett, running back, 1977–1987

Tony Dorsett finished his career as the second-leading rusher in NFL history and played in five NFC Championship Games, two Super Bowls, and four Pro Bowls. After guiding the University of Pittsburgh to the 1976 national title, and claiming the Heisman Trophy, Dorsett captured Rookie of the Year honors in 1977. He also holds the NFL record with a 99-yard touchdown run. Inducted into the Ring of Honor in 1994, Dorsett was elected to the Pro Football Hall of Fame in 1994.

COWBOYS SUPER BOWL ROUNDUP

Super Bowl V
January 17, 1971 at Miami

Dallas' first trip to the big one was a disappointing one. The Cowboys faced the legendary Johnny Unitas and a veteran Baltimore Colts team. Ten turnovers prompted some wags to dub the game the Blooper Bowl.

The Cowboys scored first, on a 14-yard field goal by Mike Clark in the first quarter, then went ahead 6–0 in the second quarter on another. But Baltimore scored on a fluke play. Baltimore legend Johnny Unitas threw a long pass to receiver Eddie Hinton; the ball bounced off Hinton's hands, back up into the air, appeared to brush the fingertips of Dallas cornerback Mel Renfro, and came down at midfield into the hands of surprised Baltimore tight end John Mackey, who raced downfield into the end zone. The Cowboys blocked the extra point to keep the score knotted at 6–6. On Baltimore's next possession, defensive end George Andrie tackled Unitas hard enough to jar the ball loose on his own 29-yard line and send him out of the game with sore ribs. Dallas quarterback Craig Morton moved his team down to the 7-yard line. A short pass to back Duane Thomas and Clark's extra point made the score 13–6.

In the second half, the Colts' Jim Duncan fumbled the opening kickoff deep in their own territory. Dallas drove from the 31-yard line to the 2 in 5 plays. Thomas, who had gained most of those yards, then fumbled the ball. The Colts screamed they

had it, and the officials awarded them the ball on the one-foot line, although Dallas center Dave Manders came up with it. Neither Morton nor Earl Morrall, filling in for Unitas, could move their team the rest of the quarter. Eight minutes into the third quarter, the Cowboys still led 13–6.

But then a Morton pass bounced off fullback Walt Garrison's fingers into the hands of safety Rick Volk, who returned the ball 17 yards to the Cowboys' three-yard line. Tom Nowatzke bulled over for the touchdown, and Jim O'Brien's extra point tied the score. Then, with only 1:09 left in the game, Baltimore linebacker Mike Curtis intercepted a Morton pass on the Dallas 41, and returned it to the 28. Two running plays later, there was time for one more play. Rookie kicker Jim O'Brien booted a 32-yard three-pointer to give the Colts an ugly but acceptable 16–13 win.

Super Bowl VI
January 16, 1972 at New Orleans

New quarterback Roger Staubach had guided the mission-minded Cowboys to nine straight victories since Landry had named him the permanent starting quarterback halfway into the season. The Cowboys faced a talented young Miami Dolphins team coached by Don Shula.

It was no contest from the start. Miami fullback Larry Csonka, normally surehanded, fumbled a first-period handoff from quarterback Bob Griese on the Dallas

258

48-yard line. Dallas recovered, and Staubach drove the Cowboys to a Mike Clark field goal. The Cowboys defense completely canceled the Miami ground game, and in the second quarter, a seven-yard touchdown pass from Staubach to Lance Alworth climaxed a long Dallas drive. But a Garo Yepremian field goal cut the lead to 10–3 at the half.

The Cowboys took the kickoff and drove downfield behind strong running by Duane Thomas. He took a pitchout from three yards out and scored, to extend the lead to 17–3. In the fourth quarter, Miami finally started moving downfield, but Cowboy linebacker Chuck Howley intercepted a Griese pass meant for Jim Kiick at midfield. Behind a phalanx of blockers, Howley charged downfield, but he tripped at the Miami 9. Three plays later, Staubach hit tight end Mike Ditka in the end zone with a seven-yard pass to put the game out of reach. Clark's conversion made the score 24–3. The Dolphins began a long drive into Dallas territory, but a Griese fumble ended the last Miami scoring threat.

Super Bowl X
January 18, 1976 at Miami

The story here was World Champions vs. Wild Card: Pittsburgh had won the previous Super Bowl, and Dallas was the first wild card team ever to reach the NFL finals. It was, or so the media insisted, brains vs. brawn, brute force against glamorous finesse. The Steel Curtain vs. the Shotgun. And the Cowboys started off with some razzle-dazzle on the opening kickoff as Thomas "Hollywood" Henderson took a handoff from Preston Pearson and raced up the sidelines 53 yards to the Pittsburgh 43-yard line—where the last man in his way, kicker Roy Gerela, knocked him out of bounds.

But it was a tight, physical ballgame through three quarters. Dallas held a 10–7 lead courtesy of a 29-yard first-quarter touchdown pass from Roger Staubach to wide receiver Drew Pearson, and a 36-yard

Toni Fritsch field goal with 15 seconds left in the half. Pittsburgh's only score was a 7-yarder, from Terry Bradshaw to tight end Randy Grossman.

Early in the final quarter, things started heating up. Pittsburgh's Reggie Harrison blocked a Mitch Hoopes punt, at the Dallas 9. The ball bounced off Harrison's face into the end zone for a 2–point safety. Then Gerela's 36-yard field goal, less than three minutes later, put Pittsburgh ahead 12–10. A few minutes later safety Mike Wagner intercepted a pass from Staubach and returned it 19 yards to the Dallas 7. A few plays later, the Steelers settled for an 18-yard Gerela field goal.

With about three minutes to go, Bradshaw got off a pass a split-second before an all-out rush knocked him out of the game. Almost sixty yards downfield wide receiver Lynn Swann made a spectacular catch and ran it five yards into the end zone. After a failed Gerela conversion, the score was 21–10 Pittsburgh.

The Cowboys took the kickoff and drove quickly down the field to score on a 34-yard TD pass from Staubach to little-used receiver Percy Howard. After the conversion, the Steelers led 21–17 with 1:48 left to play. With Terry Hanratty in for the dazed Bradshaw, the Cowboys stopped four straight Steeler runs to give the Dallas offense the ball on their own 42-yard line, with 1:22 left and no timeouts.

But Captain Comeback wouldn't pull this one out of the fire. He ran for eleven yards, then passed to Preston Pearson at the Pittsburgh 38 with 22 seconds to go. But on the last play of the game, safety Glenn Edwards intercepted a Staubach pass in the end zone to seal the Steelers' victory.

Super Bowl XII
January 15, 1978 at New Orleans

The Cowboys had lost only two games during the regular season and had destroyed playoff opponents Chicago and Minnesota.

They were a 5–point favorite to defeat Denver and their Orange Crush defense. But the Dallas Doomsday Defense II was the deciding factor, pressuring Bronco (and former Cowboy) quarterback Craig Morton into a record 4 interceptions in the first half. Randy Hughes grabbed one on the Denver 29. Four plays later, rookie Tony Dorsett's 3-yard TD run put Dallas on the board, and Efren Herrera's 35-yard three-pointer following another interception made it 10–3. Herrera missed three more field goal attempts before connecting on a 43-yarder, and Dallas led 13–0 at the half.

Early in the third quarter, a 47-yarder by Jim Turner barely scraped over the crossbar to give Denver their first score. But 5½ minutes later a diving 45-yard catch into the end zone by Butch Johnson made it 20–3 Dallas. Norris Weese replaced Morton with 6:40 left in the third quarter. His superior mobility put the Broncos in position to score their only touchdown of the game, a one-yard plunge by Rob Lytle. The finishing touch was Dallas' final score, a 29-yard spectacular catch by Golden Richards of an option pass by fullback Robert Newhouse while rolling left. In the seven minutes remaining, neither team scored. Final score: Dallas 27, Denver 10.

Super Bowl XIII
January 21, 1979 at Miami

It was a battle between two Super Bowl winners—and a fight to decide the Team of the Decade. This time Dallas was the defending champion and Pittsburgh the challenger in a rematch (the first in Super Bowl history) of what many considered the best Super Bowl ever. This one would be even better.

Dallas was up against a steamroller Steeler team that had lost only two games in the regular season, and had crushed Denver and Houston in the playoffs. The Cowboys took the opening kickoff and were moving well until Drew Pearson lost the handle on a

reverse and the ball ended up in the hands of Steeler defensive end John Banaszak. Bradshaw passed the Steelers down the field; six plays after the fumble, a 28-yard touchdown toss to John Stallworth made it 7–0 Pittsburgh. Late in the quarter, Harvey Martin sacked Bradshaw and knocked the ball loose; Ed "Too Tall" Jones recovered. Staubach took over and found Tony Hill three plays later for a 39-yard touchdown. Rafael Septien's conversion tied the score.

The Doomsday Defense II struck again in the second quarter. Hollywood Henderson broke through the Pittsburgh line to strip Bradshaw of the ball, and Mike Hegman picked it up and ran 37 yards for another touchdown. But a few plays later Stallworth took a 10-yard pass from Bradshaw, broke Aaron Kyle's tackle, and sprinted 65 yards to score. The point after tied it again. The Cowboys were moving steadily downfield. But at the Steeler 32, Staubach threw a pass to Drew Pearson that was intercepted by cornerback Mel Blount, who returned it 13 yards. Bradshaw drove his team down to the 7-yard line. With only seconds left in the half, he rolled to his right and tossed a soft pass just past D.D. Lewis's reach and into the hands of Rocky Bleier. At the half it was 21–14 Pittsburgh.

The Cowboy defense contained Pittsburgh throughout the third quarter—it didn't allow a first down in their first two possessions. Dallas ground out a drive that made it to the 10-yard line. On third and three, Staubach threw a soft, and slightly short, pass to a wide-open Jackie Smith, the veteran tight end with the sure hands. Smith stumbled slightly, and the ball went through his hands and bounced to the ground. Dallas settled for a field goal and trailed by four points.

In the final quarter, the Steelers were moving slowly under enormous pressure from the Dallas defense. At their 44-yard line, with 9:05 left to play, the Cowboys blitzed. Bradshaw threw up a wild pass in the direction of Lynn Swann. It was short and inside, and when Swann cut back for it, he ran up the back of cornerback Benny Barnes. Both players went down, and the call was pass interference. Later replays and an apology from NFL Commissioner Pete Rozelle would make clear the error of the call, but Pittsburgh was awarded a first down on the Dallas 23-yard line. Then Franco Harris ran past a blitzing Dallas defense for a 22-yard touchdown. The following kickoff was short, and fumbled by a broken-thumbed Randy White; Steeler Dennis Winston fell on it. The next play an 18-yard pass to a leaping Lynn Swann made it 35–17 Pittsburgh.

With about six minutes left Staubach went to work. After a scramble, a pass to Drew Pearson, and a run by Tony Dorsett, he found tight end Billy Joe DuPree at the Steeler 7-yard line. The big end broke two tackles and staggered into the end zone. The Steelers were ready for the obvious onside kick, but it didn't help. Rookie Dennis Thurman recovered for Dallas at midfield, and after a pass, a sack, and an incompletion, Staubach found Pearson for a 25-yard gain to the Steeler 4. A bullet to Butch Johnson in the end zone brought the Cowboys to within four points. With only 22 seconds left, the onside kick was recovered by Rocky Bleier, and Pittsburgh ran out the clock to secure a 35–31 victory and their third Super Bowl title.

Super Bowl XXVII
January 31, 1993 at Pasadena, CA

The Cowboys had endured a 14–year Super Bowl drought. The Bills were in the title game for the third consecutive year. But despite a tight game until just before halftime, in the end, it was another Super Bowl Buffalo blowout—and the beginning of a dynasty in Dallas.

Buffalo got on the board first, on a 2-yard Thurman Thomas run. The Cowboys answered with a 23-yard touchdown pass from Troy Aikman to tight end Jay Novacek and a 2-yard fumble return for a score by defensive tackle Jimmie Jones. In the second

quarter, Buffalo cut the lead to 14–10 on a 21-yard field goal by Steve Christie. But late in the first half, turnovers and two Aikman-to-Michael Irvin TD passes (one for 19 yards and one for 18 yards) made it 28–14 at the half.

Except for a 40-yard touchdown pass to Don Beebe from Frank Reich, who replaced an injured Jim Kelly in the second quarter, it was all Dallas in the second half. The fourth quarter saw three Dallas touchdowns: a 45-yard pass to Alvin Harper, a 10-yard run by Emmitt Smith, and a 9-yard return by Ken Norton of a Frank Reich fumble. Dallas defensive tackle Leon Lett almost scored on a 65-yard fumble return, but grandstanding allowed a Buffalo defender to strip the ball from him just before he reached the goal line.

Troy Aikman was brilliant, throwing four touchdowns on 22 of 30 passes for 273 yards and no interceptions, and was voted the game's MVP. Emmitt Smith rushed for 108 yards on 22 carries, and Michael Irvin gained 114 yards and 2 touchdowns on 6 receptions. But the Dallas defense was the big story: 9 turnovers by Buffalo—5 fumbles and 4 interceptions—led directly to 5 Dallas touchdowns. The final score, 52–17, was the third-largest margin of victory in a Super Bowl.

Super Bowl XXVIII
January 30, 1994 at Atlanta, GA

It was a repeat Super Bowl—Dallas for the second consecutive time, and Buffalo for an unprecedented fourth. But the result was the same as the previous year: a close game for about a half, then a Dallas blowout.

The Cowboys played sluggishly in the first two quarters, and the Bills led at halftime 13–6. In the first quarter, Dallas connected on two Eddie Murray field goals (one the result of a forced fumble by safety James Washington); Buffalo used a 54-yard Steve Christie three-pointer, a Thurman Thomas 4-yard rumble, and another Christie field goal to forge their lead. But a few minutes into the third goal, with Buffalo near midfield, tackle Leon Lett stripped the ball from Thomas, and Washington picked it up and sprinted 46 yards for the touchdown. The Eddie Murray conversion made it 13–all.

The play by Washington changed the tone of the game. When Dallas got the ball back, Emmitt Smith, playing with a separated shoulder, took over. He carried the ball on 7 out of 8 plays and scored on a 15-yard run. Then, with Buffalo threatening to tie the game, Washington intercepted a Jim Kelly pass. A one-yard run by Smith and a 20-yard field goal by Murray made the final score 30–13.

The Dallas defense was superb. They limited the Bills to 87 yards on the ground, and Thurman Thomas to another miserable Super Bowl performance: 37 yards on 16 carries and 2 fumbles. His counterpart, Emmitt Smith, had 132 yards on 30 carries running behind an offensive line that controlled the line of scrimmage in the second half.

Super Bowl XXX
January 28, 1996 at Tempe, AZ

A twenty-year-old rivalry was revived in the thirtieth Super Bowl. In the seventies it had been Dallas razzle-dazzle vs. Pittsburgh pugnacity. The Steelers had triumphed in their head-to-head confrontations in the big one—two of the best ever—but the Cowboys would gain a measure of revenge in 1996.

The Cowboys began the scoring three minutes into the game, with a Chris Boniol field goal from the 42. After Dallas held and Pittsburgh punted, new Cowboy Deion Sanders ran under an Aikman rainbow for a 42-yard gain. Three plays later, Aikman hit tight end Jay Novacek with his fourth reception on a 3-yard touchdown pass. Ahead 10–0, the Cowboys looked like they were

about to set a new Super Bowl scoring record.

But the Steeler defense stiffened and kept the Dallas offense contained. A Pittsburgh fumble led to another Boniol field goal. But after the kickoff, quarterback Neil O'Donnell drove his team downfield, mixing long passes with Bam Morris runs outside. Wide receiver Ernie Mills made a tough catch for 19 yards, then receiver Yancy Thigpen grabbed a triple-coverage pass in the end zone to put the Steelers on the board with seconds left on the clock.

In the third quarter Pittsburgh seemed to be on the move again, but O'Donnell hit Dallas safety James Brown right in the numbers; he returned the ball deep into Steeler territory. After a 17-yard reception by Irvin to the one-yard line, Emmitt Smith dived a yard into the end zone for his first TD of the game for a 20–7 lead. But Pittsburgh came right back and drove to a 46-yard Norm Johnson field goal. Next it was Dallas' turn to be surprised by razzle-dazzle, as the Steelers recovered the onside kick. The Cowboys seemed confused, and on the strength of Bam Morris's running, the Steelers drove the remaining yards to score on a one-yard plunge by Morris.

Momentum was on Pittsburgh's side, and the Cowboys couldn't establish any kind of ground attack. But the Dallas defense—or O'Donnell—struck again, with another bullet to Brown. That interception led to another Smith touchdown, this time from six yards out, and the final score, 27–17. Though the Cowboys gained sixty fewer yards on offense, and held the ball for nine fewer minutes, and Smith was held to 49 rushing yards, Aikman was 15 of 23 with no interceptions, and the Dallas defense made the big plays when it had to. Dallas' fifth Super Bowl win and eighth appearance were both unprecedented, and cemented the Cowboys' claim as Team of the Nineties.

COWBOYS PRO BOWL HONOREES

1960	(1)	Jim Doran WR
1961	(2)	Dick Bielski, TE
		Don Perkins, RB
1962	(5)	Don Bishop, CB
		Eddie LeBaron, QB
		Bob Lilly, DE
		Don Perkins, RB
		Jerry Tubbs, LB
1963	(3)	Sam Baker, P
		Lee Folkins, TE
		Don Perkins, RB
1964	(2)	Bob Lilly, DT
		Mel Renfro, S
1965	(6)	George Andrie, DE
		Cornell Green, CB
		Bob Hayes, WR
		Chuck Howley, LB
		Bob Lilly, DT
		Mel Renfro, S
1966	(9)	George Andrie, DE
		Cornell Green, CB
		Bob Hayes, WR
		Chuck Howley, LB
		Bob Lilly, DT
		Dave, Manders, C
		Don Meredith, QB
		Don Perkins, RB
		Mel Renfro, S
1967	(10)	George Andrie, DE
		Cornell Green, CB
		Bob Hayes, WR
		Chuck Howley, LB
		Lee Roy Jordan, LB
		Bob Lilly, DT
		Don Meredith, QB
		Ralph Neely, T
		Don Perkins, RB
		Mel Renfro, S
1968	(8)	George Andrie, DE
		Chuck Howley, LB
		Lee Roy Jordan, LB

		Bob Lilly, DT
		Don Meredith, QB
		John Niland, OG
		Don Perkins, RB
		Mel Renfro, CB
1969	(8)	George Andrie, DE
		Calvin Hill, RB
		Chuck Howley, LB
		Lee Roy Jordan, LB
		Bob Lilly, DT
		Ralph Neely, OT
		John Niland, OG
		Mel Renfro, CB
1970	(3)	Bob Lilly, DT
		John Niland, OG
		Mel Renfro, CB
1971	(8)	Cornell Green, S
		Chuck Howley, LB
		Bob Lilly, DT
		John Niland, OG
		Mel Renfro, S
		Roger Staubach, QB
		Ron Widby, P
		Rayfield Wright, OT
1972	(7)	Walt Garrison, RB
		Cornell Green, S
		Calvin Hill, RB
		Bob Lilly, DT
		John Niland, OG
		Mel Renfro, CB
		Rayfield Wright, OT
1973	(6)	Calvin Hill, RB
		Lee Roy Jordan, LB
		Bob Lilly, DT
		John Niland, OG
		Mel Renfro, CB
		Rayfield Wright, OT
1974	(6)	Cliff Harris, S
		Calvin Hill, RB
		Lee Roy Jordan, LB
		Blaine Nye, OG

Drew Pearson, WR
Rayfield Wright, OT

1975   (3)   Cliff Harris, S
Roger Staubach, QB
Rayfield Wright, OT

1976   (8)   Billy Joe DuPree, TE
Cliff Harris, S
Harvey Martin, DE
Blaine Nye, OG
Drew Pearson, WR
Roger Staubach, QB
Charlie Waters, S
Rayfield Wright, OT

1977   (8)   Billy Joe DuPree, TE
Cliff Harris, S
Efren Herrera, K
Harvey Martin, DE
Drew Pearson, WR
Roger Staubach, QB
Charlie Waters, S
Randy White, DT

1978   (9)   Tony Dorsett, RB
Billy Joe DuPree, TE
Cliff Harris, S
Thomas Henderson, LB
Tony Hill, WR
Harvey Martin, DE
Roger Staubach, QB
Charlie Waters, S
Randy White, DT

1979   (8)   Bob Breunig, LB
Pat Donovan, T
Cliff Harris, S
Tony Hill, WR
Harvey Martin, DE
Herb Scott, OG
Roger Staubach, QB
Randy White, DT

1980   (4)   Bob Breunig, LB
Pat Donovan, OT
Herb Scott, OG
Randy White, DT

1981   (7)   Pat Donovan, OT
Tony Dorsett, RB
Ed Jones, DE
Herb Scott, OG
Rafael Septien, K
Everson Walls, CB
Randy White, DT

1982   (7)   Bob Breunig, LB
Pat Donovan, OT
Tony Dorsett, RB
Ed Jones, DE

Everson Walls, CB
Danny White, QB
Randy White, DT

1983   (5)   Doug Cosbie, TE
Tony Dorsett, RB
Ed Jones, DE
Everson Walls, CB
Randy White, DT

1984   (3)   Bill Bates, ST
Doug Cosbie, TE
Randy White, DT

1985   (4)   Doug Cosbie, TE
Tony Hill, WR
Everson Walls, CB
Randy White, DT

1987   (1)   Herschel Walker, RB

1988   (1)   Herschel Walker, RB

1990   (1)   Emmitt Smith, RB

1991   (4)   Troy Aikman, QB
Michael Irvin, WR
Jay Novacek, TE
Emmitt Smith, RB

1992   (6)   Troy Aikman, QB
Michael Irvin, WR
Nate Newton, OG
Jay Novacek, TE
Emmitt Smith, RB
Mark Stepnoski, C

1993   (11)   Troy Aikman, QB
Thomas Everett, S
Michael Irvin, WR
Daryl Johnston, FB
Russell Maryland, DT
Nate Newton, OG
Ken Norton, LB
Jay Novacek, TE
Emmitt Smith, RB
Mark Stepnoski, C
Erik Williams, OT

1994   (11)   Troy Aikman, QB
Charles Haley, DE
Michael Irvin, WR
Daryl Johnston, FB
Leon Lett, DT
Nate Newton, OG
Jay Novacek, TE
Emmitt Smith, RB
Mark Stepnoski, C
Mark Tuinei, OT
Darren Woodson, S

1995	(10)	Troy Aikman, QB	Nate Newton, OG
		Larry Allen, OG	Jay Novacek, TE
		Ray Donaldson, C	Emmitt Smith, RB
		Charles Haley, DE	Mark Tuinei, OT
		Michael Irvin, WR	Darren Woodson, S

COWBOYS SEASON RECORDS

1960 (0–11–1)

9/24	L	28	Pittsburgh	35
9/30	L	25	Philadelphia	27
10/9	L	14	Washington	26
10/16	L	7	Cleveland	48
10/23	L	10	St. Louis	12
10/30	L	7	Baltimore	45
11/6	L	13	Los Angeles	38
11/13	L	7	Green Bay	41
11/20	L	14	San Francisco	26
11/27	L	7	Chicago	17
12/4	T	31	New York	31
12/11	L	14	Detroit	23

1961 (4–9–1)

9/17	W	27	Pittsburgh	24
9/24	W	21	Minnesota	7
10/1	L	7	Cleveland	25
10/8	W	28	Minnesota	0
10/15	L	10	New York	31
10/22	L	7	Philadelphia	43
10/29	W	17	New York	16
11/5	L	17	St. Louis	31
11/12	L	7	Pittsburgh	37
11/19	T	28	Washington	28
11/26	L	13	Philadelphia	35
12/3	L	17	Cleveland	38
12/10	L	13	St. Louis	31
12/17	L	24	Washington	34

1962 (5–8–1)

9/16	T	35	Washington	35
9/23	L	28	Pittsburgh	30
9/30	W	27	Los Angeles	17
10/7	L	10	Cleveland	19
10/14	W	41	Philadelphia	19
10/21	W	42	Pittsburgh	27
10/28	L	24	St. Louis	28
11/4	W	38	Washington	10
11/11	L	10	New York	41
11/18	L	33	Chicago	34
11/25	L	14	Philadelphia	28
12/2	W	45	Cleveland	21
12/9	L	20	St. Louis	52
12/16	L	31	New York	41

1963 (4–10)

9/14	L	7	St. Louis	34
9/22	L	24	Cleveland	41
9/29	L	17	Washington	21
10/6	L	21	Philadelphia	24
10/13	W	17	Detroit	14
10/20	L	21	New York	37
10/27	L	21	Pittsburgh	27
11/3	W	35	Washington	20
11/10	L	24	San Francisco	31
11/17	W	27	Philadelphia	20
11/24	L	17	Cleveland	27
12/1	L	27	New York	34
12/8	L	19	Pittsburgh	24
12/15	W	28	St. Louis	24

1964 (5–8–1)

9/12	L	6	St. Louis	16
9/20	W	24	Washington	18
9/27	L	17	Pittsburgh	23
10/4	L	6	Cleveland	27
10/11	T	13	New York	13
10/18	L	16	Cleveland	20
10/25	W	31	St. Louis	13
11/1	W	24	Chicago	10
11/8	W	31	New York	21
11/15	L	14	Philadelphia	17
11/22	L	16	Washington	28
11/29	L	21	Green Bay	45
12/6	L	14	Philadelphia	24
12/13	W	17	Pittsburgh	14

1965 (7–7)

9/19	W	31	New York	2
9/26	W	27	Washington	7
10/4	L	13	St. Louis	20
10/10	L	24	Philadelphia	35
10/17	L	17	Cleveland	23
10/24	L	3	Green Bay	13
10/31	L	13	Pittsburgh	22
11/7	W	39	San Francisco	31
11/14	W	24	Pittsburgh	17
11/21	L	17	Cleveland	24
11/28	L	31	Washington	34
12/5	W	21	Philadelphia	19

12/11	W	27	St. Louis		13
12/19	W	38	New York		20

PLAYOFF BOWL GAME (Miami)

1/9/66	L	3	Baltimore		35

1966 (10–3–1)

9/18	W	52	New York		7
9/25	W	28	Minnesota		17
10/2	W	47	Atlanta		14
10/9	W	56	Philadelphia		7
10/16	T	10	St. Louis		10
10/23	L	21	Cleveland		30
10/30	W	52	Pittsburgh		21
11/6	L	23	Philadelphia		24
11/13	W	31	Washington		30
11/20	W	20	Pittsburgh		7
11/24	W	26	Cleveland		14
12/4	W	31	St. Louis		17
12/11	L	31	Washington		34
12/18	W	17	New York		7

1966 CHAMPIONSHIP GAME (Dallas)

1/1/67	L	27	Green Bay		34

1967 (9–5)

9/17	W	21	Cleveland		14
9/24	W	38	New York		24
10/1	L	13	Los Angeles		35
10/8	W	17	Washington		14
10/15	W	14	New Orleans		10
10/22	W	24	Pittsburgh		21
10/29	L	14	Philadelphia		21
11/5	W	37	Atlanta		7
11/12	W	27	New Orleans		10
11/19	L	20	Washington		27
11/23	W	46	St. Louis		21
12/3	L	17	Baltimore		23
12/10	W	38	Philadelphia		17
12/16	L	16	San Francisco		24

1967 EASTERN CHAMPIONSHIP GAME (Dallas)

12/24	W	52	Cleveland		14

1967 CHAMPIONSHIP GAME (Green Bay)

12/31	L	17	Green Bay		21

1968 (12/2)

9/15	W	59	Detroit		13
9/22	W	28	Cleveland		7
9/29	W	45	Philadelphia		13
10/6	W	27	St. Louis		10
10/13	W	34	Philadelphia		14
10/20	W	20	Minnesota		7
10/28	L	17	Green Bay		28
11/3	W	17	New Orleans		3
11/10	L	21	New York		27
11/17	W	44	Washington		24
11/24	W	34	Chicago		3
11/28	W	29	Washington		20
12/8	W	28	Pittsburgh		7

12/15	W	28	New York		10

1968 EASTERN CHAMPIONSHIP GAME (Cleveland)

12/21	L	20	Cleveland		31

PLAYOFF BOWL GAME (Miami)

1/5/69	W	17	Minnesota		13

1969 (11–2–1)

9/21	W	24	St. Louis		3
9/28	W	21	New Orleans		17
10/5	W	38	Philadelphia		7
10/12	W	24	Atlanta		17
10/19	W	49	Philadelphia		14
10/27	W	25	New York		3
11/2	L	10	Cleveland		42
11/9	W	33	New Orleans		17
11/16	W	41	Washington		28
11/23	L	23	Los Angeles		24
11/27	T	24	San Francisco		24
12/7	W	10	Pittsburgh		7
12/13	W	27	Baltimore		10
12/21	W	20	Washington		10

1969 CHAMPIONSHIP GAME (Dallas)

12/28	L	14	Cleveland		38

1969 PLAYOFF BOWL GAME (Miami)

1/3/70	L	0	Los Angeles		31

1970 (10–4)

9/20	W	17	Philadelphia		7
9/27	W	28	NY Giants		10
10/4	L	7	St. Louis		20
10/11	W	13	Atlanta		0
10/18	L	13	Minnesota		54
10/25	W	27	Kansas City		16
11/1	W	21	Philadelphia		17
11/8	L	20	NY Giants		23
11/16	L	0	St. Louis		38
11/22	W	45	Washington		21
11/26	W	16	Green Bay		3
12/6	W	34	Washington		0
12/12	W	6	Cleveland		2
12/20	W	52	Houston		10

1970 DIVISIONAL PLAYOFF (Dallas)

12/26	W	5	Detroit		0

1970 NFC CHAMPIONSHIP GAME (San Francisco)

1/3/71	W	17	San Francisco		10

SUPER BOWL V (Miami)

1/17/71	L	13	Baltimore		16

1971 (11–3)

9/19	W	49	Buffalo		37
9/26	W	42	Philadelphia		7
10/3	L	16	Washington		20
10/11	W	20	NY Giants		13
10/17	L	14	New Orleans		24
10/24	W	44	New England		21
10/31	L	19	Chicago		23

11/7	W	16	St. Louis	13
11/14	W	20	Philadelphia	7
11/21	W	13	Washington	0
11/25	W	28	Los Angeles	21
12/4	W	52	NY Jets	10
12/12	W	42	NY Giants	14
12/18	W	31	St. Louis	12

1971 DIVISIONAL PLAYOFF (Minnesota)

12/25	W	20	Minnesota	12

1971 NFC CHAMPIONSHIP GAME (Dallas)

1/2/72	W	14	San Francisco	3

SUPER BOWL VI (New Orleans)

1/16/72	W	24	Miami	3

1972 (10–4)

9/17	W	28	Philadelphia	6
9/24	W	23	NY Giants	14
10/1	L	13	Green Bay	16
10/8	W	17	Pittsburgh	13
10/15	W	21	Baltimore	0
10/22	L	20	Washington	24
10/30	W	28	Detroit	24
11/5	W	34	San Diego	28
11/12	W	33	St. Louis	24
11/19	W	28	Philadelphia	7
11/23	L	10	San Francisco	31
12/3	W	27	St. Louis	6
12/9	W	34	Washington	24
12/17	L	3	NY Giants	23

1972 DIVISIONAL PLAYOFF (San Francisco)

12/23	W	30	San Francisco	28

1972 NFC CHAMPIONSHIP GAME (Washington)

12/31	L	3	Washington	26

1973 (10–4)

9/16	W	20	Chicago	17
9/24	W	40	New Orleans	3
9/30	W	45	St. Louis	10
10/8	L	7	Washington	14
10/14	L	31	Los Angeles	37
10/21	W	45	NY Giants	28
10/28	L	16	Philadelphia	30
11/4	W	38	Cincinnati	10
11/11	W	23	NY Giants	10
11/18	W	31	Philadelphia	10
11/22	L	7	Miami	14
12/2	W	22	Denver	10
12/9	W	27	Washington	7
12/16	W	30	St. Louis	3

1973 DIVISIONAL PLAYOFF (Dallas)

12/23	W	27	Los Angeles	16

1973 NFC CHAMPIONSHIP GAME (Dallas)

12/30	L	10	Minnesota	27

1974 (8–6)

9/15	W	24	Atlanta	0
9/23	L	10	Philadelphia	13
9/29	L	6	NY Giants	14
10/6	L	21	Minnesota	23
10/13	L	28	St. Louis	31
10/20	W	31	Philadelphia	24
10/27	W	21	NY Giants	7
11/3	W	17	St. Louis	14
11/10	W	20	San Francisco	14
11/17	L	21	Washington	28
11/24	W	10	Houston	0
11/28	W	24	Washington	23
12/7	W	41	Cleveland	17
12/14	L	23	Oakland	27

1975 (10–4)

9/21	W	18	Los Angeles	7
9/28	W	37	St. Louis	31
10/6	W	36	Detroit	10
10/12	W	13	NY Giants	7
10/19	L	17	Green Bay	19
10/26	W	20	Philadelphia	17
11/2	L	24	Washington	30
11/10	L	31	Kansas City	34
11/16	W	34	New England	31
11/23	W	27	Philadelphia	17
11/30	W	14	NY Giants	3
12/7	L	17	St. Louis	31
12/13	W	31	Washington	10
12/21	W	31	NY Jets	21

1975 DIVISIONAL PLAYOFF (Minnesota)

12/28	W	17	Minnesota	14

1975 NFC CHAMPIONSHIP GAME (Los Angeles)

1/4/76	W	37	Los Angeles	7

SUPER BOWL X (Miami)

1/18/76	L	17	Pittsburgh	21

1976 (11–3)

9/12	W	27	Philadelphia	7
9/19	W	24	New Orleans	6
9/26	W	30	Baltimore	27
10/3	W	28	Seattle	13
10/10	W	24	NY Giants	14
10/17	L	17	St. Louis	21
10/24	W	31	Chicago	21
10/31	W	20	Washington	7
11/7	W	9	NY Giants	3
11/15	W	17	Buffalo	10
11/21	L	10	Atlanta	17
11/25	W	19	St. Louis	14
12/5	W	26	Philadelphia	7
12/12	L	14	Washington	27

1976 DIVISIONAL PLAYOFF (Dallas)

12/19	L	12	Los Angeles	14

1977 (12–2)

9/18	W	16	Minnesota	10
9/25	W	41	NY Giants	21
10/2	W	23	Tampa Bay	7

10/9	W	30	St. Louis	24
10/16	W	34	Washington	16
10/23	W	16	Philadelphia	10
10/30	W	37	Detroit	0
11/6	W	24	NY Giants	10
11/14	L	17	St. Louis	24
11/20	L	13	Pittsburgh	28
11/27	W	14	Washington	7
12/4	W	24	Philadelphia	14
12/12	W	42	San Francisco	35
12/18	W	14	Denver	6

1977 DIVISIONAL PLAYOFF (Dallas)

12/26	W	37	Chicago	7

1977 NFC CHAMPIONSHIP GAME (Dallas)

1/1/78	W	23	Minnesota	6

SUPER BOWL XII (New Orleans)

1/15/78	W	27	Denver	10

1978 (12–4)

9/4	W	38	Baltimore	0
9/10	W	34	NY Giants	24
9/17	L	14	Los Angeles	27
9/24	W	21	St. Louis	12
10/2	L	5	Washington	9
10/8	W	24	NY Giants	3
10/15	W	24	St. Louis	21
10/22	W	14	Philadelphia	7
10/26	L	10	Minnesota	21
11/5	L	16	Miami	23
11/12	W	42	Green Bay	14
11/19	W	27	New Orleans	7
11/23	W	37	Washington	10
12/3	W	17	New England	10
12/10	W	31	Philadelphia	13
12/17	W	30	NY Jets	7

1978 DIVISIONAL PLAYOFF (Dallas)

12/30	W	27	Atlanta	20

1978 NFC CHAMPIONSHIP GAME (Los Angeles)

1/7/79	W	28	Los Angeles	0

SUPER BOWL XIII (Miami)

1/21/79	L	31	Pittsburgh	35

1979 (11–5)

9/2	W	22	St. Louis	21
9/9	W	21	San Francisco	13
9/16	W	24	Chicago	20
9/24	L	7	Cleveland	26
9/30	W	38	Cincinnati	13
10/7	W	36	Minnesota	20
10/14	W	30	Los Angeles	6
10/21	W	22	St. Louis	13
10/28	L	3	Pittsburgh	14
11/4	W	16	NY Giants	14
11/12	L	21	Philadelphia	31
11/18	L	20	Washington	34
11/22	L	24	Houston	30
12/2	W	28	NY Giants	7

12/8	W	24	Philadelphia	17
12/16	W	35	Washington	34

1979 DIVISIONAL PLAYOFF (Dallas)

12/30	L	19	Los Angeles	21

1980 (12–4)

9/8	W	17	Washington	3
9/14	L	20	Denver	41
9/21	W	28	Tampa Bay	17
9/28	W	28	Green Bay	7
10/5	W	24	NY Giants	3
10/13	W	59	San Francisco	14
10/19	L	10	Philadelphia	17
10/26	W	42	San Diego	31
11/2	W	27	St. Louis	24
11/9	L	35	NY Giants	38
11/16	W	31	St. Louis	21
11/23	W	14	Washington	10
11/27	W	51	Seattle	7
12/7	W	19	Oakland	13
12/15	L	14	Los Angeles	38
12/21	W	35	Philadelphia	27

1980 NFC WILD CARD GAME (Dallas)

12/28	W	34	Los Angeles	13

1980 DIVISIONAL PLAYOFF (Atlanta)

1/4/81	W	30	Atlanta	27

1980 NFC CHAMPIONSHIP GAME (Philadelphia)

1/11/81	L	7	Philadelphia	20

1981 (12–4)

9/6	W	26	Washington	10
9/13	W	30	St. Louis	17
9/21	W	35	New England	21
9/27	W	18	NY Giants	10
10/4	L	17	St. Louis	20
10/11	L	14	San Francisco	45
10/18	W	29	Los Angeles	17
10/25	W	28	Miami	27
11/1	W	17	Philadelphia	14
11/19	W	27	Buffalo	14
11/15	L	24	Detroit	27
11/22	W	24	Washington	10
11/26	W	10	Chicago	9
12/6	W	37	Baltimore	13
12/13	W	21	Philadelphia	10
12/19	L	10	NY Giants	13

1981 DIVISIONAL PLAYOFF (Dallas)

1/2/82	W	38	Tampa Bay	0

1981 NFC CHAMPIONSHIP GAME (San Francisco)

1/10/82	L	27	San Francisco	28

1982 (6–3)

9/13	L	28	Pittsburgh	36
9/19	W	24	St. Louis	7
			Minnesota—canceled	
			NY Giants—canceled	

			Washington—canceled	
			Philadelphia—canceled	
			Cincinnati—canceled	
			NY Giants—canceled	
			St. Louis—canceled	
			San Francisco—canceled	
11/21	W	14	Tampa Bay	9
11/25	W	31	Cleveland	14
12/5	W	24	Washington	10
12/13	W	37	Houston	7
12/19	W	21	New Orleans	7
12/26	L	20	Philadelphia	24
1/3/83	L	27	Minnesota	31

1982 SUPER OWL TOURNAMENT (Dallas)

1/9/83	W	30	Tampa Bay	17

1982 SUPER BOWL TOURNAMENT (Dallas)

1/16/83	W	37	Green Bay	26

1982 NFC CHAMPIONSHIP GAME
(Washington)

1/22/83	L	17	Washington	31

1983 (12–4)

9/5	W	31	Washington	30
9/11	W	34	St. Louis	17
9/18	W	28	NY Giants	13
9/25	W	21	New Orleans	20
10/2	W	37	Minnesota	24
10/9	W	27	Tampa Bay	24
10/16	W	37	Philadelphia	7
10/23	L	38	LA Raiders	40
10/30	W	38	NY Giants	20
11/6	W	27	Philadelphia	20
11/13	L	23	San Diego	24
11/20	W	41	Kansas City	21
11/24	W	35	St. Louis	17
12/4	W	35	Seattle	10
12/11	L	10	Washington	31
12/19	L	17	San Francisco	42

1983 NFC WILD CARD GAME (Dallas)

12/26	L	17	LA Rams	24

1984 (9–7)

9/3	W	20	LA Rams	13
9/9	L	7	NY Giants	28
9/16	W	23	Philadelphia	17
9/23	W	20	Green Bay	6
9/30	W	23	Chicago	14
10/7	L	20	St. Louis	31
10/14	L	14	Washington	34
10/21	W	30	New Orleans	27
10/28	W	22	Indianapolis	3
11/4	L	7	NY Giants	19
11/11	W	24	St. Louis	17
11/18	L	3	Buffalo	14
11/22	W	20	New England	17
12/2	W	26	Philadelphia	10
12/9	L	28	Washington	30
12/17	L	21	Miami	28

1985 (10–6)

9/9	W	44	Washington	14
9/15	L	21	Detroit	26
9/22	W	20	Cleveland	7
9/29	W	17	Houston	10
10/6	W	30	NY Giants	29
10/13	W	27	Pittsburgh	13
10/20	L	14	Philadelphia	16
10/27	W	24	Atlanta	10
11/4	L	10	St. Louis	21
11/10	W	13	Washington	7
11/17	L	0	Chicago	44
11/24	W	34	Philadelphia	17
11/28	W	35	St. Louis	17
12/8	L	24	Cincinnati	50
12/15	W	28	NY Giants	21
12/22	L	16	San Francisco	31

1985 DIVISIONAL PLAYOFF (Los Angeles)

1/4/86	L	0	LA Rams	20

1986 (7–9)

9/8	W	31	NY Giants	28
9/14	W	31	Detroit	7
9/21	L	35	Atlanta	37
9/29	W	31	St. Louis	7
10/5	L	14	Denver	29
10/12	W	30	Washington	6
10/19	W	17	Philadelphia	14
10/26	W	37	St. Louis	6
11/2	L	14	NY Giants	17
11/9	L	13	LA Raiders	17
11/16	W	24	San Diego	21
11/23	L	14	Washington	41
11/27	L	14	Seattle	31
12/7	L	10	LA Rams	29
12/14	L	21	Philadelphia	23
12/21	L	10	Chicago	24

1987 (7–8)

9/13	L	13	St. Louis	24
9/20	W	16	NY Giants	14
9/27			Buffalo—canceled	
10/4	W	38	NY Jets	24
10/11	W	41	Philadelphia	22
10/19	L	7	Washington	13
10/25	L	20	Philadelphia	37
11/2	W	33	NY Giants	24
11/8	L	17	Detroit	27
11/15	W	23	New England	17
11/22	L	14	Miami	20
11/26	L	38	Minnesota	44
12/6	L	10	Atlanta	21
12/13	L	20	Washington	24
12/21	W	29	LA Rams	21
12/27	W	21	St. Louis	16

1988 (3–13)

9/4	L	21	Pittsburgh	24
9/12	W	17	Phoenix	14

9/19	L	10	NY Giants	12	10/13	W	35	Cincinnati	23
9/25	W	26	Atlanta	20	10/27	L	10	Detroit	34
10/3	L	17	New Orleans	20	11/3	W	27	Phoenix	7
10/9	L	17	Washington	35	11/10	L	23	Houston	26
10/16	L	7	Chicago	17	11/17	L	9	NY Giants	22
10/23	L	23	Philadelphia	24	11/24	W	24	Washington	21
10/30	L	10	Phoenix	16	11/28	W	20	Pittsburgh	10
11/6	L	21	NY Giants	29	12/8	W	23	New Orleans	14
11/13	L	3	Minnesota	43	12/15	W	25	Philadelphia	13
11/20	L	24	Cincinnati	38	12/22	W	31	Atlanta	27

1991 FIRST ROUND PLAYOFFS (Chicago)

11/24	L	17	Houston	25	12/29	W	17	Chicago	13

1991 DIVISIONAL PLAYOFFS (Detroit)

12/4	L	21	Cleveland	24	1/5/92	L	6	Detroit	38
12/11	W	24	Washington	17					
12/18	L	7	Philadelphia	23					

1989 (1–15)

1992 (13–3)

9/10	L	0	New Orleans	28	9/7	W	23	Washington	10
9/17	L	21	Atlanta	27	9/13	W	34	NY Giants	28
9/24	L	7	Washington	30	9/20	W	31	Phoenix	20
10/1	L	13	NY Giants	30	10/5	L	7	Philadelphia	31
10/8	L	13	Green Bay	31	10/11	W	27	Seattle	0
10/15	L	14	San Francisco	31	10/18	W	17	Kansas City	10
10/22	L	28	Kansas City	36	10/25	W	28	LA Raiders	13
10/29	L	10	Phoenix	19	11/1	W	20	Philadelphia	10
11/5	W	13	Washington	3	11/8	W	37	Detroit	3
11/12	L	20	Phoenix	24	11/15	L	23	LA Rams	27
11/19	L	14	Miami	17	11/22	W	16	Phoenix	10
11/23	L	0	Philadelphia	27	11/26	W	30	NY Giants	3
12/3	L	31	LA Rams	35	12/6	W	31	Denver	27
12/10	L	10	Philadelphia	20	12/13	L	17	Washington	20
12/16	L	0	NY Giants	15	12/21	W	41	Atlanta	17
12/24	L	10	Green Bay	20	12/27	W	27	Chicago	14

1992 DIVISIONAL PLAYOFFS (Dallas)

1990 (7–9)

					1/10/93	W	34	Philadelphia	10

1992 NFC CHAMPIONSHIP GAME (San Francisco)

9/9	W	17	San Diego	14	1/17/93	W	30	San Francisco	20
9/16	L	7	NY Giants	28					

SUPER BOWL XXVII (Pasadena)

9/23	L	15	Washington	19	1/31/93	W	52	Buffalo	17
9/30	L	17	NY Giants	31					
10/7	W	14	Tampa Bay	10					
10/14	L	3	Phoenix	20					
10/21	W	17	Tampa Bay	13					

1993 (12–4)

10/28	L	20	Philadelphia	21	9/6	L	16	Washington	35
11/4	L	9	NY Jets	24	9/12	L	10	Buffalo	13
11/11	L	6	San Francisco	24	9/19	W	17	Phoenix	10
11/18	W	24	LA Rams	21	10/3	W	36	Green Bay	14
11/22	W	27	Washington	17	10/10	W	27	Indianapolis	3
12/2	W	17	New Orleans	13	10/17	W	26	San Francisco	17
12/16	W	41	Phoenix	10	10/31	W	23	Philadelphia	10
12/23	L	3	Philadelphia	17	11/7	W	31	NY Giants	9
12/30	L	7	Atlanta	26	11/14	W	20	Phoenix	15
					11/21	L	14	Atlanta	27

1991 (11–5)

9/1	W	26	Cleveland	14	11/25	L	14	Miami	16
9/9	L	31	Washington	33	12/6	W	23	Philadelphia	17
9/15	L	0	Philadelphia	24	12/12	W	37	Minnesota	20
9/22	W	17	Phoenix	9	12/18	W	28	NY Jets	7
9/29	W	21	NY Giants	16	12/26	W	38	Washington	3
10/6	W	20	Green Bay	17	1/2	W	16	NY Giants	13

1993 DIVISIONAL PLAYOFFS (Dallas)
1/16/94	W	27	Green Bay	17

1993 NFC CHAMPIONSHIP GAME (Dallas)
1/23/94	W	38	San Francisco	21

SUPER BOWL XXVIII (Atlanta)
1/30/94	W	30	Buffalo	13

1994 (12–4)
9/4	W	26	Pittsburgh	9
9/11	W	20	Houston	17
9/19	L	17	Detroit	20
10/2	W	34	Washington	7
10/9	W	38	Arizona	3
10/16	W	24	Philadelphia	13
10/23	W	28	Arizona	21
10/30	W	23	Cincinnati	20
11/7	W	38	NY Giants	10
11/13	L	14	San Francisco	21
11/20	W	31	Washington	7
11/24	W	42	Green Bay	31
12/4	W	31	Philadelphia	19
12/10	L	14	Cleveland	19
12/19	W	24	New Orleans	16
12/24	L	10	NY Giants	15

1994 DIVISIONAL PLAYOFFS (Dallas)
1/8/95	W	35	Green Bay	9

1994 NFC CHAMPIONSHIP GAME (San Francisco)
1/15/95	L	28	San Francisco	38

1995 (12-4)
9/4	W	35	NY Giants	0
9/10	W	31	Denver	21
9/17	W	23	Minnesota	17
9/24	W	34	Arizona	20
10/1	L	23	Washington	27
10/8	W	34	Green Bay	24
10/15	W	23	San Diego	9
10/29	W	28	Atlanta	13
11/6	W	34	Philadelphia	12
11/12	L	20	San Francisco	38
11/19	W	34	Oakland	21
11/23	W	24	Kansas City	12
12/3	L	17	Washington	24
12/10	L	17	Philadelphia	20
12/17	W	21	NY Giants	20
12/25	W	37	Arizona	13

1995 DIVISIONAL PLAYOFFS (Dallas)
1/7/96	W	30	Philadelphia	11

1995 NFC CHAMPIONSHIP GAME (Dallas)
1/14/96	W	38	Green Bay	27

SUPER BOWL XXX (Tempe, AZ)
1/28/96	W	27	Pittsburgh	17

THE ELEVEN BEST BOOKS ABOUT THE COWBOYS
(IN NO PARTICULAR ORDER)

Once a Cowboy, by Walt Garrison and John Tullius. Easily the funniest book by an ex-Cowboy. Lots of self-deprecating humor and tons of great stories, all told in Garrison's inimitable voice. Laugh-out-loud stuff.

The Crunch, by Pat Toomay. A wry, candid look at life as a Dallas Cowboy, from the excitement and uncertainty of rookie camp, to the disillusionment of stalled contract negotiations. Funny and revealing.

Hearing the Noise, by Preston Pearson. Insightful look at football with the two greatest teams of the seventies, the Dallas Cowboys and the Pittsburgh Steelers, by an intelligent, observant player who just happened to be an important cog in both machines.

Out of Control, by Thomas "Hollywood" Henderson and Peter Knobler. One of the best accounts of the seductive influences that football players face. Hollywood is candid and painfully revealing about his descent into a maelstrom of nonstop pills, weed, cocaine, sex, spousal abuse, alcohol— and that's just for starters. Not for the faint-hearted.

North Dallas Forty, by Pete Gent. Fictionalized account of Dallas and the Cowboys of the late sixties, when both the city and the team were making a name for themselves. Anyone who thinks Landry's early players were saints should read this. A fine, funny, truthful novel.

The Dallas Cowboys: The First Twenty-Five Years, by Carlton Stowers. All the standard stuff you'd expect from an authorized product—histories, profiles, great photos, etc.—but also a ton of offbeat items, like team photos (and team clown photos), plenty of amusing lists, and more. Easily the most lavish tribute to the 'Pokes.

Next Year's Champions, by Steve Perkins. The veteran newspaperman wrote two books about the Cowboys, but *Winning the Big One* rehashes a lot of material first presented here. This is a well-written, entertaining account of the 1968 season—one of the years they were supposed to win the big one and didn't. Lots of behind-the-scenes stuff and character sketches.

God's Coach, by Skip Bayless. A jaundiced view of America's Team, at least as it was under Tom Landry. Too much of the Skipper and his religious agonizing ("I often prayed for guidance before I wrote about Landry"), but irresistible behind-the-scenes juice nonetheless—mostly, it should be noted, by disgruntled former Cowboys and coaches.

First Down, Lifetime to Go, by Roger Staubach with Sam Blair and Bob St. John. A straightforward (and, save for the last chapter, sermon-free) account of Captain Comeback's life and Cowboy career through 1973. Hits all the high points of the Cowboys' glory years, in the early seventies.

The Dallas Cowboys: An Illustrated History, by Richard Whittingham. Year-by-year survey of the first two decades of America's Team, told in workmanlike fashion: unadorned prose, team records, entertaining profiles and sidebars, and a good selection of photographs.

King of the Cowboys: The Life and Times of Jerry Jones, by Jim Dent. A revealing look at the Cowboys' owner as a businessman, dice-rolling wheeler-dealer, and nonstop honkytonker. Also a fascinating, behind-the-scenes account of how the nineties Super Bowl dynasty was built.

THE FUNNIEST COWBOY QUOTES EVER

Duane Thomas, on the Super Bowl: "If this is the ultimate game, why are they playing it again next year?"

Pete Gent, to a rookie with a Cowboys playbook in hand: "Don't bother reading it, kid. Everybody gets killed in the end."

Gent, as a rookie: "I didn't know what a free agent was until I got my first paycheck."

Larry Cole, when a reporter pointed out that it had been ten years between his third and fourth professional touchdowns: "Anyone can have an off decade."

Tex Schramm, responding to Duane Thomas's charge that he was "sick, demented, and completely dishonest": "That's not bad. He got two out of three."

Steve Wilson, after fumbling a kick in the end zone (he didn't know he could have downed it for a touchback rather than run it out and be tackled at the four): "I didn't know the rule, and I didn't have time to look it up."

Thomas "Hollywood" Henderson, before Super Bowl X, about Steeler quarterback Terry Bradshaw: "He couldn't spell *cat* if you spotted him the *c* and the *a*."

Walt Garrison, when asked if Tom Landry ever smiled: "I don't know, I only played there nine years. But I know he smiled at least three times 'cause he's got three kids."

Bob Breunig: "Rooming with Roger Staubach is like rooming with my father."

Blaine Nye, after one of Tom Landry's grueling Tuesday film sessions: "It's not whether you win or lose, but who gets the blame."

275

Roger Staubach, accepting a Touchdown Club award: "I don't know what to say. I'm waiting for Coach Landry to send someone in with a statement."

Don Meredith: "Tom Landry is a perfectionist. If he was married to Raquel Welch, he'd expect her to cook."

Bob Hayes, on the tough linebackers who covered him while he was playing: "They were animals... they didn't just take their uniforms off after a game, they ripped them off... and then they'd lick themselves clean. They didn't even need to shower."

Blaine Nye, on Clint Longley's 1974 Thanksgiving Day performance in leading a comeback win over the Redskins: "The triumph of an uncluttered mind."

BIBLIOGRAPHY

Agajanian, Ben, and Paul T. Owens. *The Kicking Game*. Millbrae, CA: Celestial Arts, 1980.

Bayless, Skip. *God's Coach*. New York: Simon and Schuster, 1990.

Blair, Sam. *Dallas Cowboys: Pro or Con?* New York: Doubleday, 1970.

Chapman, Donald, Randolph Campbell, and Robert Calvert. *The Dallas Cowboys and the NFL*. Norman, OK: University of Oklahoma Press, 1970.

Coffey, Frank, and Ernie Wood with Tony Seidl. *How 'Bout Them Cowboys!* Dallas: Taylor Publishing, 1993.

Daly, Dan and Bob O'Donnell. *The Pro Football Chronicles*. New York: Macmillan, 1990.

The Dallas Cowboys Media Guides: 1960–1995.

Ditka, Mike with Don Pierson. *Ditka: an Autobiography*. Chicago: Bonus Books, 1986.

Field, Bobbi. *The Dallas Cowboys' Super Wives*. Austin: Shoal Creek, 1972.

Garrison, Walt and John Tullius. *Once a Cowboy*. New York: Random House, 1988.

Hayes, Bob with Robert Pack. *Run, Bullet, Run*. New York: Harper & Row, 1990.

Henderson, Thomas "Hollywood" and Peter Knobler. *Out of Control*. New York: Putnam, 1987.

Herskowitz, Mickey. *The Golden Age of Pro Football*. (Revised edition.) Dallas: Taylor Publishing, 1990.

Hitt, Dick. *Classic Clint*. Plano, TX: Wordware Publishing, 1992.

Johnson, Jimmy with Ed Hinton. *Turning the Thing Around*. New York: Hyperion, 1993.

Klein, Dave. *Tom and the 'Boys*. New York: Zebra Books, 1990.

Korch, Rick. *The Truly Great*. Dallas: Taylor Publishing, 1993.

Kramer, Jerry. *Instant Replay*. New York: New American Library, 1968.

Landry, Tom with Gregg Lewis. *Tom Landry: An Autobiography*. New York: HarperCollins/Zondervan, 1990.

Lilly, Bob with Sam Blair. *Bob Lilly: Reflections*. Dallas: Taylor Publishing, 1983.

Martin, Harvey. *Texas Thunder*. New York: Rawson Associates, 1988.

Meyers, Jeff. *Dallas Cowboys*. New York: Macmillan, 1974.

Neft, David S., Richard M. Cohen, and Rick Korch. *The Sports Encyclopedia: Football.* (13th Edition.) New York: St. Martin's Press, 1995.

Nelson, Mark and Miller Bonner. *The Semi-Official Dallas Cowboys Haters' Handbook.* New York: Collier Books, 1984.

The Official Dallas Cowboys Bluebook (Volumes I-X). Dallas: Taylor Publishing, 1980–89.

Panaccio, Tim. *Cowboys An' Redskins.* New York: Leisure Press, 1983.

Pearson, Preston. *Hearing the Noise.* New York: Morrow, 1985.

Perkins, Steve. *Next Year's Champions.* New York: Word Publishing, 1969.

———. *Winning the Big One.* New York: Grosset & Dunlap, 1972.

Reeves, Dan with Dick Connor. *Reeves: An Autobiography.* Chicago: Bonus Books, 1988.

Rentzel, Lance. *When All the Laughter Died in Sorrow.* New York: Saturday Review Press, 1972.

St. John, Bob. *Landry: The Man Inside.* Waco: Word Books. 1979.

———. *Tex!: The Man Who Built the Dallas Cowboys.* Englewood Cliffs, NJ: Prentice Hall, 1988.

———. *The Landry Legend.* Waco: Word Books, 1990.

Schiffer, Don. *1962 Pro Football Handbook.* New York: Pocket Books, 1962.

Staubach, Roger, with Sam Blair and Bob St. John. *First Down, Lifetime to Go.* Waco: Word Books, 1974.

Staubach, Roger, with Frank Luksa. *Time Enough to Win.* Waco: Word Books, 1980.

Stowers, Carlton. *Journey to Triumph.* Dallas: Taylor Publishing, 1982.

———. *Cotton Bowl Classic: The First Fifty Years.* Dallas: Host Communications, 1986.

———. *The Cowboy Chronicles.* Austin: Eakin Press, 1984.

———. *The Dallas Cowboys: The First Twenty-Five Years.* Dallas: Taylor Publishing, 1985.

Stratton, Gary and Robert Krug. *Dallas Cowboys Trivia Challenge.* Dallas: Taylor Publishing, 1986.

Switzer, Barry and Bud Shrake. *Bootlegger's Boy.* New York: Morrow, 1990.

Thomas, Duane and Paul Zimmerman. *Duane Thomas and the Fall of America's Team.* New York: Warner Books, 1988.

Toomay, Pat. *The Crunch.* New York: Norton. 1975.

Whittingham, Richard. *The Dallas Cowboys: An Illustrated History.* New York: Harper & Row, 1981.

Wolfe, Jane. *The Murchisons.* New York: St. Martin's Press, 1989.

Zimmerman, Paul. *The Linebackers.* New York: Scholastic Book Services, 1973.